GHOSTS OF INTERNATIONAL LAW

Heroes and villains, idealists and mercenaries, freedom fighters and religious fanatics. Foreign fighters tend to defy easy classification. Good and bad images of the foreign combatant epitomize different conceptions of freedom and are used to characterize the rightness or wrongness of this actor in civil wars. This book traces the history of these figures and their afterlife. It does so through an interdisciplinary methodology employing law, history and psychoanalytical theory, showing how different images of the foreign combatant are utilized to proscribe or endorse foreign fighters in different historical moments. By linking the Spanish, Angolan and Syrian civil wars, the book demonstrates how these figures function as a precedent for later periods and how their heritage keeps haunting the imaginary of legal actors in the present.

ALBERTO RINALDI has worked for academic and non-academic institutions in Egypt, France and currently Sweden. His research focuses on interdisciplinary approaches to law and the humanities, including law and emotions, literature, cinema and pop culture.

CAMBRIDGE STUDIES IN INTERNATIONAL
AND COMPARATIVE LAW: 191

Established in 1946, this series produces high quality, reflective and innovative scholarship in the field of public international law. It publishes works on international law that are of a theoretical, historical, cross-disciplinary or doctrinal nature. The series also welcomes books providing insights from private international law, comparative law and transnational studies which inform international legal thought and practice more generally.

The series seeks to publish views from diverse legal traditions and perspectives, and of any geographical origin. In this respect it invites studies offering regional perspectives on core *problématiques* of international law, and in the same vein, it appreciates contrasts and debates between diverging approaches. Accordingly, books offering new or less orthodox perspectives are very much welcome. Works of a generalist character are greatly valued and the series is also open to studies on specific areas, institutions or problems. Translations of the most outstanding works published in other languages are also considered.

After seventy years, Cambridge Studies in International and Comparative Law sets the standard for international legal scholarship and will continue to define the discipline as it evolves in the years to come.

Series Editors

Larissa van den Herik

Professor of Public International Law, Grotius Centre for International Legal Studies, Leiden University

Jean d'Aspremont

Professor of International Law, University of Manchester and Sciences Po Law School

A list of books in the series can be found at the end of this volume.

GHOSTS OF INTERNATIONAL LAW

The Figure of the Foreign Fighter in a Cultural Perspective

ALBERTO RINALDI
Lund University

CAMBRIDGE
UNIVERSITY PRESS

Shaftesbury Road, Cambridge CB2 8EA, United Kingdom

One Liberty Plaza, 20th Floor, New York, NY 10006, USA

477 Williamstown Road, Port Melbourne, VIC 3207, Australia

314–321, 3rd Floor, Plot 3, Splendor Forum, Jasola District Centre, New Delhi – 110025, India

103 Penang Road, #05-06/07, Visioncrest Commercial, Singapore 238467

Cambridge University Press is part of Cambridge University Press & Assessment, a department of the University of Cambridge.

We share the University's mission to contribute to society through the pursuit of education, learning and research at the highest international levels of excellence.

www.cambridge.org
Information on this title: www.cambridge.org/9781009358361

DOI: 10.1017/9781009358330

© Alberto Rinaldi 2024

This publication is in copyright. Subject to statutory exception and to the provisions of relevant collective licensing agreements, no reproduction of any part may take place without the written permission of Cambridge University Press & Assessment.

When citing this work, please include a reference to the DOI 10.1017/9781009358330

First published 2024

A catalogue record for this publication is available from the British Library.

Library of Congress Cataloging-in-Publication Data
Names: Rinaldi, Alberto, author.
Title: Ghosts of international law : the figure of the foreign fighter in a cultural perspective / Alberto Rinaldi, Sciences Po.
Description: Cambridge, United Kingdom ; New York, NY : Cambridge University Press, 2024. | Includes bibliographical references and index.
Identifiers: LCCN 2024025158 (print) | LCCN 2024025159 (ebook) | ISBN 9781009358361 (hardback) | ISBN 9781009358323 (paperback) | ISBN 9781009358330 (epub)
Subjects: LCSH: Combatants and noncombatants (International law) | War (International law) | Guerrillas (International law) | Insurgency–Law and legislation. | Non-state actors (International relations) | Civil war. | Spain–History–Civil War, 1936-1939. | Angola–History–Civil War, 1975-2002. | Syria–History–Civil War, 2011-
Classification: LCC KZ6418 .R56 2024 (print) | LCC KZ6418 (ebook) | DDC 341.6/7–dc23/eng/20240610
LC record available at https://lccn.loc.gov/2024025158
LC ebook record available at https://lccn.loc.gov/2024025159

ISBN 978-1-009-35836-1 Hardback

Cambridge University Press & Assessment has no responsibility for the persistence or accuracy of URLs for external or third-party internet websites referred to in this publication and does not guarantee that any content on such websites is, or will remain, accurate or appropriate.

CONTENTS

List of Figures   vii
Acknowledgements   viii
List of Abbreviations   x

Introduction   1
   I.1   The *Revenants* of International Law   1
   I.2   Setting the Frame   7
   I.3   The Cultural Approach: Ambivalence   12
   I.4   The Cultural Approach: The Imaginary   17
   I.5   Engaging with the Past   21
   I.6   The Stakes for International Law   28
   I.7   Content of the Chapters   34

1   The Spanish Civil War and the Legacy of Nineteenth-Century Adventurers   36
   1.1   Who Is a Genuine Volunteer?   36
   1.2   The End of Freebooters   47
   1.3   Evoking Past Heroes   60
   1.4   Brave Highlanders or Scary Adventurers?   68
   1.5   Conclusion   92

2   The Return of the Mercenaries: The 1976 Luanda Trial in Context   95
   2.1   Foreigners Sentenced in Angola   95
   2.2   What Freedom, Whose Freedom?   108
   2.3   Volunteers or Mercenaries?   129
   2.4   The Nobility of the Cause Matters   139
   2.5   Conclusion   151

3   Enemies of Humanity or Freedom Fighters? The Jihadist Combatant in the Syrian Civil War   154
   3.1   Faceless, Nameless Enemies   154
   3.2   Idealists or Fanatics?   164

3.3 Barbarism versus Heroism   180
3.4 Regular and Irregular Groups   194
3.5 Conclusion   207

Back to the Future   210
Bibliography   212
Index   241

FIGURES

1.1 Portrait of William Walker (1824–1860) by Mathew Benjamin Brady   54
2.1 Cover of the magazine *Soldier of Fortune* (summer 1975)   97
3.1 Mujahid in Afghanistan (1985)   161
3.2 Portrait of French intellectual André Malraux (1933)   169

ACKNOWLEDGEMENTS

This book originated as a doctoral thesis, which I undertook at Sciences Po Paris Law School between 2015 and 2019. I would first like to express my gratitude to my former supervisors, Emmanuelle Tourme-Jouannet and Mikhail Xifaras. The greatest gift they offered me was the freedom to choose what I could do with my doctorate. This is not to reduce their contribution, but to thank them beyond the formal aspects of their guidance. The right to take one's own path is the most valuable sign of respect a doctoral student can ask for. Thank you, Manu, and thank you, Mikhail.

In addition to my supervisors, I would like to thank the members of my jury for taking the time to engage with the text and offering valuable comments on how to improve it for possible publication: Jean d'Aspremont for pushing me to jump higher over the fence, Luigi Nuzzo for encouraging me regarding my Eurocentric fears, Martti Koskenniemi for wisely scolding me when it was necessary to do so, and Anne Orford for infusing me with hope in the academic venture. I could not have asked for a more inspiring jury.

My sincere thanks also go to my friends and colleagues in Paris: Filipe Silva, Alessandro Petti, Bruno Sousa Rodrigues, Ghazal Miyar, Sandrine Brachotte, Rashmi Dharia, Alexia Katsiginis, Selina Mac, Moritz Vinken, Vittoria Becci and Edward van Daalen. All of them have contributed in different ways to the completion of this project. A heartfelt thought to the bar L'Espérance, for many Fridays after work.

To my best friends back home, Guido and Andrea, and to the brilliant researchers with whom I have had the pleasure to work over the years: Thomas Skouteris, Ville Kari and Antoine Mégie. Although the list is longer, I know who is owed something. A loving thought to my family: my father, Massimo, my mother, Elisiana, my uncle Augusto and my sister Anna. Thank you for always being there for me.

But it would not have been possible to complete this project if I had not been given another priceless gift: time. I am grateful to Lund

University and the Raoul Wallenberg Visiting Chair project which offered me two years as a postdoctoral researcher. I am especially indebted to Jessica Almqvist, Mia Rönnmar and Thérèse Murphy for their unconditional support during the revision of the manuscript.

In Sweden, I have also found new colleagues and friends who made the writing process much more fun and enjoyable than the solitary effort required by our work: Daria Davitti, Valentin Jeutner, Ayşegül Sirakaya, Sanja Milvian, Amanda Bills, Hoda Hosseiny, Serde Atalay, Amanda Kron, Anastasiya Kotova and Mahesh Menon. Thank you for welcoming me and making me part of the Law School.

Somehow the pieces of the puzzle came together here. The journey among foreign fighters was obviously the result of my personal journey: from Florence to Cairo, from Paris to Lund. Life is a chaotic manuscript we try to sketch out and make sense of along the way. What I have tried to put here is my sincere passion. All errors of form and content naturally remain mine alone.

ABBREVIATIONS

AMT	Association de Malfaiteurs Terroriste
ANF	Al-Nusra Front
AP I	Additional Protocol I
CAA	Cour Administrative d'Appel
CIA	Central Intelligence Agency
FNLA	Frente Nacional de Libertação de Angola
FSA	Free Syrian Army
FTF	foreign terrorist fighters
GC	Geneva Convention
IAC	international armed conflict
ICEM	International Commission of Enquiry of Mercenaries
ICRC	International Committee of the Red Cross
IHL	International Humanitarian Law
IS	Islamic State
ISIL	Islamic State in Iraq and the Levant
ISIS	Islamic State of Iraq and Syria
MPLA	Movimento Popular de Libertação de Angola
NAM	Non-Aligned Movement
NIAC	non-international armed conflict
NSA	non-state actors
OAU	Organization of African Unity
PKK	Kurdistan Workers Party
POW	prisoner of war
TGI	Tribunal de Grande Instance
UN	United Nations
UNGA	United Nations General Assembly
UNITA	União Nacional para a Independência Total de Angola
UNSC	United Nations Security Council
YPG	People's Protection Unit

Introduction

> It must be remembered, too, that the belief in spirits and ghosts, and the return of the dead is far from having disappeared among educated people, and that many who are sensible in other respects find it possible to combine spiritualism with reason. A man who has grown rational and sceptical, even, may be ashamed to discover how easily he may for a moment return to a belief in spirits under the combined impact of strong emotion and perplexity.
>
> Sigmund Freud (1907)[1]

I.1 The *Revenants* of International Law

It was telling to see how the individuals coming back to Europe from the Syrian battlefield were called returnees, or *revenants*. The term *revenant* in fact indicates someone who has supposedly come back from the afterlife.[2] Since the outbreak of the Syrian Civil War, a plethora of debates has surrounded this non-state actor, debates that have amplified following the Paris and Brussels attacks.[3] The topic had gained worldwide attention when the United Nations Security Council (UNSC) openly criminalized those joining the Al-Nusra Front and the Islamic

---

[1] Sigmund Freud, 'Delusion and Dream in Jensen's Gradiva', in J. Strachey, A. Freud, A. Strachey and A. Tyson (eds.), *The Standard Edition of the Complete Psychological Works of Sigmund Freud. Vol. IX* (London: Hogarth Press 1959) 7–93, p. 71.

[2] The *Oxford English Dictionary* defines *revenant* as 'a person who has returned, especially one who is thought to have come back from the dead'. The *Larousse Dictionary* defines the term as the following: 'Âme d'un mort qui se manifesterait à un vivant sous une forme physique (apparition, esprit, fantôme).'

[3] On the security threat posed by returning foreign terrorist fighters in their home states see Phil Gurski, *Western Foreign Fighters: The Threat to Homeland and International Security* (Lanham, MD: Rowman & Littlefield 2017) and Elena Pokalova, *Returning Islamist Foreign Fighters: Threats and Challenges to the West* (London: Palgrave Macmillan 2020).

State. Conflating the problem with jihadi-led terrorism, the UNSC also offered a definition for 'foreign terrorist fighters' (FTF).[4]

As many at the time noted, no real status existed for such an actor in international law.[5] And yet foreign fighters have long been around the international scene. Historians have generally referred to the broader phenomenon of foreign volunteering, and scholarship has today recognized the involvement of volunteers in many conflicts over the last two centuries.[6] Some famous examples include the nineteenth-century wars of independence in Latin America, where Britons fought under various guises;[7] or the Greek War of Independence (1821–1832), which saw many volunteers driven by philhellenic sentiments joining the ranks of the Greek insurgents against the Ottoman empire.[8] The list continues with the American Civil War (1861–1865), the Second Boer War (1899–1902) and the Spanish Civil War (1936–1939). Recent examples include the Yugoslav Wars and the conflicts in Iraq, Somalia and Libya, where the presence of third-country nationals on the battlefield has been extensively documented.[9] To be precise, the very term 'foreign fighter' is

---

[4] Specifically resolution 2178 defined foreign terrorist fighters as 'individuals who travel to a State other than their States of residence or nationality for the purpose of the perpetration, planning, or preparation of, or participation in, terrorist acts or the providing or receiving of terrorist training, including in connection with armed conflict'. Addressing the Growing Issue of Foreign Terrorist Fighters, S/RES/2178, 24 September 2014, preamble.

[5] See generally Andrea de Guttry, Francesca Capone and Christopher Paulussen (eds.), *Foreign Fighters under International Law and Beyond* (The Hague: Asser Press 2016).

[6] See Steven O'Connor and Guillaume Piketty (eds.), *Foreign Fighters and Multinational Armies: From Civil Conflicts to Coalition Wars, 1848–2015* (Abingdon: Routledge 2022); Christine G. Kruger and Sonja Levesen (eds.), *War Volunteering in Modern Times: From the French Revolution to the Second World War* (London: Palgrave Macmillan 2013); and Nir Arielli and Bruce Collins (eds.), *Transnational Soldiers: Foreign Military Enlistment in the Modern Era* (London: Palgrave Macmillan 2013).

[7] See Moises Enriquez Rodriguez, *Freedom's Mercenaries: British Volunteers in the Wars of Independence of Latin America. Vol. I: Northern South America* and *Vol. II: Southern South America* (Lanham, MD: Hamilton Books 2006).

[8] See William St. Clair, *That Greece Might Still Be Free: The Philhellenes in the War of Independence* (Oxford: Oxford University Press 1972); Hervé Mazurel, *Vertiges De La Guerre: Byron, Les Philhellènes et Le Mirage Grec* (Paris: Les Belles Lettres 2013); and Moises Enriquez Rodriguez, *Under the Flags of Freedom: British Mercenaries in the War of the Two Brothers, the First Carlist War, and the Greek War of Independence (1821–1840)* (Lanham, MD: Hamilton Books 2009).

[9] On the Yugoslav case: Jennifer Mustapha, 'The Mujahideen in Bosnia: The Foreign Fighter as Cosmopolitan Citizen and/or Terrorist' (2013) 17 *Citizenship Studies* 742-755. For the Iraq War: Christopher Hewitt and Jessica Kelley-Moore, 'Foreign Fighters in Iraq: A Cross-National Analysis of Jihadism' (2009) 21 *Terrorism and Political Violence* 211-220. For the Somali case: Lorenzo Vidino, Raffaello Pantucci and

rather a recent invention, appearing in the academic literature and in international forums with the involvement of the Arab Mujahideen during the Soviet–Afghan War (1979–1989).[10]

One can thus suggest that the so-called foreign fighter is but a non-state actor coming back in different historical moments to fight in conflicts abroad.[11] As such, they can be added to the longer list of 'irregulars', a category already explored by legal scholars.[12] If the phenomenon of foreign volunteering is usually read in relation to the rise of modern nation-state armies, this remains but one aspect of a more

---

Evan Kohlmann, 'Bringing Global Jihad to the Horn of Africa: Al Shabaab, Western Fighters, and the Sacralization of the Somali Conflict' (2010) 3 *African Security* 216–238. For Libya: Aaron Y. Zelin, 'The Others: Foreign Fighters in Libya' (2018) 44/45 *Washington Institute for Near East Policy: Policy Notes* (2018) 1–27.

[10] See Daniel Byman, *Road Warriors: Foreign Fighters in the Armies of Jihad* (New York: Oxford University Press 2019) and Roger Warren, *Terrorist Movements and the Recruitment of Arab Foreign Fighters. A History from 1980s Afghanistan to ISIS* (Oxford: Bloomsbury 2021). For the term 'Muslim foreign fighter' see Thomas Hegghammer, 'The Rise of the Muslim Foreign Fighters: Islam and the Globalization of Jihad' (2011) 35 *International Security* 53–94. The Italian historian Marcello Flores d'Arcais retraced several instances in which the presence of foreign individuals in war was documented. Recognizing that it is difficult to give an accurate definition, d'Arcais proposes describing this actor by employing the term volunteer rather than fighter. He writes: 'The meaning and definition of "foreign fighter" has constantly evolved in light of the historical events of the past few decades, particularly because of the lack of a clear meaning and definition in the international legal framework ... Instead, the term "volunteer" was used both for nationals and foreigners, putting an emphasis on the individual – civilian and/or former (or foreign) soldier – as a participant in war (or conflict, uprising, civil war, revolution); they joined a threatened government, a non-state actor, a minority group seeking to come to power or national or diverse ethnic groups seeking their independence.' Marcello Flores, 'Foreign Fighters' Involvement in National and International Wars: A Historical Survey', in de Guttry et al. (eds.), *Foreign Fighters under International Law* 27–47, p. 28.

[11] For the purpose of this study, the terms foreign fighter/volunteer/combatant will be used interchangeably.

[12] See specifically Sibylle Scheipers, *Unlawful Combatants: A Genealogy of the Irregular Fighter* (Oxford: Oxford University Press 2015). Although Scheipers shows that various types of 'irregular fighters' (e.g., guerrillas, terrorists, etc.) have been marginalized throughout the modern codification of humanitarian law, foreign fighters are absent from her study. Emily Crawford and Helen Kinsella both contributed to problematize the division between combatants and civilians, highlighting different biases beneath the principle of distinction. See Helen M. Kinsella, *The Image before the Weapon: A Critical History of the Distinction between Combatant and Civilian* (Ithaca, NY: Cornell University Press 2011) and Emily Crawford, 'Regulating the Irregular: International Humanitarian Law and the Question of Civilian Participation in Armed Conflicts' (2011) 18 *UC Davis Journal of International Law and Policy* 163–190.

complex story.¹³ Travelling for the love of adventure, for idealism, faith, or for pecuniary reasons, there is usually a mix of causes pushing these individuals to join armed conflicts and groups abroad. One common trait points to their vision of an-other place, together with a moral urge to intervene in the world.¹⁴ 'I dream'd that Greece might still be free', writes Byron in one of his most famous poems, whereas André Malraux in *L'Espoir* describes the different motivations pushing leftist volunteers to join the ranks of the Republicans during the Spanish Civil War.¹⁵ The desire to seek a deeper meaning is often translated into action, but this impetus is always ambivalent, fractured, a harbinger of ideals and contradictions: 'I had had one craving all my life – for the power of self-expression in some imaginative form ... At last accident, with perverted humour, in casting me as a man of action had given me place in the Arab Revolt', T. E. Lawrence affirms, not without a hint of cynicism.¹⁶

To be clear, this book is not concerned with the motivations of different foreign fighters across time and space. Other scholars have successfully proposed this type of analysis.¹⁷ Rather, what is interesting

---

¹³ This point is analysed extensively by Janice Thomson, as she explains the decrease in the utilization of mercenaries compared to the rise of the nation-state army. See Janice E. Thomson, *Mercenaries, Pirates, and Sovereigns: State-Building and Extraterritorial Violence in Early Modern Europe* (Princeton, NJ: Princeton University Press 1994).

¹⁴ Roger Stéphane, *Portrait de l'Aventurier: T. E. Lawrence, Malraux, Von Solomon* (Paris: Points Editeur 2014). Based on the original text published by Éditions Grasset & Fasquelle (1965).

¹⁵ André Malraux, *L'Espoir* (Paris: Gallimard 1937).

¹⁶ T. E. Lawrence, *The Seven Pillars of Wisdom* (London: Penguin Classics 2000) pp. 640–641. In the case of white mercenaries, a mix of heroic ambitions and self-perception as noble condottieri is reflected in the way they understood their political mission on the African continent. The biographies of some well-known European mercenaries bear witness to this. See specifically Jean Schramme, *Le Battailon Leopard: Souvenirs d'un African Blanc* (Paris: Laffont 1969); Mike Hoare, *The Road to Kalamata: A Congo Mercenary's Memoir* (Lexington, KY: Lexington Books 1989); and Rolf Steiner, *Carré Rouge: du Biafra au Soudan, le Dernier Condottiere* (Paris: Laffont 1976).

¹⁷ See Nir Arielli, *From Byron to Bin Laden. A History of Foreign War Volunteers* (Cambridge, MA: Harvard University Press 2018); David Malet, *Foreign Fighters: Transnational Identity in Civil Conflicts* (Oxford: Oxford University Press 2013); and Darryl Li, *The Universal Enemy: Jihad, Empire, and the Challenge of Solidarity* (Stanford, CA: Stanford University Press 2019). For Malet, there is always a transnational identity reconnecting these individuals to certain groups and struggles abroad. In other words, there seem to be different reasons which, at different times, attract different 'types' of foreign fighters abroad. Or, as he puts it: 'in the first half of the twentieth century, most foreign fighters were members of Communist groups. In the late nineteenth century, the feared perpetrators of transnational violence were anarchists. In both these waves, the militants and insurgents shared a key common trait with mujahidin today: transnational

is the diverse range of characters one can find when looking at the recent history of this phenomenon – for example, romantic adventurers (Byron), mercenaries (Lord Cochrane), political advisers (Lafayette), revolutionaries (Garibaldi), secret agents (T. E. Lawrence) or intellectuals (Hemingway, Orwell and Malraux).

That the most diverse and renowned personalities appear on this list is not irrelevant, or just an extravagant cultural detail. Quite the contrary. Throughout this book, it will be shown how past figures of the foreign fighter are directly evoked by national and international lawmakers. The images of these and other fighters will then reappear from the past – as *revenants* – when state representatives and politicians cast decisions upon the legal status of this actor. Here is the first reason why it is crucial to go back to history: there is a whole repertoire of figures evoked in the legislative arena. Secondly, this move helps characterizing law as a social artefact, embedded within a web of cultural references. Most importantly, as a human product, moulded by the fears, desires and fantasies that traverse legal actors and their imaginary. This is the aspect that is studied in more depth in this book.

By connecting three significant moments in the recent history of civil war (Spain, Angola and Syria), the book shows how different cultural figures of the foreign fighter have informed and keep informing the legal

---

ideological affiliation'. Malet acknowledges that since the Soviet invasion of Afghanistan a new transnational identity has formed and has attracted individuals during the Bosnian wars (1992–1995), the civil war in Algeria (1991–2002), the first Chechen war (1994–1996), the Kosovo war (1998–1999) and later in Afghanistan, Iraq and Syria: the one of the Ummah, or the community of Muslim believers. According to his view, most foreign fighters are neither mercenaries nor fanatics, given that: 'rather than for greed, most mobilize in response to perceived threat . . . or the need to protect a certain group or cause' (the quotes from Malet are at pp. 207–213). Similar to Malet, Arielli argues that the decision to fight abroad is linked with forms of ideologies. These determine the volunteers' choice to leave, defining their historical contingencies. Arielli divides those ideological motivations in three grand moments, or 'waves': (1) the liberty vs. tyranny wave (nineteenth century); (2) the left-wing vs. right-wing wave (1917–1980); (3) and the so-called clashes of civilizations wave (1980–present). Arielli defines four typologies of volunteers: self-appointed ambassadors, diaspora volunteers, cross-border volunteers and substitute-conflict volunteers. Like Malet, he also distinguishes volunteers from both mercenaries and state-sponsored troops (e.g., the French foreign legion or the British colonial troops). Finally, Li's monograph focuses on one particular type of foreign fighter – the Arab Mujahedeen in the context of the Bosnian wars. By employing a mix of anthropological, historical and ethnographic methods, Li advances a fascinating argument in favour of an Islamic form of universalism. Once again, my book is not concerned with foreign fighters' motivations or ideological commitments, but rather with the figures populating the imaginary of legal actors.

conversations of state representatives, policymakers, international lawyers and national courts at different times and places. These figures, it is argued, linger at the back of various decisionmakers' positions and arguments, informing the way in which they understand the rightness or the wrongness of the foreign fighters' causes and, most importantly, the legal responses to the problem posed by Western citizens going to fight in wars abroad. Epitomizing different conceptions of freedom, these figures have an impact on the way foreign fighters are understood and judged in each historical period.

On this note, it must be added that such figures are not fixed. On the one side, they mirror the historical-political context in which the lawmakers make use of them. On the other, they move across time and space, reappearing in different settings, contexts, moments. Besides, a distinction is operated each time between the 'good' and the 'bad' foreign fighter: idealists and fascists, mercenaries and military advisers, enemies of humanity and freedom fighters, and so on. The status of foreign fighters is always played out through a lawful/unlawful dichotomy, which links to the passions, the desires and the fantasies that lawmakers project to them.

Nathaniel Berman has showed in his seminal work how rules remain essentially a human product, and likewise how human beings tend to put their 'passions and ambivalences' into the categories of law.[18] Following the same methodological path, foreign fighter status is taken here as an example to show how such status cannot explain the whole story of this non-state actor. Different lawmakers will engage in passionate fights to define who counts as a legitimate foreign combatant, as some wish to prosecute the 'bad' foreign fighters under the law, while others argue that they should not be criminalized for their actions. What is at stake is the most classical of the struggles at the core of the legislative process, which reveals how law is not a neutral tool, nor can it soften the conflicts at the root of society.[19] On the contrary, law understood *as a social and cultural construct* is embedded within the passions, the desires and the fantasies of its creators, fantasies which, every time there are attempts to expel

---

[18] Nathaniel Berman, *Passion and Ambivalence: Colonialism, Nationalism, and International Law* (Leiden: Brill 2011).

[19] Similar to the famous expression 'one man's freedom fighter is another man's terrorist', one side's lawful foreign fighter is always going to be the other side's enemy. This kind of Schmittian formula will nevertheless be problematized throughout the book. *See* Carl Schmitt, *The Concept of the Political. Expanded Edition* (Chicago: University of Chicago Press 2007).

them from the law, keep coming back, as *revenants*, here in the form of figures/images of the 'good' and the 'bad' foreign combatant.

The noble adventurer, the racist mercenary and the religious fanatic are part of a *cultural repertoire* informing the lawmaking process and related criminalization or acquittal of foreign fighters. Hence, the argument made in this book should not be misunderstood as an aesthetic or visual claim about law. Nor is the accent put on the actual roles played by Byron, Orwell, Malraux and suchlike on the battlefield. Along with De Saussure, the term 'foreign fighter' is seen as a floating signifier, with a contextual meaning. It does not matter whether they are volunteers, mercenaries or terrorists. Or rather, it matters to the extent to which the lawmakers will legitimize some and delegitimize others: idealists and fascists; soldiers of fortune and foreign advisers; fanatics and freedom fighters.[20] The interest lies in the cultural figures which haunt legal actors when they produce these kinds of binary oppositions. As much as the lawmakers would like to rationalize their passions through the law, they fail to do so. Their conscience is split, and so are the images they resort to. Yet these figures populate their imaginary and will come back to inform subsequent debates, establishing the precedents upon which the foreign fighters' status will be moulded and framed.

I.2 Setting the Frame

The present study ranges from the codification of the 1907 Hague Conventions to the Syrian Civil War, with the criminalization of foreign terrorist fighters (September 2014).[21] By following the developments on the legal status of the foreign combatant, the story highlights those moments where cultural figures enter the debate and influence lawmaking or adjudicating processes. The book should thus be read as an intervention in the legal history of the Western foreign volunteer, with the intent to analyse this non-state actor from a cultural standpoint.[22]

---

[20] Similarly see Aaron Ettinger, 'The Mercenary Moniker: Condemnations, Contradictions and the Politics of Definition' (2014) 45 *Security Dialogue* 174–191. *See* also Stéphane Baudens, Marc Dupré and Hélène Terrom (eds.), *Les Combattants Étrangers: Approches Culturelles et Juridiques* (Paris: Mare et Martin 2021).

[21] It also includes an excursus on the 1874 Brussels conference, as an important node to understand how the figure of the foreign combatant shifts from the nineteenth to the twentieth century.

[22] *See* specifically Robert W. Gordon, 'Critical Legal Histories' (1984) 36 *Stanford Law Review* 56–125. *See* also Hayden White, *Metahistory: The Historical Imagination in*

To this end, the book is built upon three civil conflicts, which mirror three historical moments and their different conceptualizations of law and of warfare.[23] These are:

(1) The Spanish Civil War (interwar period);
(2) The Angolan Civil War (decolonization);
(3) The Syrian Civil War (War on Terror).

The three civil wars are placed within ideological struggles that provide the setting from which the various figures of the foreign fighter emerge. These struggles can be summarized as follows:

(1) The fight of communism versus fascism (Spanish Civil War);
(2) The anti-colonial uprisings (Angolan Civil War);
(3) Religious fundamentalism (Syrian Civil War).

Other periods (and other wars) could have been considered, notably during the long nineteenth century. However, had the book jumped from the Greek War of Independence to the American Civil War, to Spain, the narrative would have become too episodic, losing acuity and historical accuracy. The references to Byron, Garibald or Lafayette that appear in the first chapter do indeed come from the nineteenth century, but when their images enter the debates of the interwar period, the legal and political landscape is naturally very different from that of previous centuries.

The three periods are thus chosen to reflect contemporary developments within international law, and specifically within international

---

Nineteenth-Century Europe (Baltimore, MD: Johns Hopkins University Press 1973); Hayden White, *The Content of the Form: Narrative Discourse and Historical Representation* (Baltimore, MD: Johns Hopkins University Press 1987); Keith Jenkins, *Re-thinking History* (New York: Routledge 2003); and Joan Scott, *Théorie Critique de l'Histoire. Identités, Expériences, Politiques* (Paris: Fayard 2009).

[23] The figures analysed in the chapters emerge from precise contexts. Another way of approaching the material would have been the one used by Eric Hobsbawm in his fascinating monograph on banditry. There, Hobsbawm retraces three figures of the bandit in the longue durée: the noble robbers, the avengers and the haiduks. Hobsbawm's approach has certainly influenced the present work, which however remains solidly anchored in a more traditional historical timeline. Where Hobsbawm starts his analysis from the figures (only later placed within different historical backgrounds), here the opposite process was adopted: different figures of the foreign combatant emerge each time from precise historical, political and legal contexts. See Eric Hobsbawm, *Bandits. Revised Edition* (New York: Pantheon Books 1981).

humanitarian law (IHL). The Spanish, Angolan and Syrian Civil Wars in fact represent three vantage points to explore how legal doctrines, the practice of states and the codification of the laws of war concerning foreign fighters have all been advanced in the twentieth century.[24] This is not done to retrace a history of humanitarian law, however.[25] Explaining how these individuals were taken into consideration in the codification of IHL principles, or why they have remained rather marginal figures, is not the primary intent of this book.[26]

---

[24] For some classic studies on the legal aspects of civil war: John Norton Moore and Joseph Perkovich (eds.), *Law and Civil War in the Modern World* (Baltimore, MD: Johns Hopkins University Press 1974); Stephen C. Neff, *The Rights and Duties of Neutrals: A General History* (Manchester: Manchester University Press 2000); and Eliav Lieblich, *International Law and Civil War* (New York: Routledge 2013). For a compelling historical study on the notion of civil war: David Armitage, *Civil Wars: A History in Ideas* (New York: Alfred A. Knopf 2017). This remains a non-exhaustive list, of course.

[25] The aim of this study is to show how the present foreign fighters' categorizations are linked to previous cultural archetypes. And, consequently, how the figures evoked in earlier epochs still affect and inform the imaginaries of legal actors in the present. For important critical work on the laws of war see David Kennedy, *Of War and Law* (Princeton, NJ: Princeton University Press 2006); Chris Jochnick and Roger Normand, 'The Legitimation of Violence: A Critical History of the Laws of War' (1994) 35 *Harvard International Law Journal* 49–95; Frédéric Mégret, 'The Laws of War and the Structure of Masculine Power' (2008) 19 *Melbourne Journal of International Law* 200–226; and Nathaniel Berman, 'Privileging Combat? Contemporary Conflict and the Legal Construction of War' (2004) 43 *Columbia Journal of Transnational Law* 1–71. On the colonial origin of the laws of war see Frédéric Mégret, 'From "Savages" to "Unlawful Combatants": A Postcolonial Look at International Humanitarian Law's "Other"', in Anne Orford (ed.), *International Law and Its Others* (Cambridge: Cambridge University Press 2006) 265–317.

[26] The examination of how foreign fighters were understood under the modern laws of war certainly points to the state-centric bias at the core of IHL. Foreign fighters as actors in warfare are only conceivable in relation to state armies, or groups resembling fully organized armed contingents. As we will see throughout the chapters, they will mostly be protected under the regime dealing with international armed conflicts. In a situation of civil strife; however, they tend to benefit from less protection. This bias is not exclusively targeting foreign fighters though, as they suffer from the same prejudice as other non-state armed actors. Mégret notes: 'Although the laws of war claim to have nothing to do with the jus ad bellum, they are at least the repositories of a notion of who is more fundamentally allowed to participate in war, with states at the apex, state-mimicking non-state actors a relatively close second, and pure non-state actors that do not inscribe their action within a sovereign register as distant thirds.' Frédéric Mégret, 'Theorizing the Laws of War', in Florian Hoffmann and Anne Orford (eds.), *The Oxford Handbook of the Theory of International Law* (Oxford: Oxford University Press 2016) 762–778, p. 17. For some relevant literature on non-state actors, please refer to: Andrea Bianchi (ed.), *Non-state Actors and International Law* (Aldershot: Ashgate 2009); Math Noortmann and Cedric Ryngaert (eds.), *Non-State Actor Dynamics in International Law: From Law-Takers to Law-Makers* (London: Routledge 2016); Jean d'Aspremont (ed.), *Participants*

Here, another clarification is needed. The discussion is on two levels: the national and the international. It is particularly interesting to follow the discourse of legal actors, as it shifts from the domestic to the international plane and back. Lawmakers in the domestic context refer to the international sphere to solve the issue of foreign fighters; conversely, international actors point to the domestic level to pass and enforce legislation against them. This is not only indicative of the interconnections between the two frameworks, but it also reinforces the argument about the difficulty of producing any clear-cut categorization for this non-state actor.[27]

Related to this is the choice of the material. French and British sources have been privileged. Focusing on the case studies of France and United Kingdom was not only due to the possibilities of conducting research, but above all for the richness of the material and for the cultural figures which keep recurring in the debates on foreign volunteers. One of the apparent shortcomings of this work might be that this material remains strictly legal: for example, doctrines, parliamentary debates, preparatory works. While the genealogical method envisages finding the hidden ways in which the legal material is moulded, here the reverse approach was adopted. Within the discourse of legal actors, I deliberately chose to trace those figures that bring a focus *from law elsewhere*. The objective is to bring out an alterity from the legal material itself, by showing how law is embedded within a web of cultural references in the imaginary of its creators. This is also the reason why the text makes extensive use of direct quotes – attempting to offer a sense of the fantasies, fears and related cultural images that actors use when speaking about foreign fighters.[28]

---

in the International Legal System: Multiple Perspectives on Non-State Actors in International Law (London: Routledge 2011); and Ezequiel Heffes, Marcos D. Kotlik and Manuel J. Ventura (eds.), *International Humanitarian Law and Non-State Actors: Debates, Law and Practice* (The Hague: Asser Press 2020).

[27] It must also be emphasized that legal actors themselves move from the national to the international context and vice versa. State representatives and policymakers often sit in parliamentary debates and in UN venues. Or they are briefed by international experts, before drafting legislation at the national level. This should be taken as a further confirmation of the strong interrelations between the two stages. I am aware that there are fundamental differences between the domestic and international spheres in how norms are produced and enforced. But this book does not deal with the function and nature of legal systems. The story unfolds through sites where the issue of foreign fighters is dealt with from a legal point of view.

[28] On this point see Marianne Constable, *Our Word Is Our Bond: How Legal Speech Acts* (Stanford, CA: Stanford University Press 2014).

Naturally, in each of the three periods analysed, only certain sources were considered. The problem of Western subjects going to fight in wars abroad has been discussed in many different forums and by different actors over the last century. Yet not all voices could be included.[29] Let me state an important caveat. I am aware that there is a multiplicity of stories on the ground in every historical era. Not all leftist volunteers in Spain merged with the International Brigades. There were other right-wings troops and battalions apart from the ones sent by Germany and Italy to help Franco.[30] One side of the argument is that it is difficult, if not impossible, to reflect all historical complexities. The other, more compelling I believe, is that not all foreign fighters had the same weight in the legal arena. In this sense, the book traces those events which contributed to significant debates and changes in legislation. As I explain in detail in Section I.5, the idea is to detect moments of rupture. To offer another example, the focus on British mercenaries in Angola is useful to the national and international debates triggered by the trial in Luanda (June 1976). That is why the debates at the United Nations (UN) or in Geneva are more persuasive than, say, those of the 1977 African Convention on Mercenarism. Because they are revealing of the conflicting cultural visions underneath the categorization of 'good' and 'bad' foreign combatants during the decolonization period.

At this point, it must be stressed that the purpose of this work is not to write a global history of the foreign fighter, but only a partial one. Partial, because deliberately Eurocentric. The focus is kept on Western countries,

---

[29] To offer an example, the issue of foreign volunteers is discussed at the Institut de Droit International, specifically at the Session de Florence in 1908. Nonetheless, in Chapter 1 it is preferred to give precedence to the *travaux preparatoires* of the 1907 Hague Conventions: on the one hand because the discussions at the Institut followed those that took place only one year earlier in the Netherlands and, on the other, because The Hague is a more advantageous venue to observe the figures at play behind the conceptual positions of states' delegations. In Chapter 1, the debates at the League are privileged over those at the Committee of Non-Intervention in London. This was done to establish a thread with the discussions at the General Assembly and the Security Council in the subsequent chapters.

[30] See Sylvain Roussillon, *Les 'Brigades internationales' de Franco. Les Volontaires Étrangers du Côté National* (Versailles: Via Romana 2012); Michael Alpert, *The Republican Army in the Spanish Civil War, 1936–1939* (Cambridge: Cambridge University Press 2013); and Lisa A. Kirschenbaum, *International Communism and the Spanish Civil War: Solidarity and Suspicion* (Cambridge: Cambridge University Press 2015). For two recent studies on the Spanish Civil War and its socio-political background see specifically Stanley G. Payne, *The Spanish Civil War* (Cambridge: Cambridge University Press 2012) and Gerald Brenan, *The Spanish Labyrinth* (Cambridge: Cambridge University Press 2014).

doctrines and actors.³¹ In this sense, the figures of *other* foreign fighters – that is, those populating the imaginaries of non-Western actors – are left out of this book. Nonetheless, the three chapters reveal that the colonial question is an integral part of the modern history of the Western foreign combatant, both before and after decolonization. Such a question is, however, filtered through figures pertaining to a Eurocentric imaginary. Let us now explore how.

I.3 The Cultural Approach: Ambivalence

Revenants, they have been called. The idea of the return of images of the foreign fighter is of crucial importance to rewrite the history of this non-state actor from a cultural standpoint. As much as lawmakers would like to confine foreign fighters within a certain legal category, they do not manage to do so, because of their deep ambivalences towards this figure.³² I take the psychoanalytic notion of ambivalence from Nathaniel Berman, who, in his reading of the passions that cross the modern construction of internationalism, is informed by Kleinian thought.³³ Melanie Klein retraced the fundamental idea of the individual as split between 'good' and 'bad' objects of desire, or aspects of the self:

> The concept of splitting is central to Klein's theory in which the individual begins life with the developmentally essential task of achieving a binary split between the 'good' and 'bad' aspects of himself . . . Klein's view is that the first act of the ego is to split off and project out into the object its

---

[31] On the notion of Eurocentrism see Arnulf Becker-Lorca, 'Eurocentrism in the History of International Law', in Bardo Fassbender and Anne Peters (eds.), *The Oxford Handbook of the History of International Law* (Oxford: Oxford University Press 2012) 1034–1057. On the choice of prioritizing certain events see specifically Fleur Johns, Richard Joyce and Sundhya Pahuja (eds.), *Events: The Force of International Law* (London: Routledge 2010).

[32] I use the term 'figure' interchangeably with 'image' and 'characters' in order not to overload the text.

[33] I refer to the term 'splitting' as used by Melanie Klein. Melanie Klein, *Contributions to Psychoanalysis 1921–1945* (London: Hogarth Press 1948) pp. 288 and 346. 'In dividing its mother into a "good" mother and a "bad" one and its father into a "good" father and a "bad" one, it attaches the hatred it feels for its object to the "bad" one or turns away from it while it directs its restorative trends to its "good" mother and "good" father and, in phantasy, makes good towards the damage it has done its parent-imagos in its sadistic phantasies.' Melanie Klein, *The Psychoanalysis of Children* (New York: Grove Press 1932) p. 222.

destructive impulses and its loving libidinal impulses; the object is correspondingly split into a 'bad' and a 'good' part.[34]

Berman utilizes the idea of the ego's identity construction and applies it via analogy to the self-constructed identity of internationalism, as: '[international lawyers] attempt to construct an image of the self ... by splitting between good and bad images of that self – for example, in Basch's distinction between the good colonialism of the French and the bad colonialism of other Europeans, or in Brown's distinction between bad "imperialism" and good "trusteeship colonialism"'.[35] Even if Berman's analysis focuses on the construction of internationalism as an ambivalent passion played out on binary oppositions, this model can be used for other types of legal constructs and discourses. It is the same kind of ambivalent discourse that is found when legal actors try to give an identity to our foreign fighters: these become split into good and bad 'volunteers', good and bad 'mercenaries', good and bad 'jihadists', and so on.

Yet Berman goes further in his analysis by claiming that '[international lawyers] attempt to create an *image* by splitting between good and bad images of [the] other – for example, between "undisciplined" and "disciplined" nationalism ... between not yet men and men'.[36] In other words, there are figures at play in projecting good and bad versions of the same object, figures which are attached to the desire to see war waged in a certain way, or to the nobility of the cause fought in a conflict abroad.

---

[34] Elizabeth Bott Spillius, Jane Milton, Penelope Garvey, Cyril Couve and Deborah Steine (eds.), *The New Dictionary of Kleinian Thought* (New York: Routledge 2011) p. 491.

[35] Berman, *Passion and Ambivalence*, p. 425. Jouannet explains the process in a very helpful way: 'Put more simply, it refers to the fact that an individual can experience contradictory feelings of love and hate for the same object ... Klein referred to the phenomenon of ambivalence in order to characterize one of the fundamental psychological mechanisms operative from the very first months of a human being's life, from this moment the individual – as a being of desire – is caught between the drives of life and death. In Klein's view, if the drive – as the energy that animates each individual – is fundamentally ambivalent, it will construct the objects to which it is addressed in its own image (that is, as ambivalent). Yet, the ambivalence of this constructed object (in particular the mother for the young child), is unbearable for the subject; the individual, therefore, "splits" the object into a "good" and "bad" version. In doing so, the relation to the "good" object involves an element of idealization, and the relation to the "bad" object entails, for its part, anguish and fear. The dynamics of ambivalence are inseparable from the self-construction of the subject. The two versions of the object, the "good" and the "bad", inevitably emerge together, giving rise to mechanisms of repression and conflicting fantasies.' Emmanuelle Jouannet, 'A Critical Introduction', in Berman (ed.), *Passion and Ambivalence*, pp. 9–10.

[36] Berman, *Passion and Ambivalence*, pp. 425–426. Emphasis added.

As such, the foreign fighter gets split every time into 'good' and 'bad' versions of the same: brave highlanders and scary adventurers, noble volunteers and racist white men, perverted romantics and war heroes.

Once again, these figures are not static; they travel in time, and they undergo modifications. As Berman clarifies: 'so often in "*splitting*", the lines between identities "good" and "bad", "true" and "false" are contingent and indeterminate – an unsurprising feature of constructions that seek "to manage the anxiety" provoked by irreducible ambivalences'.[37] The notion of ambivalence as developed by Berman through Klein is thus crucial to understand how various legal actors are caught up in a web of cultural references, which they cannot get rid of: 'I will use the notion of ambivalence to refer to the inability of an individual, a group, or a culture to rid themselves of ideas, passions, or relationships that they nevertheless claim to condemn or deny.'[38] In our case, the inability of national and international actors of getting rid of cultural images of the foreign combatant which each time symbolize, mirror and epitomize different desires and fantasies projected over them.[39]

The idea that the (legal) identity of foreign fighters passes from certain fantasies which unfold through a historical scenario is supported by the reading of gender historian Joan Scott.[40] Scott reflects upon the formation of the feminist self through a series of 'fantasies [which] were produced to consolidate' such an identity.[41] Utilizing the axes of 'fantasy' and 'echo', she shows how: 'identity as a continuous, coherent, historical phenomenon is revealed to be a fantasy, a fantasy that erases the divisions and the discontinuities, the absences and the differences ... Echo provides a gloss on fantasy by reminding us that identity is constructed in complex and diffracted relation to others'.[42]

---

[37] *Ibid.*, p. 429.

[38] *Ibid.*, p. 414.

[39] 'Desire is irreducible. Don't deny your desire, tell me of its quality.' Nathaniel Berman, 'In the Wake of Empire' (1999) 14 *American University International Law Review* 1515–1569, p. 1551.

[40] Joan Scott, 'Fantasy Echo: History and the Construction of Identity' (2001) 27 *Critical Inquiry* 284–304.

[41] For instance, the female orator 'which projects women into masculine public space', or the maternal fantasy 'with its acceptance of rules that define reproduction as women's primary role'. *Ibid.*, p. 293.

[42] *Ibid.*, p. 292. It is interesting that the myth of Echo is linked with the one of Narcissus. Pierre Legendre might help in elucidating this point better: 'the human would be unthinkable without the instance of representation ... This suggests that the structure of the human subject is a structure of representation'. Pierre Legendre, 'Introduction to

I.3 THE CULTURAL APPROACH: AMBIVALENCE

In every era, foreign fighters are furnished with a plot, or a scenario that settles the desires and fantasies of their creators. In other words, certain passions win over others; they operate as a narrative and contribute to form 'individual and collective identity', as Scott explains.[43] But the original tension (the Kleinian splitting) inherent in all processes of identity-formation cannot be contained, precisely because identities are built upon the marginalization of other desires which propagate over time, as an echo. And so the combatants returning today from Syria are *revenants*, as much as are past, heroic volunteers – with their barbaric, cynical, racist counterparts. As put by de Certeau: 'Psychoanalysis recognizes the past *in* the present ... any autonomous order is founded upon what it eliminates; it produces a "residue" condemned to be forgotten. But what was excluded re-infiltrates the place of its origin.'[44] The term *revenant* reconnects well both with psychoanalytical theory, and with that form of genealogy that Jacques Derrida had referred to as 'hauntology'.[45] Hauntology as a genealogical method is devoted to exploring the characteristic that ghosts seem to possess: the perpetual returning in the form of haunting.[46] If ghosts come back from the past to haunt us, they also re-infiltrate the historical scene. Reading the history of foreign fighters as a history of phantasmatic figures which populate the imaginary of legal actors across times and spaces can be seen properly as an hauntology.[47] In this sense, the history of the various juridical

---

the Theory of the Image: Narcissus and the Other in the Mirror' (1997) 8 *Law and Critique* 3–35, pp. 10–13.

[43] Scott, 'Fantasy Echo', p. 289.

[44] Michel de Certeau, *Heterologies: Discourse on the Other* (Minneapolis: University of Minnesota Press 1986) p. 4.

[45] See Jacques Derrida, *Spectres of Marx: The State of the Debt, the Work of Mourning and the New International* (New York: Routledge 1994). A clarification is needed. Derrida's hauntology, as I understand it, is a stance in favour of the living spectres of Marxism. His aim is to re-engage with and reopen that history, in a time which saw the end of the Cold War and the birth of the Washington Consensus. I make use of hauntology not to sustain a Marxist position, but rather to keep the idea of the living heritage of the past in the present. This point will further be explained in the next section.

[46] As the Oxford Dictionary puts it, haunting is 'a persistent and disturbing presence ... something unpleasant [that] continue to affect or cause problems'. In the French sense of the word *l'hantise*, 'est un obsession, ou preoccupation constante'.

[47] On the etymological convergences of the terms 'ghost', 'imagination' and 'fantasy', Sébastien Rongier writes: 'le mot *image* est hanté par la notion de fantome ... trois termes essentiels se partagent la plus grande part de la discussion: *eikon, eidolon, phantasia* ... le terme le plus courant est *eidolon*. Les premiers sens d'eidolon sont "images" et "fantome" ... par glissement, le terme définit l'imagination ... En rapportant la phantasia au regard à partir de la lumiére, le fantome devient une figure

categories utilized to label foreign fighters cannot do without the contribution of psychoanalysis, as '[psychoanalysis] introduces the agency of the unconscious ... psychoanalysis ... look beyond the literal and the rational, to entertain the idea that not all actions express the reasoned self-interest of the actors'.[48] This is of particular relevance to demonstrate how the legal status of the foreign combatant is certainly created via ideologies and state interest, but also via the resort to fantasies, desires and fears. In other words, the cultural archetypes of the foreign fighter might well be used as rationally defensible categories, but that is only one part of the story. To be clear:

> this is not to condemn law as a simple reflection of our passions and our unconscious psychological mechanisms, but rather to show that it can never be the product of our reason alone ... the suggestive force of Berman's work lies in its demonstration of the importance and the inevitability of the play of passions at the very heart of international law ... The same analysis can be applied to states and their governments ... both as national communities and as governments they have their own share of irrationality and passion that guide their actions [which] are not simply a function of their 'interests' alone ... instead, considerations of morality, of culture, of passion are unavoidably intertwined.[49]

Berman understands law as a part of a larger mosaic, formed by a whole set of cultural, moral and social tiles. Furthermore, he suggests an interconnection between the phenomenon of splitting relevant to individual self-formation of identity, and those of players in larger legal arenas. This is a significant indication of how ambivalence is not only confined to the single, private conscience of juridical actors, but crosses the whole liberal system of international law.[50] I will return to this point later when discussing the idea of indeterminacy, in relation to the way one can write the history of the foreign fighter and of international law more generally. For the moment, what needs to be assessed is how the

---

qui permet de penser l'image'. Sébastien Rongier, *Theories des Fantômes. Pour Une Archéologie des Images* (Paris: Les Belles Lettres 2016) pp. 19–21.

[48] Victoria Hesford and Lisa Diedrich, 'On "The Evidence of Experience" and Its Reverberations: An Interview with Joan W. Scott' (2014) 15 *Feminist Theory* 197–207, p. 204.

[49] Jouannet, in Berman, *Passion and Ambivalence*, pp. 11–13.

[50] 'This kind of ambivalence is associated with doubling ... these two aspects of ambivalence have profoundly marked the discourse and practice of colonialism and other forms of the exercise of power by the strongest countries of the world over those less powerful.' Berman, *Passion and Ambivalence*, pp. 414–415.

cultural figure of the foreign combatant populates the minds of different legal actors, who are part of social groups. That is how to transport the analysis of ambivalence to larger social entities and their imaginary.

I.4 The Cultural Approach: The Imaginary

The concept of the imaginary has a long history in Western thought, beginning with its modern systematizations operated by Hume and Kant, passing from French phenomenology (in the works of Sartre and Merleau-Ponty), and being appropriated by Freud and Lacan and more generally by twentieth-century psychoanalysis.[51] It is within psychoanalytic theory that this concept is of interest for the scope of this study.

If Freud and Lacan have worked extensively with the imaginary, however, they both maintained a negative vision of such a concept: for Freud, in fact, *phantasia* is the place of self-representation, the place of passions and emotions that make up the construction of the ego. These passions and emotions must however be tempered and managed because they can pose problems for human beings in their social relations. Lacan takes the teaching of Freud and develops in more detail the phases of the construction of the identity of the ego, for instance in his famous recounting of the mirror-stage.[52] For Lacan, the formation of identity passes from a whole series of images that are both fascinating and

---

[51] For an excellent study please refer to Kathleen Lennon, *Imagination and the Imaginary* (New York: Routledge 2015). *See* also Jacques Lacan, *Écrits: The First Complete Edition in English* (New York: Norton 2010) and Sigmund Freud, *Civilization and Its Discontents* (New York: Norton 2010). The concept has also been discussed with reference to law: James Boyd White, *The Legal Imagination* (Chicago: University of Chicago Press 1985), Peter Goodrich, *Oedipus Lex: Psychoanalysis, History, Law* (Berkeley: University of California Press 1995) and Peter Goodrich and David Gray Carlson (eds.), *Law and the Postmodern Mind: Essays on Psychoanalysis and Jurisprudence* (Ann Arbor: University of Michigan Press 1998).

[52] The creation of the subject – and thus of its consciousness – is a fluid, ambivalent process that involves other, uncanny elements. The child, Lacan explains, seeks in the mirror for its own image in order to constitute itself as a unitary person. But its self-image is subjected and gets seduced by other images, desires, passions and fears (like its mother's voice, gestures, facial expression, etc.). In other words, the child starts to recognize then that its own ego, its own self-image is in fact fragmented, inherently neurotic and alienated. As the French psychoanalyst explains: '[the mirror stage] is a structural crossroads at which one has to take one's bearings; [the mirror stage] turns out fantasies, produces an alienating identity, an inexhaustible squaring of the ego's audits. The subject ends up recognizing that this being has never been anything more than his construct in the imaginary'. The subject thus perceives his ego as inherently divided, fragmented and incomplete, and at the same time crossed by all sorts of 'other' elements which contribute

seductive, fearful and joyful, and so on.[53] As much as for Freud, the imaginary remains for Lacan a necessary illusion, a misrepresentation that must essentially be subsumed at the level of the 'Symbolic': the Freudian totemic, civilizing role of culture, is then translated for Lacan into the realm of language, of signs.[54]

Yet if we hold to the notion of ambivalence, we should not understand law as a mere weapon of repression, but as a 'multifaceted instrument of regulation, emancipation and illusion – as well as of satisfaction, repression and control of individual and social passions, drives and fantasies'.[55] A position that closely resembles that of social theorist Cornelius Castoriadis.[56]

Castoriadis' approach to psychoanalytic theory offers an understanding of the imaginary that is not necessarily illusory (something that must be corrected), but with the capacity to produce images in a creative sense: 'psychoanalysis obliges us to see that the human being is not [an animal possessing reason] but essentially an imagining being ... in the unconscious, representation, affect, desire are mixed together ... it is

---

to its own formation. The child, seeking for its self-representation in the mirror, finds many 'others' selves, crossing and shaping its own image. Eventually, that very image will bear an original sense of void and incompleteness, an absence of stable grounds which has contributed to its very constitution. In other words, the image that the subject sought in order to recognize itself as a fully-fledged human being will always bear the stamp of those 'other' unsettling elements. *See* specifically Jacques Lacan, 'The Mirror Stage as Formative of the I Function as Revealed in Psychoanalytic Experience', in Lacan, *Écrits*, pp. 75–81.

[53] Lennon, *Imagination and the Imaginary*, pp. 53–54.

[54] This is not to undermine the fundamental contributions of other theorists in developing a theory of the imaginary. As Bottici explains: 'Psychoanalysis and structuralism both contributed to this development – the former with a new emphasis on the complexity of psychic life and the latter with a new attention to the products of imagination. Myths, fables, fairy tales, rituals, totemic practices, all have been analysed as part of the social imaginary – one just has to think of Freud's and Jung's contributions in this direction or, more recently, of the structuralist analysis inspired by Lévi-Strauss ... the most important result is perhaps the move away from a view of the self as a mere sum of separated faculties.' Chiara Bottici, 'From Imagination to the Imaginary and Beyond: Towards a Theory of Imaginal Politics' in Chiara Bottici and Benoît Challand (eds.), *The Politics of Imagination* (London: Birkbeck Law Press 2011) 16–37, p. 22.

[55] Jouannet, in Berman, *Passion and Ambivalence*, p. 19.

[56] *See* Cornelius Castoriadis, *The Imaginary Institution of Society* (Cambridge, MA: MIT Press 1997) and Cornelius Castoriadis, *World in Fragments: Writings on Politics, Society, Psychoanalysis, and the Imagination* (Stanford, CA: Stanford University Press 1997).

I.4 THE CULTURAL APPROACH: THE IMAGINARY

impossible to separate them'.[57] Additionally, Castoriadis suggests a viable route to think of the imaginary not only as a singular, individual enterprise, but as having a 'social' dimension:

> The merit of Castoriadis' concept of social imaginary is to point out that the *instituting* social imaginary is always at the same time *instituted*. No society could ever exist if individuals created by the society itself had not created it. Society can exist concretely only through the fragmentary and complementary incarnation and incorporation of its institution and its imaginary significations in the living, talking and acting individuals of that society.[58]

This vision of the social imaginary is extremely important, because it offers a framework to analyse individuals as active participants in the creation of society itself.[59] International lawyers, state representatives, national policymakers, all these groups come with certain figures of the foreign fighter in their mind: be it the adventurer international lawyers refer to during the interwar years, or the Spanish Civil War heroes state representatives evoke at the UN, or the freedom fighters in contemporary parliamentary debates. Yet these individuals do not operate in a vacuum. They are part of larger institutions or social groups that function through their own instituted imaginaries: international lawyers in the 1930s will thus frame the problem of volunteers through the laws of neutrality; state

---

[57] 'For Castoriadis, the imaginary is not constituted out of a relation to an external, and illusory, image. It is instead the product of the originary and creative capacity for making and grasping image or form in what is presented to us. Although such imaginary formations are multiple and historically variable, they are not necessarily distorting and illusory ... The point of the imagination is not simply to provide images which will satisfy fundamental drives universally present in each psyche. It is rather that the nature of such psychic drives is not fixed independently of the images which express them. These images can be multiple and variable, and constitute the affective texture of the psyche's interior world.' Lennon, *Imagination and the Imaginary*, p. 76.

[58] Bottici, 'From Imagination to the Imaginary', p. 25.

[59] 'The social imaginary significations of any society form an immensely complex web of meanings, which nonetheless, for Castoriadis, display some unity and internal cohesion. This network of meanings he termed a magma of "social imaginary significations that are carried by and embodied in the institution of a given society and that, so to speak, animate it" ... For Castoriadis, social imaginaries also yield a sense of what constitutes the society itself and what constitutes our own identity as members of the society ... social groupings require a shared imaginary about that grouping ... a sense of a "we" transparent between individual and collective which constitutes both individual and group identity. "Every society up to now has attempted to give an answer to a few fundamental questions: Who are we as a collectivity".' Lennon, *Imagination and the Imaginary*, p. 81.

representatives in the 1970s discuss the outlawing of mercenaries in contraposition to the combatant's privilege; today's policymakers operate under the global counter-terrorism agenda when deciding which of their citizens shall be prevented from leaving for Syria.

Nonetheless, as Castoriadis posits, men are imagining being and, in the unconscious, representation, affect, desire are all mixed together. If individual and collective imaginaries are interdependent, then all those passions, desires and fantasies that Berman sees as constituting the raw material of the lawmaking process are indissolubly part of the same story.[60] And this is the decisive point which reconnects the cultural history of the foreign combatant as presented in this book and the figures evoked in various juridical settings. The idea is to offer a link to the way certain figures epitomize the fantasies, the desires and the passions of legal actors distant in time, and the idea of the social imaginary outlined by Castoriadis.[61] In this regard, I find it useful to turn to Canadian philosopher Charles Taylor, who has developed a workable definition of the social imaginary as the following:

> the ways people imagine their social existence, how they fit together with others, how things go on between them and their fellows, the expectations that are normally met, and the deeper normative notions and images that underlie these expectations ... this is not often expressed in theoretical terms, but is carried in images, stories, and legends.[62]

It is important to underline the normative aspect of the social imaginary, given that legal actors are constantly involved in the production of rules to capture foreign fighters' status. As we shall see, the various forms of normative projects that inform the debates on foreign fighters (both

---

[60] See specifically Castoriadis, *The Imaginary Institution of Society*, pp. 184–189. Bottici further explains: 'Otherwise put, the definition of the "real" is the result of the dialectics between the instituted and the instituting side of the social imaginary. Behind this idea there is a complex view of the relationship between individuals who cannot but exist within imaginary significations, and a social imaginary which cannot but exist in and through individuals themselves.' Bottici, 'From Imagination to the Imaginary', p. 27.

[61] 'Castoriadis offers a picture of the relation between the psyche and the social in which neither is reduced to the other. There is rather a relation of interdependency which he terms "leaning on". The psyche maintains a certain independence of the social, while necessarily being modified by the social imaginaries to which it is exposed. Nonetheless these social imaginaries are reinterpreted in its own terms. An individual is always socially formed, but also bears the distinctiveness of its own psychic formation.' Lennon, *Imagination and the Imaginary*, pp. 77–78.

[62] Charles Taylor, *Modern Social Imaginaries* (Durham, NC: Duke University Press 2004) pp. 23–24.

nationally and internationally) are flooded with images that emerge from the actors' inner life. These form the magma of the social imaginary, and become a *repertoire* that in Taylor's words 'is carried in images, stories, and legends': the nobility of the adventurers à la Byron, the paternalism of the former European colonizers, the twisted romanticism of contemporary jihadists. An ambivalent repertoire, as it emanates from the fears and fantasies of the various legal actors who try to subsume foreign fighters within the rational endeavour of lawmaking. As Berman reminds us:

> the cultural approach explores the way international lawyers and policy-makers construct their images ... in accordance with their own implicit, culturally and historically contingent fears and fantasies ... one should not seek to get rid of cultural images but to make them explicit, evaluate them substantially, allow them to compete with alternative images.[63]

And so international lawyers and policymakers construct the law related to foreign fighters by resorting to their own culturally and historically contingent fantasies and fears. These crystallize into images of the 'good' and 'bad' foreign combatant, which help them to characterize *how* civil war should be conducted, *who* is a legitimate fighter, or *which side* of the trench is the right one to die for. Read this way, the imagination of legal actors should not be seen as a purely negative enterprise. If legal categories are necessarily ambiguous, this could in fact be seen, according to Berman, as an opportunity to 'allow [images] to compete with alternative images'. This approach is a way to rethink the story one is accustomed to, and most importantly to include other narratives. What is at stake is not only how one can write the history of the foreign fighter per se, but the histories of international law more generally. I will try to elucidate this point further in the next two sections.

I.5 Engaging with the Past

The historical work presented in this book has been influenced by the genealogical method developed by a variety of authors commonly

---

[63] Nathaniel Berman, 'Legalizing Jerusalem: Or, of Law, Fantasy, and Faith' (1996) 45 *Catholic University Law Review* 823–835, pp. 830–831. For an earlier – different – attempt to analyse the conscious and unconscious resort to images used by international lawyers see Georg Schwarzenberger, 'Images and Models of International law' (1966) 19 *Current Legal Problems* 192–207.

associated with French post-structuralism.[64] This has provided the background for articulating my claim around the different figures of the foreign combatant, via a reading of history centred on the study of discourse.[65] Broadly conceived, genealogy not only investigates how certain ideas and concepts are always rooted in specific historical, political and linguistic contexts, but it also suggests a vision of history in terms of accidents, ruptures and discontinuities.[66] Specifically, it seeks to identify the deviations which contributed to the formation of certain apparently stable and well-rounded truths. Or as Foucault put it: 'genealogy does not pretend to go back in time to restore an unbroken continuity ... it seeks to make visible all of those discontinuities that cross us'.[67]

If genealogy focuses on the ruptures, the suppressions and the exclusions that cross us, Foucault himself remained cautious about the purpose of this method: 'its duty is not to demonstrate that the past actively exist in the present'.[68] At first glance, this seems to contravene the project of a theorist whose aim had always been to write a history of the present. But that the past can represent a means to understand the present is an idea that must be handled with due care.[69]

Every historical period comes with its own *episteme*, with a system of significations which introduces a form of radical discontinuity within any underlying idea of continuity of forms and concepts.[70] The interwar reliance on neutrality laws to read the phenomenon of foreign volunteers is very different from the post-Geneva 1949 landscape, to offer a blunt

---

[64] It would be impossible to sum up the diverse contributions of this movement. The works of the authors cited throughout the text represent those on which I have built the methodological framework of this study. For a general reference: Catherine Belsey, *Poststructuralism: A Very Short Introduction* (Oxford: Oxford University Press 2002).

[65] *See* generally Michel Foucault, *The Archeology of Knowledge* (Abingdon: Routledge 2002).

[66] Michel Foucault, 'Nietzsche, Genealogy, History', in Donald F. Bouchard (ed.), *Language, Counter-Memory, Practice: Selected Essays and Interviews* (Ithaca, NY: Cornell University Press 1977) 139–164.

[67] *Ibid.*, pp. 146 and 162.

[68] *Ibid.*, p. 146.

[69] One must not fall into the naïve misunderstanding against which de Certeau warned: '[d'identifier] une permanence de surface [qui] maintient identiques les mots, les concepts les thèmes symboliques ... les mêmes mots ne désignent pas les mêmes choses. Des idées, des thèses, des classifications surnagent, passant d'un univers mental à un autre, mais chaque fois affectées par les structures qui les organisent et leur donnent une signification différente'. *See* Michel de Certeau, *Histoire et Psychanalyse Entre Sciences et Fiction* (Paris: Gallimard 1987) pp. 194–196.

[70] On this point see generally Michel Foucault, *The Order of Things* (New York: Routledge 2001).

example. This is not something undesirable, but rather enriching for the genealogist. In this sense, his task is to work at the hedge of continuity and discontinuity.[71]

I find the idea of working between continuity and discontinuity one of the peculiar traits of the so-called historical turn started by Martti Koskenniemi's *Gentle Civilizer*, which has since developed in multiple directions.[72] The historical turn has brought about one of the most significant shifts of international legal scholarship, especially because it translated into a critical strand that was able to problematize mainstream views of progress and modernization typically attached to the discipline.[73] This turn has produced breaks and ruptures, revealing a series of alternative stories, together with shedding light on instances that seemed forgotten, taken as natural or – and this is important – fell outside international law's traditional boundaries.[74]

The idea of working between continuity and discontinuity does not sound completely foreign to lawyers either. This is common practice in our profession. The fact that in the legal field the past is constantly retrieved as a source of rationalization of the present has been described by Anne Orford as the 'anachronistic' nature of the (international) legal method: 'the study of international law requires attention to the movement of meaning. International law is inherently genealogical depending as it does upon the transmission of concepts, languages and norms across

---

[71] 'La tâche de l'histoire n'est donc pas de choisir entre continuité et discontinuité, elle est d'assumer leur équivoque, d'examiner comment ces choses passées sont toujours présentes mais autrement qu'elles n'étaient, d'essayer de raconter le mieux possible cette altérité.' Mikhail Xifaras, 'Comment rendre le passé contemporain?', in Nicolas Laurent-Bonne and Xavier Prévost (eds.), *Penser l'ancien droit privé, volume II* (Paris: LGDJ 2018) 13–38, p. 32.

[72] Martti Koskenniemi, *The Gentle Civilizer of Nations: The Rise and Fall of International Law 1870–1960* (Cambridge: Cambridge University Press 2004). *See* also Matthew Craven, 'Theorizing the Turn to History in International Law', in Hoffmann and Orford (eds.), *The Oxford Handbook of the Theory of International Law* 21–37.

[73] *See* specifically Thomas Skouteris, *The Notion of Progress in International Law Discourse* (The Hague: Asser Press 2010).

[74] For a selection see Anthony Anghie, *Imperialism, Sovereignty and the Making of International Law* (Cambridge: Cambridge University Press 2006); Sundhya Pahuja, *Decolonizing International Law: Development, Economic Growth and the Politics of Universality* (Cambridge: Cambridge University Press 2011); Martti Koskenniemi, Walter Rech and Manuel Jimenez Fonseca (eds.), *International Law and Empire: Historical Explorations* (Oxford: Oxford University Press 2017); and Matthew Craven, Malgosia Fitzmaurice and Maria Vogiatzi (eds.), *Time, History and International* (Leiden: Brill 2007). *See* also Philip Allot, 'International Law and the Idea of History' (1999) 1 *Journal of History of International Law* 1–21.

time and space. The past, far from being gone, is constantly being retrieved as a source or rationalization of present obligation'.[75] This is to say that, unlike historians, legal scholars are interested in how concepts move across time and space, rather than seeking for a pure contextualization of the so-called historical archive.

Orford thus posits an important methodological distinction with both the Cambridge school and a vision of history as a product purely of the historian.[76] 'Between the meaning that has become an object, and the meaning that allows to understand it today', as Foucault notes, there is the juncture where it is possible to situate a workable methodological position.[77] Let me now offer an example which points to the idea of working between continuity and discontinuity that I have just evoked.

The three historical periods chosen in this study can be seen as moments of rupture – that is, moments where the discourse of legal

---

[75] Anne Orford, 'On International Legal Method' (2013) 1 *London Review of International Law* 166–197, p. 175.

[76] The writing of history – to use de Certeau's expression – passes inevitably from forms of emplotment dictated by the context and not ultimately by the author's views, an idea reiterated also by Collingwood and by the Annalistes. *See* Michel de Certeau, *The Writing of History* (New York: Columbia University Press 1992). *See* also Peter Burke, *The French Historical Revolution: The Annales School 1924–2014* (Cambridge: Polity Press 2015); Robin G. Collingwood, *The Idea of History* (Oxford: Oxford University Press 1994); Georg G. Iggers, *Historiography in the Twentieth Century: From Scientific Objectivity to the Postmodern Challenge* (Middletown, CT: Wesleyan University Press 2005); and Elizabeth A. Clark, *History, Theory, Text: Historians and the Linguistic Turn* (Cambridge, MA: Harvard University Press 2004).

[77] I side with Orford when she states: 'I want to stress that the contextualist school of intellectual history and international lawyers find common ground in their focus on interpreting texts in "context". Much of the best recent work engaging with the relation between past and present in international law is in sympathy with Skinner's arguments for interpreting classic texts in that respect. For Skinner, legal, philosophical, or political texts should not be read as sources of timeless truths or authoritative statements about fundamental concepts. In order to understand a particular statement, utterance, or text, the historian needs to reconstruct what its author was doing in making that statement, uttering that utterance, or writing that text ... But the polemical argument for "contextualism" in the work of intellectual historians is tightly bound up with an idea about time that marks the point at which international law and contextual intellectual history part company ... it is important for lawyers to engage with the context of past texts or utterances, but that it is also appropriate for historical jurisprudence or those attempting to understand current law to trace the evolution or transformation of concepts across time.' Anne Orford, 'International Law and the Limits of History', in Wouter Werner, Marieke de Hoon and Alexis Galán (eds.), *The Law of International Lawyers: Reading Martti Koskenniemi* (Cambridge: Cambridge University Press 2015) 297–320, pp. 5–6. *See* also Anne Orford, *International Law and the Politics of History* (Cambridge: Cambridge University Press 2021).

actors drastically change. This is especially evident when analysing the argumentations of international lawyers around the three civil wars: the Spanish, Angolan and Syrian wars are in fact described as different from 'all that has happened previously'. This is also translated into how lawyers and experts understand the problems of foreign fighters. For instance, during the Spanish Civil War, many internationalists would begin their dissertations by claiming that 'adventurers of all sorts have always fought in wars abroad', yet the present situation had to be understood differently due to the presence of fascist volunteers on the ground (something that altered the way in which the problem was traditionally understood). The same line of argumentation goes with mercenaries during decolonization and with terrorists today.

In a sense, this is the story of international law as a discipline built upon subsequent crisis or, to put it otherwise, obsessed with crisis discourse.[78] If this is an integral part of the preoccupations that legal actors project over foreign fighters, their change of register is important to confirm a twofold aspect. On the one hand, lawmakers want to break away from the past, to conclude that the present historical period (with its own foreign fighters) is radically different from what has occurred previously. On the other hand, their imaginary is held hostage to certain figures who keep coming back, and from which they cannot free themselves: the adventurer à la Byron, the heroes of the Spanish Civil War, the freedom fighters of decolonization. Figures that rise to their contextual meaning when placed in a historical context.[79] Figures which must not be seen only as imprisoned in that context, however, but that travel through time and reappear in subsequent epochs.

The idea that the past is not to be considered as a dead letter, but rather something which informs present legal obligations, is also one of the workhorses of Third World Approaches to International Law (TWAIL).[80] If the aim of this scholarship is to revive past practices,

---

[78] 'A crisis provides a focus for the development of the discipline and it allows international lawyers the sense that their work is of immediate, intense relevance . . . crisis structure our thinking about international law . . . international law's obsession with crisis leads us to concentrate on a single event or series of events and often to miss the larger picture.' Hilary Charlesworth, 'International Law: A Discipline of Crisis' (2002) 65 *Modern Law Review* 377–392, pp. 377, 382 and 384.

[79] For the idea that consciousness must always be historicized see specifically Thomas Khun, *The Structure of Scientific Revolutions* (Chicago: University of Chicago Press 1970).

[80] Among the vast TWAIL literature: Makau Mutua and Anthony Anghie, 'What Is TWAIL?' (2000) 94 *Proceedings of the Annual Meeting (American Society of*

institutions and discourses to show how they might form the basis of legal obligations in the present, its strand of critique remains rooted in a postcolonial approach to law.[81] As such, there is a tendency to emphasize the various encounters with the colonial 'other' and to put such encounters at the centre of their investigations. Although this critique is of fundamental importance for any stance against the universality of international law, the approach followed in this book does not go in that direction. I will try to explain this point by resorting again to the three contexts upon which this study is built.

Spain in the 1930s, Angola in the 1970s and contemporary Syria are undoubtedly *other* places with respect to the centrality of European consciousness, actors and institutions. They represent an alterity (for example, a 'barbaric/backward place', a 'space for adventure', a 'promised land') where different actors project their fantasies. The decisive point, however, is not to retrace an encounter with a colonial subject out there, or to unravel how legal discourses or practices have developed through the exclusion of certain others. The goal is rather to look at the *otherness* inherent in the figure of the foreign combatant itself. So that the 'barbarity', the 'fanaticism' or the 'heroism' attached to this figure are all fantasies that inhabit the consciousness of the actors who use and deploy them for different purposes.

International Law) 31–40; B. S. Chimni, 'Third World Approach to International Law: A Manifesto' (2006) 8 *International Community Law Review*; B. S. Chimni, 'The Past, Present and Future of International Law: A Critical Third World Approach' (2007) 8 *Melbourne Journal of International Law* 499–514; James Thuo Gathii, 'Imperialism, Colonialism and International Law' (2007) 54 *Buffalo Law Review* 1013–1066; James Thuo Gathii, 'TWAIL: A Brief History of Its Origins, Its Decentralized Network, and a Tentative Bibliography' (2011) 3 *Trade Law and Development* 27–64; Obiora Chinedu Okafor, 'Critical Third World Approaches to International Law (TWAIL): Theory, Methodology, or Both?' (2008) 10 *International Community Law Review* 371–378; and Obiora Chinedu Okafor, 'Newness, Imperialism, and International Legal Reform in Our Time: A TWAIL Perspective' (2005) 43 *Osgoode Hall Law Journal* 171–191. This remains of course a non-exhaustive list.

[81] *See* Alpana Roy, 'Postcolonial Theory and Law: A Critical Introduction' (2008) 29 *Adelaide Law Review* 315–357. *See* also Gayatri Chakravorty Spivak, *A Critique of Postcolonial Reason: Towards a History of the Vanishing Present* (Cambridge, MA: Harvard University Press 1999); Bart Moore-Gilbert, *Postcolonial Theory: Contexts, Practices, Politics* (London: Verso 1997); Henry Schwarz and Sangeeta Ray (eds.), *A Companion to Postcolonial Studies* (Malden, MA: Blackwell Publishing 2005); and Dipesh Chakrabarty, *Provincializing Europe: Postcolonial Thought and Historical Difference* (Princeton, NJ: Princeton University Press 2000).

Gerry Simpson has suggested something in a similar vein when analysing the pirate, as a figure underpinning the legal category of the 'enemy of humanity'.[82] As pirates started to be back in vogue with the advent of the global war on terror, Simpson seemed at first inclined towards a grand narrative about international law and the ever-present problem of piracy: 'the international community fights humanitarian wars against outlaws and pirates'.[83] This would have been a story of how the figure of the pirate is used to mobilize particular legal regimes (such as universal jurisdiction or humanitarian intervention). Yet Simpson moves towards another kind of narrative within his recital about pirates. By claiming that pirates were not always seen as criminals, but also as a 'mode of production supported by great Powers and Empires', or as active participants in rebellions, wars and revolutions, the Australian scholar ends up telling a different story, one which goes in the direction of ambivalence:

> it is important here to do more than simply make an argument about the return of the pirate or, indeed, produce a Schmittian salvo in the direction of Empire. What I want to suggest is that the pirate is a deeply ambiguous figure ... this ambiguity emerges precisely because of efforts to inject clear moral distinction into our dealings with enemies while at the same time erasing some of international law's most enduring demarcations ... if the pirate is [a] foundational category ... then it is little wonder that categories are blurring as this figure resurfaces. Indeed, the return of the pirate is a return to ambiguity ... pirates turn out to be not enemies of humankind but humankind in its plural guises.[84]

And so for our foreign fighters. Recounting their recent history could have resulted in looking at how this actor has been mobilized, by whom, and for what purposes: the Russian Comintern at the time of the Spanish Civil War, Third World states throughout decolonization, Western countries in today's war on terror. One would therefore be tempted to seek the usual suspects of international law: foreign intervention, the crime of aggression, the laws of neutrality and the duties of states in civil war, or indeed the combatant's privilege. Let me be clear, all of these are integral and essential parts of the narrative, and the three chapters of this book make explicit references to such a legal context. But my story veers in

---

[82] *See* Gerry Simpson, 'Piracy and the Origins of Enmity', in M. Craven et al. (eds.), *Time, History and International Law* (Leiden: Brill 2007) 219–230.
[83] *Ibid.*, p. 224.
[84] *Ibid.*, pp. 225–230.

another direction. In this regard, and to make my position more explicit, a few words on the issue of indeterminacy.

I.6 The Stakes for International Law

I am of course very much indebted to Martti Koskenniemi's critique of the international legal argument.[85] The indeterminacy of norms and the binary opposition which structure legal rules are evident in the way actors engage in passionate fights to establish who is the 'good' and who is the 'bad' foreign combatant. Leaving aside the fact that such a model is built upon a liberal theory of politics, the story of how foreign fighters enter legal debates points to the inherent political premises of law.[86] For critics such as Koskenniemi, 'modern international law is an elaborate framework for deferring substantive resolution elsewhere'[87] – only to realize that 'a demonstration that "it all depends on politics" does not move one inch towards a *better* politics'.[88] Engaging in the language of expertise is certainly a tactic, and David Kennedy has demonstrated that strategy masterfully.[89] But what about the short-circuits of power, its grey areas, its ambiguities?[90] What about the inner passions, the

---

[85] See Martti Koskenniemi, *From Apology to Utopia: The Structure of International Legal Argument. Reissue with a New Epilogue* (Cambridge: Cambridge University Press 2005).

[86] For a critique of Koskenniemi see Emmanuelle Jouannet, 'Koskenniemi: A Critical Introduction', in Martti Koskenniemi, *The Politics of International Law* (Oxford: Hart 2011) 1–32.

[87] Martti Koskenniemi, *The Politics of International Law* (Oxford: Hart 2011), p. 58.

[88] Of course, Koskenniemi realizes the different (political) projects which have informed his trajectory: 'If 20 years ago it seemed intellectually necessary and politically useful to demonstrate the indeterminacy (and, thus, political preference) within the idiom of public international law, today's critique will have to focus on the clash of different idioms – public international law just one competitor among many to global authority – and highlight the way their competing descriptions work to push forward some actors or interests while leaving others in the shadows.' *Ibid.*, pp. 64–68.

[89] David Kennedy, *A World of Struggle. How Power, Law and Expertise Shape Political Economy* (Princeton, NJ: Princeton University Press 2016).

[90] 'Martti Koskenniemi discussed the double aspiration of international lawyers in relation to power in terms of the competing discourses of "apology" and "utopia"; Richard Falk diagnosed it in terms of the twin desires for "normativity" and "relevance"; I have often referred to it as the relationship between "power" and "principle." International lawyers often dream of the final absorption of sovereign power by internationalist principle, of conflict by cooperation, of atomization by community ... At a general level, these dynamics sometimes tip international lawyers over in the direction of "apology," in which the inequalities of wealth and power are simply denied in favor of abstract legalism; at other times, they tip international lawyers over in the direction of "utopia," in which

1.6 THE STAKES FOR INTERNATIONAL LAW

ambivalences of discourses, the fantasies that populate them? And why not reconsider our ambiguous relationship with power itself? This should not be read as an invitation to relativism, or to political disengagement, but rather to restart a dialogue with our own fractured self. Writing a purely Marxist or TWAIL or feminist history of international law are very important enterprises. But so is reflecting more on the ambivalences and contradictions of each of the above positions (and so of pro- and anti-colonial positions, pro- and anti-imperial positions, pro- and anti-jihadist positions, before pointing them out simply as fanatical, racist, sexist, or imperialist).[91]

To be fair, Koskenniemi's turn towards history has already directed critique from the analysis of ahistorical structures to the moving landscape of a whole diverse set of actors, places and chronologies.[92] What

---

the unjust present is juxtaposed with a future world in which the conditions for the rule of law would finally prevail. By contrast, especially in relation to specific problems, the dynamics of ambivalence often produce fascinating, multi-leveled discourses, rich in contradiction, paradox, and complex imagery.' Berman, *Passion and Ambivalence*, pp. 419–420.

[91] 'The basic paradox within international law meant that it could combine a universalist façade with discriminatory and imperialistic practices. Indeed, its extension to the universal level was not possible without completely recasting all non-Western political entities into the mould of modern European states, which in turn required the irreparable destruction of all traditional forms of polity in existence.' Emmanuelle Jouannet, 'Universalism and Imperialism: The True–False Paradox of International Law?' (2007) 18 *European Journal of International Law* 379–407, pp. 380–382. Berman also elucidates this point in relation to the ambivalences permeating the idea of self-determination: 'On one level, the lesson of this story is the elementary Legal Realist point that no formal distinction, like that between "self-determination" and "secession," is determinate without reference to auxiliary cultural and political judgments. The Legal Realist would show that the question of whether the Algerian FLN was a movement for "secession" or "self-determination" depended on competing theories of colonialism and that the doctrinal distinction only looks self-interpreting during periods when these kinds of judgments are not challenged. Yet the vicissitudes of self-determination do not simply demonstrate the indeterminacy of such distinctions, but rather, the ways in which the ever-renewed attempt to gain control over nationalism seems to generate the very forms of the resistance that threaten that control ... In a very concrete way, the challenge emerges out of the dynamics of the internationalist ambivalence toward nationalism; in projecting the feared elements of nationalism into a forbidden zone, internationalists should not be surprised at the eventual "return of the repressed".' Nathaniel Berman, 'Nationalism "Good" and "Bad": The Vicissitudes of an Obsession' (1996) 90 *Proceedings of the Annual Meeting of the American Society of International Law* 214–218, p. 216.

[92] As Emmanuelle Jouannet points out: 'the denunciation of political liberalism within international law also reflects one possible principle driving the evolution of Koskenniemi's thought since *From Apology to Utopia*, a more complex development than can be accounted for by structuralism alone. The discourse is not self-contained, it is

remains to be seen is how to mould the historical material, how to expand the histories of international law.[93] On the one side, 'we do not need to always look at Westphalia',[94] and on the other, 'by confining themselves to the very same terms, categories and vocabularies of the linear disciplinary histories [they seek to disrupt], these new critical histories uphold more than they disrupt or displace'.[95] As one soon realizes, the limits of our imagination *are* the limits of history.

And so one can well advance the claim that categorizing foreign fighters as 'good' and 'bad' is a common trope used by states to legitimize/delegitimize forms of intervention in a foreign war. Or that the law in relation to foreign volunteers reflects the change in worldviews from the age of positivism and neutrality to postcolonial left-wing euphoria, to the fight against an absolute evil (such as Islamic terrorism). No one is denying such arguments. I have already mentioned international law's usual suspects as examples of histories one can write following those lines. Yet the present study wants to go beyond the dictates of the *raison d'état*, the pragmatic decisions of realpolitik, or law's ideological developments.

---

not only structure; international law cannot be analysed as a language alone. It is also a set of utterances that produce social effects; it is an instrument that can be manipulated; and it is a practice that can be the bearer of much promise. It is not only a language; it is also a discourse. It is a politics every bit as much as it is a language; and this political dimension opens up new perspectives that become, for Koskenniemi, new fields of investigation. Law is politics just as law is culture; law is alive. It is not the metaphor of the game, so commonly used today, that is appropriate to describe the manner in which Koskenniemi conceives of international law; rather, it is without doubt – as his works make clear – the old metaphor of the "tongue" that is best suited to this task; a tongue by now moulded by many centuries of culture, religion and history; a common tongue, constructed progressively, that has enriched other domains even as it has sombrely colonised them. Law belongs to the realm of the tongue, of lived experience, of history. To compare it to a game or to a system of rules, or even to a set of networks would without doubt appear reductionist to Koskenniemi, as it would be to ignore that in law which goes beyond the rules and the systems, beyond the networks, beyond the instruments used.' Jouannet, 'Koskenniemi: A Critical Introduction', p. 15.

[93] See Martti Koskenniemi, 'Expanding Histories of International Law' (2016) 56 *American Journal of Legal History* 104–112 and Martti Koskenniemi, 'Histories of International Law: Significance and Problems for a Critical View' (2013) 27 *Temple International and Comparative Law Journal* 215–240.

[94] See Alexandra Kemmerer, '"We Do Not Need to Always Look at Westphalia…" A Conversation with Martti Koskenniemi and Anne Orford' (2015) 17 *Journal of the History of International Law* 1–14.

[95] Jean d'Aspremont, 'Critical Histories of International Law and the Repression of Disciplinary Imagination' (2019) 7 *London Review of International Law* 98–115, p. 103.

1.6 THE STAKES FOR INTERNATIONAL LAW

To retrace a cultural history of the foreign fighter might then well be a history of the phantasmatic figures which populate the imaginary of legal actors in different contexts and places. This is done by taking the concept of ambivalence as a pillar, and as such rejecting 'international legal history as an ever-advancing dialectic of restatement and renewal'.[96] The genealogist à la Berman does not see law merely as a repressive tool of power and control, but as a multifaceted instrument of regulation, emancipation and illusion: 'it is precisely international law's lack of coherence, the instability of its transitory configurations of rules and players that makes it a hopeful enterprise';[97] a discipline haunted by passions, fantasies and desires, which must necessarily reflect those of its creators.[98] It is in this sense that ambivalence should be understood, as traversing the whole structure of apologetic and utopian claims of international law.[99]

To restart a conversation on law's ambivalent side is a way to investigate further how and why certain norms are produced the way they are.[100] I believe there is a need to move away from technical expertise and to open other perspectives out of the hyper-procedural way in which international law is produced and enforced.[101] In this sense, the categorizations of foreign fighters are also the product of ambivalent passions,

---

[96] Berman, 'In the Wake of Empire', p. 1523.
[97] Ibid., p. 1524.
[98] Yishai Blank has worked on the idea of 'legal reenchantment', a position which I find particularly interesting to frame my own: 'contemporary antirealists are less interested in resisting the rehashed themes regarding law's indeterminacy and power – the familiar legal-realist challenges. Rather, they are offering the idea that there is "more" to law than its instrumentality, power, and distributive impact. This insistence on "more," I argue, lies at the heart of legal reenchantment.' Yishai Blank, 'The Reenchantment of Law' (2011) 63 *Cornell Law Review* 633–670, p. 643.
[99] 'Let's think about the meaning and uses ... of break and continuity, let's think about the project's ambivalent history.' Berman, 'In the Wake of Empire', p. 1527.
[100] One should not misread this argument as posing a dichotomy between reason and emotions. On this point see specifically Antonio R. Damasio, *Descartes' Error: Emotion, Reason, and the Human Brain* (New York: Avon Books, 1995). On the cognitive structure of emotions and their relevance for decision-making see in particular Andrew Ortnoy, Gerald L. Clore and Allan Collins (eds.), *The Cognitive Structure of Emotions* (Cambridge: Cambridge University Press 1988). In relation to international law see Andrea Bianchi and Anne Saab, 'Fear and International Law-Making: An Exploratory Inquiry' (2019) 32 *Leiden Journal of International Law* 351–365.
[101] In a similar vein, Gerry Simpson writes: 'Maybe it's time then to search again for international law's unconscious soul ... to bring out the unexpected, perhaps unconscious, expressions of political desire at the base of the legal-technocratic procedure: international law's intimate subterfuges, its exiled subjects.' Gerry Simpson, *The*

fears and desires, and not of politics and self-interest alone.[102] This occurs because international law – like any other type of law – is finally a human product. As such it is influenced by the passions and the ambivalences of its creators. Hence the constant recourse to something *other than law*.

That approach can be enriching not only as a matter of history-writing, but also for the practitioner and the expert. My book can in fact push them to face their own inner tensions and ambiguities as something not to discharge, but to reconnect with. My suggestion is that coming to terms with this aspect of lawmaking could be beneficial, rather than hiding behind technical legalese. There is something to gain here in recognizing that our cultural biases, fantasies and fears come into play when we engage with certain non-state actors, for instance, and with international law more generally.

To offer some clearer markers, resorting to such an approach can be useful to: (1) de-exoticize today's foreign fighters under the recent global war on terror, and thus expand their histories and consequently the histories of international law; (2) clarify where our normative values come from, and what the assumptions are that we resort to when we look at the involvement of third-country nationals in armed conflicts; (3) show how the figure of the foreign combatant is always differentiated into a 'good' and a 'bad' version; (4) propose a broader reflection upon the reasons why the status of foreign fighters remains one of the problematic nodes of international law.[103]

One final yet essential point. As we shall see through the chapters, foreign volunteers' choices to join wars abroad point to the ambivalent

Sentimental Life of International Law: Literature, Language, and Longing in World Politics (Oxford: Oxford University Press 2021) pp. 10–11.

[102] 'If various emotions have the structure of cognition, and cognition itself often functions in an intuitive, affective way, then bringing the two together by recognizing the place of emotions in law does not seem anomalous after all.' Kathryn Abrams and Hila Keren, 'Who's Afraid of Law and the Emotions', in Susan A. Bandes, Jody Lyneé Madeira, Kathryn D. Temple and Emily Kidd White (eds.), *The Edward Elgar Research Handbook on Law and Emotion* (Northampton, MA: Edward Elgar 2021) 566–600, p. 580.

[103] The argument holds even more, given that it is still impossible for states to reach a definitive compromise over the legal status of foreign individuals in wars abroad: at various times, different definitions have been adopted, without however clarifying the legitimacy of foreign fighters for subsequent conflicts. See on this point Marnie Lloydd, 'Framing Foreign Fighting: Exploring the Scope of Prevention and the Categorisation of Fighters in International Law', in Christophe Paulussen and Martin Scheinin (eds.), *Human Dignity and Human Security in Times of Terrorism* (The Hague: Asser Press 2020) 207–238.

landscape of commitments related to various liberating projects. Their presence on the battlefield is framed through a good/bad dichotomy, this dichotomy translates into normative responses of different scales and, most importantly, it reflects moral–political stances of diverse kinds. These reveal how Europeans have certainly gone to fight in wars abroad before, but for quite different reasons. Most importantly, they have gone to fight against and for fascism, they have gone to fight for and against communism, and they have gone to fight against present-day dictatorships, though with different projects in mind. Read this way, we could ask how the presence of these individuals is contributing to shape our own perception of civil war and, consequently, how we think about our values and beliefs when we encounter any legislative measure on foreign fighters. If volunteering abroad has epitomized different political visions and passions, perhaps this can help us think about the larger picture, rather than apply a deficit model. Apart from any postmodern posture, shouldn't we ask ourselves what liberating projects we can commit to? What stances are we able to accept, or even hear? And how do we understand the claims made by present-day non-state armed groups, especially those pointing beyond the contours of the nation-state? The figures which populate the imaginary of legal actors are a way to reconnect with our own ambivalent conscience in this regard.[104] Perhaps leaving that space open is the most genuine emancipatory venture we can hope for in the anxious times that come after the fall of utopias.

---

[104] Butler recognizes for instance the ambivalent position of Klein with regards to love and aggression: 'In the work of Melanie Klein, guilt appears to emerge, not in consequence of internalizing an external prohibition, but as a way of preserving the object of love from one's own potentially obliterating violence. Guilt serves the function of preserving the object of love and, hence, of preserving love itself. What might it mean to understand guilt, then, as a way in which love preserves the object it might otherwise destroy? ... It is in this sense that guilt emerges in the course of melancholia not only, as the Freudian view would have it, to keep the dead object alive, but to keep the living object from death, where death means the death of love, including the occasions of separation and loss ... In order to preserve the object from one's own aggression, an aggression that always accompanies love (as conflict), guilt enters the psychic scene as a necessity ... Because love and aggression work together, the mitigation of aggression through guilt is also the mitigation of love. Guilt works, then, both to foreclose and to continue love, or rather, to continue love (less passionately, to be sure) as the effect of a foreclosure.' Judith Butler, *The Psychic Life of Power: Theories in Subjection* (Stanford, CA: Stanford University Press 1997) pp. 25–26.

I.7 Content of the Chapters

Each of the three chapters starts *in medias res*, with a story immersing the reader in the historical context and delineating the legal contours of the civil war analysed. These narratives set the tone of the ideological struggles fought and offer a background to the legal concepts related to that particular war and its actors. The concepts treated are not left solely to these introductory stories, of course. They are organically developed during each chapter, taking the reader through the various sites where the figures of the foreign fighter eventually emerge.

Chapter 1 opens in May 1937 at the Council of the League of Nations (the Council). There, the Spanish representative is pleading his case to sustain the legitimate volunteers fighting on the Republican side, while denouncing the presence of fascist troops sent by Rome and Berlin. The chapter moves on to analyse the Anglo-American doctrine during the same years, as well as domestic discussions in France and the United Kingdom over the adoption of ad hoc legislation to prevent their citizens going to fight in Spain. It ends with an excursus on the Hague Peace Conferences of 1907, where early norms on volunteers were codified. The purpose of the first chapter is to delineate the legal, cultural and political terrain to understand how foreign volunteering was understood in the interwar period. It shows how the figure of the adventurer as a legacy of the long nineteenth century underpins the conversations of legal actors of the time, and the changes this figure undergoes through the Spanish Civil War years.

Chapter 2 opens with the mercenaries' trial in Angola (June 1976). This trial provides an entry point to the decolonization period, showing how foreign fighters are understood in a new historical context. The chapter moves on to analyse crucial debates at the UN General Assembly and at the Security Council in the period 1960–1976, as well as national responses to the condemnation of the British mercenaries in Luanda. It ends with an excursus on the advancement of the laws of war in Additional Protocol I to the Geneva Conventions (1977). The aim of Chapter 2 is to show the persistence and modification of the figure of the foreign volunteer (that is, the adventurer of Chapter 1). It highlights an interesting inversion of perspective from the Spanish Civil War era: now the noble volunteers of the International Brigades are taken as an example by the representatives of European states to legitimize the presence of their citizens in Africa. This figure will be contrasted with that of the soldier of fortune, who resembles and embodies an older one:

the white colonial ruler against whom wars of national liberation are being fought.

Chapter 3 focuses on the Syrian Civil War. In this context, the criminalization by the Security Council of the foreign terrorist fighter (2014) once again sparked passionate debates among experts, state representatives and politicians around the legal status of foreign volunteers. Chapter 3 retraces the debates at the Security Council and in domestic parliaments, and moves on to analyse some crucial court decisions in France and the United Kingdom concerning the jihadist foreign fighter. It puts in question the proscription of this actor as the current enemy of humanity. This final chapter shows how ad hoc legislation and court decisions on foreign terrorist fighters are still filled by a series of figures from the past. These figures contribute to making the legislative and adjudicative processes deeply ambiguous. Such images inform the legal conversations and point once again to the foreign fighter as an unsettling category.

1

The Spanish Civil War and the Legacy of Nineteenth-Century Adventurers

1.1 Who Is a Genuine Volunteer?

May 1937. When the Spanish minister of foreign affairs Julio Álvarez del Vayo sent to the League of Nations a White Book containing evidence of regular presence of Italian troops on Spanish soil, the civil war had been going on for about a year.[1] Having started as a revolt against the government of the Popular Front, the rebellion was soon joined by military generals and factions opposed to the Republican government in Madrid.[2] First with the help of Mussolini and then of Hitler, Francisco Franco – at the time commander-in-chief of the Army of Africa – had been able to transport his troops from Morocco to Europe, and was soon recognized as the most experienced general to lead the Nationalist army.[3] What began as a mutiny resulted in a civil war, thanks also to the aid furnished by foreign powers in various forms.

In March 1937, del Vayo had sent a note to the League's Secretary General denouncing the presence of Italian troops as 'constituting an attack upon the territorial integrity of Spain' and requesting the note be communicated to all member states.[4] The Council confronted the issue during its ninety-seventh session held in Geneva on 28–29 May.

---

[1] League of Nations, Official Journal, Special Supplement 165, White Book (1937) pp. 4–140.

[2] For a detailed account see Hugh Thomas, *The Spanish Civil War: Third Edition. Revised and Enlarged* (London: Penguin 1977). See also Michael Alpert, *A New International History of the Spanish Civil War* (London: Macmillan 1994) and Guy Hermet, *La Guerre d'Espagne* (Paris: Éditions du Seuil 1989). For a detailed legal analysis of the war see Ann Van Wynen and A. J. Thomas Jr., 'International Legal Aspects of the Civil War in Spain, 1936-39', in Richard Falk (ed.), *The International Law of Civil War* (Baltimore, MD: Johns Hopkins University Press 1971) 111–175.

[3] *See* John F. Coverdale, *Italian Intervention in the Spanish Civil War* (Princeton, NJ: Princeton University Press 1975) and Robert H. Whealey, *Hitler and Spain: The Nazi Role in the Spanish Civil War, 1936–1939* (Lexington: University of Kentucky Press 1989).

[4] *See* on this point Francis O. Wilcox, 'The League of Nations and the Spanish Civil War' (1938) 198 *Annals of the American Academy of Political and Social Science* 65–72, p. 65.

1.1 WHO IS A GENUINE VOLUNTEER? 37

Although this was not the first attempt made by Spanish representatives to denounce the interventions of Italy and Germany to sustain Franco's army, the League had never previously been confronted with such evidence. The White Book was in fact the result of a series of documents found in the possession of Italian officers during the battle of Guadalajara, one of the fiercest fought during the war (8–23 March 1937). The Book gave a detailed account of the war materiel, military structure and instructions sent by Rome to its volunteer units. It included payrolls, roadmaps, the numbers of weapons assigned to the various brigades, as well as copies of their military badges.

Certainly, the presence of foreign contingents on Spanish soil had been known for some time. The Non-Intervention Committee based in London had already implemented a land and sea borders control plan to stop the influx of volunteers in February 1937.[5] Hence the League was certainly not the only venue to look at the problem of foreign fighters during those years. Yet it was there that the Spanish representatives kept bringing their claims, denouncing the Non-Intervention Agreement as a 'legal monstrosity'.[6]

On 28 May del Vayo started his speech in front of the Council by referring to the last extraordinary session held in December 1936, which had culminated in the adoption of the first resolution on the Spanish situation.[7] He stated that the evidence collected during the previous months proved beyond doubt that an armed intervention was underway.[8] Then he turned to the White Book, which in his view clearly demonstrated the following:

> (1) The existence on Spanish territory of complete units of the Italian army whose personnel, material, liaison and command are Italian; (2) The fact that these Italian military units behave in the sectors assigned to them as a veritable army of occupation; (3) The existence of services organized by the Italian Government for these military units on Spanish territory as if they were in a finally conquered country; (4) The active participation of the most eminent personalities in the Italian Government, who have

---

[5] *See* Patricia A. M. Van Der Esch, *Prelude to War: The International Repercussions of the Spanish Civil War (1936–1939)* (The Hague: Martinus Nijhoff 1951) p. 77.

[6] *See* the original speech by del Vayo in September 1936. League of Nations, Official Journal, Special Supplement 155, 17th Ordinary Session, sixth plenary meeting (1936) pp. 49–50.

[7] League of Nations, Official Journal 18, 97th Session of the Council, fifth meeting (1937) p. 317.

[8] *Ibid.*

addressed messages to the invading forces, giving them advice and encouragement in their aggression.[9]

The Spanish representative made some crucial categorizations in his speech, classifying the contingents as 'complete units' forming an 'army of occupation', and having a clear line of command attributable to the Italian government. In other words, the organized and structured character of the volunteers sent by Mussolini constituted for him an armed aggression. Yet, beyond these technicalities:

> it is painful for the Spanish Government to accept the use of the title 'volunteers' for two different categories of men; on the one hand, those who are sent from countries where every free expression of will is crushed by the iron tyranny of the totalitarian regimes and who are not even volunteers in name ... On the other hand, those who came of their own free will to fight side by side with us ... A clear and noble ideal brought these volunteers into the struggle in Spain because of its universal aspect.[10]

The distinction made between regular and irregular military units is here framed by a clear moral divide. The real volunteers are understood as those men fighting for an ideal: that is, they had come to Spain not following the orders of a government, but rather of their own free will. Moreover, the struggle fought in Spain was to del Vayo universally recognized as a 'just' cause for engaging within the ranks of the Republicans. Here is an indication of how the status of foreign fighters depends primarily on an ideological stance.

This differentiation between 'good' and 'bad' volunteers can be better understood if one looks at the political context of the time. The civil war was generally perceived in Europe as a conflict between two contesting ideologies: communism against fascism.[11] This was evidenced by the arrival of thousands of volunteers ready to fight on one side or the other.[12] In a historical moment that was witnessing the consolidation

---

[9] *Ibid.*, p. 318.

[10] *Ibid.*, p. 319.

[11] See Koskenniemi, *The Gentle Civilizer*, pp. 338–342. See more generally Alun Kenwood (ed.), *The Spanish Civil War: A Cultural and Historical Reader* (Providence, RI: Berg Publishers 1993).

[12] The literature on foreign volunteers during the Spanish Civil War is vast. For some compelling studies see Peter Carroll, *The Odyssey of the Abraham Lincoln Brigade: Americans in the Spanish Civil War* (Stanford, CA: Stanford University Press 1994); Richard Baxell, *British Volunteers in the Spanish Civil War: The British Battalion in the International Brigades, 1936–1939* (London: Routledge 2004); Christopher Othen, *Franco's International Brigades: Adventurers, Fascists and Christian Crusaders in the*

of totalitarianism, the liberal European powers were deeply worried that the Spanish scenario could result in a world war, and did not wish to expose themselves militarily.[13] Hence the Franco-British plan of non-intervention. Conversely, the Soviet Union hoped to intensify the hostilities in order to gain a greater sphere of influence on the world stage.[14]

Politics aside, the Iberian Peninsula also became the battlefield for wider cultural struggles: between fascism and communism, certainly, but also between civilization and barbarism.[15] The war thus had great resonance among European and American intelligentsia, with many renowned personalities expressing their support, or joining the battlefield. George Orwell, Simone Weil, Ernest Hemingway and André Malraux were among those leftist intellectuals who stood with the Republicans. Drieu la Rochelle, Evelyn Waugh and Ezra Pound were sympathizers of Franco.[16] Their open commitment to the Spanish conflict is far from insignificant. It is precisely this cultural heritage that would flood the

---

Spanish Civil War (London: Hurst 2013); Rémi Skoutelsky, *L'Espoir Guidait Leur Pas: Les Volontaires Français Dans les Brigades Internationales* (Paris: Grasset & Fasquelle 1998); Giles Tremlett, *The International Brigades: Fascism, Freedom and the Spanish Civil War* (London: Bloomsbury 2020); and Judith Keene, *Fighting for Franco: International Volunteers in Nationalist Spain during the Spanish Civil War* (London: Hambledon Continuum 2007).

[13] This point is explained in Nathaniel Berman, 'Between "Alliance" and "Localization": Nationalism and the New Oscillationism' (1994) 26 *New York University Journal of International Law & Politics* 449–492.

[14] See Dan Richardson, *Comintern Army: The International Brigades and the Spanish Civil War* (Lexington: University of Kentucky Press 1982) and Stanley G. Payne, *The Spanish Civil War, the Soviet Union, and Communism* (New Haven, CT: Yale University Press 2004).

[15] It is no coincidence that important internationalists of the time took opposing positions on the war. Louis Le Fur, for instance, supported the legitimate resistance of Franco's army and thus the lawful intervention of Germany and Italy: 'On comprend ... le jugement d'Unamuno, souvent cité: "Dans l'Espagne actuelle, il y a d'un côté la civilisation et de l'autre la barbarie", ou celui plus récent du cardinal Verdier en réponse à la Lettre collective des Evêques d'Espagne: "La lutte titanesque qui ensanglante le sol de la catholique Espagne est en réalité la lutte entre la civilisation chrétienne et la prétendue civilisation de l'athéisme soviétique".' Louis le Fur, *La Guerre d'Espagne et le Droit* (Paris: Les Editions Internationales 1938) p. 25. On the opposite side, one can find the position of Scelle. See George Scelle, 'La Guerre Civile Espagnole et le Droit des Gens' (1939) 13 *Revue Générale de Droit International Public* 197–228.

[16] *See* generally Valentine Cunningham (ed.), *The Spanish Front: Writers on the Civil War* (Oxford: Oxford University Press 1986) and Stanley Weintraub, *The Last Great Cause: The Intellectuals and the Spanish Civil War* (New York: Weybright and Talley 1968). *See* also James D. Wilkinson, 'Truth and Delusion: European Intellectuals in Search of the Spanish Civil War' (1987) 76 *Salmagundi* 3–52. For some notable literary works which include personal accounts of the war, *see* George Orwell, *Homage to Catalonia* (London:

imaginaries of legal actors in the following decades. The images of these personalities would reappear in other contexts and times, influencing how foreign fighters' causes would later be understood. But for the moment, let's return to the Council in May 1937.

After del Vayo completed his speech, the French minister of foreign affairs Yvon Delbos took the floor. First, Delbos reiterated the achievements made by the Non-Intervention Committee, praising especially the frontier control plan.[17] Then, he stressed that there was a clear duty facing the League, to recall 'the foreign combatants, whose presence in Spain ... serves to feed the flames of civil war and threatens to extend the conflict'.[18] These words were echoed by the British foreign secretary Anthony Eden, who himself praised the Non-Intervention Agreement. On the question of the withdrawal of volunteers, Eden pointed out that 'foreigners engaged in hostilities, whether on one side of the other, have no business on Spanish soil'.[19] He concluded his speech by stressing that the Committee was presently negotiating solutions to implement a viable plan for the withdrawal of non-Spanish combatants.

Of a quite different tone was the intervention by the Soviet representative Litvinoff. As he condemned the 'violent intrusion of foreign armed forces into the territory of a Member of the League of Nations', he also called it an 'aggression in its crudest form'.[20] The Russian diplomat went on to emphasize how Franco's rebellion would not have been possible without the aid coming from abroad, and that the White Book clearly proved that 'tens of thousands of well-armed and trained foreigners poured into Spain to help the rebels ... foreigners who were on active service in the armed forces of other States'.[21]

This was hardly surprising. Russia had firmly opposed the Italian and German intervention in Spain since the very beginning of the hostilities. Already in December 1936, when del Vayo appealed to the League on the basis of Art. 11 of the Covenant, the Russians had clearly voiced their

---

Penguin 2013); Georges Bernanos, *Les Grands Cimetières Sous la Lune* (Paris: Plon/Seuil 1995); and Ernest Hemingway, *For Whom the Bell Tolls* (London: Vintage Books 2005).

[17] League of Nations, Official Journal 18, 97th Session of the Council, fifth meeting (1937) p. 321.
[18] *Ibid.*
[19] *Ibid.*, p. 324.
[20] *Ibid.*, p. 321.
[21] *Ibid.*, p. 322.

support for the Spanish government.²² Back then, the Soviet representative had made clear that 'certain foreign Powers have openly intervened in the interests of the rebels ... supplied them with war material, airplanes and *experts* now assisted by whole formations from abroad'.²³

The term of art utilized by the Russian representative is noteworthy, and returned in the period of decolonization. Then, foreign advisers and experts sent by Cuba and Russia to their allies in Africa would be endorsed as a legitimate form of aid, unlike the groups of white mercenaries pointed to as unlawful combatants. Yet this passage calls for a further parallel. In December 1936, the French representative Viénot had underlined that 'for a long time, the arrivals of volunteers in Spain were individual and intermittent; and many Governments were not able to interfere to restrict such activities ... this is no longer the position. Large formations – and even organized units – are now appearing in the war area'.²⁴

While Viénot's vision was certainly influenced by the 1907 Hague Conventions – as we shall see – it is interesting to note this contraposition between the single individual leaving their country to fight abroad and the organized nature of foreign aid. The dichotomy between 'organized' and 'non-organized' groups is another of the poles on which the lawfulness of foreign fighters plays out, especially in contemporary counter-terrorism discourse.

At the time, the organized aid sent by Rome and Berlin in the form of war materiel, experts and technicians was a serious matter for the Spanish government. Franco had been able to transport part of his army from Africa to Spain thanks to the aeroplanes delivered by Mussolini. And it is not irrelevant that the two champions of non-intervention – France and the United Kingdom – were the first two nations to prohibit public and private exports of all war materiel to both sides, as early as August 1936.²⁵ In this regard, it is interesting to see how that Army of

---

[22] League of Nations, Official Journal 18, 95th Session of the Council, third meeting (1936) pp. 11–14. Article 11 of the League Covenant stated: 'Any war or threat of war, whether immediately affecting any of the Members of the League or not, is hereby declared a matter of concern to the whole League, and the League shall take any action that may be deemed wise and effectual to safeguard the peace of nations. In case any such emergency should arise the Secretary General shall on the request of any Member of the League forthwith summon a meeting of the Council.' League of Nations, Covenant of the League of Nations (Paris, 28 April 1919) Art. 11.
[23] *Ibid.*, p. 16. Emphasis added.
[24] *Ibid.*, p. 13.
[25] Portugal, Italy and Germany also joined the Non-Intervention Agreement, although with important reservations, and breached it almost immediately, together with Russia.

Africa was characterized. These were the troops which had been moved on the continent with the help of Italy in July 1936. In September of the same year, in a note sent to the members of the Non-Intervention Agreement, the Spanish government stated the following:

> In their inability to enlist in the rebellion real Spanish contingents, the rebel generals, besides assuring themselves of this foreign aid, had recourse to the recruitment of mercenary Moroccan troops, mobilized against the Spanish people precisely because of their fame for cruelty and their sanguinary renown, a proceeding which by itself should have scandalized the civilized world.[26]

It is fascinating to see how the Moors were singled out as mercenaries, but also as barbarian troops who would render war more savage. This certainly gives an account of the racialized discourse informing the interwar period.[27] At the same time, the categorization of the Moors as barbaric troops offers an idea of the ambivalence permeating the figure of the foreign fighter: during decolonization, there would be a shift in such racialized conceptions, with the anti-colonial fighters being portrayed as battling for self-determination, and the white, right-wing mercenaries pointed to as neocolonial and racist soldiers of fortune. Indeed, the colonial question would resurface again along three historical moments: in the Hague in 1907, in the United Kingdom in 1976 and in contemporary debates on the Syrian Civil War.

Back to the question of foreign aid: del Vayo himself returned to this issue in September 1937. The Spanish representative once again pressed his colleagues: '[Could] anyone deny that the sending of arms, ammunition and whole divisions to the rebels constitutes a scandalous violation of international law?'[28] He then lashed out at the policy of non-intervention, asking the other delegates whether such a policy made

---

[26] See Norman J. Padelford, *International Law and Diplomacy in the Spanish Civil Strife* (New York: Macmillan Company 1939) pp. 231–232.

[27] On this point see Pierre-Alexandre Cardinal and Frédéric Mégret, 'The Other "Other": Moors, International Law and the Origin of the Colonial Matrix', in Ignacio de la Rasilla del Moral and Ayesha Shahid (eds.), *International Law and Islam: Historical Explorations* (Leiden: Brill/Nijhoff 2018) pp. 165–198. *See* also Elisabeth Bolorinos Allard, 'The Crescent and the Dagger: Representations of the Moorish Other during the Spanish Civil War' (2016) 93 *Bulletin of Spanish Studies* 965–988 and Ali Al Tuma, 'The Participation of Moorish Troops in the Spanish Civil War (1936-39): Military Value, Motivations, and Religious Aspects' (2011) 30 *War & Society* 91–107.

[28] League of Nations, Official Journal, Special Supplement 175, 18th Ordinary Session. Sixth Committee, eighth meeting (1937) p. 57.

sense at all, given that Italy and Germany were blatantly violating the agreement.[29] Finally, he went back to the issue of the withdrawal of non-Spanish combatants by asserting that, for the Spanish government, the International Brigades were 'the only genuine foreign volunteers'.[30] To testify once more to the moral divide between 'good' and 'bad' volunteers, it suffices to go back to a few days earlier at the eighteenth ordinary session of the League's Assembly. There, the Spanish Prime Minister Juan Negrín had taken the floor for a long tirade against the fascist intervention: 'The only volunteers are those fighting in our ranks. [They have been] driven from home by ... the Fascist terror, and [are] convinced that the cause of Spain is that of world freedom.'[31] This statement should be compared with that of Count Ciano, Mussolini's right-hand man, who had previously declared: 'We put no pressure on the volunteers. The national spirit of Italy is such that even without an appeal from the Government all Italian youth desires, as soon as it feels itself engaged in an anti-Communist struggle, to take part in the fight.'[32]

Fascist terror and anti-communist struggle. There could not be two more different conceptions of freedom, and thus of the reasons for going to fight in Spain. This perspective shifted during decolonization, when the Soviet Union became the sworn enemy of American imperialism. White mercenaries then professed an open aversion to Russia and vowed to stop a communist takeover of the African continent. Conversely, the autocratic nature of the Islamic State pushed many Western volunteers to join Kurdish groups during the Syrian Civil War. The point is that the status of foreign fighters is in fact impossible to understand unless opposing conceptions of freedom are considered. As will be shown in the following sections, cultural figures are often associated with these opposing visions.

Back to the plenary meeting of September 1937. The representatives of France and the United Kingdom again defended the policy of non-intervention. This time, however, they also made clear the real purpose of such a policy. While recognizing the rhetorical force of del Vayo's speech, Delbos stated in fact that 'all Europe realized how important it

---

[29] *Ibid.*, p. 58.
[30] *Ibid.*, p. 56.
[31] League of Nations, Official Journal, Special Supplement 169, 18th Plenary Session, fifth meeting (1937) p. 57.
[32] Malcolm Muggeridge and Stuart Hood (eds.), *Ciano's Diplomatic Papers* (London: Odhams Press 1948) p. 77.

was to prevent Spain from becoming the theatre of ... conflicting interventions'.[33] Elliot (United Kingdom) asserted instead that 'the urgent and essential need was to prevent the Spanish conflict from overflowing the borders of Spain and engulfing the whole of Europe'.[34] Much has been written about the policy of non-intervention, and it is not the aim here to return to it. But these words sum up extremely well the political attitude of the two countries that made all possible efforts to establish a parallel system to the League, fearing that the Spanish Civil War could spark a world conflict.

Conversely, the Russian representative Litvinoff reminded his colleagues that 'in accordance with international law, it was to give no help to the rebels against the lawful Government'[35] but that 'immediately after signing the Non-Intervention Agreement it became known to the whole world that supplies were still being sent to the rebels'.[36] Litvinoff concluded his speech by remarking how the non-intervention had bluntly failed. While Norway, Austria and Poland sided with France and the United Kingdom, the speech of the Mexican representative Isidro Fabela was perhaps the most critical about the shortcomings of the League. At the same time, Fabela focused on the issue of volunteers. After denouncing the 'war of aggression'[37] at the hands of a 'foreign army fighting in Spain against the lawful government',[38] Fabela again noted the distinction between legitimate and illegitimate volunteers:

> They are volunteers, we are told ... We know that thousands of so-called volunteers who are fighting the Spanish Government have been trained abroad. Is it imaginable that thousands and thousands of 'volunteers' can be 'organized' – I stress the word 'organized' – by their own resources in one country to invade another without the help or protection of their Government. To accept that view would be tantamount to admitting that such a Government exercises no authority or control over what is happening in the territory under its jurisdiction.[39]

Significantly, the differentiation between organized and non-organized groups returns in the Mexican representative's speech. In particular, in

---

[33] League of Nations, Official Journal, Special Supplement 175, 18th Ordinary Session. Sixth Committee, ninth meeting (1937) p. 59.
[34] Ibid., p. 60.
[35] Ibid., p. 63.
[36] Ibid.
[37] Ibid., p. 60.
[38] Ibid., p. 61.
[39] Ibid.

his view, the large number of troops trained abroad made their home states directly responsible.[40] To prove this point, Fabela affirmed that the tribute received in the countries of origins clearly made these volunteers organs of the state. Conversely, if they were soldiers leaving their countries to serve in a foreign army, they would have been outlawed:

> Army regulations all over the world contain definite rules making it an offence for soldiers to serve a foreign Government without official authorization and severely punishing such action. Therefore, if it is to be admitted that the foreign soldiers fighting in Spain are volunteers, they would have to be regarded as having left their country illegally – that is to say, as offenders. It is common knowledge, though, that these soldiers are not only not regarded as offenders, but as *heroes* deserving the cordial congratulations of their Government. Consequently, their acts are the acts of the Government and involve the latter's responsibility.[41]

The remark made by Fabela is interesting precisely because it points to the homage received by the fascist volunteers upon their return to Italy.[42] Two visions of the heroic nature of the foreign combatant are made clear: on the one hand the leftist idealists who joined the International Brigades, and on the other the brave legionaries who fought in Spain to defeat the Bolshevik enemy.

Nothing resulted from that September session, however, and no formal act was passed.[43] It took another seven months for the League to hold another session on the Spanish question. Del Vayo first sent a letter from

---

[40] In his speech, Fabela made reference to the 1933 Treaty of London, which outlawed different acts of aggression. The treaty contained the expression 'armed bands', a term which will become in vogue among international lawyers after World War II. *See* Convention for the Definition of Aggression (London, 3 July 1933) Art. II (5).

[41] League of Nations, Official Journal, Special Supplement 175, 18th Ordinary Session. Sixth Committee, ninth meeting (1937) p. 61. Emphasis added.

[42] This was also highlighted by Negrín during the Assembly meeting: 'in the Popolo d'Italia, Signor Mussolini's organ, we read of "the Italian generals who led the legionary troops to victory in Spain, north of Santander" ... Every cinema in Geneva gives Italian news reels showing those same troops singing "Giovinezza" as they enter the towns of Northern Spain'. League of Nations, Official Journal, Special Supplement 169, 18th Ordinary Session, fifth plenary meeting (1937) p. 58.

[43] A subsequent controversy arose over a vote on a resolution on the Spanish situation containing a specific paragraph about non-Spanish combatants. The various states' positions were exacerbated precisely when it came to discuss whether to include paragraph 4 of the said resolution, which stated: 'there are veritable foreign army corps on Spanish soil, which represents foreign intervention in Spanish affairs'. *See* League of Nations, Official Journal, Special Supplement 169, 18th Ordinary Session, eleventh plenary meeting (1937) pp. 99–108.

Barcelona on 19 April 1938, and then a formal telegram to the Secretariat on 30 April, requesting the issue be placed on the agenda. Restating all the main issues concerning the situation in Spain, during the 101st session of the Council, held in Geneva on 11–13 May 1938, the Spanish representative also emphasized how the conditions of the war had worsened. There, del Vayo gave his final passionate speeches, stressing once again that characterizing the conflict in Spain as a civil war did not do justice to the actual situation on the ground:

> We reject the characterization of the Spanish war as a civil war, because this term is used to create the impression that the conflict is limited to two Spanish groups and that there is therefore no foreign intervention . . . This is proved by acts such as the bombardment of Guernica, Almeria and Barcelona, and many others of a like nature of which the barbarity has aroused the indignation of the whole world.[44]

The cruelty of the fascist troops was at the heart of the matter. Once again, no resolution was adopted. Lord Halifax (United Kingdom) and Henri Bonnet (France) reassured the League that a plan for the withdrawal of volunteers was in the hands of the Committee of Non-Intervention.[45] But it was only in September 1938 that an agreement was finally reached. This time a resolution was approved, which included the dispatch of an International Commission, with the United Kingdom, France and Iran appointed as the three members to supervise its work.[46] The very last meeting on the Spanish situation held by the countries still standing at the League was held in January–February 1939. It was there that the International Commission presented the Council with a provisional report on the 'Withdrawal of Non-Spanish Combatants from Spain'.[47] Two years had passed since the border closure plan was set up by the Non-Intervention Committee in February 1937. The withdrawal of volunteers was the last act in a dramatic situation that had lasted for

---

[44] League of Nations, Official Journal 19, 101st Session of the Council, seventh meeting (1938) pp. 354–355. A few days earlier, del Vayo had addressed the floor by stating that. 'Hitler's Germany and Fascist Italy are fulfilling in Spain their sinister destiny' and that 'despite the Non-intervention Agreement, large scale Italo-German intervention is to-day a fact'. Fourth meeting, p. 327.

[45] Ibid., p. 331.

[46] League of Nations, Official Journal 19, 103rd Session of the Council, second meeting (1938) p. 883.

[47] League of Nations Official Journal 20, 104th Session of the Council. Provisional Report of the International Military Commission Entrusted with the Verification of the Withdrawal of non-Spanish Combatants from Spain (1939) pp. 125–141.

almost four years. A few months later, in April 1939, Franco proclaimed his victory over the Republicans, putting an end to the civil war. In September of the same year, Hitler invaded Poland, opening a new page in the history of warfare and of armed intervention.

1.2 The End of Freebooters

While the League's discussions provide the ideological background to frame the dichotomy between 'good' and 'bad' volunteers, it is significant to note how the Spanish Civil War ignited debates among famous international lawyers of the time. McNair, Padelford, Lauterpacht and Jessup are among those Anglo-American scholars who published articles and books on the topic.[48] These debates give a first-hand account of the sources, conventions and principles utilized during the interwar era, together with offering a good entry point to the doctrine of neutrality.[49] Yet these discussions are also revealing of important cultural aspects lingering behind the legal characterizations of volunteering abroad. In particular, one can see how the predominant figure at play in the imaginary of these internationalists is that of the adventurer, understood as a free individual not pursuing any state policy. In contrast to this, the image of the freebooter is indicative of a discomfort at the idea of citizens of third states venturing into civil wars for pecuniary reasons or to seize other nations' territories. But let us look into these aspects more closely.

A first, significant article that came out in January of 1937 was one by Philip Jessup.[50] Distancing himself from political quarrels and from any discussion on the 'present political alignments of Europe . . . with fascism

---

[48] Charles Rousseau, Georges Scelle and Louis le Fur were their most renowned French counterparts.

[49] Significantly, these international lawyers in effect refer to the classical doctrine of neutrality, as codified in the Hague Conventions, overshadowing any early idea of collective security under the League system. On this point see generally Morris Greenspan, *The Modern Law of Land Warfare* (Berkeley: University of California Press 1959).

[50] Philip C. Jessup, 'The Spanish Rebellion and International Law' (1937) 15 *Foreign Affairs* 260–279. In a surgical analysis, Jessup traces the steps that can lead to a civil war. From a situation of mere domestic violence (or riots), to one of open rebellion (equated with insurrection or revolution), to the recognition of the rebel group by foreign states. The American scholar clarifies that recognition of insurgency does not confer special rights on the insurgents, and it does not impose on foreign states any special obligations. Only later on, 'if the insurgents have reached a very considerable degree of organization and stability . . . they may attain the status of belligerency', pp. 270–272.

arrayed against democracy',[51] the well-known American jurist focused instead on the most pressing legal problems arising from the situation on the Spanish peninsula. For lawyers like Jessup, the object of contention was first to assess the legal status of both factions in the war; whether the conflict in Spain was to be considered a civil war (or only an internal rebellion); and what rights and obligations other states held towards the belligerents.[52] In his article, Jessup argues that there existed a difference in international law between 'helping the established government and helping a revolutionary group which has not yet been accorded recognition'.[53] Recognition of belligerency, he explains, put the two factions in the war on an equal footing, conferred them the same rights and duties, and entailed neutrality by other foreign states.[54] Jessup then continues by listing the ways in which the belligerency of a rebel group can be recognized, not ultimately by enforcing a blockade, as he recalls the famous precedent of the American Civil War.[55]

Here one can have a sense of the legal background in which the debates over foreign volunteers were taking place. As seen at the League, these were pressing issues for the Spanish government, given the aid Rome and Berlin had provided to the rebels, together with their recognition of Franco's government. As Jessup notes: 'the extension of recognition by Italy and Germany is that ... for them the Franco government is the government of Spain and the established government is merely a rebellious group ... following the principles outlined above, Italy and Germany would now be legally free to supply aid to the Franco group just as previously any states would have been free to supply aid to the established government'.[56] Naturally, Jessup is aware of the Non-Intervention Agreement which should have precluded any foreign aid reaching either party in the war, yet he also acknowledges the purpose of that policy: prevent the spillover of the conflict in Europe.[57]

---

[51] Ibid., p. 260.
[52] In a similar vein see Charles Fenwich, 'Can Civil Wars Be Brought under the Control of International Law' (1938) 32 *American Journal of International Law* 538–542.
[53] Jessup, 'The Spanish Rebellion', p. 265.
[54] 'If their belligerency is recognized, they thereupon acquire the same rights which are granted to a sovereign state when it is at war. In other words, recognized belligerents may establish blockades, may visit and search the ships of third powers on the high seas, may size and confiscate contraband goods, and the like.' Ibid., p. 272.
[55] Ibid.
[56] Ibid., p. 274.
[57] Ibid.

1.2 THE END OF FREEBOOTERS

We have already seen how the pact of non-intervention was highly criticized by the Spanish government. What is more interesting for our purpose is looking at how Jessup deals with the problem of volunteers. He does so in few lines, recalling that 'the enlistment of volunteers is within the control of any government' and that 'if the laws of neutrality are applicable, all governments are under a duty to prevent such forms of assistance'.[58] Quite concise, to say the least. At the same time, Jessup does not miss the opportunity to point out how the present situation differed from what has happened in the past: 'it cannot be denied that one of the burdens which must be accepted by totalitarian state or dictatorial government is an enhanced international responsibility for the acts of its individual citizens'.[59]

This is one of the recurring tropes used by lawyers and experts discussing the reappearance of foreign fighters in war scenarios. While recognizing that volunteers have always taken part in conflicts abroad, they tend to distinguish the current situation (be it of mercenaries during decolonization or of terrorists today) from what occurred previously. This break between the past and the present is always done with the purpose of advancing a particular project: emphasizing enhanced state control over its citizens – as in the case of Jessup – or differentiating between old and new actors on the battlefield. Yet this tactic of distancing from the past is accompanied by the persistence of certain figures lingering in their imaginary, as we shall see.

The British legal scholar Arnold McNair discussed the problem of volunteers more extensively than his American counterpart.[60] Adopting a similar attitude to Jessup's, he distances himself from the politics of the Spanish Civil War. McNair starts his discussion by recalling the

---

[58] *Ibid.*, p. 269.

[59] *Ibid.*, p. 268. Jessup continues by discussing the recognition of the de facto government. The very issue of recognition of insurgents as the de facto government was analysed by Hersch Lauterpacht in a famous article of June 1939, just at the end of the Spanish Civil War. Yet the two most famous international lawyers of the Anglo-American tradition do not seem very interested in the problem of volunteers, and rather kept their focus on the doctrine of neutrality, and how it applied to the various stages of the civil war. *See* Hersch Lauterpacht, 'Recognition of Insurgents as a de facto Government' (1939) 3 *Modern Law Review* 1–20. On the same issue see also Wyndham Legh Walker, 'Recognition of Belligerency and Grant of Belligerent Rights' (1937) 23 *Transactions of the Grotius Society* 177–210 and H. A. Smith, 'Some Problems of the Spanish Civil War' (1937) 18 *British Yearbook of International Law* 17–31.

[60] Arnold McNair, 'The Law Relating to the Civil War in Spain' (1937) 53 *Law Quarterly Review* 471–500.

principles laid out by the Institut de Droit International concerning the duties of foreign powers during an insurrection. McNair asserts that in the event of a civil war third states have an obligation not to interfere, for instance by sending weapons, ammunition, military equipment, or financial aid. Likewise, no duty exists to help the legitimate government suppress an insurrection.[61] He then moves on to discuss the very central legal problem: the recognition of belligerency by a foreign government and its consequences.[62] Again, it is not the purpose here to enter into a technical debate concerning the recognition of belligerency, or how such a doctrine developed during the long nineteenth century. Mention of these principles are intended to offer an idea of the context in which legal debates on foreign volunteers were taking place.

What really preoccupies McNair is how to justify the British attitude towards the Spanish Civil War.[63] He points out that under international law the United Kingdom had a right to recognize the belligerent status of Franco's faction, yet his government opted for a policy of non-intervention. He praises this latter option by recalling that 'recognition of belligerency would have been entirely consistent with a policy of "neutrality" ... but ... our Government and the French Government took the view that the grant of any such recognition ... would in fact bring considerable prestige to General Franco and be tantamount to an intervention in his favour'.[64] McNair is of course aware that the Spanish Civil War was not fought on purely legal grounds, but also in the sphere of international diplomacy.

His analysis of the current law in relation to foreign volunteers is more elaborated than Jessup's. McNair starts from the general acknowledgement that 'a foreigner who enlists in the forces of either belligerent when an international war is in progress ... commits no crime against the other belligerent, who is not entitled to punish him if captured'.[65] Yet he also recalls that many countries had passed specific legislation to criminalize those who join a foreign war. He mentions the UK Foreign Enlistment Act of 1870, which was re-enacted in January 1937. Such acts

---

[61] *Ibid.*, pp. 472–473. For an opposite view see Scelle, 'La guerre civile espagnole', p. 223. Discussing the policy of non-intervention, Scelle argued that third states had a right to intervene in supporting the legitimate government in a civil strife.

[62] *Ibid.*, pp. 474–484.

[63] On McNair's and other British international lawyers' attitudes during the Spanish Civil War see specifically Ignacio de la Rasilla del Moral, 'In the General Interest of Peace? British International Lawyers and the Spanish Civil War' (2016) 18 *Journal of the History of International Law* 197–238.

[64] McNair, 'The Law Relating to the Civil War in Spain', pp. 491–492.

[65] *Ibid.*, p. 494.

1.2 THE END OF FREEBOOTERS

were common in nineteenth-century British foreign policy and were directed at preventing citizens enlisting in foreign armies, but were also intended as a manifest form of neutrality towards a foreign conflict.[66] Having discussed the meaning of the act, McNair turns to examine the question of volunteers. His words mirror those spoken at the League by various states' representatives. In particular, he asserts that:

> In almost every war will be found fighting foreign volunteers attracted by the desire of employment or love of adventure or sympathy with the cause of one of the belligerents ... the present conflict in Spain is no exception. But it is exceptional in another aspect ... that from certain countries, sometimes called 'totalitarians', in which the Government controls the actions of its citizens ... there have gone to Spain to fight for one side or the other military and air units or formations, definitely organized ... their degrees of organization constitute them at any rate 'hostile expeditions', such as it is illegal for a neutral Power to permit to leave its territory.[67]

McNair makes no distinction here between the volunteers fighting for personal gain and those going to fight abroad following their ideals, as they are a common feature of many civil wars. In this sense, the figure of the volunteer evoked by McNair is a hybrid between an adventurer, a mercenary and a committed idealist. Like Jessup, he is more interested in establishing a separation between the past and the present: volunteers from the so-called totalitarian states possess for him a degree of organization that makes them part of a 'hostile expedition'.[68]

McNair substantiates his arguments by resorting to the 1907 Hague Conventions which made legal the crossing of frontiers by single persons willing to join one of the belligerents. We have already encountered this idea in the proceedings of the League. Specifically, in the intervention by Viénot in December 1936, when the French representative reiterated the idea of small groups of men crossing borders, as opposed to entire and

---

[66] Foreign Enlistment Acts were used in many civil wars during the nineteenth century to prevent British subjects from going to fight in Latin America or in the Greek War of Independence. See Nir Arielli, Gabriela A. Frei and Inge Van Hulle, 'The Foreign Enlistment Act, International Law, and British Politics, 1819–2014' (2016) 38 *International History Review* 636–656. With reference to the Spanish Civil War, see S. P. Mackenzie, 'The Foreign Enlistment Act and the Spanish Civil War, 1936–1939' (1999) 10 *Twentieth Century British History* 52–66.

[67] McNair, 'The Law Relating to the Civil War in Spain', p. 497.

[68] McNair then returns to the problem of recognition of belligerency, explaining that if a foreign power had recognized both parties to the conflict, then neutrality would apply and any such expeditions would be illegal. On the contrary, if a foreign power had not recognized belligerent status, those expeditions would be legal if directed to help the legitimate government, but not the insurgents *Ibid.*, pp. 498–499.

organized military units. McNair is careful to remind his readers that a hostile military expedition prepared in the territory of a neutral state is to be considered illegal. The expeditions evoked by McNair represent a cornerstone against which the problem of volunteers was being read and understood by the Anglo-American internationalists of the 1930s.[69] It is thus essential to elucidate this point further.

The topic is addressed by Hersch Lauterpacht in an article published in the *American Journal of International Law* in 1928.[70] His study is noteworthy because it discusses the meaning of 'hostile acts' of private persons directed towards a foreign state. Lauterpacht outlines a difference existing between the Russo-German attitude on the one side and the Anglo-Saxon one on the other. For the former countries, hostile acts included a large pool of activities (such as revolutionary propaganda and conspiracies), whereas for the latter, these were 'organized acts of force directed against a foreign territory' (which included military expeditions).[71] Lauterpacht then regroups states' responses to such acts into two main categories, underlining that the United Kingdom and United States adopted a 'rigid distinction between the duties of the state and those of its subjects'.[72] On the contrary, countries like Russia, Germany, or Austria are described by Lauterpacht as reactionary, given that they treated 'revolutionary acts of a treasonable character against a foreign government . . . as criminal offences'.[73] Reference is made to the German,

---

[69] For the sake of clarity, it must be pointed out that even when American jurists acknowledge a duty for governments not to allow hostile military expeditions to be formed within their borders, this remains a marginal problem in the overall discussion of non-intervention and recognition of belligerency.

[70] Hersch Lauterpacht, 'Revolutionary Activities by Private Persons Against Foreign States' (1928) 22 *American Journal of International Law* 105–130.

[71] 'This means that whereas the state itself is prohibited by international law from committing acts amounting to assisting revolutionary movements abroad, its subjects are not, with one exception, so prohibited. The second is that, in consequence of that exception, private persons are forbidden by municipal law, enacted in performance of a clear international duty, from committing such acts as amount to making the national territory a base for military or naval operations against a friendly state.' *Ibid.*, p. 113.

[72] *Ibid.*, p. 113. Lauterpacht mentions a third group of states represented by France, Italy and Spain: 'The criminal codes of the countries belonging to this group do not state *expressis verbis* what are the acts which are deemed likely to disturb the external peace of the state and which are accordingly prohibited by law. They content themselves with stigmatizing as crimes such acts as are described as being against international law, or as exposing the country to the danger of war or reprisals, or, in general, as compromising its foreign relations.' *Ibid.*, p. 118.

[73] The acts of private individuals, Lauterpacht explains, could be subsequently criminalized under municipal law, e.g., the British Foreign Enlistment Acts and the US neutrality laws. *Ibid.*, p. 116.

Austrian and Russian penal codes, which all contained extremely strict provisions regarding the actions of their citizens at home and abroad. Thus, Lauterpacht notes a strict centralization by this group of states regarding their own citizens, including the duties owned to foreign governments.

Seeking to define what principles states should generally follow when it comes to preventing hostile military expeditions, Lauterpacht opts for the Anglo-Saxon tradition of neutrality laws. However, he does recognize a limit to the freedom given to the subjects of neutral countries, in such a way that 'it must prevent them from committing such as acts as would result in the neutral territory becoming directly a base for the military operations of either party. They must not build or fit out ships to the order of belligerents ... they must not leave the neutral territory in organized military units'.[74] In other words, a neutral state must not host or become the base for military operations in foreign countries, and – most importantly for our purpose – individuals who wish to fight abroad should not cross borders in organized military units. But where did this idea come from, and on what cultural background is it based?

The answer is offered by Emerson Curtis in a fascinating article dated 1914.[75] There, Curtis discusses the American legal responses to such expeditions in the nineteenth century. By resorting to some famous examples, Curtis aims to demonstrate the crystallization of a duty preventing these activities in international law.[76] What is most significant, though, is how these expeditions are characterized. By equating them with the actions of privateers, Curtis draws a distinction between these actors and the volunteers going to fight in wars abroad. The American William Walker is used to make the point:

> Perhaps the most notorious expeditions were those of William Walker. In his first attempt, he planned to gain possession of the Mexican territory of Lower California. He set sail in October 1853 with an expedition from San Francisco, invaded the territory, killed a few people, and wounded others ... On May 4, 1855, Walker again set sail from San Francisco, this time for Nicaragua ... Walker made three more attempts at invasion of Central America ... He was shot at Truxillo in September 1860.[77]

---

[74] *Ibid.*, p. 127.
[75] Roy Emerson Curtis, 'The Law of Hostile Military Expeditions as Applied by the United States' (1914) 8 *American Journal of International Law* 1–37.
[76] Curtis cites the Texas Revolution, the Canadian Rebellion of 1837 and the Nicaraguan Revolution of 1855 (among others), where American citizens had taken active part in military expeditions abroad.
[77] *Ibid.*, pp. 243–244.

Figure 1.1 Portrait of William Walker (1824–1860) by Mathew Benjamin Brady
Source: Library of Congress Prints and Photographs Division, Brady–Handy Photograph Collection, DC 20540 USA.

1.2 THE END OF FREEBOOTERS

The figure of Walker is used to show how expeditions aimed at conquering the territory of other states were extremely dangerous to peaceful relations among sovereign states. It is not the point of this study to retrace the history of piracy and privateering in the long nineteenth century. Suffice to say that these actors – which were more or less tolerated by states in previous times – contributed to structuring diplomatic and foreign relations among countries.[78] But the figure of the pirate does not remain confined to that era and reappears in other periods. However, for scholars like Curtis, freebooters were seen as a dangerous legacy of the past. His position thus attests to a discomfort with their activities, as opposed to the image of the adventurer engaging in wars abroad following higher ideals. The dichotomy between 'good' and 'bad' foreign fighters is drawn based on moral judgements concerning the cause pushing people to take up weapons abroad, and is supported by precise cultural figures, in this case Walker.

Going back to the Spanish Civil War, if during the first months of hostilities the focus was on the recognition of belligerency, as the numbers of foreigners increased, references to the problem of volunteers became more frequent. In an article by Francis O. Wilcox in the *American Political Science Review* in April 1938, one can see how the topic is given increasingly more space.[79] Referring back to the Hague Conventions, and the principles of the Institut of Droit International, Wilcox reasserts the idea that there is no responsibility on a neutral state in a civil war when separate individuals are crossing borders. States are however free to pass legislation to prevent that from happening, or to criminalize such conduct.[80] Oppenheim in particular is a central source for international lawyers of the time, since he devoted the whole second book of his famous *Treatise* to war and neutrality. Interestingly,

---

[78] This is not to equate filibusters/freebooters/privateers with pirates. There are legal as well as conceptual differences between the two actors. *See* J. D. Ford, *The Emergence of Privateering* (Leiden: Brill/Nijhoff 2023), Daniel Heller-Roazen, *The Enemy of All: Piracy and the Law of Nations* (New York: Zone Books 2009) and Sonja Schillings, *Enemies of All Humankind* (Hanover, NH: Dartmouth College Press 2016).

[79] Francis O. Wilcox, 'The Localization of the Spanish War' (1938) 32 *American Political Science Review* 237–260.

[80] 'Neutrality is thus an attitude of impartiality on the part of states, and not on the part of individuals. ... On the other hand, each government may, within its own discretion, impose upon its citizens those restrictions which seem advisable in order to ensure neutrality.' *Ibid.*, p. 240.

Oppenheim confirms the doctrine in relation to foreign volunteers in these terms:

> Although several States, as, for instance Great Britain and the United States of America, by their Municipal Law prohibit their subjects from enlisting in the military or naval service of belligerents, the duty of impartiality incumbent upon neutrals does not at present include any necessity for such prohibition, provided that the individuals concerned cross the frontier singly and not in a body; moreover, as has already been mentioned, the subjects of neutral States who thus enlist do not thereby commit any offence against the rules of International Law.[81]

This point will be elucidated when looking at the *travaux* of the 1907 Hague Conventions, which reveal a certain laissez-faire attitude on the part of states towards their citizens taking up arms abroad.[82] As seen in Lauterpacht, this way of looking at the problem is mainly drawn from the Anglo-Saxon tradition on neutrality, a tradition which prevailed over those of the German-speaking countries and of Russia. This points to a division in the former countries between the private and public spheres, with the legal scenario changing the moment organized groups move across borders. That has perhaps radically changed today, if one considers the security concerns informing current legislation on foreign fighters in the global war on terror. This aspect will be analysed in more detail later, but it is important to start drawing some parallels to see what of the original neutrality doctrine has endured and what has drastically changed. It is interesting to note how the private/public distinction – a pillar of the interwar period – starts to shift during the

---

[81] Lassa Oppenheim, *International Law: A Treatise, Fifth Edition Vol. II*. Edited by Hersch Lauterpacht (New York: Longmans, Green 1935) p. 555 § 322.

[82] Garcia-Mora, in a study devoted to hostile acts of private persons against foreign states, discusses the issue of volunteers in these terms: 'The only prohibition imposed is the formation of combatant corps to assist any of the belligerents as found in Article IV of the Convention [Hague Convention N. V, Art. VI]. It has been seen quite clearly that this Article really prohibits the organization of military expeditions in neutral territory, and that the obligation contained in it does not go beyond the prevention of such expeditions in the manner indicated. As previously submitted, the cardinal distinction embodied in these two articles reflected the nineteenth century *laissez-faire* philosophy whereby a line of demarcation was drawn between the sphere of the government and that of the individual, thus implicitly assuming that purely private actions of the individual could not be imputed to the state.' Manuel R. Garcia-Mora, *International Responsibility for Hostile Acts of Private Persons Against Foreign States* (The Hague: Martinus Nijhoff 1962) p. 68.

Spanish Civil War, as a direct effect of the fascist/totalitarian volunteers present on the Iberian Peninsula.[83] Let us delve into this aspect further.

We have seen how foreign volunteers were generally read by the international lawyers of the time through the prism of neutrality. For most of those lawyers, volunteers should have been dealt with using ad hoc legislation, such as the British Foreign Enlistment Acts, or the US neutrality laws.[84] If one takes a look at the latter, it can be seen how the delivery of war materiel was much more central than the volunteers themselves. Under such laws, American citizens were forbidden to travel on belligerent ships during war, but were not strictly forbidden to enlist in foreign armies.[85] An article by James W. Garner published in January 1937 asserts that:

> If it be said that the duty of non-intervention has reference only to the conduct of governments in directly assisting the rebels and has no application to the conduct of private individuals ... this distinction, if it was ever applicable in civil wars, is now antiquated, and is today repudiated by the best writers on international law, and has been rejected by the most recent legislation, such as the American neutrality legislation of 1935 and 1936.[86]

Garner thus aligns himself with those international lawyers who wanted to break with the past. He points nonetheless to a division existing between the private and public spheres, given that the duty of non-

---

[83] On this point see W. Friedmann, 'The Growth of State Control over the Individual, and Its Effect upon the Rules of International State Responsibility' (1938) 19 *British Yearbook of International Law* 118–150.

[84] Neutrality laws generally prohibited the export of arms, ammunition and instruments of war from the United States to foreign nations at war, and also private loans from American citizens to belligerent nations. They functioned therefore as a sort of embargo. Specifically, the act of May 1937 forbade US citizens from travelling on belligerent ships, and American merchant ships were prevented from transporting arms to belligerents. However, they did not criminalize the enlisting of private citizens per se. See Francis Deák and Philip C. Jessup (eds.), *A Collection of Neutrality Laws, Regulations and Treaties of Various Countries (2 vols.)* (New York: Columbia University Press 1939). See also Charles G. Fenwich, *The Neutrality Laws of the United States* (Washington, DC: Carnegie Endowment for International Peace 1913).

[85] Although the participation of American citizens in the Spanish War was generally regarded as unpatriotic. See on this point Edwin Borchard, 'The Power to Punish Neutral Volunteers in Enemy Armies' (1938) 32 *American Journal of International Law* 535–538. See also George A. Finch, 'The United States and the Spanish Civil War' (1937) 31 *American Journal of International Law* 74–81. The point is analysed historically by Thomson, *Mercenaries, Pirates, and Sovereign*, pp. 79–84.

[86] James W. Garner, 'Questions of International Law in the Spanish Civil War' (1937) 31 *American Journal of International Law* 66–73, p. 68.

interference in a foreign conflict was traditionally put solely on the state, and not on private individuals trading with the factions at war.[87] Another American internationalist, Vernon O'Rourke, discusses the private nature of the aid to be furnished to insurgents in these terms:

> A position of neutrality in a civil war interdicts only official governmental aid to the insurgents; help of a private nature is usually not considered violative of neutrality ... But non-intervention, as announced at London, involves the control of activities of private individuals to a much greater extent than is necessitated by a declaration of neutrality. In pursuance of this policy all governments in Europe have passed laws forbidding the direct or indirect exportation of arms, munitions and materials of war destined for Spain.[88]

O'Rourke also shares the opinion that private trade with the belligerents is now to be forbidden and welcomes the Non-Intervention Agreement. Then he turns to discuss the acts passed in the United Kingdom and France to prevent citizens from going to fight abroad. This comes as a confirmation that the two issues – trade and fighting – were seen as distinct spheres. Hence, for many international lawyers of the time, single, private citizens were free to enlist abroad, unless national legislation prevented them from doing so. But there is a curious ambivalence in the figure of the private citizen evoked by these American jurists. On the one side, they acknowledge that modern law requires a shift from a duty of non-intervention put solely on states to one addressing single, private individuals; on the other hand, the private character they refer to seems to involve only the material transactions of subjects with the belligerents, remaining silent on physical engagement in war. In this sense, the figure that underpins their vision is still the one of the nineteenth-century adventurer, devoid of any financial motivation. An ideal kind of fighter

---

[87] *See* the Final Act of the Hague Peace Conference 1907 (18 October 1907): 'The Conference expresses the opinion that, in case of war, the responsible authorities, civil as well as military, should make it their special duty to ensure and safeguard the maintenance of pacific relations, more especially of the commercial and industrial relations between the inhabitants of the belligerent States and neutral countries.' James Brown Scott (ed.), *The Hague Conventions and Declarations of 1899 and 1907: Accompanied by Tables of Signatures, Ratifications and Adhesions of the Various Powers, and Texts of Reservations. Second Edition* (New York: Oxford University Press/Humphrey Milford 1915) p. 29.

[88] Vernon O'Rourke, 'Recognition of Belligerency and the Spanish War' (1937) 31 *American Journal of International Law* 398–413, p. 409.

who has nothing to do with privateering activities, as we have seen with reference to the image of Walker.

To conclude with the Spanish Civil War, perhaps the most complete work produced by a legal scholar at the time is that by Norman Padelford. The American academic addresses all the main legal problems of the war, while examining extensive material taken from the archives of the Non-Intervention Committee.[89] His take on volunteers is objective and neutral. By confining himself to the actual practice of states, he concludes that:

> [before the war] the majority of the states of Europe did not regard volunteering for or engaging in military service in a foreign civil strife as contrary to or forbidden by existing international law ... Subsequent to the 14th of February, 1937, restrictive measures were adopted by twenty-five of the twenty-eight states adhering to the non-intervention policy ... Judging from the ad hoc form of the measures which were taken by the other twenty-four states above noted, it would appear that the states had no thought of establishing a new principle of international law generally binding in all future cases of civil strife.[90]

Padelford regards volunteers as a problem to be addressed using ad hoc legislation, affirming that there was no urgent need for a norm in international law to regulate the question – perhaps a further confirmation that foreign fighters at the time were not making the headlines in international legal scholarship. The fact that most of these internationalists referred to the domestic context is not to be overlooked, however. On the contrary, it proves how the legal dynamics connected to foreign fighters inevitably passed from the national level as well. In fact, it was in January 1937 that countries started to discuss legislation to prevent their citizens' recruitment and departure for Spain. The British Houses and the French Parliament are privileged venues to understand how states were dealing internally with these individuals, particularly because they reveal

---

[89] See Padelford, *International Law and Diplomacy*, Appendices, pp. 203–674. Charles Rousseau also devotes a long and comprehensive study to the Non-Intervention Agreement, its origins and nature, its application and practical content as well as its functioning. His characterization of the agreement as a '*no man's land* juridique' remains well-known. Similarly to Padelford, Rousseau deals with the main legal questions related to the Spanish Civil War in a neutral and analytical tone. Different from his American counterpart, however, when it comes to discussing the issue of volunteers, Rousseau is much more attentive to national debates. Charles Rousseau, 'La Non-Intervention en Espagne' (1939) 19 *Revue de Droit International et de Législation Comparée* 217–280, p. 237.

[90] Padelford, *International Law and Diplomacy*, pp. 74–75.

significant cultural aspects informing the discourse of policymakers, aside from the doctrine of neutrality as seen in the work of the Anglo-American internationalists.

1.3 Evoking Past Heroes

Following a new influx of Italian troops into Spain in autumn 1936, many European states began to debate internally the problem of volunteers.[91] Belgium, Switzerland and Poland were among those countries where strict legislation to prevent the recruitment and departure of volunteers was enforced. Our focus will be on the United Kingdom and France, not only because these were the two main promoters of the Committee of Non-Intervention, but also because the numbers of their citizens going to fight in Spain were the highest during those years.[92] Additionally, many of the volunteers were reaching Spain through France, making the country an important place of transit. As already pointed out, some important personalities who were active on the Iberian Peninsula were British and French. The focus on these two countries is thus useful on the one hand to show a continuation with the League's debates and, on the other hand, because French and British parliamentary debates reveal fascinating cultural aspects framing the figure of the foreign fighter in the interwar period.

In France, a law for the interdiction of volunteers is discussed at the Chamber of Deputies on 15 January 1937. A proposal to criminalize French nationals going to fight in Spain had already been filed in December by Council President Louis Rollin.[93] By the end of the month, Jean Desbons, a deputy from the Haute-Pyrénées had deposited formal draft legislation to outlaw French nationals fighting in Spain with either side. The draft included the stripping of their nationality, six months' imprisonment with a fine of 10,000 francs for those who helped the

---

[91] See le Fur, *La Guerre d'Espagne et le Droit*, p. 48.
[92] Technically France comes first for numbers of volunteers joining the International Brigades, followed by Italy, Germany, Poland, the United States, the Soviet Union and only then the United Kingdom. See specifically Thomas, *The Spanish Civil War*, Appendix 7, pp. 974–985.
[93] A previous debate was held on 5 December, when the problem of French citizens going to fight in Spain was addressed in terms of the dangers posed to France's foreign policy. See Journal officiel de la République française. Débats parlementaires. Chambre des députés. Séance du samedi 5 Décembre 1936.

1.3 EVOKING PAST HEROES 61

recruitment process, and the banning of all propaganda activities in France.[94]

The proposal by Desbons was examined on 12 January 1937, but it was later abandoned. The government of Leon Blum wished to remain in line with the United Kingdom, and more generally with the decisions taken by the Non-Intervention Committee. Blum himself, on 13 January, filed a draft bill on volunteers, which was approved a few days later. It is interesting to look at the parliamentary debate following this proposal, as it gives a first-hand account of the arguments deployed by the various blocs of the Parliament, and as they contextualize the cultural references flooding the imaginary of the French legislator.

The session of 15 January was opened by Raymond Vidal, the special rapporteur of the civil and criminal commission. Vidal reminded the audience that although at the beginning foreign volunteers were just 'des isolés qui, mus par leur seul idéal, allaient combattre sous le drapeau de leur choix, pour une cause qu'ils croyaient juste et bonne',[95] after some time their character had changed: 'nous avons assisté à l'arrivée en Espagne de techniciens, d'ingénieurs; de pilotes; récemment, les départs sont devenus collectifs, ils ont même paru inspirés, suscités, organisés'.[96]

Here one can see the idea already contained in the League's debates and highlighted by the Anglo-American internationalists: the actions of individual foreign volunteers could not be deemed illegal. Conversely, the moment they organized in military units, the legal scenario changed. What is crucial to highlight in this debate, however, is how a distinction was drawn between the volunteers and those who recruited them. Having briefly commented on the retroactivity of the law for those already on Spanish soil, Vidal takes a clear stance by pointing out that:

> nous avions pensé pouvoir instaurer une échelle de peines ... nous avions pensé qu'il fallait faire une différence entre le volontaire qui part combattre pour son idéal, avec sa foi, son ardeur, sa générosité – car l'idéal, quel qu'il soit, est toujours éminemment respectable – et, au contraire, celui qui faisait profession d'enrôler, celui qui, systématiquement, recrutait

---

[94] For a recent overview on the stripping of nationality see Laura Van Waas, 'Foreign Fighters and the Deprivation of Nationality: National Practices and International Law Implications', in Andrea de Guttry, Francesca Capone and Christopher Paulussen (eds.), *Foreign Fighters under International Law and Beyond* (The Hague: Asser Press 2016) 469–487.
[95] Journal officiel de la République française. Débats parlementaires. Chambre des députés. Séance du vendredi 15 Janvier 1937, p. 42.
[96] *Ibid.*

dans un but plus ou moins avoué, plus ou moins vénal, et qu'il importait de punir davantage.[97]

Vidal is suggesting introducing different punishments for the volunteers who travelled to Spain and those who recruited them, judged as individuals who sought to profit from the actions of the volunteers. This could be an early suggestion of the main division which would later on distinguish volunteers from mercenaries. But it is interesting to note that the same figure which underlaid the discourse of the Anglo-American international lawyers remerges here: the free, committed adventurer who is engaging in a war abroad not for material reasons. It is by following this line of thinking that Vidal wished to punish the recruiters more severely than the actual volunteers.

Next, Grumbach, the rapporteur for the Commission of Foreign Affairs, reminded his colleagues that the Spanish situation was endangering the peace of Europe, and the hostilities were exacerbated by the presence of foreigners on both sides. Taking a seemingly pacifist stance, he sided with Blum's proposal, stating that: 'd'accord avec le Gouvernement, la commission des affaires étrangères, à l'unanimité, estime que l'état de choses actuel constitue un immense danger pour la paix'.[98] To that end, Grumbach contrasted the proposal made by Vidal for establishing a different degree of criminal offences for the volunteers and the recruiters. Although realizing that 'si cruellement injuste qu'il soit d'être oblige ... de mettre sur le même plan les volontaires – les vrais volontaires – quelle que soit leur nationalité, quelles que soient leurs opinions, qu'ils se battent par conviction et enthousiasme républicains, dans les rangs des gouvernementaux, ou mus par un idéal opposé au nôtre, dans le camp des rebelles'[99], Grumbach saw no other way to end the conflict but to ban all forms of volunteering, perhaps one of the clearest statements of *realpolitik* of those years.

It was then the turn of Marcel Héraud, representative of the Républicains indépendants et d'action sociale, who took a strong stance against the proposal by Blum, praising instead the original draft prepared by Desbons. In particular, Héraud saw the stripping of nationality as the right penalty to deter volunteers from volunteering in Spain: 'ne vous rendez-vous pas compte combien ces sanctions sont dérisoires? ...

---

[97] *Ibid.*, p. 43.
[98] Séance du vendredi 15 Janvier 1937, p. 44.
[99] *Ibid.*

1.3 EVOKING PAST HEROES 63

Pensez-vous qu'un homme qui va risquer sa vie pour son idée puisse être empêché de le faire par la menace d'une amende? Pouvez-vous imaginer que recule devant la prison celui qui ne recule pas devant la mort?'[100]

These interventions make clear what criminal sanctions the French legislator was envisaging for foreign volunteers. It is also here that some famous cultural references start to appear. Another deputy, Brun, responded vehemently to Héraud's intervention with the following question: 'Qu'attendez-vous alors pour dire que Garibaldi a eu tort et pour condamner La Fayette?'[101] The famous communist deputy Gabriel Péri was even more direct than his colleague:

> Je suppose que la majorité de la Chambre trouvera aussi choquante que nous-mêmes l'assimilation que, sous ce terme générique de 'volontaires' on établit entre des forces et d'origine et de qualité différente ... Il n'y a, à côté de l'armée républicaine espagnole, des volontaires qui, après tout, peuvent se réclamer des plus généreuses traditions, celle de La Fayette, celle de Garibaldi, celle de Byron. Il y a des hommes qui se sentent menacés chaque fois qu'ils savent que la liberté est en péril ... des hommes qui, lorsqu'ils sont Français et qu'ils se battent aux côtés de la république espagnole, témoignent qu'ils ont de la sécurité française une notion beaucoup plus juste et beaucoup plus correcte que celle des pèlerins de Burgos.[102]

The images of former foreign fighters are evoked to characterize the French nationals fighting for freedom, and to distinguish them from those totalitarian volunteers sent by Italy and Germany. Garibaldi, Byron and Lafayette are regarded as honourable volunteers, and are used to draw a moral divide with the military expeditions sent to Spain by totalitarian states.[103]

Leon Blum was not averse to such references either. In recalling to the Chamber how both the British and French governments wanted to push for a common policy to prevent their citizens from going to Spain, he stated:

> [la loi] assimile ... deux formes d'engagement ou d'enrôlement qui sont cependant bien différentes: le libre don de la personne à un idéal, à une

---

[100] *Ibid.*, p. 46.
[101] *Ibid.*
[102] *Ibid.*, p. 49.
[103] As Péri continues his speech: 'Le danger provient de l'afflux, sur le territoire espagnol, d'effectifs paramilitaires ou militaires envoyés en service commandé, en corps expéditionnaire par des gouvernements étrangers ... Ce sont des "volontaires totalitaires" ou, plus exactement, suivant une définition originale, en régime hitlérien un volontaire est un homme qui reçoit l'ordre de demander l'autorisation de s'engager volontairement.' *Ibid.*, p. 49.

foi, selon ces exemples légendaires que l'on a cités aujourd'hui à maintes reprises à la tribune, l'exemple de La Fayette, celui de Byron, celui de Garibaldi, celui de Villebois-Mareuil, ou bien un départ en service commandé; d'une part, le libre exercice de la volonté ou de la conviction individuelle, qui jusqu'à ce jour, au regard des engagements internationaux, était pleinement licite, ou bien, de l'autre part, l'intervention indirecte d'un Etat ... Nous sentons cette difficulté et nous comprenons les appréhensions qu'elle peut provoquer; mais, avant tout, il s'agit de préserver l'Europe de la guerre.[104]

Two opposed notions of freedom – and thus of reasons for fighting abroad – are at play here: embracing an ideal or following the commands of a government. Two versions had already been discussed at the League, and that will return, reversed, in the period of decolonization.

Nonetheless, it is important to note that not everyone in the room shared Péri's view. A few moments earlier some right-wing representatives had reacted to the comparisons drawn by the communist deputy, shouting from their benches: '[M. François de Saint-Just] c'est votre avis, ce n'est pas le notre [M. Charles des Isnards] Et les pèlerins de Moscou?'[105] In other words, the figure of the good foreign fighter evoked by some politicians is split: on the one side, there might well be the Garibaldis, the Lafayettes, the Byrons, taken as examples of an honourable form of volunteering; while on the other, the figure of the Soviet soldier is thrown into the discussion to show that their vaunted heroism may contain a dark, twisted side. These two versions of the foreign combatant (the idealist volunteer and the cynical/opportunist soldier) reappear decades later, both at the UN General Assembly, and in contemporary debates over foreign terrorist fighters.

The point is that political actors stand on different moral grounds, and as Blum was trying to convince the Chamber of Deputies to vote in favour of the proposed bill on volunteers, the representatives of the right felt compelled to react to the unlawful invasion of Spain at the hands of the Bolshevik enemy. As already seen at the League, civilization and barbarism were the two poles around which the legitimacy of foreign fighters was debated: be it the savagery of the Moorish troops, the cruelty of fascist soldiers, or conversely the fear of an end to Christian civilization at the hands of the Russians.[106]

---

[104] Séance du vendredi 15 Janvier 1937, p. 52.
[105] *Ibid.*, p. 42.
[106] On the differentiation between the 'bad' Comintern soldiers and 'good' foreign volunteers see specifically George Esenwein, 'Freedom Fighters or Comintern Soldiers?

1.3 EVOKING PAST HEROES 65

The draft law proposed by Blum was finally passed on 21 January. It ended up being more far-reaching than the one proposed by Desbons. It authorized the French government to take 'all the necessary measures' to hamper (a) the engagement and acts tending to the engagement of persons in either of the fighting forces of Spain; (b) the departure and transit of all persons going to Spain in order to fight; (c) the engagement in the above forces of French nationals who were outside of the national territory. It did not, however, include the removal of nationality.

Reference to past volunteers is also present on the other side of the Channel. The problem of British citizens going to fight abroad was addressed by Westminster in winter 1936. On 1 December, while the House of Commons was discussing the implementation of a specific bill outlawing the carriage of munitions to Spain on merchant shipping, Philip Noel-Baker – representative of the Labour Party – raised the issue of volunteers. Fiercely criticizing the pact of non-intervention and suggesting that the League was instead the right venue to deal with the Spanish situation, he pointed the finger at the troops fighting on the side of Franco.[107] In particular, Noel-Baker feared that when the Non-Intervention Committee extended the embargo on volunteers, Italy and Germany would maintain their battalions on Spanish soil. As noted by the communist representative William Gallacher: 'if you stop the volunteers from this country [Russia] the Germans will still be there. If Germany signed a Non-intervention Pact which included no volunteers, the Germans would still be there, and so would the Italians'.[108]

A few days before, on 25 November, the Secretary of Foreign Affairs Anthony Eden had made clear that 'the question of the enlistment of

---

Writing about the "Good Fight" during the Spanish Civil War' (2010) 12 *Civil Wars* 156–166.

[107] HC Deb, 1 December 1936, Vol. 318, c1068. Philip Noel-Baker continued: 'I believe that if our Government had then invoked the League and had endeavoured to establish a really effective system for preventing such infractions by Signor Mussolini and others, a really effective system of non-intervention, that they would have rendered a great service to Europe. But, unfortunately, they did not ... If the embargo had been applied all round it would have deprived the Spanish Government of their legal rights, but it might have solved the general problem. But, unfortunately, we applied it at once, and we allowed the Fascists five weeks in which to pour in arms in quantities which they thought were sufficient to win the war.' For a compelling analysis of British diplomatic efforts during the Spanish Civil War *see* Tom Buchanan, 'Edge of Darkness: British "Front-line" Diplomacy in the Spanish Civil War, 1936–1937' (2003) 12 *Contemporary European History* 279–303.

[108] HC Deb, 1 December 1936, Vol. 318, cc1148–1149.

volunteers is not covered by the Agreement regarding Non-Intervention in Spain, which relates only to the prohibition of the export of war material',[109] while advancing the idea that the Committee in London was taking into consideration a general prohibition on all volunteers. A certain distrust of such provisions was evident – especially from the Labour Party's side – as made clear by the words of the Welsh representative Morgan Jones: 'I should be glad to see volunteers and all instruments of warfare stopped, so long as they are stopped all round ... If there is to be a ban on volunteers therefore, let it not be unilateral, but multilateral, all nations taking part in it.'[110]

Nevertheless, the Foreign Enlistment Act came into force on 11 January 1937. It proscribed British subjects from going to Spain. Anthony Eden returned to the question of volunteers on 19 January, the same day that the French National Assembly was discussing Blum's draft law. Eden made reference to the discussions held at the Committee of Non-Intervention, highlighting how the issue of volunteers had become a more serious matter. As well as introducing the idea of a frontier control system, Eden focused on an aspect that we have already seen debated in the French context – the differentiation between volunteering and recruiting. In the words of the British prime minister:

> within the last few weeks, the attention of the Government has been called to the development of recruiting activities in this country. I deliberately say 'recruiting', and not 'volunteering', because it is the activities of recruiting agents to which our attention has been directed, rather than the purely voluntary enlistment of individual supporters of one side or the other wishing to go to fight in Spain.[111]

Eden replied to a remark that those being paid were the volunteers fighting for Franco: 'it is not a question here of someone going to fight in Spain for their political principles; it is a question of recruiting going on, of offering individuals money to go and take part'.[112] In other words, Eden stressed that the legality of British citizens going to fight abroad was initially raised because of the issue of recruitment.[113] This position attests

---

[109] HC Deb, 25 November 1936, Vol. 318, c394.
[110] HC Deb, 18 December 1936, Vol. 318, c2826.
[111] HC Deb, 19 January 1937, Vol. 319, c98.
[112] Ibid.
[113] 'The point was that, once recruiting had begun in this country, the Government were bound to be asked whether it was legal or not; and, the legal position having been ascertained, it was no less clear that it was the duty of the Government to make it plain. Admittedly we are in this respect in a different position from other countries which have

to a significant cultural detail. On the one side, it shows how the UK authorities were more worried about the organized enrolment of individuals on British soil, an aspect that might be linked to the prohibition of hostile military expeditions. On the other hand, the net distinction made by Eden between recruiters and volunteers points once again to the images found in the writings of the internationalists: the idealist adventurer fighting abroad following his political faith, as opposed to the freebooter seeking personal profit from wars and revolutions.

In the session of 19 January, the discussion was diverted to the question of volunteers already present on Spanish soil. Clement Attlee, president of the Labour Party, challenged Eden: 'now we have the question of volunteers. You cannot call the German and Italian troops in Spain and Morocco volunteers. You cannot volunteer, if you belong to a Fascist State, unless you manage to escape from it. They are in no sense volunteers; they are instruments of dictatorship'.[114] The differentiation between totalitarian and genuine volunteers is once again drawn and it reflects the tense political climate of those years. The session of 19 January essentially continued with the discussions concerning the most suitable rule to stop all volunteers, whether the Foreign Enlistment Act was passed in time, and if Italy and Germany would have respected the Non-Intervention Agreement.

Noel-Baker – one of the strongest adversary of non-intervention – again questioned Anthony Eden in a subsequent session: 'can [Mr. Eden] give the House any information concerning the last meeting of the Non-Intervention Committee, and the proposals made in the notes from Germany and Italy concerning the despatch of volunteers from Spain?'[115] To the answer provided by Eden, that both Germany and Italy had declared themselves favourable to the prohibition on sending their volunteers, the Labour representative replied: 'shall we not have the same situation as there was previously, with one-sided observance at the expense of the Madrid Government?'[116] And in a heated debate at the House of Lords in March 1937, Baker evoked those noble figures who had already been mentioned in the French Chamber of Deputies:

---

no Foreign Enlistment Act. We are in a different position from the French, who have had to pass this Bill in order to enable them to act at all.' *Ibid.*, c100.
[114] *Ibid.*, c110.
[115] HC Deb, 1 February 1937, Vol. 319, c1272.
[116] *Ibid.*, c1273.

> They are not volunteers. You cannot put on the same footing as those troops the other volunteers, the 20,000 or so of the international column on the Government side who are engaged in what Lord Palmerston encouraged 10,000 Britishers to do for the Government of Spain in 1837. They are doing only what was done by people like Lafayette, Byron and Garibaldi, whose names Englishmen, not less than others, now honour. You cannot put these men on the same footing as the hired levies from Italy and Germany.[117]

Many other discussions about foreign volunteers were held during those years. From proposing specific legislation to hamper their recruitment and departure, to the stripping of their citizenship, to the question of repatriation at the end of the hostilities, a complete review of state practice would be impossible. France and the United Kingdom were chosen as the main promoters of the policy of non-intervention, but also for the important cultural references evoked in their Parliamentary debates. The images of past, noble adventurers stand as proof of how the foreign fighter is a category which cannot be reduced to technicalities alone. The figure of the foreign volunteer is constantly evoked in law-making processes, to help characterize the legitimacy and the illegitimacy of their cause. If the debates at the League were played mainly on ideological grounds, the writings of the internationalists revealed a set of cultural ideas behind the outlawing of certain practices related to volunteering abroad. Here, the images of former adventurers reappeared from the past, flooding the imaginary of British and French policy-makers, and epitomizing different conception of freedom. However, an analysis of how the foreign fighter as a cultural category entered the scene of modern international law cannot ignore the Hague Conventions of 1907. It is there that a first codification of its status is found, and the two opposing figures of the adventurer come into play. The Hague Peace Conferences represent a logical step to show how the volunteers of the interwar era moved on to the codification in the Geneva Conventions, before the next historical period, and the appearance of other foreigners fighting in wars abroad.

1.4 Brave Highlanders or Scary Adventurers?

The Hague Peace Conferences provide a privileged venue to explore the codification of early norms on volunteering abroad, but also to capture

---

[117] HC Deb, 17 March 1937, Vol. 321, c2143.

1.4 BRAVE HIGHLANDERS OR SCARY ADVENTURERS? 69

different cultural references relating to foreign fighters, as a mirror of specific fears, desires and fantasies at play in the delegates' discourses. The Conferences of 1907 are also the only humanitarian conventions in which the question of foreign volunteers was openly debated, given that in the subsequent Geneva talks, volunteers would be assimilated into the armed forces of one of the contracting parties.

An aspect worth mentioning is how these early codifications were strongly influenced by the doctrine of neutrality. Therefore, one can advance the argument that they have been formally replaced by the Geneva texts and especially by Additional Protocol I (AP I). Their present relevance also remains doubtful because the doctrine of neutrality has been gradually overshadowed by the collective security system under the UN Charter.[118]

Conversely, it is interesting to note how neutrality has reappeared today: some academics and policymakers have in fact advanced the argument that a return to neutrality laws would represent a practical way to counteract the phenomenon of foreign fighters in our time.[119] That the doctrine of neutrality did not completely disappear – even with the advent of the UN – is a topic extensively discussed in the literature, and which goes beyond the scope of this book.[120] But neutrality was a

---

[118] For a debate *see* T. Komarnicki, 'The Problem of Neutrality under the United Nations Charter' (1952) 38 *Transactions of the Grotius Society* 77–91, Laurent Goetschel, 'Neutrality, A Really Dead Concept?' (1999) 34 *Cooperation and Conflict* 115–139, Detlev F. Vagts, 'The Traditional Legal Concept of Neutrality in a Changing Environment' (1998) 14 *American University International Law Review* 83–102, Alfred P. Rubin, 'The Concept of Neutrality in International Law' (1988) 16 *Denver Journal of International Law & Policy* 353–375 and Patrick M. Norton, 'Between the Ideology and the Reality: The Shadow of the Law of Neutrality' (1976) 17 *Harvard International Law Journal* 249–312.

[119] *See* specifically Marnie Lloydd, 'Retrieving Neutrality Law to Consider "Other" Foreign Fighters under International Law' (2017) 9 *ESIL Conference Paper Series* 1–28, John Ip, 'Reconceptualising the Legal Response to Foreign Fighters' (2020) 69 *International and Comparative Law Quarterly* 103–134, Elizabeth Chadwick, 'Neutrality Revised' (2013) 22 *Nottingham Law Journal* 41–52 and Craig Forcese and Ani Mamikon, 'Neutrality Law, Anti-Terrorism, and Foreign Fighters: Legal Solutions to the Recruitment of Canadians to Foreign Insurgencies' (2015) 48 *University of British Columbia Law Review* 305–360.

[120] It is with the advent of the League that a new way of framing the relations of sovereign states had been put in place. Nonetheless, the writings of the international lawyers during the Spanish Civil War contain no reference to the principles laid down in Arts. 10 and 11 of the Covenant, which are taken as the foundation of the modern collective security system. A few years after the creation of the UN, Erik Castrén will devote one of his most important works to the question of neutrality in warfare. *See* Erik

pivotal concept in the early modern period for assessing the relations of states at war, as evidenced by the works of important internationalists like Oppenheim.[121] Again, the aim is not to retrace the debates around this doctrine, but rather to understand how it formed the legal lens through which volunteering abroad was understood in The Hague.[122]

In particular, Convention V relating to the Rights and Duties of Neutral Powers and Persons in War on Land contains six articles on foreign volunteers. Interestingly, an important distinction was made at the time between the rights and duties of a neutral *power* (a state) and of neutral *persons* (individuals). Although this differentiation has been criticized by many international lawyers, it remains central to the debates and to the subsequent codification in 1907.[123] Chapter I of Convention V – headed 'Rights and Duties of Neutral Powers' – contains at least two important articles in relation to volunteers:

> **Article 4**
> Corps of combatants cannot be formed nor recruiting agencies opened on the territory of a neutral Power to assist the belligerents.

Castrén, *The Present Law of War and Neutrality* (Helsinki: Suomalainev Tiedeakemia 1954).

[121] 'It was not until the eighteenth century that theory and practice agreed that it was the duty of neutrals to remain impartial, and of belligerents to respect the territories of neutrals. Bynkershoek and Vattel formulated adequate conceptions of neutrality. Bynkershoek does not use the term "neutrality", but calls neutrals *non hostes*, and he describes them as those who are of neither party – *qui neutrarum partium sunt* – in a war, and who do not, in accordance with a treaty, give assistance to either party. Vattel, on the other hand, uses the term "neutrality", and gives the following definition: "Neutral nations, during a war, are those who take no one's part, remaining friends common to both parties, and not favouring the armies of one of them to the prejudice of the other". But although Vattel's book appeared in 1758 ... his doctrines are in some ways less advanced than those of Bynkershoek. Bynkershoek, in contradiction to Grotius, maintained that in the absence of a previous treaty promising help, neutrals had nothing to do with the question as to which party in a war had a just cause; that neutrals, being friends to both parties, have not to sit as judges between them, and consequently, must not give or deny to one party or the other more or less accordance with their conviction as to the justice or injustice of the cause of each.' Oppenheim, *International Law*, pp. 494–495 § 288.

[122] 'Such States as do not take part in a war between other States are neutrals. The term "neutrality" is derived from the Latin *neuter*. Neutrality may be defined as *the attitude of impartiality adopted by third States towards belligerents and recognised by belligerents, such attitude creating rights and duties between the impartial States and the belligerents.*' *Ibid.*, p. 519 § 293.

[123] 'Neutrality is an attitude of impartiality on the part of States, and not on the part of individuals. Individuals derive neither rights nor duties according to International Law from the neutrality of those States whose subjects they are.' *Ibid.*, p. 522 § 296.

1.4 BRAVE HIGHLANDERS OR SCARY ADVENTURERS? 71

Article 6
The responsibility of a neutral Power is not engaged by the fact of persons crossing the frontier separately to offer their services to one of the belligerents.

Article 7
A neutral Power is not called upon to prevent the export or transport, on behalf of one or other of the belligerents, of arms, munitions of war, or, in general, of anything which can be of use to an army or a fleet.[124]

Here we can finally see the rules mentioned in the previous sections of the chapter, and that were alluded to in the writings of the internationalists and in the debates at the League: the idea that corps of combatants (such as hostile military expeditions) should not be organized in the territory of a neutral state; or conversely, that a state's neutrality in a foreign war was preserved when there were few single individuals crossing the frontier to join one of the belligerents.[125] Additionally, as we read Art. 7, it is clear that the neutrality of a state is not called into question for commercial transactions with one of the belligerents.[126] Here lies that

---

[124] Convention (V) Respecting the Rights and Duties of Neutral Powers and Persons in Case of War on Law (The Hague, 18 October 1907). Full text in Brown Scott, *The Hague Conventions and Declarations of 1899 and 1907*, pp. 133–134. The first articles of the Convention recite as follows: 'Article 1. The territory of neutral Powers is inviolable; Article 2. Belligerents are forbidden to move troops or convoys of either munitions of war or supplies across the territory of a neutral Power; Article 3. Belligerents are likewise forbidden to: (a) Erect on the territory of a neutral Power a wireless telegraphy station or other apparatus for the purpose of communicating with belligerent forces on land or sea; (b) Use any installation of this kind established by them before the war on the territory of a neutral Power for purely military purposes, and which has not been opened for the service of public messages ... Article 5. A neutral Power must not allow any of the acts referred to in Articles 2 to 4 to occur on its territory. It is not called upon to punish acts in violation of its neutrality unless the said acts have been committed on its own territory.'

[125] As explained by Castrén: 'Hague Convention V forbids the formation of armed forces and the setting up of enlistment bureaux in the territory of a neutral state for the benefit of belligerents ... a neutral State is not, however, bound to prevent private individuals intending to join the services of a belligerent from crossing its frontier separately. This provision has ... been interpreted to mean that individuals may leave neutral territory even in small groups as long as no organization is connected with their move ... if volunteer movements arise in neutral territory, the neutral State may not support them by organizing or assisting the departure of the volunteers.' Castrén, *The Present Law of War and Neutrality*, pp. 481–482.

[126] Concerning the export or transport of war and other materiel, Castrén makes clear that a neutral state cannot deliberately furnish such materiel to one of the belligerents. However, its private citizens are free to engage in commerce with the parties to a war:

distinction between the public and the private spheres evoked earlier, as private individuals could enlist in the army of one of the belligerents but could also continue their normal business transactions with them.[127] Let us turn then to the first two articles – those relating to the formation of corps of combatants and to the individuals crossing borders – to see their genesis and codification.

It was on the suggestion of the French delegation that the subject was brought to the fore during the conferences' meetings. In particular, the French were dissatisfied with the 1899 Hague Regulations, which in

'a neutral State may not itself deliver weapons and other war material to belligerents ... The Hague Convention (V) does not, to be sure, contain any direct prohibition to this effect. In only provides that a neutral power need not prevent the export or transport from or through its territory, on behalf of either of the belligerents, of anything which can be use to an army or a navy ... the neutral State may only allow ordinary business activities by private individuals'. *Ibid.*, pp. 474–475.

[127] On this last point, it suffices to take the second *voeu* of the Final Acts of the Hague Conferences (18 October 1907), which recites: 'The Conference utters the *voeu* that, in case of war, the responsible authorities, civil as well as military, should make it their special duty to ensure and safeguard the maintenance of pacific relations, more especially of the commercial and industrial relations between the inhabitants of the belligerent States and neutral countries.' Brown Scott, *The Hague Conventions and Declarations of 1899 and 1907*, p. 689. This is the position criticized in the 1930s by many Anglo-American international lawyers. In two of the most important studies on law and neutrality published in the 1950s, such those of Castrén and Greenspan, there was still much disagreement on this very point. For Castrén, in fact, private persons should be prevented from sending war materiel to one of the belligerents, whereas for Greenspan a doubt arose in considering a difference between a state-owned company and purely private business owners. 'If ... private persons begin to send war material from neutral territory direct to the armed forces of a belligerent Power, these deliveries must be stopped in order to prevent the neutral territory concerned from becoming a base for the belligerents.' Castrén, *The Present Law of War and Neutrality*, p. 475. Greenspan writes instead: 'A question of some difficulty ... arises with regard to commercial enterprises owned by the state ... If commercial enterprises owned by the neutral state are prohibited from supplying war material to a belligerent, then the power with a state-owned economy is placed at a disadvantage compared with a neutral state where private enterprise still flourishes. The law of neutrality in this respect requires clarification ... the reason for the rule permitting private neutral trade in war material with belligerent states lies in the right of neutrals to maintain commercial relations with belligerents in spite of war. There would, therefore, appear to be no logical reason for any distinction in this regard between purely commercial enterprises in neutral countries whether owned by private individuals or by the state ... whether a neutral state will permit its nationals to supply war material to belligerents is a matter which lies within the discretion of the government of the neutral state.' Greenspan, *The Modern Law of Land Warfare*, pp. 550–552. Finally, for Castrén, the issue was to be deferred to domestic law since the Hague Conventions were not clear on this point. See Castrén, *The Present Law of War and Neutrality*, p. 447.

1.4 BRAVE HIGHLANDERS OR SCARY ADVENTURERS? 73

their opinion dealt with the question too vaguely. Their delegation took inspiration from various municipal laws on neutrality, with the aim of codifying them in international law.[128] The original French proposal read as follow:

Article 1
A neutral State cannot be responsible for acts of its subjects of which a belligerent complains unless the acts have been committed on its own territory.

Article 2
A neutral State must not allow in its territory the formation of corps of combatants nor the opening of recruiting agencies to assist a belligerent. But its responsibility is not engaged by the fact of certain of its citizens crossing the frontier to offer their services to one or other of the belligerents.

Article 3
A neutral State is not called upon to prevent its subjects from exporting arms, munitions of war, or, in general, from furnishing anything which can be of use to an army, for the account of one or other of the belligerents.[129]

Supporting the French text, the Belgians stressed that neutral Powers not only had duties but also rights: 'being themselves strangers to the hostilities they have the primordial right to demand that they be not implicated in them directly or indirectly'.[130]

The Belgian delegation wanted to emphasize that the territory of a neutral state should remain free from any involvement in the hostilities and, as they put it, '[be] inviolable'.[131] Colonel Borel from the Swiss delegation expressed his agreement with the Belgian view, but reminded the other delegates that 'a neutral State has no other obligation than to repress acts in violation of neutrality which might be committed on its

---

[128] James Brown Scott, *The Proceedings of the Hague Conferences. Volume 3* (Oxford: Oxford University Press 1921), Meetings of the Second, Third and Fourth Commissions. Second Commission, Second Subcommission, fourth meeting (19 July 1907) pp. 173–174.
[129] *Ibid.*, p. 255.
[130] *Ibid.*, p. 174.
[131] *Ibid.* This would then become Art. 1 of the Convention: 'The territory of Neutral Powers in inviolable.'

territory, and this obligation is limited by its frontiers'.[132] The view of the Swiss delegate is interesting – given the traditional attitude of his country – as Borel put forward the distinction between 'the recruiting or organizing of groups of combatants on the territory of the neutral State' (as acts that would entail responsibility) and 'the crossing of the frontier separately by individuals' (towards which the neutral state had no obligation).[133] In support of his latter point, Borel added that: 'the control of individual passages can, moreover, never be carried into practice for it is impossible to scrutinize the intentions of each one and an attempt to exercise such control would raise intolerable obstacles to the passage of individuals from one State to another'.[134]

This passage is fascinating if compared with the security concerns of the post-9/11 landscape. As states increasingly possess extensive information on their citizens, this can be used at border controls and airports to detect potential foreign fighters. The idea of scrutinizing the intentions of individuals is today much debated in counter-terrorism discourse, especially when used to identify radicalized individuals operating in Western states. Certainly, the expansion of the technological apparatus has changed the rules of the game since 1907. But it is fascinating to see how these very problems were already present back then when dealing with citizens crossing borders to join a belligerent abroad.[135]

It was the Germans that raised one of the most important issues in relation to volunteers. Baron Mareschall von Bieberstein made clear that there had to be a distinction between neutral powers and neutral persons. In particular, the reservation made by Germany aimed at forbidding 'neutral persons from rendering war services to belligerents ... the second part of the French text does not make this point sufficiently clear'.[136] This was indeed a very strong counterclaim. It contradicted the whole idea of freeing states from their responsibility when numbers

---

[132] The French proposal contained also a fourth article. Article 4: 'Prisoners who, having escaped from the territory of the belligerent which held them, arrive in a neutral country shall be left free.' *Ibid.*, p. 255.

[133] *Ibid.*, p. 176.

[134] *Ibid.*, p. 177.

[135] Japan was among those states willing to extend the responsibilities of neutral powers also to their protectorates. However, its proposition was dismissed, as a majority of delegates agreed that the responsibility of a neutral ended at the limits of its jurisdiction (e.g., only its national territory). *See* on this point Antonio S. de Bustamante, 'The Hague Convention Concerning the Rights and Duties of Neutral Powers and Persons in Land Warfare' (1908) 2 *American Journal of International Law* 95–120, p. 100.

[136] Brown Scott, *The Proceedings of the Hague Conferences. Volume 3*, p. 177.

of individual citizens were crossing borders to join a belligerent abroad. The issue was not pushed forward by the German representative, and it was dropped during the fourth meeting on 19 July, but it became central during the subsequent one on 26 July. There, the German delegation proposed to include in the Convention a chapter relating to the rights and duties of neutral persons, by filing the following proposition:

CHAPTER I. – Definition of a neutral person
Article 61
All the *ressortissants* of a State which is not taking part in the war are considered as neutral persons.

Article 62
A violation of neutrality involves loss of character as a neutral person with respect to both belligerents. There is a violation of neutrality:

(a) If the neutral person commits hostile acts against one of the belligerent parties;
(b) If he commits acts in favor of one of the belligerent parties, particularly if he voluntarily enlists in the ranks of the armed force of one of the parties (Article 64, paragraph 2).

Article 63
The following acts shall not be considered as committed in favor of one of the belligerent parties in the sense of Article 62, letter b:

(a) Supplies furnished or loans made to one of the belligerent parties, so far as these supplies or loans do not come from enemy territory or territory occupied by the enemy.
(b) Services rendered in matters of police or civil administration.

CHAPTER II. – Services rendered by neutral persons
Article 64
Belligerent parties shall not ask neutral persons to render them war services, even though voluntary. The following shall be considered as war services: Any assistance by a neutral person in the armed forces of one of the belligerent parties, in the character of combatant or adviser, and, so far as he is placed under the laws, regulations or orders in effect by the said armed force, of other classes also, for example, secretary, workman, cook. Services of an ecclesiastical and sanitary character are excepted.

Article 65
Neutral Powers are bound to prohibit their *ressortissants* from engaging to perform military service in the armed force of either of the belligerent parties.

Article 66
Neutral persons moreover shall not be required, against their will, to lend services, not considered war services, to the armed force of either of the belligerent parties. It will be permitted, nevertheless, to require of them sanitary services or sanitary police services, not connected with actual hostilities. Such services shall be paid for in cash, so far as it is possible to do so. If cash is not paid, requisition receipts shall be given.[137]

The German proposal is probably one of the most comprehensive in terms of banning foreign volunteers in the armies of one of the belligerents. This time von Bieberstein took the floor for a long introduction, stressing that there was a need to regulate the status of neutral persons in the territory of the belligerents: 'in the majority of States there are hundreds of thousands of inhabitants belonging to another nationality ... what is then their position with respect to belligerents? What treatment shall they receive? Can they be enrolled in the ranks of the belligerents' armies and render to them other person services in promoting the war?'[138] For the Germans, such individuals were to lose their neutral status if they enlisted in the ranks of either side conducting hostilities. Conversely, furnishing the belligerents with loans or other material/supplies was not regarded as an action endangering the status of being neutral. Thus, if Art. 63 remained in line with the idea shared by many other states (leaving their citizens free to conduct commerce with the belligerents in time of war), Art. 62 was in direct contradiction with the original French proposal. It is here that a particular cultural image emerges. This is summarized by the words of von Bieberstein:

> First of all, the subjects of neutral States should not be admitted into the armies of belligerents ... If their participation in the war were recognized as lawful one should expect to see *adventurers from all parts of the world* flock to the colors of the belligerents. The presence of such elements in national armies would constitute a danger to discipline and would make it impossible for belligerents to guarantee conscientious application of the humanitarian rules prescribed by the Convention of 1899.[139]

The German delegation was worried not only that allowing the possibility of enlisting would open the door for any sort of adventurers, but that the presence of foreign individuals in another nation's army would endanger the proper conduct of hostilities. The figure of the adventurer evoked by the German delegation is very different from the idealized

---
[137] *Ibid.*, pp. 266–267.
[138] *Ibid.*, Second Commission, Second Subcommission, fifth meeting (26 July 1907) p. 187.
[139] *Ibid.* Emphasis added.

image of the noble volunteer we have encountered in the Anglo-American doctrine or in domestic debates. The figure of individuals flooding into a civil war 'from all parts of the world' reappeared many decades later, when the Security Council passed resolutions to stop the influx of 'faceless, nameless terrorists' joining jihadist groups in the Syrian Civil War. At the same time, such a characterization points to a tangible fear among the Germans that the inflow of foreigners to wars abroad posed a potential threat to good relations among states.[140] Certainly, this position confirms the analysis by Lauterpacht about those reactionary countries which saw no separation between their citizens and the rights and duties of the state on the international arena. As already pointed out, countries like the United Kingdom and France were instead adopting a more liberal view, and so did their delegations in The Hague.

It was in fact the British representative Lord Reay who first opposed the German proposition: '[it] forbids a Government to compel a neutral resident within its territory to take up arms; but [it permits it] to treat a neutral, as far as concerns his property or lands, or the payment of taxes, in time of war, in the same manner and to the same extent as it does its own citizens'.[141] The British delegate was thus glossing over the issue of foreigners travelling to join another state's army abroad, and rather focused on the status of those foreigners already present in the territory of one of the belligerents. This is not surprising, given the large colonies with many non-British citizens who could have enlisted in the army, if they wanted to.[142] As Lord Reay continued his intervention, the British delegation wished to clarify 'whether it is desirable that the neutrals established on the territory of a belligerent be put ... on a footing of complete equality with the *ressortissants* of the State in which they reside or whether they should be accorded a distinct position'.[143] The British were mainly interested in understanding how to treat neutral citizens in their colonies, rather than worrying about the question of foreigners going to fight abroad.

---

[140] 'Moreover, the fact that subjects of a neutral State bear arms against one of the belligerents would not be without influence on the relations between the Governments and might lead to serious complications.' *Ibid.*
[141] *Ibid.*, Second Commission, Second Subcommission, fifth meeting (26 July 1907) p. 188.
[142] The point is explained in A. Pearce Higgins, *The Hague Peace Conferences and Other International Conferences Concerning the Laws and Usage of War. Texts of Conventions with Commentaries* (Cambridge: Cambridge University Press 1909) p. 293.
[143] Brown Scott, *The Proceedings of the Hague Conferences. Volume 3*, Second Commission, Second Subcommission, fifth meeting (26 July 1907) p. 188.

However, the German proposal found a strong ally in the US delegation. Although praising the original French draft, General Davis thought that the German proposal was more advanced in establishing a clear status for neutral inhabitants in a belligerent territory: 'the rules which have been submitted by the German delegation ... define the rights, the duties, and the immunities of a neutral inhabitant of a belligerent State in time of war ... immunity from burdens of a specifically military nature ... in all other respects his situation is not changed. His property is taxed to support the civil administration'.[144] The Americans were also overlooking the issue of foreigners going to fight abroad, and rather focused their attention on those citizens of neutral states already residing in belligerents' territory. The reason given to support the German proposal is interesting though, as the American delegate stressed that the status of foreigners was to 'conform to the conditions of modern commerce'[145] and that 'commercial operations are no longer confined to a single State, but extend to several States'.[146] The Americans were thus particularly concerned with maintaining normal commercial relations during warfare, as they agreed with the idea of authorizing 'supplies furnished or loans made to one of the belligerent parties' by their own nationals. This position was very much in line with the US Neutrality Acts, which prevented the state from supplying and trading war materiel, but not commercial transactions by private individuals, as previously seen.

So much for the general discussion, the various delegates started to debate the specific articles of the German proposal and suggested possible amendments to it. In particular, various delegations wanted to clarify the meaning of *ressortissants*, so as to elucidate whether the term concerned 'persons ... domiciled in the territory of a belligerent State but who [were] not its nationals'.[147] The doubt was soon resolved thanks to the intervention of Colonel Borel, and the delegates agreed to change the word *ressortissants* to *nationals*.[148] The Swiss delegate then proposed an interesting amendment to the text. He advanced the idea that, when

---

[144] *Ibid.*, p. 189.
[145] *Ibid.*
[146] *Ibid.*
[147] *Ibid.*, p. 190. As further explained by Pearce Higgins: 'the word ressortissants appears to have a wider meaning than subject, and to include all over whom a state claims to exercise jurisdiction either by virtue of allegiance or domicile'. Pearce Higgins, *The Hague Peace Conferences*, p. 266.
[148] Brown Scott, *The Proceedings of the Hague Conferences. Volume 3*, Second Commission, Second Subcommission, fifth meeting (26 July 1907) p. 190.

1.4 BRAVE HIGHLANDERS OR SCARY ADVENTURERS? 79

deciding no longer to observe neutrality, a neutral person should not be treated differently, or deemed 'guilty of a special infraction'.[149] As he praised the efforts of the German delegation to ameliorate the negative effects of the hostilities, Borel emphasized that 'his failure to observe neutrality implies in itself alone no other consequence for the neutral than the loss of his neutrality in itself'.[150] This proposition is important, as it put the person who enlisted in a foreign army on an equal footing with the nationals of the belligerent party. Here one can see crystallizing a particular attitude towards foreign fighters of the time, something that has perhaps radically changed under today's counter-terrorism discourse.

The discussion soon returned to the problem of the enlistment in a foreign army. In particular, the French delegate Louis Renault opposed the propositions contained in both Art. 64 and Art. 65, as they prevented belligerents enlisting foreigners in their army. In the words of the French delegate:

> neutrals can freely enlist and that the belligerents can accept their services without the neutral State [being consulted]. The consequence of this right will naturally be their complete assimilation to the soldiers of the belligerent ... The only thing that can be required of a neutral State is that it shall not make it easy for them in this respect by allowing on its territory the formation of corps of combatants or the opening of recruiting agencies. ... But outside of these limits the neutral State cannot be held to control the actions of its subjects, though it is able to claim from their enrolment whatever consequences it will by reason of its internal legislation, which in certain countries provides loss of nationality in such a case.[151]

As much as for the British, the French delegation saw no issue in enlisting foreigners in their army, the only real obligation being to prevent the formation of organized groups within their territory. In the event that a country wanted to stop the departure of its own citizens, it could resort to the provisions of domestic law. The Belgian delegate found himself in line with his French colleague, as he deplored the German proposal by stating that '[it was] going too far; such a general and absolute prohibition arbitrarily limits the authority of the belligerent while at the same time infringing the right of individual liberty of the neutrals'.[152] The Japanese delegate aligned himself with Germany, stating that it was not desirable to have foreign elements in a regular army. For

---

[149] Ibid.
[150] Ibid., p. 191.
[151] Ibid., p. 195.
[152] Ibid., p. 196.

their part, the delegates of the United States and the United Kingdom limited their intervention by restating the examples of their Neutrality Laws and Foreign Enlistment Acts.

Faced with mounting opposition, the German delegate tried to soften his position by admitting that 'it would not be possible for the neutral State to prevent its subjects, by Draconian methods, from enlisting in the service of such or such belligerent ... but one might imagine the case where thousands of neutral *ressortissants* come to enlist voluntarily in the ranks of one of the belligerent armies'.[153] The French delegation immediately replied by saying that what was worrying the Germans was 'the fact that the subjects of a neutral State might cross its frontier *en masse* to go into the service of one or the other of the belligerents', but that scenario was already been envisioned by Art. 2 of the original proposal. It placed an obligation on the state not to allow the formation of organized groups of combatants to leave its territory to fight abroad.[154]

The fifth meeting ended with France and the United Kingdom reaffirming their disagreement with the Germans, specifically on the proposed Art. 65, which envisaged a strict prohibition on the part of neutral powers towards their citizens in performing military services in the armed forces of either belligerent. In the last words before the meeting was adjourned Lord Reay stated: 'we believe we should maintain with respect to the neutrals only this negative obligation not to favor any of the belligerents and not to depart from a strict impartiality with regard to them'.[155]

But the tone of the conversation was not reconciled in the next discussion, held on 2 August. There, the Dutch delegation returned to the original problem of citizens of a neutral state already in the territory of one of the belligerents. The Dutch were as worried as the British that if the German proposal was accepted, their colonial troops would be hampered from enlisting volunteers. General Jonkheer den Beer Poortugael made his country's position clear:

> Our army is one composed of militia ... but we have in addition a small corps, a reserve of our colonial army. This reserve, like our whole colonial army, is composed of volunteer enlisted soldiers, of which some are natives ... *These are intrepid men loving dangers like the mountain climbers*; furthermore they seek to make a career, as many have done. Well! Why force a State to do without services for which it has such need

---

[153] *Ibid.*, Second Commission, Second Subcommission, fifth meeting (26 July 1907) p. 197.
[154] *Ibid.*, p. 199.
[155] *Ibid.*, p. 200.

1.4 BRAVE HIGHLANDERS OR SCARY ADVENTURERS? 81

and restrain these persons from accomplishing a service which they love and have contracted for?[156]

Quite an interesting statement, especially if compared with how Alvaro del Vayo would some years later characterize the Army of Africa, as a group of barbaric mercenaries 'shocking the conscience of the civilized world'. Here one can see emerging a very different image from the adventurer evoked some days earlier by the German delegation. The figure of the *bon sauvage*, depicted as an intrepid man who loves danger and mountain climbing, is clearly imbued with patronizing tones. This image reveals the visceral attachment of the Dutch to their colonies, a sentiment that will re-emerge strongly during decolonization in the discourse of certain European states. There, it will be significant to see how the same image imbued the discourse of British policymakers when they will take pride in the services rendered by their colonial troops.

Going back to The Hague, the Dutch delegation suggested an amendment to Art. 64, excluding the citizens of a neutral State who at the beginning of the hostilities were already in the ranks of the army of a belligerent.[157] The point was backed by the Norwegian delegation, as his representative Hagerup underlined that: 'when war breaks out, a country cannot deprive itself of the services of all those who are not its nationals'.[158] If the situation was not complicated enough, the Italian representative brought to the fore the problem of double nationals. In particular, he found it problematic to reconcile their status in light of Art. 65. How could the obligations of the state where they resided at the beginning of hostilities be solved if they had to be forced to fight against their country of nationality? Faced with mounting difficulties, most states at The Hague finally voted to reject the German proposal, although not in its entirety.[159] The status of neutral persons in the Hague Convention V would finally be codified in three articles, forming Chapter III and regulating the Neutral Powers and Persons in Land Warfare:

---

[156] *Ibid.*, sixth meeting (2 August 1907) p. 202. Emphasis added.
[157] *Ibid.*, Second Commission, Second Subcommission, sixth meeting (2 August 1907) p. 275.
[158] *Ibid.*, p. 203.
[159] James Brown Scott, *The Proceedings of the Hague Conferences. Volume 1* (Oxford: Oxford University Press 1920), fifth plenary meeting (7 September 1907) and sixth plenary meeting (21 September 1907) pp. 123–129 and 162–172.

Article 16
The nationals of a State which is not taking part in the war are considered as neutrals.

Article 17
A neutral cannot avail himself of his neutrality (a) If he commits hostile acts against a belligerent; (b) If he commits acts in favor of a belligerent, particularly if he voluntarily enlists in the ranks of the armed forces of one of the parties. In such a case, the neutral shall not be more severely treated by the belligerent as against whom he has abandoned his neutrality than a national of the other belligerent State could be for the same act.

Article 18
The following acts shall not be considered as committed in favour of one belligerent in the sense of Article 17, letter (b): (a) Supplies furnished or loans made to one of the belligerents, provided that the person who furnishes the supplies or who makes the loans lives neither in the territory of the other party nor in the territory occupied by him, and that the supplies do not come from these territories; (b) Services rendered in matters of police or civil administration.[160]

As can be seen, the most difficult questions were removed from the final text. The articles did not contain much detail in defining the meaning of hostile acts, or what to do with double nationals. Contrary to the German proposal, a neutral person was free to enlist voluntarily in an army, at the cost of 'availing himself of his neutrality'. However, following the Swiss amendment, such a person would not risk a worse treatment than was reserved to the nationals of the countries at war. Finally, the supplies and loans furnished by single individuals to both parties in the conflict were not seen as endangering their neutrality.

If paired with final Arts. 4 and 6 of the same Convention, these three additional articles give a comprehensive view of how the foreign volunteer was codified in the early laws of war. As a general laissez-faire attitude prevailed among states at The Hague, under international law citizens of neutral countries were free to enlist in a foreign army. However, no groups or expeditions with the intent to join a belligerent were to be formed within a neutral state's territory. All in all, most European delegations understood the problem of volunteers as something to be dealt with via domestic legislation, when and if it was deemed necessary. This points to a distinction existing at the time between the private and public spheres, an aspect further exemplified by the

---

[160] Brown Scott, *The Hague Conventions and Declarations of 1899 and 1907*, p. 136.

1.4 BRAVE HIGHLANDERS OR SCARY ADVENTURERS?

separation between the state and its citizens with regard to the furnishing of supplies and loans to one of the belligerents. As already pointed out, this vision was already being questioned in the 1930s and then radically changed in the 1950s, when internationalists like Brownlie would lament the vagueness and ineffectiveness of the Hague Conventions, calling for their revision.

Nevertheless, one important aspect emerging from the Hague was the contrasting and ambivalent images of the foreign fighter, as expressed by the German, Dutch and British delegations. On the one side, one can find the figure of the adventurer who can endanger the normal conduct of warfare; on the other, the image of the *bon sauvage* was evoked by those representatives whose states included colonial troops in their armies. But the figure of the foreign fighter in the early modern period would not be complete without looking at the codification of this actor as part of the personnel a state can resort to in warfare. After all, this was the point raised by both the British and Dutch delegations in the Hague. For them, the problem was not so much about foreigners travelling to fight abroad, but rather not to exclude the volunteers already residing in their colonies or enlisted in their armies. The qualification of 'militia or volunteer corps' as a lawful actor within the rules of humanitarian law came from the Lieber Code of 1863, and reached Art. 4 of the 1949 Geneva Conventions. To be clear, the following digression will not enter into the specific historical details.

The early modern norms on belligerent qualification are found in the Lieber Code of 1863, including the first distinction between civilians and combatants.[161] In particular, the Code recognized 'partisans' as regular troops that could be used in warfare, and it distinguished them from irregular fighters not belonging to an organized army, such as scouts or single soldiers (to be treated as spies), armed prowlers (to be treated as robbers) and war-rebels.[162] Although the intention of the Lieber Code

---

[161] *See* for instance Art. 22: 'Nevertheless, as civilization has advanced during the last centuries, so has likewise steadily advanced, especially in war on land, the distinction between the private individual belonging to a hostile country and the hostile country itself, with its men in arms. The principle has been more and more acknowledged that the unarmed citizen is to be spared in person, property, and honor as much as the exigencies of war will admit.' Instructions for the Government of Armies of the United States in the Field (Lieber Code) 24 April 1863, originally Issued as General Orders No. 100 (Washington 1898: Government Printing Office). On this point see also Scheipers, *Unlawful Combatants*, pp. 69–104.

[162] Respectively Art. 83 (scouts), Art. 84 (armed prowlers) and Art. 85 (war rebels). Art. 81 recites: 'Partisans are soldiers armed and wearing the uniform of their army but belonging to a corps which acts detached from the main body for the purpose of making inroads into the territory occupied by the enemy. If captured, they are entitled to all the privileges of the

was to differentiate between partisans and other (irregular) combatants, one can imagine how the former could have included the many volunteers who enrolled with both sides during the four years of the conflict.[163] Naturally, the Code remains a first incomplete draft of the modern laws of war, and it was affected by the context of the American Civil War.[164] In fact, it was with the Brussels Peace Conference of 1874 that European powers started to take into consideration a wider and more encompassing project for the codification of international norms to be respected in warfare. And it was in this venue that an article recognizing 'militia and volunteer corps' as lawful belligerent was codified:

Article 9
The laws, rights, and duties of war apply not only to armies, but also to militia and volunteer corps fulfilling the following conditions:

1. That they be commanded by a person responsible for his subordinates;
2. That they have a fixed distinctive emblem recognizable at a distance;
3. That they carry arms openly; and
4. That they conduct their operations in accordance with the laws and customs of war.

In countries where militia constitute the army, or form part of it, they are included under the denomination 'army'.[165]

This article contains the four criteria that need to be fulfilled by 'volunteers and militia corps', and which survived more or less intact until the

---

prisoner of war.' Interestingly, Lieber further explains his position with reference to partisans: 'The terms partisan and free corps are vaguely used. Sometimes, as we shall see farther on, partisan is used for a self-constituted guerrillero; more frequently it has a different meaning. Both partisan-corps and free-corps designate bodies detached from the main army; but the former term refers to the action of the troop, the latter to the composition ... Free-corps, on the other hand, are troops not belonging to the regular army, consisting of volunteers, generally raised by individuals authorized to do so by the government, used for petty war.' Francis Lieber, 'On Guerrilla Parties', in Francis Lieber (ed.), *The Miscellaneous Writings of Francis Lieber: Contributions to Political Science, Volume II* (Philadelphia: J. B. Lippincott 1881) 275–292, pp. 282–283.

[163] On this point see Tracey Leigh Dowdeswell, 'The Brussels Peace Conference of 1874 and the Modern Laws of Belligerent Qualification' (2017) 54 *Osgoode Hall Law Journal* 805–850, pp. 816–824.

[164] Additionally, the Code at Art. 52 recognized that: 'so soon as a man is armed by a sovereign government and takes the soldier's oath of fidelity, he is a belligerent'. In this sense, volunteers who enlisted in one of the armies could be recognized as legitimate solider – thus benefiting from prisoner of war status – as long as they wore uniforms and were recognized to be part of one of the two armies.

[165] Project of an International Declaration Concerning the Laws and Customs of War (Brussels, 27 August 1874) Art. 9.

1.4 BRAVE HIGHLANDERS OR SCARY ADVENTURERS? 85

Geneva Conventions of 1949.[166] At the time of the Brussels Conference, two of the most pressing problems were represented by the *levée en masse* and the role of *franc-tireurs*.[167] It was with the Franco-Prussian war of 1870–1871 that these issues had risen to the fore, and as such they informed the discussions of states representatives.[168] What worried the German delegation was to regulate the spontaneous taking up of arms of a local population (*levée en masse*).[169] In other words, the Germans, in their desire to see anyone who could take arms against them in uniform, in order to be able to identify them, wished to regulate the *levée en masse* as much as possible through the criteria set out by Art. 9. The issue became animated, especially because states such as Belgium, Spain and the Netherlands did not want to relinquish the possibility, in case of an invasion, of making use of other kinds of troops outside of their standard army. The discussions in Brussels thus saw two contrasting sentiments at play. On the one side, the patriotism asserted by smaller states to support their population and the right to defend their motherland. On the other, the German fear of brigands and looters flooding the battlefield.[170] This

---

[166] As explained by Dowdeswell: 'An early formulation of these rules was delivered in a paper read by Henry Richmond Droop, a barrister of Lincoln's Inn Fields, to the Juridical Society of London on 30 November 1870. Droop's paper addressed the most pressing topic in international law of the day – the status of the francs-tireurs – and he articulated many of the key concepts of modern international humanitarian law ... Droop recognized that sovereign authorization remained, at that time, the generally accepted rule for belligerent qualification. However, he argued that this rule was no longer desirable for regulating present-day conflicts, and he proposed instead a rule for belligerent qualification based upon objective and readily observable criteria. Droop rejected the sovereign authorization rule on the grounds that sovereign authorization alone would make it impossible to distinguish between troops and civilians, or to enforce respect for the laws of war on the part of belligerents. Civilians should not be attacked in war, and protecting them is the responsibility of the armed forces who would wage that war ... The modern definition of a "lawful combatant" first appeared in its essential form in Article 9 of the Draft Declaration presented at Brussels, and was based upon Droop's organizational criteria, including wearing a distinctive insignia, carrying arms openly, and being subsumed under a nation state's military chain of command so that the laws and customs of war can be enforced by a qualified public authority.' Dowdeswell, 'The Brussels Peace Conference of 1874', pp. 828–830.
[167] On this point see Crawford, 'Regulating the Irregular', pp. 170–171.
[168] Dowdeswell, 'The Brussels Peace Conference of 1874', p. 807.
[169] Actes de la Conférence de Bruxelles de 1874 sur le Projet d'Une Convention Internationale Concernant la Guerre. Protocoles des Séances Plenieres. Protocoles de la Commission Déléguée par la Conférence. Annexes (Paris: Librairie Des Publications Législatives 1874) pp. 28–34.
[170] The German delegation wished that such spontaneous upheaval should nonetheless be organized through a line of command, by making people wear recognizable uniforms:

was the same kind of feeling that was manifest in The Hague through the figure of the adventurer endangering the good conduct of hostilities.[171]

The Germans would eventually relinquish their dream, understanding that it was impossible to demand that an entire population could be provided with uniforms during an occupation in times of war.[172] Nevertheless, what needs to be emphasized here is: when state representatives in Brussels included volunteers and militia corps under Art. 9, no mention was made of foreign fighters. Evidently, they were not the problem that the delegates had in mind, and the fact that volunteers could have been foreign did not make the headlines in 1874. In fact, the same article was transposed in an almost identical form in both the 1899 and 1907 Hague Regulations on the Laws and Customs of Land Warfare. Again, no mention was made of foreign volunteers or foreign militia troops. The article on belligerent qualification as codified in the Hague Convention IV of 1907 read as follows:

Article 1
The laws, rights, and duties of war apply not only to armies, but also to militia and volunteer corps fulfilling the following conditions:

1. To be commanded by a person responsible for his subordinates;
2. To have a fixed distinctive emblem recognizable at a distance;

'mais il faudra que ces hommes portent un signe certain qui les distingue des brigands et des pillards'. *Ibid.*, 28–29.

[171] Although the Germans came to their senses, they were still worried that leaving the levée en masse completely unregulated would have been problematic for the problem of brigandage: 'En terminant, M. le délégué d'Allemagne dit que la levée en masse est une chose légitime, parfois nécessaire, et qu'il ne peut venir à la pensée de personne de l'empêcher ou du l'entraver; ce que l'on demande, c'est qu'elle soit organisée d'une manière quelconque, afin de ne pas dégénérer en brigandage. La question doit être examinée sérieusement et consciencieusement: il est de l'intérêt de la patrie de chacun et de la défense commune à tous les Etats qu'elle soit résolue affirmativement.' *Ibid.*

[172] Finally, an article codifying the levée en masse was included (Art. 10). This article was transposed in an almost identical form into both the 1899 and 1907 Hague Conventions (Art. 2) and also found its way into the 1949 Geneva Conventions under Art 4 (A) (6). The case of the *franc-tireurs* remained pending. To the questions posed by the Belgian delegation on the status of those individuals not belonging to collective groups, the answer was that the overall project of the Convention was not meant to deal with the special case of single individuals. 'M. le délégué de Belgique avait demandé quel serait le sort d'un citoyen qui, agissant isolément et dans la partie non occupée du pays, ferait des actes do guerre destinés, par exemple, à entraver la marche de l'ennemi. Il lui a été répondu que le projet ne prévoyait pas de tels cas spéciaux. En conséquence, il est resté entendu que la question de savoir si l'individu, agissant dans les conditions ci-dessus indiquées, doit ou non être considéré comme belligérant, n'est pas tranchée par le projet et reste dès lors da dans le domaine du droit des gens non écrit.' *Ibid.*, p. 45.

3. To carry arms openly; and
4. To conduct their operations in accordance with the laws and customs of war.

> In countries where militia or volunteer corps constitute the army, or form part of it, they are included under the denomination 'army'.[173]

Volunteers who respected these four criteria – no matter if foreigners or not – were equated with the soldiers of a standard army.[174] Moreover, in those countries where volunteers and other militias formed the national armed forces – like Switzerland – those troops would have been recognized as the lawful regular army.[175]

Despite two world wars and notably the Spanish Civil War, the story of this article did not undergo significant changes, at least from the point of view of foreign fighters. The representatives of the states gathered in post-war Geneva dealt with a wider, more encompassing codification for the status and the treatment of prisoners of war, following the previous text of 1929.[176] This time the *francs-tireurs* would no longer be the central preoccupation of the various delegates, but rather how to include resistance movements and partisans, for their fundamental role played in World War II. As noted by Jean Pictet in the famous commentaries to the Geneva Conventions: 'the problem was finally solved by the assimilation of resistance movements to militias and corps of volunteers'.[177]

---

[173] Text in Brown Scott, *The Hague Conventions and Declarations of 1899 and 1907*, p. 107.

[174] This point is confirmed also by the Institute de Droit International in 1908: 'La condition juridique internationale des étrangers, civils ou militaires, n'appartenant par leur nationalité à aucun des Etats belligérants et engagés au service de l'un d'eux, sera absolument identique, en ce qui concerne l'application des lois de la guerre, à celle des nationaux de l'Etat au service duquel ils se trouvent.' Institut de Droit International, Resolution. 'De la Condition Juridique Internationale des Étrangers Civils ou Militaires, au Service des Belligérants' (Florence, 28 September 1908).

[175] The question had already been raised in Brussels in 1874 by Colonel Staaff, delegate representative of Norway and Sweden: 'M. le colonel Staaff trouve que cette question est fort délicate et mérite d'être prise en considération. Si l'on admet que les quatre conditions réunies de l'article 9 ont leur raison d'être, il faudra évidemment faire une distinction entre les corps improvisés et les milices existant en vertu de la constitution de certains pays, surtout lorsque, comme en Suisse, elles forment l'armée même.' Actes de la Conférence de Bruxelles de 1874, p. 29.

[176] Convention de Genève du 27 juillet 1929 Relative au Traitement des Prisonniers de Guerre (Geneva, 27 July 1929).

[177] 'During the preparatory work for the Conference, and even during the Conference itself, two schools of thought were observed. Some delegates considered that partisans should have to fulfil conditions even stricter than those laid down by the Hague Regulations in order to benefit by the provisions of the Convention. On the other hand, other experts or

The final Art. 4 section (A) (1) (2), which included the new wording of resistance movements and the four criteria for belligerent qualification, as codified in Geneva Convention III, is as follows:

> **Article 4**
>
> A. Prisoners of war, in the sense of the present Convention, are persons belonging to one of the following categories, who have fallen into the power of the enemy:
>
> (1) Members of the armed forces of a Party to the conflict as well as members of militias or volunteer corps forming part of such armed forces.
>
> (2) Members of other militias and members of other volunteer corps, including those of organized resistance movements, belonging to a Party to the conflict and operating in or outside their own territory, even if this territory is occupied, provided that such militias or volunteer corps, including such organized resistance movements, fulfil the following conditions:
>
> (a) that of being commanded by a person responsible for his subordinates;
> (b) that of having a fixed distinctive sign recognizable at a distance;
> (c) that of carrying arms openly;
> (d) that of conducting their operations in accordance with the laws and customs of war.[178]

Naturally, other issues surrounding militia and corps of volunteers occupied a good part of the preparatory works of Art. 4, yet not that of foreign volunteers.[179] It seems that from 1907 the problem had vanished. What

---

delegates held the view that resistance movements should be given more latitude. The problem was finally solved by the assimilation of resistance movements to militias and corps of volunteers "not forming part of the armed forces" of a Party to the conflict. However, contrary to the interpretation generally given to the corresponding provision in the Hague Regulations, it was recognized that such units might operate in occupied territory. That was an important innovation which grew out of the experience of the Second World War.' Jean Pictet (ed.), *Commentary to the Geneva Convention III Relative to the Treatment of Prisoners of War* (Geneva: ICRC 1960) pp. 49–50. This is of course an oversimplification and the discussions by the Committee in charge of Art. 4 (originally Art. 3) were much longer and denser in content. Again, the point here is not to retrace the history of Art. 4, but rather to look at whether the issue of foreign volunteers had entered the discussions either in Geneva or beforehand. *See* Final Record of the Diplomatic Conference of Geneva of 1949, Vol. II A, Committee II, thirtieth and thirty-sixth meetings, pp. 383–390 and pp. 410–412.

[178] Convention (III) relative to the Treatment of Prisoners of War (Geneva, 12 August 1949) Art. 4(A)(2).

[179] Notably some countries raised the problem of state armies composed by volunteers and militia corps, while others questioned whether there had to be a distinction between 'militias and volunteer corps' which formed part of the armed forces and 'members of

1.4 BRAVE HIGHLANDERS OR SCARY ADVENTURERS? 89

was the legacy left by those three dramatic years (1936–1939) which had held Europe and the League in suspense? As noted by many commentators, the Spanish Civil War was central in the development of another, no less important norm coming out of the Geneva talks: common Art. 3.[180] Codifying the existence of non-international armed conflicts, this article represented a great incremental step in the protection of the victims of the warfare that had devasted the Spanish peninsula.[181] Perhaps the bloodshed and the sacrifice of the International Brigades – and of the many Italian and German troops sent to Spain by their governments – was not completely in vain.[182]

But what of foreign fighters after the Spanish Civil War? As we move from the League to the United Nations system and towards the decolonization era, a young assistant lecturer at the University of Leeds advances some reflections on volunteering abroad. That young lecturer is Ian Brownlie.[183] As previously explained, the vagueness of Hague Convention V relating to the status of neutral powers and persons in warfare had come under fierce critique already during the interwar years.[184] Back in 1939 Friedmann had commented on Art. 6 of the convention: 'this rule presupposes a community in which an individual

---

other militia' and 'other volunteer corps'. See Pictet, *Commentary to the Geneva Convention III*, pp. 51–56.

[180] David A. Elder, 'The Historical Background of Common Article 3 of the Geneva Convention of 1949' (1979) 11 *Case Western Reserve Journal of International Law* 37-69. See also Giovanni Mantilla, *Lawmaking under Pressure. International Humanitarian Law and Internal Armed Conflict* (Ithaca, NY: Cornell University Press 2020) pp. 58–97.

[181] Final Record of the Diplomatic Conference of Geneva of 1949, Vol. II B, Summary Records of Meetings, pp. 40–48, 75–79, 82–84, 90–95 and 97–102.

[182] As Antonio Cassese noted: 'States, in deciding to apply some international norms to the Spanish civil war, expressed the legal conviction that these rules should be applied to all internal armed conflicts with the same characteristics of intensity and length as the Spanish war. We can conclude that by the end of the 1930s far-reaching international norms on internal armed conflicts were created and these norms were substantially modelled on the ones applicable to inter-State conflicts. The Spanish civil war thus represented a watershed in the legal conceptions of the international community.' Antonio Cassese, *The Human Dimension of International Law: Selected Papers* (Oxford: Oxford University Press 2008) p. 115.

[183] Ian Brownlie, 'Volunteers and the Law of War and Neutrality' (1956) 5 *International and Comparative Law Quarterly* 570–580.

[184] The laissez-faire attitude endorsed by a majority of states in the Hague seemed unattainable, especially when liberal European powers were confronted with totalitarian/fascist volunteers. Padelford himself had expressed his reservations over the evident state of confusion of the law generally relating to civil war, stating that 'it would be highly desirable ... to draw up and accept an international convention defining clearly the rights and duties and obligations of armed forces in time of civil strife'. Norman

may make a decision, such as volunteering for a foreign war on his own responsibility, independently of his government. That this condition no longer exists generally among the members of the family of nations became obvious in the Spanish Civil War'.[185] Shifting from neutrality towards the collective security system, the idea of a volunteer detached from any form of state control also starts to crumble. Far from disappearing, the issue of volunteers re-emerged twice in the years immediately following the creation of the UN: the Israeli War of Independence of 1948 and especially the Korean War of 1950–1953. It was exactly three years after the armistice ending the Korean War that Brownlie devoted a sharp, compelling article on the question of foreign volunteering. He makes clear that the purpose of his study is to criticize the 'ambiguities, gaps and opportunities for abuse' of the present law.[186] One can thus find a clear parallel with those international lawyers who, already in the 1930s, wanted to break with the past. Most importantly, Brownlie asserts that: 'the use of pseudo-volunteers as an instrument of government policy and for purposes of aggression gives increasing significance to the shortcomings of . . . the law'.[187]

What catches the attention is the categorization of our actor as an 'instrument of government policy'. We are very far from the image of the idealist adventurer going to fight abroad following his ideals. Volunteers are now depicted as linked to a governmental plan, ideally closing that public/private gap which existed at the beginning of the century.[188]

J. Padelford and Henry G. Seymour, 'Some International Problems of the Spanish Civil War' (1937) 52 *Political Science Quarterly* 364–380, p.380.

[185] Friedmann, 'The Growth of State Control over the Individual', p. 141.

[186] Brownlie, 'Volunteers and the Law of War and Neutrality', p. 570.

[187] *Ibid.*

[188] 'The toleration of departure of large numbers of volunteers accompanied by bad faith probably amounts to aggression . . . It might fall within other offences usually discussed in relation to aggression – the harbouring of armed bands, fomenting civil strife, or other forms of intentional interference in internal affairs.' *Ibid.*, p. 578. Brownlie would return to this point in his first book devoted to the use of force. By recalling the example of the Korean War, he asserted that: 'the use of volunteers under government control for launching a military campaign or supporting active rebel groups will undoubtedly constitute "use of force". It is the question of government control and not the label "volunteer" . . . which is important'. Ian Brownlie, *International Law and the Use of Force by States* (Oxford: Clarendon Press 1963) pp. 371–372. One more layer is added by Brownlie to the discussion on volunteers. In trying to describe these actors and especially the offences they can be punishable for, he uses the term 'armed bands'. These would become very popular after World War II under the rubric of aggression, as much as hostile military expeditions were in the decades before. In another of his early articles,

1.4 BRAVE HIGHLANDERS OR SCARY ADVENTURERS? 91

To sustain his point, Brownlie further argues that: 'the individualism and *laissez-faire* once prevalent [is] now increasingly replaced by the integration of the individual on the State corpus. With an increase in the definition and comprehensive nature of the citizen's rights and duties *vis-à-vis* the State, there must be a change in the character of the volunteer'.[189] In other words, the volunteer can no longer be understood as detached from the state apparatus. In fact, he is seen as an actor advancing some governmental policy: 'other historical instances of threats to the peace caused by the operations of volunteers include the occupation of Karelia and Olonets by Finnish volunteers in 1919, and D'Annunzio occupation of Fiume'.[190] The figure of D'Annunzio evoked in this passage points to a shift from the image of the noble adventurer as a legacy of the nineteenth century, towards one of an actor under the direct patronage of a state's foreign policy.[191]

To conclude, one can see how in the first years of the Cold War a clear change over the cultural understanding of volunteering abroad was taking place. Brownlie's position attests to the inadequacies of the Hague Conventions and more generally to the perceived gaps in the law. Still in 1962, Manuel Garcia-Mora conducted an in-depth study centred on the international responsibility for hostile acts of individuals against foreign states.[192] In his book, Garcia-Mora dedicates an entire chapter to volunteers. There, he asserts that: 'the years that have elapsed since the adoption of the Hague Conventions have made crystal clear that volunteers are really instruments of international policy and

---

Brownlie inscribes the history of armed bands within the larger history of hostile military expeditions. Ian Brownlie, 'International Law and the Activities of Armed Bands' (1958) *International and Comparative Law Quarterly* 712–735.

[189] Brownlie, 'Volunteers and the Law of War and Neutrality', p. 577.
[190] *Ibid.*, p. 578.
[191] Few years before Brownlie, the Australian international lawyer Julius Stone, had written: 'any large-scale movement such as that of the army which moved from China into the Korean theatre in the winter of 1950 could scarcely proceed without such organization as would engage the neutral's responsibility'. Julius Stone, *Legal Controls of International Conflict: A Treatise on the Dynamics of Disputes and War-Law* (New York: Rinehart 1954) p. 389.
[192] 'Moreover, the present-day state control over the movement of persons is so pervasive and complete that the departure of a vast number of individuals to participate in a foreign or civil war must necessarily count upon the approval of the state, thus engaging its international responsibility.' See Garcia-Mora, *International Responsibility for Hostile Acts*, pp. 76–77.

not simply innocent foreigners who for ideological reasons join belligerent forces'.[193]

This quote seems appropriate to end the first chapter and to move to the next historical period. Between 1960 and 1963, the Katangese province of the Congo started a rebellion to gain its independence. Nigeria, Rhodesia and Angola experienced violent civil wars in the same years. The period commonly known as decolonization began a few years before with Algeria and would now set on fire the rest of the African continent. It is here that other foreign fighters are found in the battlefield. Yet they are portrayed very differently from their predecessors on the Iberian Peninsula. They do not seem to fight for an ideal, but rather for mere personal profit. The mercenaries have made their reappearance on the world's stage.

1.5 Conclusion

The Spanish Civil War was a vantage point to examine how the figure of the foreign fighter entered the legal debates in the early twentieth century. Fought around two opposing ideologies, namely fascism and communism, this war was also described as a battle between Christian civilization and the barbarity of Bolshevism. Overall, these ideological struggles were important to understand foreign policy decisions, and to foreground the cultural figures through which legal actors defined who was a lawful and who an unlawful foreign combatant.

The chapter opened in May 1937 at Council of the League of Nations (Section 1.1). There, the Spanish minister of foreign affairs del Vayo was pleading his case against the Italian aggression. To mark the difference between legitimate and illegitimate volunteers, del Vayo characterized the legitimate ones as those idealists who came to Spain following their political faith, and not the dictates of a government. The differentiation between 'good' and 'bad' volunteers were reiterated during the League's discussions, taking diverse connotations: barbaric and civilized troops, organized and disorganized contingents, heroic fighters and fascist militias. Through these distinctions, a battle was waged between different notions of freedom.

Section 1.2 looked at the debates in the Anglo-American doctrine during the Spanish Civil War years. Although Jessup, Lauterpacht and

---

[193] *Ibid.*, p. 78.

1.5 CONCLUSION 93

McNair devoted less attention to the issue of volunteers, when compared to the regulation of armed conflict, one can still trace what figure lingered in their imagination. The organized and state-sponsored nature of fascist militias fighting in Spain was in fact perceived by these internationalists as highly problematic. When differentiating the legitimate volunteers from hostile military expeditions, interesting cultural references appeared. The figure of the American freebooter William Walker was evoked to support the argument that expeditions organized within the territory of a state and aimed at conquering or looting other states' territories should now be considered illegal. The activities of freebooters – vestiges of the long nineteenth century – were thus contraposed with the image of the noble adventurer fighting for his political beliefs.

The figure of the adventurer could also be traced in domestic discussions in France and the United Kingdom in the early months of 1937 (Section 1.3). It was here that, along with the usual foreign policy concerns, cultural references entered the lawmaking process. The figures of Byron, Garibaldi and Lafayette were evoked by the French and British legislators: they were taken as a reference to characterize the good side of the Spanish struggle, and thus to legitimize those French and British subjects who were joining the Republicans. Nonetheless, some reacted to this noble lineage by pointing the finger at the cynical and opportunist Russian Comintern soldier. Thus, the figure of the volunteer was split in two: on the one side, there were idealists travelling to the Iberian Peninsula to follow their political faith; on the other hand, opportunist soldiers were also present. This differentiation highlighted a split in the consciousness of the legislator, an aspect that would reappear in subsequent periods.

Finally, the chapter traced a further genealogy at the international level (Section 1.4). As such, it offered a window on the *travaux préparatoires* of the 1907 Hague Peace Conferences, where specific rules on volunteers were codified. At The Hague, opposing images were at play in the discourse of representatives of states. The fear of seeing 'adventurers of all sorts' endangering the good conduct of hostilities underlay the discourse of the German delegation. This version of the 'bad' adventurer was distinguished from that of the *bon sauvage* evoked by the British and the Dutch to portray the foreigners present in their colonial armies.

The end of the chapter placed the figure of the foreign fighter in connection with other important humanitarian debates, specifically the Brussels Peace Conference of 1874 and the 1949 Geneva Conventions. This was done on the one hand to explain the passage from the doctrine of neutrality towards the codification of the famous combatant status and, on the other hand, to attest to a shift in the cultural perception of the foreign fighter. As we reach the 1950s, the romantic, idealist adventurer which haunted the imagination of a large part of international lawyers and national policymakers had disappeared. The example of the Italian intellectual Gabriele D'Annunzio was used by Ian Brownlie to prove that volunteers could no longer be understood as detached from a state's foreign policy, but rather was a direct manifestation of it. We thus moved into a new era with a new sensibility. And Brownlie was extremely receptive to these changes: by sketching a new figure of the foreign fighter he claimed that 'the volunteer is the relic of the eighteenth-century toleration of the supply of mercenaries'.[194]

---

[194] Brownlie, 'Volunteers and the Law of War and Neutrality', p. 575.

2

The Return of the Mercenaries

The 1976 Luanda Trial in Context

2.1 Foreigners Sentenced in Angola

This trial of mercenaries opened on 11 June in Luanda, the capital of the newly independent state of Angola. In front of the five judges there stood thirteen accused: nine Britons, three Americans and one Irish. Colonel Callan (*nom de guerre* of Costas Georgiou) an ex-British paratrooper, was identified as the leader of the squadron. Among the list of 139 indictments were those of crimes against peace, murder of civilians, robbing and looting and, most importantly, of mercenarism. The proceedings lasted for little more than a week. The final judgment was carried out on 28 June, with a death sentence for four of the accused (including Callan), and prison terms ranging from sixteen to thirty years for the remaining nine.[1] Although serving clear political interests, this trial remains a milestone in the process of decolonization and a useful angle to look at how the

---

[1] The trial has been recounted by a variety of authors, as well as by the international press. Here I base the analysis specifically on the writings of Mike J. Hoover, 'The Laws of War and the Angolan Trial of Mercenaries: Death to the Dogs of War' (1977) 9 *Case Western Reserve Journal of International Law* 323–406 and George H. Lockwood, 'Report on the Trial of Mercenaries: Luanda, Angola – June, 1976' (1977) 7 *Manitoba Law Journal* 183–202. A Canadian lawyer and member of Amnesty International, Lockwood was also one of the members of the International Commission of Inquiry on Mercenaries appointed by the Angolan government to supervise the fair conduct of the trial. Another important first-hand source is the book written jointly by Australian journalist Wilfred Burchett and British law professor and member of the International Commission, Derek Roebuck. See Wilfred Burchett and Derek Roebuck, *The Whores of War: Mercenaries Today* (Harmondsworth: Penguin 1977). Mockler provides another first-hand version of the trial as well as recounting the story of Colonel Callan's squadron. See Anthony Mockler, *Gli Ultimi Mercenari* (Milano: Sugarco 1987), based on the original text *The New Mercenaries* (London: Sidgwick & Jackson 1985). Two additional, original sources are: *O Povo Acusa: Julgamento dos Mercenários: Alegações Finais do Procurador Popular* (Luanda: INA 1976) and Raúl Valdés Vivó, *Angola: Fim do Mito dos Mercenários* (Luanda: África editora 1976).

problem of foreign fighters reappeared in international law after World War II.² But what was the context in which it took place?

A former colony of Portugal, Angola was formally granted independence in November 1975, after a fierce struggle that began in 1961. Torn by an ongoing civil war, three main national liberation movements were still contending power: the Movimento Popular de Libertação de Angola (MPLA) led by Agostinho Neto, the Frente Nacional de Libertação de Angola (FNLA) led by Holden Roberto, and the União Nacional para a Independência Total de Angola (UNITA), led by Jonas Savimbi.³ Each movement controlled a part of the country and was supported by important foreign allies: Cuba and Russia for the MPLA, the United States for both the FNLA and UNITA.⁴ Hence, the background story at the time of the Luanda trial is that of an African nation which has recently achieved independence but is still struggling to find its political stability. Moreover – as it was four decades earlier for Spain – in the case of Angola foreign powers were also involved in the battlefield through various forms of assistance. The country thus represents one of the favoured terrains to look at the battle that opposed communism to American imperialism, a battle epitomized by the Cold War years.

And yet, with a shift of the political landscape seen in the Spanish case, which had previously pitted the Soviet Union against the totalitarian states of Italy and Germany. This inversion of ideologies is quite interesting not only to understand the bigger geopolitical context of the Luanda trial, but also to characterize the foreign actors on the ground. Many of the Europeans going to fight in various parts of the Third World

---

² However, this was not the first trial of mercenaries held on African soil. Colonel Rolf Steiner was tried and sentenced in 1971 in Khartoum (Sudan), although he was not charged directly with mercenarism. Steiner was accused of having: (1) entered and stayed illegally in Sudan; (2) fomented subversive activities on behalf of foreign powers; and (3) led an armed rebellion. See Steiner, *Carre Rouge*, pp. 408 and 420. See also Eric David, 'Les Mercenaires en Droit International (Développements récents)' (1977) 13 *Revue Belge de Droit International* 197–237, p. 224.

³ See generally David Birmingham, *A Short History of Modern Angola* (London: Hurst 2015).

⁴ While the MPLA was in control of the capital Luanda and its neighbouring areas, the FNLA exercised power over the northern part of the country (with the help of Zairean troops). Conversely, UNITA was stronger in the south, thanks to the support of South African troops. See Edward George, *The Cuban Intervention in Angola, 1965–1991: From Che Guevara to Cuito Cuanavale* (London: Frank Cass 2005); John Stockwell, *In Search of Enemies: A CIA Story* (New York: Norton 1978); Ernst Harsch and Miah Malik, *Angola: The Hidden History of Washington's War* (New York: Pathfinder Press 1976). For the role played by China in Angola see specifically Govind P. Deshpande and Harmala K. Gupta, *United Front against Imperialism: China's Foreign Policy in Africa* (Bombay: Somaiya Publications 1986).

Figure 2.1 Cover of the magazine *Soldier of Fortune* (summer 1975)
Source: Internet Archive (https://archive.org/details/soldieroffortunemagazine/Soldier%20of%20Fortune%20%5B1975%20Summer%5D/).

during the decolonization period adhered to an open anti-communist, neocolonial, right-wing political ideology, aside from the pecuniary motivation for which they have become renowned.[5]

December 1975 was an important turning point in the story that involved Colonel Callan and his group of white mercenaries. During that month, the US Congress had decided to halt any more direct financial or military aid to Angola, both for internal political reasons and for fear of transforming the country into another Vietnam.[6]

Previously, the US Central Intelligence Agency (CIA) had been a major supporter of both the FNLA and UNITA, training their troops and delivering weapons and other war materiel.[7] Still these efforts had not translated into any long-term political success. On the contrary, they had the opposite effect of mobilizing the Cubans, whose help had been requested on several occasions by Neto, an important ally of Castro in Africa.[8] At this moment the leaders of both UNITA and FNLA started to look for foreign individuals who were willing to enlist in their respective armies.[9] As recalled by John Stockwell, former CIA chief of the Angola Task Force, in his 1978 memoirs: 'we searched the world for allies who could provide qualified advisors to put into the conflict ... preferably Europeans with the requisite military skills and perhaps experience in Africa. As long as they were not Americans, the Committee approved'.[10] Remarkably, Stockwell utilizes a term which came into vogue during the decolonization period, that is of foreign advisers. The dividing line between advisers and mercenaries would give way to tense ideological confrontations and epitomize once more the impossibility of a clear-cut

---

[5] *See* generally Serge Dumont, *Les Mercenaires* (Berchem: EPO 1983).
[6] *See* John A. Marcum, 'Lessons of Angola' (1976) 54 *Foreign Affairs* 407–425. *See* also Burchett and Roebuck, *The Whores of War*, pp. 23–25.
[7] *See* Stockwell, *In Search of Enemies*, pp. 176–182.
[8] It was thanks to the dispatch of large numbers of Cuban troops and artillery that the MPLA had resolved a complicated battlefield situation, reversing the fate of the civil war in autumn 1975. Being pressured from both the north and the south, the MPLA succeeded in halting the advance of FNLA/Zairean troops, and fought back the UNITA/South African contingents, maintaining control over the capital Luanda. Overall, the Cuban–Soviet backing was crucial for Neto and served an important strategic function when independence was declared in Luanda by the MPLA on 11 November. *See* Jiri Valenta, 'The Soviet–Cuban Intervention in Angola, 1975' (1978) 9 *Studies in Comparative Communism* 3–33, pp. 27–28. *See* also Basil Davidson, 'Angola: A Success That Changes History' (1976) 28 *Race and Class* 23–37.
[9] In the United Kingdom recruitment was taking place through advertisements in newspapers and through specialized agencies, such as the SAS (Security Advisors Service).
[10] Stockwell, *In Search of Enemies*, p. 182.

definition for foreign fighters.[11] To point to another interesting inversion of perspective from the Spanish case, the Soviet representative had deplored the presence on Spanish soil of Italian and German 'experts' sent by Mussolini and Hitler to help Franco, considering that act a blunt aggression. On the other hand, the volunteers travelling by their own initiative from every corner of Europe to join the International Brigades had been placed on a different moral scale.

Returning to the Angolan story, the trial of mercenaries opened on 11 June.[12] Although the accused had spent more than four months in prison they all seemed in good health, well fed and rested.[13] They also had been given the choice to be represented by either Angolan or foreign lawyers. The courtroom was filled with Western and Third World guests – including journalists, legal academics and jurists – who had been invited by the government to assist in the trial. Fifty-one of them were part of the International Commission of Enquiry of Mercenaries (ICEM), expressly requested by the MPLA to observe the proceedings, to testify to the trial's fairness, and to produce recommendations on the transnational problem of mercenarism. Neto thus presented an image of the purity of the leftist revolution he was leading in Angola – including respect for the rule of law – against the imperialist and counter-revolutionary enemies from abroad.[14]

---

[11] During the preparatory work for Additional Protocol I, many states pointed to this problematic division as a possible loophole in the definition of mercenarism. On this point see Sarah Percy, *Mercenaries: The History of a Norm in International Relations* (Oxford: Oxford University Press 2007) p. 173.

[12] For a detailed account of Callan's actions on the battlefield see specifically Scott Fitzsimmons, *Mercenaries in Asymmetric Conflicts* (Cambridge: Cambridge University Press 2012) pp. 109–161. For a first-hand account of the events recounted by two mercenaries from Callan's group see Chris Dempster and Dave Tomkins, *Fire Power* (London: Corgi Books 1978). The group's vicissitudes are also recounted in Mockler, *Gli Ultimi Mercenari*, pp. 168–169, 172–174 and 183–198.

[13] Mockler, *Gli Ultimi Mercenari*, p. 210.

[14] Angola had adopted a new Constitution after the 1975 declaration of independence. Various legislation was passed to enact the different branches of the government, including Law No. 7/76 (1 May 1976), constituting the People's Revolutionary Court and outlining its competences, composition and rules of procedure. In particular, the Revolutionary Tribunal could judge crimes carried out against the Angolan people, against the sovereignty of the People's Republic of Angola and its territorial integrity, as well as war crimes and crimes against humanity. Hoover, 'The Laws of War and the Angolan Trial of Mercenaries', Appendix III (Law 7/76) and Appendix IV (Constitution of 1975).

The public prosecutor started by highlighting the role of white mercenaries who had arrived in Angola since November 1975, in the ranks of both the FNLA and UNITA. Although Callan's squadron had been short-lived, the emphasis was soon put on the recruitment of his men. The defendants were questioned not so much about their actions on the battlefield, but as representatives of the politics of their countries of origin. Take this exchange between the public prosecutor Manuel Rui Alves Monteiro and the American mercenary Gustavo Marcelo Grillo:

[PROSECUTOR]: Don't you think that the real reason that you and the others are unfortunate enough to be here is the fault of your society, the fault of your government?
[GRILLO]: I'd say it's half and half. The government and society are half responsible and I am half responsible. I came here for greed, for money. That's the US system. . . .
[PROSECUTOR]: how do you see the society in which you live? . . . Institutions like the FBI and CIA?
[GRILLO]: US society, of which I am a product, is a monster.[15]

What it is evident from this exchange is the willingness to impute to the mercenaries some wider accusations, to take them as examples (and as products) of the corrupt, imperialist societies that had sent them to Angola to fight on the wrong side. Yet when Daniel Gearhart, a US citizen who had found his way to Africa through a job advertisement, was questioned, a more nuanced story surfaced:

[PROSECUTOR]: In the advertisement you offered yourself as a full-time mercenary?
[GEARHART]: Yes . . . At the time I was looking for information – not necessarily employment.
[PROSECUTOR]: What sort of information?
[GEARHART]: Political information. What people were fighting – who they were fighting. Things not usually available in books. On all of Africa.
[PROSECUTOR]: For this Court, it's a little strange that someone who wants to study the political situation in a country comes as a mercenary.
[GEARHART]: You ask me whether my coming as a mercenary was a cover for something else? No, I came as a mercenary to stop, as I thought, a Russian Communist takeover of Angola. I came to help the people of Angola.[16]

---

[15] Burchett and Roebuck, *The Whores of War*, pp. 73–74.
[16] *Ibid.*, pp. 75–76.

If the advertisement left no doubt that Gearhart was seeking employment, somehow an idealistic motivation was also present in his decision to embark for Angola. In other words, the American soldier of fortune was delineating the profile of a political mercenary, colliding with the greedy, neocolonial image that the prosecutor wanted to deliver to the audience. At the same time, Gearhart's answer put in question the role of the Cuban troops in Angola: weren't those men in fact sent to the battlefield for political reasons as well? Weren't they also to be understood as political mercenaries? The thin line between mercenaries and foreign advisers was thus crumbling, with the risk of hijacking the outcome of the trial. That is when the prosecutor turned to the indictments against the thirteen accused:

> **Indictment**
> The PEOPLE'S PROSECUTOR of the PEOPLE'S REVOLUTIONARY COURT, – in the name of the ANGOLAN PEOPLE and the PEOPLE'S REPUBLIC OF ANGOLA, makes the following INDICTMENT against: COSTAS GEORGIOU, known as 'CALLAN'; ANDREW GORDON McKENZIE, MALCOLM McINTYRE, KEVIN JOHN MARCHANT, JOHN LAWLOR, COLIN CLIFFORD EVANS, MICHAEL DOUGLAS WISEMAN, CECIL MARTIN FORTUIN, DEREK. JOHN BARKER, JOHN JAMES NAMMOCK, GUSTAVO MARCELO GRILLO, known as 'GUS', DANIEL FRANCIS GEARHART and GARY MARTIN ACKER ... for the CRIME OF BEING MERCENARIES and for CRIMES AGAINST PEACE, committed by enemies of the ANGOLAN PEOPLE and the PEOPLE'S REPUBLIC OF ANGOLA, in a mercenary war of aggression carried out with the aim of extinguishing the independence of the country, enslaving, oppressing, and dividing the ANGOLAN PEOPLE and pillaging the natural resources of the territory for the benefit of foreign, neocolonialist and imperialist interests.[17]

Carrying out a 'mercenary war of aggression' with the aim of 'enslaving, oppressing' the Angolan people and 'pillaging their natural resources', for 'neocolonialist and imperialist interests'. These charges certainly leave no room for the imagination, and they transport us directly into the heated context of decolonization and the Third World's national liberation struggles. Yet such inflammatory language does not end there. Let's look at the narrative built by the prosecutor to portray those 'foreign invaders',

---

[17] Text translated into English is reported in full length in Hoover, 'The Laws of War and the Angolan Trial of Mercenaries', Appendix I.

and the role played by the United States and the United Kingdom in their recruitment and dispatch to Angola:

Second
At the end of 1975, faced with the victorious advance of FAPLA, the National Army of the PEOPLE'S REPUBLIC OF ANGOLA, which was defeating the simultaneous and concerted attack of the racist South African army, and the imperialist puppets FNLA and UNITA on all fronts, the colluding forces of American imperialism, racist South African fascism, bankrupt colonialism and the traitorous FNLA and UNITA bands, with the support and complicity of governments subject to the dictates of imperialism, decided to intensify the use of mercenaries. This new and criminal warlike aggression was a vain attempt to prevent the inexorable victory of the ANGOLAN PEOPLE, united in the establishment, maintenance and progress of the PEOPLE'S REPUBLIC OF ANGOLA.

Third
To this end these forces undertook a shameful public recruitment campaign in the UNITED STATES OF AMERICA and BRITAIN, through the mass media, to bring together ex-soldiers with military experience in other wars of aggression.
...

Fifth
Offices were opened and functioned in NEW YORK and LONDON in which the interviews, contracting, classification and assembling of mercenaries were done, to augment the criminal group that were coming to attack the PEOPLE'S REPUBLIC OF ANGOLA and the ANGOLAN PEOPLE.

Sixth
These organised offices allocated the enlisted mercenaries . . .

Seventh
They contracted their criminal services against payment of a sum in dollars or pounds sterling, as well as other pecuniary advantages.

Eighth
They negotiated the air transport of AFRICA of the recruited mercenaries, they dealt with all emigration and customs formalities, such as passports, visas, etc. (in which the diligent activities of the SECURITY ADVISORY SERVICES (SAS) organisation in BRITAIN is notable), they assembled the mercenaries in previously arranged places, such as the London hotels PARK COURT HOTEL and TOWER HOTEL, sending them in different groups, some of more than a hundred people, to KINSHASA via BRUSSELS, PARIS or ATHENS, using SABENA AIRWAYS and AIR FRANCE planes.

Ninth

Shamefully, all this took place with every facility in broad daylight, without any preventive or, at least, restraining action being taken by the authorities of the countries where mercenary recruitment was going on. This strikingly demonstrates the acquiescence and complicity of the various governments, particularly those of Britain and America, in the preparation and development of the criminal conspiracy.. . .

Thirteenth

The mercenaries were all armed and equipped with war material of American, British, French, Belgian, Portuguese, and Chinese origin, by which is also shown the nature of the international 'holy alliance' which criminally armed these enemies of the ANGOLAN PEOPLE.[18]

The public prosecutor built his plea upon the vast amount of evidence provided by newspapers advertising mercenaries' recruitment. Pointing the finger to the open complicity of police border controls and the acquiescence of Western governments, he deprecated the 'international holy alliance' established to overthrow the newly independent state of Angola.[19] As he reached the conclusion of the charges, he reported that the mercenaries 'enlisted voluntarily, for a sum of money in wages' and that they did so 'to participate in a war of aggression ... by full consciousness of its illegality ... in the service of neo-colonialism and imperialism'.[20] The accusations against imperialism as a form of fascism are reminiscent of those made by del Vayo against the totalitarian volunteers sent by Italy and Germany. But if these accusations do not sound particularly new, it is here that things start to get interesting, at least from a legal standpoint. Paragraph 134 contains the legal basis of the abovementioned charges:

The facts constitute the CRIME OF BEING A MERCENARY, as is specifically set out in the STATEMENT OF THE HEADS OF STATES AND GOVERNMENTS OF MEMBER COUNTRIES OF THE OAU – ORGANISATION OF AFRICAN UNITY – held in KINSHASA, in 1967;

---

[18] *Ibid.*, pp. 353–355.
[19] On top of the evidence collected to build the case file, other evidence of the charges was produced from three main sources: (1) the confessions of the mercenaries themselves; (2) twenty-one witnesses that were called to testify during the proceedings; and (3) reports from psychiatric, clinical and forensic doctors. Lockwood, 'Report on the Trial of Mercenaries', p. 188.
[20] Hundred and Thirty-Fourth Indictment, in Hoover, 'The Laws of War and the Angolan Trial of Mercenaries', p. 371.

in the STATEMENT ON MERCENARY ACTIVITIES IN AFRICA, ADDIS ABEBA [sic] 1971, and RESOLUTIONS NO. 2395 (XXIII), 2465 (XXIII), 2548 (XXIV), and 3103 (XXVII) OF THE UNITED NATIONS GENERAL ASSEMBLY.[21]

Here there is a link to specific United Nations General Assembly (UNGA) and Organization of African Unity (OAU) Resolutions which were taken as the legal bases to criminalize the activities of white mercenaries in Africa.[22] In the next section, we will explore in more detail the debates at the UN General Assembly and the Security Council throughout the 1960s and 1970s, because these documents help to contextualize the figures evoked by legal actors to frame those foreigners taking up arms abroad in such a tense political period. What is important to highlight, though, is that in June 1976 mercenarism was still not recognized internationally as a crime. This was one of the main points of contention of the trial, as well as the main line used by the defence.[23] Bob Cesner, an American attorney in Angola to defend US citizens Martin Acker and Daniel Gearhart, performed a brilliant pleading mentioning the 1949 Geneva Conventions (GC) and questioning the validity of the UN resolutions.[24] If mercenarism was still not recognized as a crime internationally, the accused would technically fall under Art. 4(2) of Geneva III, which, as seen in the previous chapter, granted prisoner of war (POW) status to combatants enlisting in the armies of foreign governments. On top of that, Cesner added that the public prosecutor had not proven the existence of such an offence in Angolan domestic law.

The purpose here is not to produce a detailed analysis of the charges and the defending arguments, or to launch into a discussion about the relevance of the UN and its resolutions and their legal force. The aim is rather to take a closer look at the outcome of the trial, as it elucidates the

---

[21] *Ibid.*
[22] *See* specifically: Question of Territories under Portuguese Administration, A/RES/2395 (XXIII), 29 November 1968, paragraph 9. Implementation of the Declaration on the Granting of Independence to Colonial Countries and Peoples, A/RES/2465 (XXIII), 20 December 1968, paragraph 8. Implementation of the Declaration on the Granting of Independence to Colonial Countries and Peoples, A/RES/2548 (XXIV), 11 December 1969, paragraph 7. Basic Principles of the Legal Status of the Combatants Struggling against Colonial and Alien Domination and Racist Regimes, A/RES/3103 (XXVIII), 12 December 1973, paragraph 4. Resolution on Mercenaries, AHG/Res. 49 (IV), 14 September 1967, paragraph 5. Declaration on the Activities of Mercenaries in Africa, CM/St. 6 (XVII), 15 June 1971, heading.
[23] Vivó, *Angola: Fim do Mito dos Mercenários*, pp. 174–178.
[24] Mockler, *Gli Ultimi Mercenari*, pp. 224–225.

reasoning built to indict the accused with the crime of mercenarism and to substantiate the responses given to their lawyers.

Delivered on 28 June, the verdict started by reiterating the charges against Callan's group; it explained how the evidence collected proved the links with recruitment agencies in the United Kingdom, how the enlisting took place through national newspapers, but also via the involvement of the CIA and the tacit complicity of the British government. All of which led the Court to the conclusions that: 'the major capitalist powers were agreeing among themselves on a programme for the overthrow of the People's Republic of Angola and that, having realized that direct military intervention was unviable, they resorted to private armies. Which they regimented, armed, and paid. And the defendants were in fact the instruments for the action of this political orchestration'.[25]

Subsequently, the verdict described in detail the mercenaries' contracting period and pay rates, stating that the purpose was to enlist them in the ranks of the FNLA to overthrow the legitimate Angolan government, and highlighting that 'the defendants were perfectly conscious of that mission'.[26] It went on to recall the actions of the mercenaries on the ground, summarizing their roles, dwelling particularly on the responsibilities of Callan.[27] Finally, it discussed the applicable law and in particular the basis for the charge of mercenarism.

The Court started by generally stating that 'mercenarism was not unknown in traditional penal law, where it was always dealt with in relation to homicide', and that a mercenary 'was an agent that committed a crime for wages'.[28] It went on to recall how in the history of nineteenth century, it was much debated whether it was the actual individuals who should be punished, or those who had recruited them, and that finally a consensus had been reached on incriminating both.[29] This type of reasoning served well the purpose of the Court, which moments later stated that 'this Tribunal does not heed the note often struck by the defence that it was not the defendants who were those most responsible for the crimes they committed, but governments and organizations

---

[25] Hoover, 'The Laws of War and the Angolan Trial of Mercenaries', Appendix II, paragraph 15.
[26] *Ibid.*, paragraphs 18–23.
[27] *Ibid.*, paragraphs 24 and 33–45.
[28] *Ibid.*, paragraphs 46–47.
[29] *Ibid.*, paragraphs 50–51.

which, for pecuniary compensation, made them commit such offences'.[30] Having offered a historical resume – albeit in a minimal form – the Court defined mercenarism in the present time:

> [53] Yet it is important that in modern penal law, and in the field of comparative law, the mercenary crime lost all autonomous existence and was seen as a common crime, generally speaking aggravated by the profit motive which prompts it. And this mercenary crime, which is known today as 'paid crime to order', comes within the laws on criminal complicity, it being through them that the responsibility of he who orders and he who is ordered is evaluated. [54] In our case, mercenarism is provided for in Art. 20 No. 4 of the Penal Code in force. [55] This annuls the objection of the defence that the crime of mercenarism has not been defined and that there is no penalty for it. [56] It is in fact provided for with penalty in most evolved penal systems. As a material crime, of course![31]

Although many commentators were not convinced by this reasoning, the Court had found a shortcut to respond to the objection raised by Cesner. Mercenarism was equated with the common crime of homicide, with the aggravating factor represented by the pecuniary motive. Having established this, the verdict took on the tones of a political pamphlet, which are nonetheless significant here, as they offer a sense of the context in which the Luanda Tribunal was delivering its historic ruling:

> [57] Previously in Congo and Biafra. Only yesterday in Angola. Today in Rhodesia. [58] In the convulsed history of the past 20 years, and always serving neo-colonial plans, there have always been packs of dogs of war with blood-stained muzzles, engaged in acts of aggression, in crimes against peace and against humanity, decapitating or trying to decapitate revolutions, wrecking or trying to wreck the freedom of peoples ... Therefore, they have been systematically involved in the commission of international crimes. ... Looking back at its wounds of yesterday, Africa feels that mercenaries are a danger to peace for its children and to the security of its states. ... [62] Hence those who commit the crime of mercenarism, in its consummate form, are all those who, for personal profit, enlist in a group or in forces intending, by military means, to counter the achievement of a foreign people's self-determination or, by the same means, to impose neo-colonial designs on them.[32]

No words could better summarize the political context of African struggle for self-determination. Yet this passage is significant because it

---

[30] *Ibid.*, paragraph 52.
[31] *Ibid.*, paragraphs 53–56.
[32] *Ibid.*, paragraphs 57–62.

shifts the discussion in relation to the crime of mercenarism from the national to the international level. By referring to 'acts of aggression' and 'crimes against peace and humanity', and by stating how those are perpetrated to 'decapitate revolutions and wreck the freedom of peoples', the Court succeeded in establishing a link with the international order in which the mercenaries were operating. A few paragraphs later, the UN resolutions and OAU documents were once again mentioned as the proper legal basis for proving that 'mercenarism is considered a crime in the view of nations and is expressly stated to be one in resolutions 2395 (XXIII), 2465 (XXIII), 2548 (XXIV) and 3103 (XXVII)'.[33]

As expected, an attack on the imperialist governments that 'encouraged [the mercenaries'] recruitment, armed and paid them wages' and by doing so '[persisted] in their racist philosophies ... blinded by imperial delirium' was included in the final verdict, which ended with an important note, at least from a legal point of view.[34] At paragraph 67 in fact, it was stated that the defendants could not invoke POW status, as they were 'irregular members of an army'.[35] This passage is interesting, not only because it comes one year ahead of the codification of Additional Protocol I (AP I), but also because it utilizes the term 'irregular'. This term – which has become popular in our time to characterize international terrorists – was back then reserved for mercenaries. Third World states would evoke it in the context of the Geneva talks to differentiate mercenaries from other types of combatants, and to classify them as the 'enemy of humanity' of the decolonization period. We will return to this point later, particularly when analysing the *travaux preparatoires* of AP I; yet it was interesting to note how the Court dismissed Cesner's plea regarding the relevance of Art. 4(2) of GC III.

Having excluded the accused from benefiting from POW status, the judges delivered the final sentence. Nammock, Acker and McIntyre were given sixteen years; Lawlor, Evans and Fortuin twenty-four; Wiseman, Marchant and Grillo thirty; McKenzie, Barker, Gearhart and Callan were sentenced to death.[36] The judgment did not provide for an appeal, and

---

[33] *Ibid.*, paragraph 63.
[34] *Ibid.*, paragraph 64.
[35] *Ibid.*, paragraph 67. This was also echoed in the Draft Convention on the Prevention and Suppression of Mercenarism, prepared by the ICEM. *See* Art. 4: 'Mercenaries are not lawful combatants. If captured, they are not entitled to prisoner of war status.' Overall, the Draft Convention replicates the language and the sources of the Tribunal's verdict. *Ibid.*, Appendix VIII.
[36] *Ibid.*, Appendix II, paragraphs 76–81. The public prosecutor also charged the mercenaries with 'crimes against peace' – referring to the Statute of the Nuremberg Tribunal – and

despite a demand for clemency was sent to Angola by the UK and US governments, Agostinho Neto confirmed the verdict.[37] As the curtains fall on the stage of the Luanda mercenaries' trial, it is crucial to see how and why it arrived at such a dramatic end. What were the salient moments and discussions happening at the international level around these combatants? And why was the People's Tribunal so keen to resort to the resolutions of the General Assembly to convict those foreigners taking up arms abroad? To do that, we must move to the United Nations, in the heated period of national liberation struggles.

2.2 What Freedom, Whose Freedom?

As previously mentioned, the Luanda trial took place at the peak of the decolonization period, when for more than two decades many of the so-called Third World countries were engaging in a fierce struggle to free themselves from their colonizers.[38] In December 1960, the UN General Assembly through Resolution 1514 (XV), spelled out the will of a majority of member states to grant independence to those territories still

---

declared that their actions were in violation of the Angolan 'Combatants Disciplinary Law' of 10 July 1966, and as such demanded the death penalty for all of the accused. *Ibid.*, pp. 371–372.

[37] Apart from the clear political undertone of the prosecutor's accusations, the trial was overall conducted fairly. With the ICEM supervising the proceedings, all the accused had the opportunity to question the witnesses called to court, they could benefit from proper legal defence and had more than one occasion to confront the judges. In their final declarations, most of the defendants publicly expressed thanks for the fair and objective way in which they were treated both in prison and in court. See Vivó, *Angola: Fim do Mito dos Mercenários*, pp. 174–178. Reflecting on the trial and its proceedings, Lockwood writes: 'I am satisfied that from a purely procedural point of view, the trial was a fair trial. All the basic principles agreed upon at the outset by the Judicial Committee were complied with.' Lockwood, 'Report on the Trial of Mercenaries', p. 193. Hoover is more critical: 'The judgment of the People's Revolutionary Court called attention to a political problem and to the need for effective legislation. The procedural fairness of the trial was commendable, but the countervailing substantive unfairness resulted in a miscarriage of justice. With this trial as one poor example, it would seem essential that future bodies affirm in advance the laws to be applied, the rules of procedure to be followed and the nature of evidence to be presented.' Hoover, 'The Laws of War and the Angolan Trial of Mercenaries', p. 374.

[38] Here I work upon a very conventional idea of decolonization, understood as a historical moment ranging from the liberation of India in 1947 and running through the whole Cold War era. I recognize that this is non-exhaustive, yet it serves a precise intellectual intent of placing the legal talks concerning mercenaries against a historical background.

subject to colonial domination, and acknowledged the right to self-determination of all peoples.[39]

It is against this political background that we witness a resurgence of talks about foreigners going to fight abroad, and that the newly independent African states start to point to the problem of white mercenaries and raise their complaints at the international level. Of course, Africa was not the only place where decolonization was taking place, or where the mercenaries' issue was present – in addition to the fact that differences existed among various types of mercenaries themselves.[40] However, Africa's struggle for self-determination became inexorably linked with the mercenaries' problem, and African states were the first promoters of the fight against these 'irregular' combatants in the new world order shaped by Resolution 1514.[41]

Furthermore, it should also be remembered that the objective here is to seek for a background to contextualize our actors, while at the same time limiting the field of inquiry. In this sense, the focus on the UN General Assembly and Security Council must not be seen as exclusive. The issue of white mercenaries in Africa were discussed in many other venues during those years, including the newly established OAU, the summits of the Non-Aligned Movement (NAM) and – as we shall see – in Geneva. However, the United Nations remains a useful venue to look at the opposing positions of member states regarding mercenaries, especially because these positions were exacerbated by the Western/Eastern blocs' confrontation, and by the growing number of Third World states present in the Assembly. Therefore, the idea is to look for the most salient moments for understanding how the discussions on mercenaries reached the international level, and how these discussions subsequently formed the basis of the Luanda trial.[42]

---

[39] Declaration on the Granting of Independence to Colonial Countries and Peoples, A/RES/1514 (XV), 14 December 1960.

[40] Mercenaries were also present in the Middle East, South-East Asia and Latin America. Not all were Europeans or from Western countries. For an overarching study see specifically Guy Arnold, *Mercenaries: The Scourge of the Third World* (Basingstoke: Macmillan 1999). Additionally, not all mercenaries were following the same patterns of recruitment or were performing the same functions. For the distinction between 'white-collar' mercenaries mostly present in the Middle East and performing the function of advisers, and the 'blue-collar' mercenaries involved on the battlefield in Africa, see specifically Pertti Joenniemi, 'Two Models of Mercenarism; Historical and Contemporary' (1977) 7 *Instant Research on Peace and Violence* 184–196, p. 191.

[41] Percy, *Mercenaries*, p. 185.

[42] It should be clear that each example has its own history and context. The idea is not to report a succession of names and dates, but rather to see the evolution of the discourse on

In fact, the story introduced with reference to Angola is just one of many that saw our actors present on the ground: the judgment issued by the Revolutionary Tribunal had mentioned other instances in which Western mercenaries were interfering in wars of national liberation. Dozens of other examples can be located over the three decades between July 1960 (the date of Congo's independence) and December 1989 (when the UN Mercenary Convention was finally concluded). Congo, Nigeria, Rhodesia, Benin, and later on the Comoros Islands and the Seychelles, are all African countries which, in a thirty-year timespan, witnessed the presence of white mercenaries, including well-known personalities such as Bob Denard, Jean Schramme, Mike Hoare and Rolf Steiner.

However, it seems logical to start with the example of Congo, not only for obvious chronological reasons, but also because it is the first instance in which the United Nations was called upon to take a stand against mercenaries in a war of national liberation.[43] The 'Congo crisis' (1960–1967) was indeed one of the most difficult situations faced by the UN in the first wave of Africa's decolonization, and it also saw the dispatch of troops on the ground through the United Nations Operation in the Congo.

Soon after having been granted formal independence from Belgium in July 1960, the southern province of Katanga declared its secession from the central government.[44] The secession was led by the pro-Western businessman and politician Moïse Tshombe, who in order to maintain power made extensive use of mercenaries of many different nationalities (including British, French, Belgian, German, South African and Rhodesian).[45] At the time, many Belgian citizens were still present in the country. Katanga being an area rich in natural resources, it became for Belgium a base from where to challenge the independence of its former colony.[46] Events escalated quickly; the help of the Soviet Union was requested by the Congolese central government, and the UN itself was called to intervene to restore order and combat the secessionists.

---

mercenaries at the international level (specifically at the UN), while taking into account the particularity of each situation for what is possible.

[43] For an excellent summary of the Congo crisis and the main legal issues at stake, see Donald W. McNemar, 'The Postindependence War in the Congo', in Richard Falk (ed.), *The International Law of Civil War* (Baltimore, MD: Johns Hopkins University Press 1971), 244–302.

[44] Ibid., p. 252.

[45] Arnold, *Mercenaries*, pp. 1–2.

[46] Ibid.

2.2 WHAT FREEDOM, WHOSE FREEDOM? 111

It was at this moment that discussions concerning the presence of white mercenaries in Katanga reached the Security Council and member states started to vehemently debate their role and function on the battlefield.

A first resolution was passed in February 1961, generally urging the 'withdrawal and evacuation from Congo of all Belgian and other foreign military and paramilitary personnel and political advisers ... and mercenaries',[47] and it was only months later that the Security Council would take the issue of mercenaries more seriously into consideration. The situation on the ground was becoming more complicated, especially due to the increasing number of white mercenaries who were reaching Katanga and engaging in active combat against UN troops.[48] By mid-November of the same year, the Security Council was drafting a resolution on the ongoing situation in the newly independent African country. Presided over by the Soviet Union and with the presence of the representatives of Belgium and Congo in the room, the Council held three of its tensest meetings on the issue of mercenaries (15–17 November 1961).

The first meeting was opened by Liberia, whose representative left no one in the room wondering about the real problem at stake: 'I address myself to the situation of continuing unrest in the Congo ... I cannot help observing, however, that the problem that faces this Council now is ... the world's colonial legacy.'[49] Making explicit reference to UNGA Resolution 1514 and recalling the principles of territorial integrity and national unity as set forth in that document, the Liberian delegate went straight to the point by claiming that 'the whole problem of Katanga was created by foreigners, who from sordid interests, are trying to perpetuate colonial domination in Africa'.[50] There could not be clearer words to transport us into the heated period of decolonization, and to understand how European intrusion into African internal affairs was represented at the time.

A few moments later, the same delegate made a compelling point, stating that 'the backbone of Tshombe secession is not the people of Katanga ... the backbone of this secession is the foreign support and assistance which the provincial government continues to receive [from] mercenaries'.[51] And here we come to one of the first characterizations of our actors: 'in my view ... these missionaries of evil are no better than

---

[47] The Congo question, S/RES/161, 21 February 1961, paragraph 2.
[48] Arnold, *Mercenaries*, pp. 3–6.
[49] UN Security Council Official Records, 974th meeting (15 November 1961) p. 2.
[50] *Ibid.*, p. 3.
[51] *Ibid.*, p. 6.

criminals and they should be treated as such ... their trial and punishment, when proved guilty, will serve not only the ends of justice but will also serve to deter others'.[52] Almost fifteen years before the Luanda trial, we already find a call to bring mercenaries before a court of law.

The Liberian representative was among those who supported a resolution which could have authorized the United Nations forces to put mercenaries in jail 'until legal action [could] be taken against them'.[53] Although he did not provide further insights on *who* should judge them and *where* to host their trials, the Liberian representative seemed to have already gained confidence in the UN Charter, as he then suggested that under Art. 25, 'States concerned were under a legal obligation to adapt their national legislation to the extent necessary to give effect to [UN] resolutions'.[54] The Liberian delegate reminded the representative of Belgium, who was present in the room, that in the previous UNSC Resolution the Council had asked states to take measures to prevent the departure of military, paramilitary and mercenaries to the Congo.[55] He finally suggested that 'now we should go further and should call upon all Member States to so adapt their legislation as to prevent entry of such mercenaries into Katanga'.[56]

Subsequently, the representative of the United Arab Republic restated how Tshombe – by declaring a secession – had certainly committed an illegal act, but that it was only through 'the colonialists and international financiers' and with the 'material assistance and military support of foreign elements' that he was able to do so.[57] Pointing his finger at the Belgian and French soldiers of fortune enlisted to serve with Katangese troops, he supported the proposal of the Liberian delegate for a more comprehensive and encompassing resolution and he concluded that 'all necessary measures [have to] be taken to prevent the entry of arms, equipment or other material in Katanga'.[58]

It was then the turn of France, whose representative wisely began his speech by recalling how his country had supported the legitimate authorities of Congo and was committed to its independence and sovereign unity. He also reminded the audience how France had been driven by an

[52] *Ibid.*, pp. 6–7.
[53] *Ibid.*, p. 7.
[54] *Ibid.*
[55] *Ibid.*, p. 3.
[56] *Ibid.*, p. 7.
[57] *Ibid.*, p. 9.
[58] *Ibid.*, p. 12.

attitude of non-interference in the internal affairs of the newly independent state.[59] The French delegate seemed upfront on the question of mercenaries, reminding everyone in the room that in his country 'recruiting for foreign armed forces is prohibited and punished under the Penal Code', and stressing how 'the French Government [had] banned any recruiting in its territory for the Katangese forces'.[60] As proof of the good faith of his country, he declared that an amendment introducing the sanction of losing nationality for those who were to enlist had been inserted into the French penal code. However, only a few moments later, he added that: 'if a handful of French adventurers such as are to be found wherever there are disturbances, have nevertheless managed to reach Katanga, their country of origin cannot be blamed for their activities'.[61] This is a first indication of how the figure of the adventurer has not completely disappeared from the imagination of legal actors and how it still permeates the discourse of representatives of Western states like France. This type of discourse is reminiscent of the *travaux* of Hague Convention V in 1907, when – contrary to the intention of Germany – the British, French and Swiss delegates made it clear that it was impossible to criminalize (and thus to control) the departure of all their citizens for war zones. In other words, those adventurers were not the state's responsibility; In going to fight abroad they were only following their ideals. And yet it seems out of place if used to characterize those foreign combatants who were plundering the Third World. One can witness here a clear reversal of perspectives from the Spanish Civil War: on the one hand, the image of the Western adventurer persists and justifies the discourse of Western states vis-à-vis the presence of their citizens on African soil. On the other hand, those scary adventurers already evoked by the Germans in The Hague seem to have reappeared, but under a different guise – of the white, racist soldier of fortune in the service of imperialist states. That image brings with it an older one, of the white colonialist man who '[is] trying to perpetuate colonial domination in Africa', as the representative of Liberia noted during his first speech at the Security Council.

Going back to the meeting, it was the Belgian delegate Paul-Henri Spaak who then asked permission to intervene in the debate. From this moment onwards, a proper confrontation took place between the Belgian

---

[59] *Ibid.*, p. 13.
[60] *Ibid.*, p. 14.
[61] *Ibid.*

representative and those of other nations, especially Russia and African countries.

Spaak started his speech by stating boldly that 'I do not come here as a defendant accused of a crime, still less as a guilty man', adding a few moments later that 'I am not willing to be condemned for certain relationships between countries which existed during the last century'.[62] Claiming that he was not a colonialist and that the government he was representing was not either, Spaak continued with a tone that would enrage a good number of governments in the room: 'we practised paternalism for too long and perhaps ... we granted independence too suddenly'.[63]

The image of the colonialist white man is therefore itself fractured, and Spaak's speech clearly highlights this aspect: his reference to the paternalistic attitude of his country over the previous century, as well as the idea of having retreated from Africa too soon, points very much to the white man's burden made famous by Kipling's poem.

Although one can easily understand how these statements were not taken lightly by African states present at the Council, perhaps Spaak thought in good faith that the formal independence granted to the Congolese authorities had not been a wise political choice, given how the situation had developed. In any case, the Belgian representative then turned to a more technical discussion, stating how his government had done everything possible to withdraw all the political advisers, but reminding the audience that 'there are several thousand Belgians in Katanga; there are hundreds of women and children. If things turn out badly, we may be obliged to undertake a full-scale evacuation at very short notice'.[64] There is no need to speculate on Spaak's real intentions, or on his political attitude, and the Belgian representative was possibly making a claim of realpolitik here. What is more interesting, however, is how he then dealt with the issue of mercenaries: 'finally there is the question of mercenaries ... but what is a mercenary? ... I condemn this practice. But it is a far cry from that to being held responsible ... for the fact that there may still be some Belgian mercenaries there'.[65]

Spaak seems to walk in the footsteps of the French delegate by questioning his country's responsibility for the mercenaries present on Katanga's soil. Reminding the audience that Belgium too had long been

[62] *Ibid.*, p. 18.
[63] *Ibid.*
[64] *Ibid.*, p. 22.
[65] *Ibid.*

2.2 WHAT FREEDOM, WHOSE FREEDOM? 115

implementing laws to forbid its citizens enlisting in foreign armies, the Belgian delegate responded firmly to those countries that wanted to apply stricter sanctions against mercenaries with the following words: 'I do not believe that [these are] altogether adequate for it is really too easy to circumvent the law', and then he asked: 'what practical measures would you advise a democratic government to take in a country where freedom of movement exists?'[66] As the representative of the French government had done before him, Spaak made it clear that Belgium – a democratic country where citizens enjoyed full rights – could not be held responsible for those soldiers of fortune who sought adventure abroad.

Naturally, Spaak was also trying to protect his fellow citizens still trapped in the Congo. Worried by the fact that no real definition of a mercenary yet existed, and that Congolese authorities could have indiscriminately targeted anyone on the ground, Spaak vehemently opposed the resolution being drafted, asking: 'so the United Nations is now going to take action against all mercenaries and all hostile elements? But I ask you, gentlemen, with what safeguards? ... What you are doing today by considering a draft resolution like this ... is a hunt for whites, a hunt for unprotected whites who cannot defend themselves, can give no explanations and cannot be assisted'.[67]

Essentially the first of the three meetings ended there, with a firm response by the representative of the Congo, who questioned the good faith of Belgium and its ambivalent role in Congolese internal affairs.[68] Just as it had been four decades earlier with Spain, also in the case of these foreigner fighters, the absence of a real definition and the opposing states' attitudes towards their citizens were all factors contributing to such confrontation. But the problem of white mercenaries in Africa is a more complex issue than might seem at first, because it catalyses a whole series of other questions directly related to Western colonialism and its ambivalent imaginary.

The very next day, the representative of Ceylon reopened the debate in much harsher tones. Leaving no room to wonder that what was happening in Katanga was a '[foreign] intervention of some colonial and neo-colonial forces', he also confronted Spaak's somehow defiant attitude by reminding the room that 'there are now some twenty-five Member States from the African continent for which the United Nations

---

[66] Ibid., p. 23.
[67] Ibid., p. 29.
[68] Ibid., pp. 33–35.

is their second country and for which the success or failure of the United Nations in the Congo is a paramount criterion of what this Organization can and cannot do'.[69] One of the promoters of the Bandung conference understood very well the favourable moment that Third World states were enjoying at the United Nations at the time. Subsequently, the Sri Lankan representative dispelled Spaak's fear of a 'hunt for whites' by bluntly stating that 'there will be no hunt for whites. The only white men who will be hunted will be the mercenaries'.[70] Contrary to the Belgian representative, it seemed very clear to him who should have been criminalized: 'why should there be so much difficulty about this term? ... The hostile elements are those people who have declared open war against the sovereignty of the Congo ... and these people are by no means difficult to identify'.[71]

It was then the turn of the United States, whose representative supported the role of the United Nations and sided with the central government against the secession of Katanga, before dropping one brief reference to the issue of mercenaries, deprecating the 'irresponsible soldiers of fortune ... who are not subject to any effective national control'.[72]

The meeting continued in rather neutral tones, especially when it came to France and the United Kingdom, whose representatives attempted to divert the attention of their colleagues to other aspects of the delicate political situation in the Congo, and thus diverging from the hot topic of white mercenaries in Katanga.[73] However, a few minutes later, the delegate of Soviet Union took the floor to refocus the debate where it had started. Aware of the Western states' attempt to shift the discourse, he launched into a fierce attack on Spaak,[74] blaming the Belgian representative for avoiding responsibility and directly accusing Belgium of using mercenaries in Katanga for clear political purposes.[75] Quoting from an official report prepared for the Secretary General – which

---

[69] UN Security Council Official Records, 975th meeting (16 November 1961) pp. 1–4.
[70] Ibid., p. 6.
[71] Ibid., pp. 4–5.
[72] Ibid., p. 10.
[73] Ibid., pp. 11–12.
[74] 'It is no accident that Mr. Stevenson and the distinguished representative of the United Kingdom should wish to divert the Council's attention, for Katanga is a "hot spot" for the Colonial Powers and they would like to get away from this "hot spot" and direct the Council's attention elsewhere.' Ibid., pp. 21–22.
[75] Ibid., pp. 16–17.

contained the interrogations of thirty foreign mercenaries captured in the Congo by UN forces during the previous months – the Soviet representative mocked Spaak's concerns about the identity of white mercenaries in Katanga: 'Mr. Spaak asked us a question, saying that he did not quite understand what "mercenaries" were and that this term was really not clear to him ... But if Mr. Spaak does not know what mercenaries are, I will take the liberty of giving him some help.'[76]

The report delivered by Zorin, the Soviet representative, contained precise details on the names and countries of origin of the mercenaries, and even comprehensive information on their employment contracts, as well as proof that they had been hired by Belgian military officers: 'Do you not know Major Bergenhaus, Mr. Spaak? I think you should know him. He is also a Belgian and, what is more, a Belgian officer ... why did you tolerate this illegal situation ... when the Security Council had on 21 February 1961 adopted a decision calling for the immediate withdrawal of all foreign advisers: foreign military, paramilitary and political personnel? Why?'[77]

The tone had become heated. And at that moment the Russian representative took the opportunity to strike the fatal blow:

> the whole world has changed. Colonialism is in its death-throes. And today the African and Asian States no longer cringe before the Foreign Ministers of any State; they voice, openly and frankly, their criticism of the colonialists. And I think this cultured Foreign Minister should welcome the change, for the twentieth century is the century of the liberation of colonial peoples; a cultured Belgian statesman should be glad of this world-wide progress.[78]

One can only imagine the atmosphere in the Council after such a speech. The Soviet Union was assuming the main role as an advocate for the oppressed peoples around the world, as it had tried to do four decades earlier by siding with the Republicans in Spain. Nevertheless, that day Belgium – and perhaps all the Western countries involved in the Congo crisis – had received a resounding defeat. Spaak, as a wise political man, decided not to reply: 'I am your guest here, I shall not for a single moment try to act contrary to your desires, and I am quite willing to postpone my speech until tomorrow.'[79] The meeting was adjourned to the next day.

---

[76] *Ibid.*, p. 18.
[77] *Ibid.*, p. 19.
[78] *Ibid.*, pp. 20–21.
[79] *Ibid.*, p. 23.

There, the Belgian representative started his speech by thanking the Council for having granted him the opportunity to oversee the proceedings of the draft resolution. He then moved on to reject Ceylon's accusations of the previous day, denying the charges of responsibility for Belgian mercenaries in Katanga, and explaining how his country had collaborated with the UN to expel all the troops still present on the ground: 'I think I can say that at present there is no longer a single Belgian solider in Katanga and that at least 200 to 250 Belgian soldiers have been recalled.'[80] Perhaps Spaak had understood that it was necessary to adopt a different strategy in an Assembly where the ex-European colonies were clearly starting to outnumber their former colonizers. He then pointed out that, of the list of the thirty mercenaries presented the day before to the Council, no one was Belgian. He closed his speech reaffirming that 'the Belgian Government condemns the secession of Katanga'.[81]

India's representative then took the floor and in a long and powerful speech once again condemned foreign interference in Congo's internal affairs, also blaming Western countries (especially France) for selling arms and other materiel to the Katangese government.[82] The Indian delegate was definitely not convinced by Spaak's condescending demeanour, and he returned to the issue of mercenaries by stating that 'there should be no quarter, there should be no relaxing of our views as regards the mercenaries'.[83] This time, however, the speech was not purely political, as the Indian representative started to put on the table more specific propositions on how to deal with the problem: 'mercenaries ... are being sent away, it is true, but they go out by one road and come back by another ... if that is the case, what is the use of sending them away? ... let the protection of [their] government[s] be withdrawn from these people and these people should become subject to the domestic law of that country'.[84] Again we find the idea – later confirmed in Luanda – of prosecuting mercenaries under the national laws of the country where they went to fight.

While the representative of Turkey restated all the points of contention regarding Congo's unity and independence, the representative of the United Kingdom seemed more concerned to clarify certain other matters:

---

[80] UN Security Council Official Records, 976th meeting (17 November 1961) p. 7.
[81] *Ibid.*, p. 8.
[82] *Ibid.*, pp. 9–24.
[83] *Ibid.*, p. 23.
[84] *Ibid.*, pp. 18–19.

2.2 WHAT FREEDOM, WHOSE FREEDOM? 119

'you, Mr. President, yesterday made great play with the nationalities of some mercenaries, including British ... the fact is that in all these assertions no distinction has been drawn between the actions of Governments and the actions of their nationals'.[85] In other words, the British delegate – like his French and Belgian colleagues – wanted to make clear that his government was not responsible for those soldiers of fortune embarking on expeditions abroad. With a hint of irritation, Mr. Dean also made clear to the Council that the British government did not want to support unconditional interventions of UN troops on the ground: 'the United Nations would be at the beck and call of any State faced with the problem of a dissident minority within its own borders'.[86] However, with many colonial territories still under British rule, one can well imagine that such an appeal was probably not voiced to spare UN officers' lives.

Without venturing too far into the geopolitical dynamics of the time, right at the end of the 976th meeting there was a fascinating exchange of views between the representative of Congo and the Belgian delegate. As the former recognized the efforts made by France and Belgium to amend their legislation, he also questioned the Belgian representative over whether some of those mercenaries expelled from the Congo had in fact been punished: 'the question arises whether ... the mercenaries who have been expelled ... have been punished ... under the laws of those countries'.[87] Worried by certain information his government had received about tributes paid to Belgian mercenaries killed in Congo, he pressed Spaak: 'our information indicates ... that certain mercenaries killed in Katanga ... have been the subject of national demonstrations. It has even been said that a Belgian officer was buried with national honours. I therefore ask: is that not an encouragement to secession ... a man to whom honor is paid by his country as a hero. Can the mercenaries be regarded as heroes?'[88]

It was here that things became interesting. As the Belgian delegate clarified how it was not mercenaries themselves who were put in jail, but only their recruiters, Spaak added:

> You seem to forget all history and to believe this is the first time that people have gone to fight in foreign armies. Have you forgotten certain events which took place before the Second World War, when men from

[85] *Ibid.*, p. 30.
[86] *Ibid.*, p. 34.
[87] *Ibid.*, p. 39.
[88] *Ibid.*

all countries went to defend *freedom* in other countries? What would have happened then, if those men who had gone to fight in another country had been punished when they returned home. It is easy to laugh, but this is history.[89]

This could not have been just a Freudian slip. Spaak was making direct reference to the Spanish Civil War, comparing the Belgian mercenaries with those idealist volunteers who went to Spain to fight alongside the Republicans in the name of freedom. In other words, the greedy, racist soldiers of fortune could even have ideals. Most importantly, the heroic volunteers who fought on the Iberian Peninsula had come back to haunt the imaginary of certain delegates, contributing to produce an ambivalent stance with regard to those foreigners who were now looting and pillaging the newly independent African states.

At this point we might remember how Daniel Gearhart – one of the US mercenaries sentenced in Luanda – had confessed to the public prosecutor that he had gone to Angola to fight against a communist takeover. To add another interesting reference, the writings and interviews collected from some of the leading European mercenaries active in Africa at the time show a mix of motivations behind the decision to fight abroad. In particular, these soldiers of fortune professed a strong attachment to the 'old and virtuous' military values and shared an ideal of white supremacy.[90] Western mercenaries such as Jean Schramme and

---

[89] Ibid., p. 44. Emphasis added.

[90] I am referring to the writings of Jean Schramme, Mike Hoare and Rolf Steiner, already cited in the introduction. See also the interesting insights of John de St. Jorre, 'Looking for Mercenaries (and Some Pen-Portraits of Those We Found)' (1967) 33 *Transition* 19–25 and Akbarali H. Thobhani, 'The Mercenary Menace' (1976) 23 *Africa Today* 61–68. See for instance the statement released by Bob Denard during the Congo crisis: 'Ce n'est pas parce qu'on nous fait porter l'étiquette de mercenaires qu'il faut penser que nous sommes prêts à suivre n'importe quelle aventure, en faisant fi des engagements que nous avons pris envers le gouvernement de la RDC. Je suis fier de pouvoir dire que la grande majorité de mes hommes partagent mes sentiments vis-à-vis du respect des engagements pris, vous avez pu vous rendre à mon état-major et avez pu constater que notre devise est "honneur et fidélité". Je pense qu'elle a été respectée. J'espère que le peuple congolais et les troupes de l'ANC en particulier en ont pris conscience. Je profite de l'occasion pour vous demander ... de bannir le mot "mercenaire".' The interview is reported in Walter Bruyère-Ostells, 'La Révolte des Mercenaires Contre Mobutu en 1967' (2012) 247 *Guerres mondiales et conflits contemporains* 91–104, pp. 95–96. For the role of French soldiers of fortune in Congo, see more specifically Walter Bruyère-Ostells, 'L'Influence Français Dans la Sécession Katangaise: Naissance d'Un Système Mercenaire' (2015) 162 *Relations internationales* 157–172 and Vincent Genin, 'La France et le Congo ex-Belge (1961–1965). Intérêts et Influences en Mutation' (2013) 91 *Revue Belge de Philologie et d'Histoire* 1057–1110. For the role of the United States in Congo see Piero Gleijeses,

2.2 WHAT FREEDOM, WHOSE FREEDOM? 121

Rolf Steiner identified themselves as descendants of a noble lineage of 'condottieri'.[91] This figure of the adventurer was present not only in their own writings, but also and most importantly in the speeches of certain European delegates, as we have seen. Certainly, supporting neocolonial, racist regimes and professing a clear right-wing political faith may be at odds with the ideals championed by the volunteers who went to fight against Franco. Yet Spaak's reference seems to suggest precisely the opposite. Or rather, that there might be very different conceptions of freedom at stake. The figure of the adventurer encountered in the previous chapter is then split into two again: the 'good' soldier of fortune who fights for noble ideals, and the neocolonial, racist mercenary.

Such ideals were of course fiercely opposed by Third World states. And the issue of mercenaries' motivation reappeared strongly in the discussions at Geneva. We will see this aspect in more detail later in the chapter, but it seemed relevant to point to it now, given the interesting cultural references found in Spaak's speech.[92]

The volatile political situation in the Congo continued until 1967, when all remaining foreign mercenaries were finally evacuated from the country.[93] The Security Council voted on an important resolution on this issue in July of the same year.[94] The discussions leading up to the vote followed those already seen in previous years, with Third World states asking for stronger legal solutions to tackle the problem of mercenaries

---

"'Flee! The White Giants are Coming!'": The United States, Mercenaries, and the Congo, 1964-1965' (1994) 18 *Diplomatic History* 207-237.

[91] See specifically Steiner, *Carre Rouge*.

[92] Essentially, things did not change much in the following meetings. A more substantial resolution was passed (with France and the United Kingdom abstaining), which authorized the Secretary General to use 'the requisite measures of force ... for the immediate apprehension, detention pending legal action and/or deportation of all foreign military and paramilitary personnel and political advisers ... and mercenaries'. The Congo question, S/RES/169, 24 November 1961, paragraph 4.

[93] The Congo crisis was discussed extensively also at the General Assembly during those years. See specifically, UN General Assembly Official Records, 967th plenary meeting (24 March 1961), 975th plenary meeting (4 April 1961), 977th plenary meeting (5 April 1961), 978th plenary meeting (6 April 1961), 980th plenary meeting (7 April 1961), 983rd plenary meeting (14 April 1961), 987th plenary meeting (18 April 1961), 1035th plenary meeting (13 October 1961), 1060th plenary meeting (21 November 1961), 1292nd plenary meeting (7 December 1964), 1293rd plenary meeting (7 December 1964), 1307th plenary meeting (18 December 1964), 1575th plenary meeting (2 October 1967) and 1590th plenary meeting (13 October 1967).

[94] Question concerning the Democratic Republic of the Congo, S/RES/239, 10 July 1967.

and Western countries trying to soften the tone, while formally supporting the principle of non-interference and condemning such acts as 'aggression'.[95]

Moving forward, it was the Nigerian Civil War (1967–1970) that again attracted Europeans fighting to support the new secessionist state.[96] For various political reasons, including a strong opposition from the United Kingdom, the United Nations stayed out of this conflict, and no real talks were held at the General Assembly or the Security Council on the issue of mercenaries in Biafra.[97] Interestingly, a few years later Nigeria proposed the draft article at the Geneva talks, and promoted the first UN Convention against mercenaries.

Significantly, in June 1976 the Angolan Revolutionary Tribunal had mentioned specific General Assembly resolutions to incriminate Callan and his group of white mercenaries. Resolutions 2395 (1968), 2465 (1968), 2548 (1968) and 3103 (1973) were in fact taken as the basis to demonstrate that mercenarism was recognized as a crime internationally, and that Angola was therefore bound by these legal obligations. We have already seen how Western commentators had not been convinced by such arguments, or simply saw no legal force in these UN documents.[98] Nevertheless, it is significant that in each of these resolutions – which concerned disparate aspects of the colonial question – specific mention of mercenarism was included.[99] There is no need to go into further detail here. It suffices to highlight that, in those resolutions, mercenaries were

---

[95] UN Security Council Official Records, 1376th meeting (10 July 1967). Particularly the speeches of Brazil, Congo, Argentina, Nigeria and Bulgaria.

[96] *See* specifically Arnold, *Mercenaries*, pp. 18–25. For the involvement of French mercenaries see Christopher Griffin, 'French Military Policy in the Nigerian Civil War, 1967–1970' (2015) 26 *Small Wars & Insurgencies* 114–135.

[97] For main reference see John J. Stremlau, *The International Politics of the Nigerian Civil War, 1967–1970* (Princeton, NJ: Princeton University Press 1977). *See* also J. Isawa Elaigwu, 'The Nigerian Civil War and the Angolan Civil War Linkages between Domestic Tensions and International Alignments' (1977) 12 *Journal of African and Asian Studies* 215–235.

[98] On top of that, the MPLA had still not been granted recognition by many Western states. The United States had even vetoed Angola's admission to the United Nations during the proceedings of the Luanda trial. *See* UN Security Council Official Records, 1932nd meeting (23 June 1976) record of the vote, pp. 23–24.

[99] 'Urgently appeals to all States to take all measures to prevent the recruitment or training in their territories of any persons as mercenaries for the colonial war being waged in the Territories under Portuguese domination and for violations of the territorial integrity and sovereignty of the independent African States.' A/RES/2395, paragraph 9.

essentially being cast as 'outlaws' (Res. 2465)[100] and that a net separation between two types of combatants was being drawn (Res. 3103).[101] On the one side were those fighters struggling against colonial domination, and as such benefiting from POW status; on the other were the mercenaries, depicted instead as criminals.

Provisions against mercenaries were increasingly spelled out, as shown by two other important UNGA resolutions of that period: the Declaration of Friendly Relations among States (1970) and the Definition of Aggression (1974).[102] In these documents, mercenaries were added to the list of those armed bands for whose organization and dispatch states could be held responsible. The more we advance towards the discussions at Geneva, then, the more the legal characterization of the mercenary as an unlawful type of combatant is crystallized at the international level. This demonstrates how the demonization carried out by Third World countries against these actors was gaining widespread recognition on the international arena.

However, despite the strong political pressure from these countries, not all states agreed with such a proscription. Or, to put it differently, it was not clear to everyone at the General Assembly what was to be achieved – legally speaking – when defining mercenaries as outlaws.

---

[100] 'Declares that the practice of using mercenaries against movements for national liberation and independence is punishable as a criminal act and that mercenaries themselves are outlaws, and calls upon the Governments of all countries to enact legislation declaring the recruitment, financing and training of mercenaries in their territory to be a punishable offence and prohibiting their nationals from serving as mercenaries.' A/RES/2465, paragraph 8.

[101] 'The combatants struggling against colonial and alien domination and racist regimes captured as prisoners are to be accorded the status of prisoners of war and their treatment should be in accordance with the provisions of the Geneva Convention relative to the Treatment of Prisoners of War, of 12 August 1949 ... The use of mercenaries by colonial and racist regimes against the national liberation movements struggling for their freedom and independence from the yoke of colonialism and alien domination is considered to be a criminal act and the mercenaries should accordingly be punished as criminal.' A/RES/3103, paragraphs 4–5.

[102] 'Every State has the duty to refrain from organizing or encouraging the organization of irregular forces or armed bands, including mercenaries, for incursion into the territory of another State.' See Declaration on Principles of International Law concerning Friendly Relations and Co-operation among States in accordance with the Charter of the United Nations, A/RES/2625 (XXV), 24 October 1970, preamble. Among the acts qualifying as an act of aggression there is: 'The sending by or on behalf of a State of armed bands, groups, irregulars or mercenaries, which carry out acts of armed forces against another State of such gravity as to amount to the acts listed above, or its substantial involvement therein.' Definition of Aggression, A/RES/3314 (XXIX), 14 December 1974, Art. 3(g).

This is evident for instance in the discussions around operative paragraph 8 of Resolution 2465, where for the first time such a characterization was made and introduced in an official UN document.[103] Although this addition (originally a Soviet amendment) was finally passed, a total of forty-three states abstained from the vote, with eight voting against. Without venturing too far into the voting proceedings, if states like South Africa, the United States and Belgium objected strongly to the insertion of the paragraph, Italy and Ireland were among those countries that asked for explanations of the legal nature of the term 'outlaws'.[104] The Italian delegate, for instance, voiced his doubts in the following terms: 'does it mean that such criminals find themselves outside the legal order? If it is so, the concept is utterly contrary to the Italian Constitution ... nobody in my country can be outside the law. Even the criminal is under the law and must be judged according to the law and through a fair trial'.[105] The Irish delegate echoed his colleague by remarking that 'we do not see how it would be possible to reconcile a declaration "that the mercenaries themselves are outlaws" with Article VI of the Universal Declaration of Human Rights, which reads: "Everyone has the right to recognition everywhere as a person before the law"'.[106]

At the time these were important questions, above all because mercenaries were being represented as the sworn opponents of African self-determination, and therefore some kind of enemies of humanity.[107] That

---

[103] *See* UN General Assembly Official Records, 1743rd plenary meeting (16 December 1968), 1749th plenary meeting (19 December 1968) and 1751st plenary meeting (20 December 1968).

[104] The Belgian representative stated for instance that: 'The authorities and public opinion in Belgium unequivocally condemn the use of mercenaries. The recruitment of mercenaries has long been punishable under article 135 of our penal code. That legislation has been supplemented by the introduction of a bill which subjects the activities of the mercenaries themselves to severe penalties. Nevertheless, the Belgian delegation was not able to vote in favour of the paragraph set out in the amendment because of a wording which seems questionable to us, whatever the intentions of the sponsors may have been. I am referring, more particularly, to the use of such expressions as "outlaws". In a system based on law, whatever crimes an individual may commit, he cannot be convicted except in accordance with the legal rules.' UNGA, 1751st plenary meeting (20 December 1968) p. 14.

[105] *Ibid.*, pp. 12–13.

[106] *Ibid.*, p. 13.

[107] The Italian delegate in fact noted that: 'One cannot escape the impression that objectives that have nothing to do with mercenaries and with decolonization in general are being pursued and that, thanks to the anti-colonial vote, an attempt is being made at smuggling legal abnormalities that are contrary to the constitution of most countries.' UNGA, 1751st plenary meeting (20 December 1968) p. 13.

accusation can be compared to today's characterization of foreign terrorist fighters, as we will see in the next chapter.

Another point of contention was represented by the alleged difference between mercenaries and foreign advisers: this had been mentioned during the Luanda trial, yet the massive presence of Cuban and Soviet troops supporting the MPLA had not allowed this argument to emerge fully before the court. Interestingly, this would become one of the main contentious topics discussed at Geneva, also because it represented a loophole in the definition of who was to be understood as a mercenary. It is here then that we need to make a further leap forward, to March 1976.

We are again at the Security Council. In Angola, Callan and his squad had already been captured, but a formal trial had not yet been decided. Kenya was now bringing a complaint against the act of aggression perpetrated by South Africa against the People's Republic of Angola.[108] Four intensive meetings were being held on the issue, meetings in which everyone seemed to understand what the real topic on the table was. However, the MPLA was not yet recognized as the official government of the country, nor did Angola have a seat at the United Nations. The best that could be achieved was to point the finger at the South Africans, who had lined up with UNITA and controlled the south of the country.[109] These meetings were interesting not so much for the usual accusations made by the Eastern bloc against the 'imperialist and neocolonial' aggression perpetrated by South Africa against a fellow African country, but rather because they highlighted different cultural details underpinning the proscription of mercenarism.

China launched the first accusation. Raging against the Soviet 'social-imperialism', the Chinese representative asserted that: 'some 1,000 Soviet military troops and over 10,000 foreign mercenary troops supported by Soviet Union are still hanging on in Angola and refuse to withdraw ... the Chinese government strongly condemn ... the Soviet military personnel and its foreign mercenary troops'.[110] While the Russian delegate refused to comment on that allegation, the Cuban representative

---

[108] UN Security Council Official Records, 1900th meeting (26 March 1976), 1901st meeting (29 March 1976), 1902nd meeting (29 March 1976), 1904th meeting (30 March 1976), 1906th meeting (31 March 1976).

[109] This, however, suited the Russians, who were increasingly focusing their attention on the southern cone of Africa, against states like South Africa and Rhodesia, which for them stood as allies of American imperialism.

[110] UNSC, 1902nd meeting (29 March 1976) p. 7.

clarified: 'for Cuba, to give assistance to the fraternal people, victim of the combined aggression of imperialists, racist and mercenaries ... was simply to fulfil an elementary duty of solidarity ... of course Ambassador Huang Hua said not one word about the real mercenaries, the paid assassins with long criminal experience in the Congo, Nigeria, Rhodesia and other African countries'.[111]

The Soviet and Cuban foreign advisers were not perceived by all states in the same way. Indeed, there were some at the Security Council who even dared to depict them as mercenaries. Perhaps that was why the Cuban delegate felt compelled to explain the difference between the idealism of its troops sent in support of the 'heroic soldiers of the Angolan national army ... that have stood against colonialism',[112] and the real mercenaries paid to plunder Africa.

Yet where did we hear a similar tune before? Is this not reminiscent of what was seen at the League of Nations between the 'genuine' volunteers who came to Spain following their ideals and the fascist troops sent by totalitarian states? History repeats itself, though changing its mask. At the time of the Spanish Civil War, in fact, the real volunteers were those who travelled to Spain without being affiliated formally with any state; Cuba justified sending its soldiers as an act of international solidarity against those neocolonial and imperial homelands of the mercenaries.[113]

But the situation was about to become even more tense. The Soviet Union took the opportunity to directly challenge the delegates of the United States and the United Kingdom: 'if anyone has any doubts as to what a mercenary is, he can go to London where the mercenaries were recruited. But if he does not have any spare money, he can simply take the subway here in New York to the place where he will also find that mercenaries, white mercenaries, are being recruited'.[114] A fierce battle ensued, with the two blocs of countries essentially trying to prove how their men were the most virtuous – and thus legitimate – combatants.[115]

---

[111] *Ibid.*
[112] *Ibid.*, p. 6.
[113] At the beginning of the 1960s, Cuba was accusing the United States of aggression by organizing and sending bands of mercenaries. *See* General Assembly Official Records, 995th plenary meeting (21 April 1961) pp. 490–493.
[114] UNSC, 1904th meeting (30 March 1976) pp. 4–5.
[115] Or, as the representative of Benin added, it was unthinkable to 'place on a footing of equality the heinous crime committed by the disgusting apartheid regime [of South Africa] and the presence in Angola of troops invited by the lawful government at Luanda to come to its assistance'. UNSC, 1906th meeting (31 March 1976) p. 23.

Nothing had really changed from the Spanish Civil War. A few moments later, however, the Saudi Arabian delegate embarked on a remarkable speech:

> With regard to aid that comes from the outside ... Who can forget Lafayette? Somebody might say it was because the French were revolutionaries ... On the other hand ... many British historians thought that Lafayette came here in order to [weaken the] British in their colony ... For example, who aided the Greeks in 1824, when they got their independence? The British sent Lord Byron, the poet, to Greece to liberate them from the Ottoman Empire, and many extolled the British for that matter. Of course, the Turks did not like that, but those who believed that liberty should be served thought that the British did something good.[116]

Our heroes have reappeared. Lafayette and Byron, whom we encountered during the Spanish Civil War, had made their entrance at the United Nations. And yet, with a twist of realpolitik, the Saudi Arabian representative challenged his colleagues' endless fight by highlighting that how Byron and Lafayette were viewed depended very much on which side was looking at them. For some they were mercenaries, for others foreign advisers; for some thirsty imperialists and neocolonial slavers, for others virtuous troops dispatched to help their comrades' quest for freedom.

Conversely, one should not forget how the figures of Byron and Lafayette evoked by the Saudi representative remain ambiguous, because they are tinged with the passions of the players who evoke them. Very different conceptions of freedom, and thus of wars of national liberation, are in fact attached to these images. As much as the European colonizer underpinning the discourse of African states carries with it its counterpart, that of the paternalistic white man, so is the figure of the noble adventurer. Were mercenaries to be understood as neocolonialist, racist combatants, or were they instead the heirs of the Spanish Civil War heroes, continuing the long tradition of the Byrons and the Lafayettes, reincarnated in Jean Schramme, Bob Denard and Rolf Steiner? There can be no clear answer to this question. What is evident though is that figures of past volunteers permeated the imaginary of states representative and keep coming back to characterize the legitimacy or illegitimacy of foreign fighters' causes.

Yet one must not be oblivious of the context where these debates happen. Epitomized by the Luanda trial, a specific balance of power crystallized during decolonization, channelling certain passions, directing

---

[116] UNSC, 1904th meeting (30 March 1976) p. 21.

the ambivalences. The Soviet representative continued only moments after the Saudi delegate's speech: 'the first half of the 1970s [saw] the collapse of the colonial system of the African continent. An important international task is the full elimination of all vestiges of ... colonialism, of oppression and of inequality, the attainment of the independence of peoples and the elimination of all hotbeds of racism and colonialism'.[117] It is thus sufficiently clear how white mercenaries became a symbol of the colonial powers' intervention and sphere of influence in the Third World, particularly on the African continent. The General Assembly and Security Council debates help us understand not only how the discourse around these actors reached the international level, but also the various arguments (with their related figures) deployed by the two blocs of countries in responding to the mercenaries' problem. These discussions also highlighted ambiguities, which would be reiterated both at the national level and in Geneva.

To conclude, Angola was finally granted a seat at the United Nations in December 1976.[118] The issue of Western mercenaries in the Third World certainly did not end there, as many other instances involving these actors can be identified after the Luanda trial. Frictions between Western and Eastern states continued, attested by the case of Southern Rhodesia while the Geneva talks were fully underway, for instance.[119] The attempted coup led by Bob Denard and his group of mercenaries in Benin in January 1977 (five months before the Additional Protocol was signed) reopened fierce discussions at the Security Council, with Third World countries pleading for concrete legal solutions to end the mercenary plague.[120] Particularly since the events in the Congo, African states

---

[117] Ibid., p. 7.

[118] For the Angolan representative's speech, see General Assembly Official Records, 84th plenary meeting (1 December 1976) pp. 1284–1289.

[119] See for example the discussions held at the Fourth Committee of the UN General Assembly: UN General Assembly Fourth Committee, 46th meeting (13 December 1976) and 49th meeting (14 December 1976). During the latter, the Soviet delegate Kharlamov remarked: 'The representative of the United Kingdom had also stated that United Kingdom nationals were free to leave the country at any time. It was a strange freedom which allowed nationals to leave the country in order to serve in the army of another State. Obviously, the British and Soviet concepts of freedom were different. Furthermore, the United States press, and other sources had confirmed the recruitment of British nationals in the United Kingdom to serve as mercenaries in Southern Rhodesia, even while the Geneva talks were in progress.' 49th meeting, p. 9.

[120] For a brief analysis on the Benin coup see Arnold, *Mercenaries*, 56–64. *See also* UN Security Council Official Records, 1987th meeting (8 February 1977), 2005th meeting (14 April 1977), 2049th meeting (24 November 1977).

had been wondering how and where to try the mercenaries, and under whose responsibility these actors should fall. Condemning mercenaries *tout court* was not enough, and the Luanda trial had offered a concrete attempt to bring these soldiers of fortune to justice. Yet since the Spanish Civil War, states had questioned how they could prevent the departure of their citizens for war zones, and what to do if they were to return. From the British reactions to the indictments of their citizens in Angola it is clear how the dynamics of state responsibility had evolved, how the attitudes of Western states had changed, and how these debates were framed by returning to former cultural figures. It is again at the national level that our journey among foreign fighters will continue.

2.3 Volunteers or Mercenaries?

We have seen how the Luanda courtroom was filled with Westerners, expressly requested by Neto to participate, and oversee the trial's proceedings. American and British lawyers were given the possibility to defend those mercenaries who wished to be represented by their attorneys. In sum, the Luanda trial attracted worldwide attention and it was impossible for the mercenaries' countries of origin to ignore it. Unlike the Spanish Civil War, however, no legislation was enacted in either the United Kingdom or the United States to stop the recruitment or departure of these men.[121] While British authorities had prevented new groups

---

[121] In August 1976 the US House of Representatives hold formal meetings on the question of mercenaries in Africa. The Hearings before the Special Subcommittee on Investigations retrace the chronology of the events in Angola in the years 1957–1976, and show the ambivalent role played by the US government in the Angolan civil war. But the Hearings are also compelling from a legal standpoint. The government representatives mention the relevance of the 1949 Geneva Conventions, questioning the recent indictment of the American citizens Gearhart, Acker and Grillo in Luanda. They also summarize the relevant US jurisprudence and Congressional acts concerning the issue of loss of nationality, pointing to a discrepancy among the two. Where the latter provided for such a penalty, a 1967 USSC case forbade it (*Afroym* v. *Rusk*). The government representatives further developed neutrality laws. These had been in place since the time of the Spanish Civil War, and subsequent statutes were adopted to criminalize enlistment and recruitment in a foreign army. However, US jurisprudence had taken the opposite direction. Putting emphasis on the need to prove the intentional character of the action undertaken by private citizens, it made it difficult to charge people with such an offence. This evident lack of clarity between the written law and courts' decisions was noted by the members of the Special Subcommittee: 'these laws ... they are pretty vague ... there should be a tightening or changing of those laws ... it looks like they are kind of contradictory in what they are saying'. These words are reminiscent of those

reaching Angola, overall Western states had a laissez-faire attitude towards the actions of their citizens abroad.[122]

This does not mean that the situation in Angola was not being closely monitored. Reports about the involvement of ex-British Army members were a matter of concern for Downing Street from December 1975.[123] As more men were departing, the Prime Minister Harold Wilson addressed the House of Commons on 10 February 1976. He also announced that an in-depth inquiry would be conducted by the eminent judge Lord Diplock.[124] What became the Diplock Report was presented to Parliament in August 1976, informing the government of the main legal issues concerning mercenaries and their recruitment.[125]

During Wilson's speech in February, the prime minister made clear that his government was considering passing legislation to stop further recruitment of mercenaries. This entailed re-enacting the Foreign Enlistment Act, already seen at the time of the Spanish Civil War.[126] Interestingly, it was the leader of the opposition, Margaret Thatcher, who asked for clarification on the meaning of the Act. The Conservative

---

written by Ian Brownlie at the end of the 1950s, when he was lamenting the ambiguity of The Hague provisions on foreign volunteers. In that case, of course, international law was in the spotlight for its apparent deficiencies, whereas here national legislation was the target of the criticism of the subcommittee members. Nonetheless, it is interesting to note how with different place, time and actors, legal problems concerning foreign fighters persisted. See Mercenaries in Africa: Hearing before the Special Subcommittee on Investigations of the Committee on International Relations, House of Representatives, Ninety-fourth Congress, Second Session, 9 August 1976, p. 11. For an overview of the role of American soldiers of fortune in Africa see Klaas Voß, 'Plausibly Deniable: Mercenaries in US Covert Interventions during the Cold War, 1964–1987' (2016) 16 *Cold War History* 37–60 and Ward Churchill, 'U.S. Mercenaries in Southern Africa: The Recruiting Network and U.S. Policy' (1980) 27 *Africa Today* 21–46.

[122] On British foreign policy see specifically Geraint Hughes, 'Soldiers of Misfortune: The Angolan Civil War, the British Mercenary Intervention, and UK Policy towards Southern Africa, 1975-6' (2014) 36 *International History Review* 493–512.

[123] 'Miss Richardson asked the Secretary of State for Defence whether any precautions are being taken or are contemplated to prevent former members of the British Armed Services from placing the benefits of their training at the disposal of foreign Governments for the purpose of attacking countries with which the United Kingdom is not at war, or in helping to maintain regimes whose existence Her Majesty's Government do not officially recognise.' HC Deb, 19 December 1975, Vol. 902, c819.

[124] HC Deb, 10 February 1976, Vol. 905, cc236–247. Technically, the issue of mercenaries' recruitment started to be addressed at the end of January 1976. HC Deb, 28 January 1976, Vol. 904, c411.

[125] Report of the Committee of Privy Counsellors appointed to inquire into the recruitment of mercenaries ('Diplock Report'), Cmnd. 6569 (August 1976).

[126] HC Deb, 10 February 1976, Vol. 905, c236.

leader was in fact concerned about whether the Act was to cover all British citizens going abroad to fight: 'British citizens have within present recollection fought for many different causes overseas ... Will the right hon. Gentleman confirm that the Foreign Enlistment Act makes no distinction between whether those who fight overseas are paid or are volunteers?'[127]

This is a significant question raised, because it points to that previously mentioned inversion of ideologies from the Spanish Civil War time. If in fact the white mercenaries present in Africa during the decolonization period seemed to adhere to a racist, conservative and neocolonial ideology, here this stance takes on a political connotation. Thatcher saw a clear difference between a volunteer and a mercenary, suggesting that she understood the British citizens going to Angola as volunteers. Wilson took the opportunity to clarify: 'I agree with the right hon. Lady that there are different occasions, reasons, motives, and inspirations for people going abroad to fight. [This situation] is entirely different ... within a few days a small group of people – whatever their background – have been able to raise a vast private army. That this is possible could be a threat to democracy in this country'.[128]

Although the prime minister acknowledged that the issue of foreign fighters had occurred before, he also drew a clear line between past instances and the present situation, establishing a net division between those purely private actors and foreign volunteers. This differentiation between the present and the past had already been seen in the writings of the internationalists in the 1930s (as they wanted to draw a line between fascist troops and other, previous forms of volunteering) and has become part of counter-terrorism legislation in our time. But at the House of Commons things were only starting to get heated.

Another member of the Conservative Party – Julian Amery – intervened with a more explicit remark: 'is the Prime Minister aware that many of us feel that the Western Powers collectively should be organizing help to the pro-Western and anti-Communist forces in Angola and that, in the absence of such help, to interfere with the flow of *genuine volunteers* to the pro-Western forces in Angola would be tantamount to becoming accomplices of the Cuban and Soviet aggressors?'[129] This suggested again that the line between who counted as a true volunteer

---

[127] *Ibid.*, c238.
[128] *Ibid.*, c239.
[129] *Ibid.*, c243. Emphasis added.

and who did not was a thin one. Interestingly, on 9 February, Amery had given a speech at the Foreign Policy and Morality Commons Sitting, where he deplored the role of Cuban troops in Angola and even went as far as comparing Lord Byron to a mercenary:

> We must not deprecate mercenaries too much. *Lord Byron was a mercenary.* I should have thought that many people in the Labour Party would take a pride in the record of the Attlee battalion in the International Brigade ... Of course, they were mercenaries ... The Gurkhas have done tremendous service for this country. They are mercenaries too.[130]

The emblematic figure of Lord Byron (together with those of the Spanish International Brigades) have returned, once more transmuted. This reminds us of the words of Spaak at the United Nations, when the Belgian delegate portrayed his fellow countrymen going to the Congo as genuine volunteers fighting for freedom. In addition, Amery recalls those colonial troops which we have already encountered at the Hague in 1907. The image of the *bon sauvage* underlining the discourse of the Dutch and British delegations is here replaced by that of the honourable soldier of fortune which has long fought on the side of the British army (for example, the Gurkhas).

Lord Byron, the International Brigades and even the colonial troops are alive and present in the imaginary of British legislators. Their images haunt its discourse and contribute to tinge the lawmaking process with deep ambivalence, because the passions actors project over them while trying to clarify legal categories are ambivalent. Finally – as was the case four decades earlier with the Soviets – Amery made it clear that the Cubans were the villains in the Angolan affair.

But Wilson was immovable. After stating that no matter which side people fought for, his government would take the same stance, he ended his speech by asserting that it was necessary 'to draw a distinction

---

[130] Amery continued: 'The hon. Gentleman referred to the Sultanate of Oman. He showed an abysmal ignorance of the history of that country. Up to 1970 I absolutely agree that the regime was not a progressive regime, because the Sultan had no money. The oil had not then been struck. The country is now pushing rapidly ahead. Thanks to not only Regular British officers who have gone there but also to some British mercenaries, contract officers, the Sultan's forces have secured internal stability. Thanks to that, the oil from the Persian Gulf is safe – and the hon. Gentleman's constituents and all our constituents have at least a chance of seeing the wheels of industry and of our motor cars turning. However, when it comes to Angola, surely if there be any scandal about mercenaries it is the mass invasion by at least 12,000 – it may be more – Cubans with Soviet technical support.' HC Deb, 9 February 1976, Vol. 905, c47. Emphasis added.

between volunteers ... especially those stirred by a deep religious faith or by any other faith, and people recruiting mercenaries for the sake of personal profit, the profit being to the group who sent them off. I think that there is a vast difference and that the House should be concerned that anyone can raise a private army by this means for service at home or abroad. That is why we are setting up the inquiry'.[131]

Although many in the opposition did not believe Wilson's general condemnation – given the alleged political support of the Labour Party for the MPLA – the prime minister had made an important point: the overt pecuniary motive linked with the recruitment of mercenaries was to differentiate these actors from all other types of volunteer.[132] Additionally, what concerned Wilson was the possibility of a private army being raised within UK borders to fight abroad.

One cannot fail to note how Wilson was uncomfortable with the idea of a private army, while he did not seem concerned with the volunteers moved by a 'deep religious faith or by any other faith'. A few decades later such concerns would change. The reactions of Western governments would in fact shift in tolerating the presence of private armies in war zones, while accusing individuals going to fight abroad with a religious agenda of international terrorism.[133] At the same time, Wilson's words imply that the figure of the noble adventurer is still very much lingering in the imaginary of policymakers. What most preoccupies the prime minister are the commercial enterprises set up to recruit men for fighting abroad (reminiscent of such activities already intolerable for international lawyers in the 1930s), as he differentiates recruiting agencies from other forms of volunteering.

Although the British prime minister seemed willing to act decisively on the issue of mercenaries, the Diplock inquiry took several months to be conducted and handed back to the government. During the session held on 10 February, many in the Parliament had asked if a more rapid and comprehensive legislative Act could have been passed, given that the Foreign Enlistment Act appeared out of date and largely

---

[131] HC Deb, 10 February 1976, Vol. 905, c246.
[132] In the session of 28 January, for instance, many representatives of the House of Commons had questioned the Labour Party's involvement on the side of the MPLA. See Callaghan's intervention in HC Deb, 10 February 1976, Vol. 905, c412.
[133] *See* generally Peter Warren Singer, *Corporate Warriors: The Rise of the Privatized Military Industry* (Ithaca, NY: Cornell University Press 2003) and Simon Chesterman and Chia Lehnardt (eds.), *From Mercenaries to Market: The Rise and Regulation of Private Military Companies* (Oxford: Oxford University Press 2007).

ineffective.[134] However, no clear legal responses were made by the government that day or in the months that followed. If it is true that further groups of mercenaries ready to embark for Angola were stopped at Heathrow airport and that the passports of those returning from the field were withdrawn, it remains unclear how many investigations were opened in the subsequent months.[135] As confirmed later by the findings

---

[134] For instance, David Steel, a member of the Liberal Party, commented: 'I fully support the setting up of the inquiry, but will the Prime Minister clarify what at first sight seems to be a contradiction in his statement? He said that the inquiry is to consider whether sufficient control exists over the recruitment of United Kingdom citizens, but later in his statement he said that the existing law on the issues involved is unsatisfactory. Is it the Government's view that the law should be changed to prevent the enlistment of mercenaries in this country by foreign Powers?' HC Deb, 10 February 1976, Vol. 905, c240. Robert Hughes made the point even clearer: 'Is my right hon. Friend aware that there will be considerable disappointment in Britain and in Africa that the setting up of the inquiry will lead to delays in activating measures to stop mercenaries being recruited? Would it not be possible to put an Act through this House in 24 hours, at least making it illegal openly to recruit mercenaries in this country? The facts are very well known and action is needed now.' Ibid., c241.

[135] See for instance the sessions of 19 February and 10 March at the House of Commons on the ongoing investigations into the mercenaries' business in Angola and on the issue of passport withdrawal: '[Mr. Newens] asked the Secretary of State for Foreign and Commonwealth Affairs if he will make a further statement on the outcome of the investigations made by his Department to seek to elicit the facts about the massacre of 14 British mercenaries in Angola on the instructions of their own officers. [Mr. Ennals] No investigation has been undertaken by my Department. A report on an investigation by the Metropolitan Police into these allegations was submitted to the Director of Public Prosecutions ... [Mr. Newens] asked the Secretary of State for Foreign and Commonwealth Affairs how many additional British mercenary soldiers are known to have left Great Britain for service in Angola since the Prime Minister's statement of 10th February; and if he will make a statement. [Mr. Ennals] No records are kept of individuals leaving the United Kingdom. Applications for passports from people who are going to Angola as mercenaries or who are known organisers of mercenary activities will be refused. My right hon. Friend has also authorised the withdrawal of passports from such mercenaries and from known organisers of Angolan mercenary activities. Passports have been withdrawn from mercenaries who have returned from Angola.' HC Deb, 19 February 1976, Vol. 905, c814. On 10 March: '[Mr. Beith] Will the Minister confirm that those which have been returned to former mercenaries have been returned on the basis of an undertaking that they will not in future go to Angola for those purposes? Does the right hon. Gentleman agree that action of that kind sets a precedent which might be used by future Governments in order to silence critics or prevent other kinds of conduct which was disapproved of on grounds that it might be controversial? [Mr. Ennals] I think that there are very limited categories in which this action can be taken. The list of categories of persons from whom passports may be withdrawn was given to the House on 15th November 1974 and included those whose past or proposed activities are so demonstrably undesirable that the grant or continued enjoyment of passport facilities would be contrary to the public interest. I remind the House and

2.3 VOLUNTEERS OR MERCENARIES? 135

of the Report itself, the British authorities seemed at an impasse on what to do. The lawmakers in both Houses were much more concerned to solve the long-standing question of whom to consider a mercenary and whom a volunteer. Another intervention during the very same session of 10 February noted:

> I notice that the terms of reference refer specifically to 'the recruitment of United Kingdom citizens for service as mercenaries'. Would this exclude the question of volunteers? Because in the past a great many citizens of this country have taken part in civil wars or internal disputes in other countries as volunteers; and one can remember, on the other side of the fence, certain Americans who joined our Forces at the beginning of the last war, for whose help we were indeed extremely grateful.[136]

especially Opposition Members that this action was taken at precisely the time when reports were coming to this country that some mercenaries had been massacred in Angola. I am happy that the recruitment of mercenaries has now ended. I also point out that if those from whom passports have been withdrawn now apply to the Passport Office their passports will be returned, provided they sign an undertaking that they will not return to Angola as mercenaries.' HC Deb, 10 March 1976, Vol. 907 c409–410.

[136] *See* the debate at the House of Lords on the same day, particularly the speeches of Lord Aberdare and Lord Shepherd: '[Lord Aberdare] I would suggest that possibly these terms of reference are rather too narrow, and that they should cover not only mercenaries but also volunteers who go of their own free will and take part in activities of a warlike nature in other countries ... [Lord Shepherd] In regard to the question of the terms of reference, it is true that the terms refer to mercenaries. I suspect that the reason for that is that we are dealing with the present and very sad situation in Angola and, if we are to deal with this situation, the Committee must act very quickly and this can be done only if the operation of their inquiry is in a very narrow field. The noble Lord, Lord Aberdare, mentioned volunteers. One thinks of those who have served with honour as volunteers in various causes. This would raise very wide issues. I should have thought that the first thing was to deal with this particular case and this is why the terms of reference have been so drafted.' HL Deb, 10 February 1976, Vol. 368, cc22–30. *See* also the discussions on 17 February, particularly the speeches of Viscount Monckton of Brenchley and Lord Goronwy-Roberts: '[Viscount Monckton of Brenchley] My intervention is solely on one small side of the question of mercenaries who, I think your Lordships will agree, have in the past had great honour in history. We could not have won most of the major wars we fought without the Hanoverian legions. At present, there are the Ghurkas, the French Foreign Legion, and the Wild Geese from Ireland who officered and commanded most of the armies of Europe at one time or another. The real mercenaries in this problem are the Cubans who are armed, fed, transported and governed by the Russians. That to me is a pure definition of mercenary.' Lord Goronwy-Roberts made an interesting statement on British foreign policy: 'I deplored every incursion, including mercenaries, when I replied from this Box. I ask the House to consider that at that time British policy and British counsel was achieving increasing credibility in Africa among the countries whom we were seeking to convince we were in earnest about non-intervention. It was at that time that this kind of sordid, bloody adventure was concocted in this country. This is what set off the fully justified condemnation of that adventure by my right honourable

Again and again, the imaginary of the British legislator is captured by the figure of the noble volunteer, a figure which has characterized the legal discussions over foreign fighters. In this case, the reference points to the US 'Eagle Squadrons', a group of American volunteers who fought on the side of the British Air Force in the early years of World War II. In short, one returns to the clashes already seen in other lawmaking venues. With the Conservative party accusing its opponents of being on the side of the MPLA, and the British mercenaries being compared to past, honourable foreign volunteers, the Cuban and Soviet troops in Angola were depicted as being the real mercenaries. It is time to leave these familiar political quarrels and concentrate instead on the content of the Diplock Report, whose aim was to instruct on the legal solutions to the mercenaries' problem.

The report started by returning to the recent events in Angola, stating that some 160 British citizens were known to be recruited in the United Kingdom to fight in the ranks of the FNLA.[137] It specified how these men were enlisted through newspaper advertisement, indicating the contracts they had been offered and highlighting how they were recruited to perform mainly combat function. The report also retraced briefly the long history of mercenarism, a practice that was said to be known for centuries and which included more recently the Gurkha regiments, the International Brigades and also the British Jews who fought in the Israeli army during the Arab–Israeli War.[138] It also provided a definition of mercenaries as 'persons who serve voluntarily for pay in armed forces other than the regular forces of their own country'.[139]

Interestingly, it made clear that it was difficult to distinguish between a mercenary and a volunteer, and that 'in nearly all cases ... the motives which induce a particular individual to serve as a mercenary will be mixed'.[140] One can therefore deduce why the foreign volunteers who fought against Franco were included in the historical examples, and why the report continued by affirming that 'mercenaries ... can only

---

friend the Prime Minister. Quite apart from the sordidness of this adventure, the total irresponsibility in its effect upon the credibility of what this country was trying to get over to black Africa.' HL Deb, 17 February 1976, Vol. 368, cc423–426 and cc437–438. On the issue of withdrawal of passports, HL Deb, 9 March 1976, Vol. 368, cc1201–1207.

[137] 'Diplock Report', p. 1.
[138] Ibid., p. 2.
[139] Ibid., p. 1.
[140] Ibid., p. 2.

be defined by reference to *what* they do, and not by reference to *why* they do it'.[141]

This is an important caveat, because it leaves out any criminalization for enlisting with a foreign army purely based on intent. This point was highly contentious not only during the Geneva talks, but also decades later when states tried to come up with legislation criminalizing the recruitment and departure to Syria and Iraq of foreign terrorist fighters.

Nonetheless, at the time, the British government felt that restricting the departure of its citizens to serve in a foreign army would have constituted a deprivation of their liberties: 'we do not think there are any means by which it would be practical to prevent a United Kingdom citizen from volunteering while he is abroad to serve as a mercenary and from leaving the United Kingdom ... any attempt to impose such a prohibition [would be] a deprivation of his freedom'.[142] Any restrictions – the report continued – could only have been justified on the grounds of public interest. As a list of these was provided – keeping good international relations, avoid expenses to repatriate mercenaries – one cannot help but think how they seem trivial if compared with the current terrorist threat, which has given states *carte blanche* to pass the broadest legislation to criminalize foreign fighters. Yet at the time, the report gave the impression of taking the rights of British citizens seriously, as attested by the explicit reference to Art. 13(2) of the Universal Declaration of Human Rights, protecting the right to leave and to return to one's home country.[143] On the same legal grounds, the report also made clear that neither the refusal nor the withdrawal of passports to prevent citizens' departure would have been an effective or justifiable legal solution.[144]

---

[141] *Ibid.* Emphases added.
[142] *Ibid.*, p. 4.
[143] *Ibid.*
[144] 'In fact passports were withdrawn from eight United Kingdom citizens who served as mercenaries in the Congo in 1961, three who served in the Congo in 1967/68, four who served in Nigeria in 1968, and fifty-four who served in Angola earlier this year. It is, in our view, significant that on each of these occasions the stable door was shut after the horse had gone – if such a metaphor is appropriate to the minor obstacle to departure that lack of a passport creates ... We are satisfied that neither the refusal of a passport nor its withdrawal can provide an effective administrative means of preventing or delaying the departure from the country of a would-be mercenary who has been informed about his legal rights ... these considerations lead us to conclude that the use of the prerogative power to withhold or withdraw a passport as a means of hindering United Kingdom citizens from leaving the country to enlist as mercenaries cannot be justified pragmatically or morally.' *Ibid.*, pp. 5–6.

Another problem was represented by the Foreign Enlistment Act. In particular, the Act made it illegal for a British subject to enlist, accepting 'any commission or engagement in the military or naval service of any foreign state at war with any foreign state at peace with her Majesty'.[145] The point of contention was whether such proscription could have been applied to the existing conditions of warfare given 'the immense changes in those conditions which have taken place in the last hundred years and particularly since World War II'.[146] Already at the time of the Spanish civil strife, the Act was considered largely ineffective. As more time had passed, it was unclear whether it applied in a situation of internal armed conflict with new actors on the ground (for example, guerrilla movements). To sum up, the very doctrine of belligerents' recognition which had legally characterized the Spanish conflict seemed at this point largely unattainable to the counsellors in charge of drafting the report. Stating that during its 106 years of existence 'there have never been a prosecution, let alone a conviction',[147] they finally concluded that 'the provisions of the Foreign Enlistment Act, 1870, which relate to illegal enlistment have become thoroughly unsatisfactory in modern conditions'.[148]

Certainly – the report continued – British citizens could have been prosecuted if in breach of a law prohibiting certain behaviours abroad. However, individuals would have faced trial only upon return to their home country, and only if there was enough 'admissible and cogent evidence to satisfy the high standard of proof of guilt that is required in criminal cases'.[149] It is therefore evident from all these formulations that the counsellors wished to make it particularly difficult to charge

---

[145] *Ibid.*, p. 7.
[146] *Ibid.*
[147] *Ibid.*, p. 10.
[148] *Ibid.*, p. 11.
[149] *Ibid.*, p. 3. The Report had also stated that: 'Independently of the difficulties of determining the status of the various armed forces that may be operating in an internal struggle ... in any trial of a person after his return for an offence under the [Foreign Enlistment Act] the prosecution would be confronted by evidential difficulties in proving what the accused had in fact done in the foreign country ... This would require oral evidence from eye-witnesses of his conduct ... The only persons in this country likely to be able to give first-hand evidence of this kind after the return of the accused to the United Kingdom are his former comrades ... The task of assembling sufficient evidence to support a conviction from other witnesses in the foreign country where the mercenary served and persuading them to come here for the trial presents practical problems that would, in our view, be insurmountable.' *Ibid.*, pp. 9–10.

British citizens for acts committed in a foreign country. Reiterating how it was not possible to criminalize enlisting as a mercenary per se, the counsellors concluded by advising legislation should be enacted prohibiting recruitment of mercenaries within UK borders.[150] Once again, it was the conscripting activity and not the voluntary enlisting which was being criminalized.

To sum up, the laissez-faire attitude typical of the interwar period was now being replaced with a professed commitment to individuals' rights, while the public interest did not seem to be endangered by the actions of a few mercenaries in foreign theatres of war.[151] Overall, British responses to the mercenaries' problem were still vague and mostly ineffective. The law relating to these foreign fighters was quite obscure and largely underdeveloped, notwithstanding the repeated calls from African states to outlaw mercenaries. Perhaps there lay the problem. Although the Luanda trial had invoked important international documents to incriminate these actors, states largely disagreed on how to define mercenarism to begin with. It is therefore again at the international level that we must look, retracing the *travaux* of Art. 47 of AP I. This article will in fact offer a definition for mercenarism, excluding these actors from POW status in international armed conflict.

2.4 The Nobility of the Cause Matters

The draft additional protocols presented by the International Committee of the Red Cross (ICRC) at the beginning of the Geneva talks contained no articles on mercenaries.[152] The proposal to add a provision relating to these actors came from the Nigerian delegation, in an effort to differentiate mercenaries from other type of combatants.[153] The proposed article, presented to the Third Committee in May 1976 was as follows:

---

[150] 'The activities prohibited under this head should be widely defined so as to include publishing information as to how or where to apply for employment as a mercenary or how to get to the place where such employment is available and making any payment or taking part in any arrangement to facilitate or promote employment.' *Ibid.*, p. 14.

[151] *Ibid.*, pp. 13–14.

[152] International Committee of the Red Cross, *Commentary on the Additional Protocols of 8 June 1977 to the Geneva Conventions of 12 August 1949* (The Hague: Martinus Nijhoff 1987) pp. 571–581. For the original text presented by the ICRC at the beginning of the Conference see International Committee of the Red Cross, *Draft Additional Protocols to the Geneva Conventions of August 12, 1949: Commentary* (Geneva, 1973).

[153] ICRC, *Commentary*, p. 573.

Article 42 quater – Mercenaries

1. The status of combatant or prisoner of war shall not be accorded to any mercenary who takes part in armed conflicts referred to in the Conventions and the present Protocol.
2. A mercenary includes any person not a member of the armed forces of a Party to the conflict who is specially recruited abroad and who is motivated to fight or take part in armed conflict essentially for monetary payment, reward or other private gain.[154]

Although the essential features of what became Art. 47 are already visible (for example, deprivation of POW status and monetary incentive behind enlisting), it is interesting to note that the proposal came rather late in the proceedings of the Conference. The delegations were occupied in defining first and foremost the armed forces (Art. 43), the combatants and prisoners of war (Art. 44) and the protection of persons who had taken part in hostilities (Art. 45). These provisions were to be placed in the new legal landscape that was supplanting the Geneva Conventions of 1949.[155] To be more specific, the Additional Protocol's aim was to bring under the protection of international law those new types of combatants that had emerged from national liberation struggles.[156]

It is here that the norm against mercenaries eventually took shape. The Nigerian proposal crystallized the willingness of several states to differentiate these actors, who otherwise would have been granted prisoner of war status. The desire to distinguish mercenaries from other types of combatants is visible in the *travaux* of Art. 44 – which dealt with the new categories of prisoners of war (draft Arts. 42, 42 bis) and prisoners not entitled to prisoners of war status (Art. 42 *ter*). Looking at the records of the thirty-fourth, thirty-fifth and thirty-sixth plenary meetings of the Conference (March 1975) one can see how the reference to mercenaries

---

[154] Official Records of the Diplomatic Conference on the Reaffirmation and Development of International Humanitarian Law Applicable in Armed Conflicts. Geneva (1974–1977), Vol. III, p. 192.

[155] Protocol Additional to the Geneva Conventions of 12 August 1949, and Relating to the Protection of Victims of International Armed Conflicts (Protocol I) (Geneva, 8 June 1977), Art. 1.

[156] *See* specifically ICRC, *Commentary*, pp. 506–542. For an in-depth study on Additional Protocol I and the influence that postcolonial discourse and social movements had on the creation of these rules see Amanda Alexander, 'International Humanitarian Law, Postcolonialism and the 1977 Geneva Protocol I' (2016) 17 *Melbourne Journal of International Law* 15–50.

finds a way into the discussions concerned with the meaning of irregular armed forces and of national liberation movements.[157]

It was the Greek delegation that made an initial comment on the topic. While debating the role of political resistance movements, its delegate pointed out that: 'adventurers and mercenaries might also be involved: it would therefore be dangerous to widen the concept of combatants entitled to the status of prisoners of war'.[158] The figure of the adventurer is evoked here in a negative light, to establish a clear differentiation from other resistance movements. A few moments later, it was the Ukrainian Soviet Socialist Republic that made the first statement on mercenaries. Reminding his colleagues that 'the purpose of article 42 was to confer the status of combatant on persons fighting against colonial and racist regimes', delegate Belousov made clear that those same colonial regimes were also trying to regain control over their former colonies precisely by using mercenaries.[159]

The Ukrainian delegate began a long tirade citing General Assembly resolutions which had denounced the recruitment and use of mercenaries in wars of national liberation. He also listed three different kinds of combatants: regular armed forces, national liberation movements and mercenaries. The delegate concluded his speech by stating that: 'to accord mercenaries the safeguards offered to the other categories would be contrary to the rules of existing international law and also to the resolutions of the United Nations General Assembly and the Security Council'.[160] This remark was immediately followed by delegate of Lesotho, who asked for a clarification of the term irregular fighter: 'it might be asked what exactly was meant by the word "irregular". Was it for instance the opposite of "regular", in which case mercenaries were "irregular forces"? Did the Conference intend to protect mercenaries? [My] Government, which had experience of atrocities committed by

---

[157] Official Records, Vol. XIV, pp. 335–385. A first, brief mention of mercenaries is present in the speech of the delegation of Ukraine already in 1974. See Official Records, Vol. V, pp. 112–113.
[158] Official Records, Vol. XIV, p. 338.
[159] 'That did not mean that those colonialist regimes would not try to reintroduce such regimes in those countries which had recently gained their independence ... In its fight against national liberation movements colonialism had resorted to the use of mercenaries: that had been the case in the Congo, Nigeria and the Arabian Peninsula.' Ibid., p. 342.
[160] Ibid., p. 343.

mercenaries in Africa, could not support any provision of the Protocol which protected them'.[161]

From then on, many non-Western delegations would include a reference to mercenaries in their speeches, to highlight the difference existing between these actors and other combatants that ought to be protected by draft Art. 42. For example, the Soviet delegate specified that: 'it should be clearly stated that the individuals known as "mercenaries" were not eligible for the benefit of any protection. Mercenaries were guilty of crimes against humanity and should be regarded as dangerous war criminals'.[162] The same was reaffirmed by the delegates of Czechoslovakia and Byelorussia, whereas the Indian delegation made clear that it: 'was opposed to the term "members of irregular forces", not knowing what was meant by that vague and ambiguous term. Perhaps it had been used to cover mercenaries, which would be unacceptable'.[163] As the debate intensified, the delegations of Nigeria, Ivory Coast, Mongolia, Madagascar and Zimbabwe left no doubt that mercenaries could not receive the same status as the fighters of national liberation movements.[164]

Not surprisingly, Western delegates remained cautious, with the delegate of Sweden reminding his colleagues that although the United Nations had clearly spoken against mercenaries, 'the meaning of "mercenary" would have to be precisely defined ... It would have to be made clear in particular, how it differed from volunteers'.[165] The ambivalent figure of the volunteer reappears here. As seen in the United Kingdom, many were still perplexed as to how to draw the line between the two types of actors. However, the vision underlying the Swedish delegate's speech is that of the good volunteer, which has nothing to do with those racist enemies of humanity who raid African countries.

---

[161] *Ibid.*, p. 344.
[162] *Ibid.*, p. 360.
[163] *Ibid.*, p. 348 (Czechoslovakia), p. 357 (Byelorussia) and p. 369 (India).
[164] *Ibid.*, p. 369 (Nigeria), pp. 373–374 (Ivory Coast), p. 375 (Mongolia), p. 377 (Madagascar), pp. 383–384 (Zimbabwe).
[165] *Ibid.*, p. 362 (Sweden). The British delegate stated that: 'Replying to the representative of the Ukrainian Soviet Socialist Republic, he said that, in the context of article 42*bis*, the references to mercenaries were a spectre without substance, since nothing in that article deprived a Party to a conflict of the right to try war criminals. Indeed, its purpose was to ensure that such trials would be conducted with all the necessary judicial safeguards, with fairness and in public. Such fundamental guarantees should be extended to everyone.' *Ibid.*, p. 351. The various states' positions are also reiterated in the statements made at the thirty-fourth meeting. *Ibid.*, pp. 487–556.

2.4 THE NOBILITY OF THE CAUSE MATTERS 143

Few expected that the issue of mercenaries would enter the conference discussions, as evidenced by the Australian delegation's final statement: 'during this debate there have been a number of references to the treatment of mercenaries. We are uncertain of what representatives have in mind on this matter and we would prefer to discuss the legal principles raised by this question after we have seen what proposals, if any, are put forward'.[166]

But the spark had been lit. Overall, the 1975 debates showed how the issue of mercenaries reappeared quite naturally in the humanitarian talks in Geneva, even if the topic was not officially on the agenda. It is therefore no coincidence that when it came to discussing new categories of combatants, many Third World countries emphasized the distinction between legitimate combatants and those neocolonial criminals in the service of imperialist states.

It was at the following year's talk (May–June 1976) that the Nigerian proposal was taken into consideration. Although supported by many states, no consensus was reached on Art. 42 *quater*, which appeared too complex to be dealt with in the time available.[167] Baxter – the representative of the United States and Rapporteur of the Third Committee in charge of it – returned to the problems encountered during the talks. He specified that while there was widespread agreement to deny mercenaries prisoner of war status, it was difficult to translate such a provision into a workable definition which 'can have life or death consequences for a person charged with being a mercenary'.[168] Recalling how some delegations preferred to adopt a shorter definition, while others seemed keen to spell out in more detail the various criteria for its qualification, Baxter clarified that a general agreement was reached among the working group in charge of Art. 42 *quater*:

> a mercenary is a person who is motivated to fight essentially or primarily by the desire for, as one representative put it, 'hard cash'. He fights for

---

[166] *See* the statement of Australia. *Ibid.*, p. 525.
[167] *See* Official Records, Vol. XV, pp. 112–113: '[Mr. Baxter. United States of America. Rapporteur] The matter had been discussed at length in the Working Group and had proved to be much more complex than expected when the study of the topic began. It had not been possible to arrive at an agreed text, despite the several attempts which he had made to prepare a draft that would be generally acceptable. The matter would have to be re-opened at the fourth session and he suggested that the Nigerian proposal on mercenaries should be circulated as a Conference document rather than as a working paper of the Working Group.'
[168] *Ibid.*, p. 405. *See* specifically CDDH/236/Rev. 1 (paragraphs 95–108) pp. 404–407.

monetary gain – whether it be higher pay than is given to the regular armed forces of the state or by way of bonuses for persons killed or captured. The definition must be so framed, however, that the individual who enlists as a regular member of the armed forces because he is attracted by good pay is not on that account deemed to be a mercenary. The establishment of a person's motivation may pose some problems of proof.[169]

Nigeria's original proposal was thus expanded, for example by the idea that a mercenary was to be paid more than a regular soldier. At the same time, the problem remained how to differentiate among individuals who enlisted in an army *also* because they were attracted by a payroll. In other words, the mixed motivations found in some defendants at the Luanda trial had re-emerged.

While it was generally accepted that a mercenary was recruited either locally or abroad to participate in a specific conflict, a further condition was proposed by some delegations: a mercenary 'was not a national of a party to the conflict'.[170] Yet the other side of the coin was constituted by foreign advisers and technicians, particularly favoured by the Soviets and Cubans.[171] Additionally, there seemed to be a loophole in the definition: states could have simply made mercenaries members of their armed forces in order to grant them prisoner of war status.[172] Callan's men were said to have been fighting within the ranks of the FNLA, and to have gone to Angola to train FNLA troops. Again, the thorny question of whether those who enlisted did so for financial gain continued to worry many.[173] The tricky point was to demonstrate the intentionality of the actors involved, and to prove that the mercenaries were paid more than the regular soldiers of a given army.[174]

---

[169] *Ibid.*, pp. 405–406.
[170] *Ibid.*, p. 406.
[171] *Ibid.*
[172] *Ibid.*
[173] *Ibid.*
[174] Finally, there was the question of the minimum protection to be granted to mercenaries. Even if they were to be excluded from prisoner of war status, some delegations believed that it was desirable to place them under the fundamental guarantees laid out by draft Art. 65, later codified as Art. 75. 'All who spoke in the Working Group believed that as a minimum, persons found to be mercenaries should be entitled to be treated humanely and in accordance with the national law of the capturing Power. But some delegations thought that this was not enough. Mercenaries, even if found to be such, should receive the protection accorded by article 65 of draft Protocol I; even the worst of sinners is entitled to basic safeguards. Other delegations opposed the application of article 65 to

2.4 THE NOBILITY OF THE CAUSE MATTERS 145

Overall, the points raised within the working group made it clear that more specific criteria were needed to identify mercenaries and to draw the necessary distinctions with other types of combatants. The talks on this article were adjourned to the next session, and the Nigerian delegation took the opportunity to redraw its original proposal and engaged in private consultations with the other delegations.[175] The result of these discussions crystallized in a new article which was presented to the Third Committee one year later (April 1977) and was this time accepted by consensus. Art. 47 qualified the role of mercenaries in international armed conflicts, excluding them from the combatant's privilege:

1. A mercenary shall not have the right to be a combatant or a prisoner of war.
2. A mercenary is any person who:

    (a) is specially recruited locally or abroad in order to fight in an armed conflict;

    (b) does, in fact, take a direct part in the hostilities;

    (c) is motivated to take part in the hostilities essentially by the desire for private gain and, in fact, is promised, by or on behalf of a Party to the conflict, material compensation substantially in excess of that promised or paid to combatants of similar ranks and functions in the armed forces of that Party;

    (d) is neither a national of a Party to the conflict nor a resident of territory controlled by a Party to the conflict;

    (e) is not a member of the armed forces of a Party to the conflict; and

    (f) has not been sent by a State which is not a Party to the conflict on official duty as a member of its armed forces.[176]

Art. 47 therefore included the points highlighted the previous year by the working group. Thanks to private consultations, Nigeria had managed to introduce a proposal on which all states could agree. As the six qualifications had to be read cumulatively, mercenaries were seen as foreigners (sub-paragraph d) going to fight abroad and taking direct action on the battlefield for material compensation. This compensation was superior to that of other combatants enrolled in the same army.[177]

---

mercenaries, whose barbarities should place them outside the protection of international law.' *Ibid.*, p. 407.

[175] See ICRC, *Commentary*, p. 574.

[176] Text is reported in Official Records, Vol. XV, p. 481.

[177] As specified in the subsequent report of the Third Committee, released after the voting on the finalized article: 'Recognizing that some ranks and functions in armed forces are likely to be paid more than others, the draft, in paragraph 2 (c) provides an objective test

During the *travaux* of the working group, it had also been declared that a 'mercenary might be a career fighter or killer, but if a person makes a career of fighting in support of one and only one State, it seems rather difficult to regard him as a mercenary'.[178] In other words, Western states could now exclude from Art. 47 those career fighters and long-lasting volunteers enrolled in the ranks of the French and Spanish Foreign Legions, the Swiss Guards or the British Gurkhas.[179]

Sub-paragraph (b) also excluded foreign advisers and technicians, if they did not take any direct part in hostilities. This provision – mirroring the interests of states from the Eastern bloc – was complemented by sub-paragraph (f), which barred from the definition of mercenarism those troops sent on behalf of a third state on official duty. Overall, these two sub-paragraphs showed how mercenaries were seen as uncontrolled, non-state actors moving from one war zone to another on their own, and not as troops invited by a party in the conflict to perform advisory or technical roles. This vision is reminiscent of the proscription of hostile expeditions, already encountered during the interwar years.

Regarding the pecuniary motivation behind enlisting (sub-paragraph c), this requirement turned out to be one of the most problematic. Some delegations still saw this condition as not pertinent to the overall scope of a humanitarian treaty which should strictly differentiate between *jus ad bellum* and *jus in bello* motives.[180] Sub-paragraph (e) appeared even more dubious. As already evidenced by some delegations during the *travaux* of the working group, states could have simply made mercenaries members of their armed forces, thus invalidating the entire anti-mercenary norm.[181]

---

to help determine motivations of persons serving with the armed forces of a Party to the conflict; such persons may not be considered to be motivated essentially by the desire for private gain unless they are promised compensation substantially in excess of that promised or paid to combatants of similar rank and function in the armed forces of that Party. Thus, pilots would be judged by the same standards of compensation as other pilots, not by the standard of infantrymen. Several representatives criticized this paragraph as providing a possible escape for some mercenaries.' *Ibid.*, specifically CDDH/407/Rev. 1, p. 455.

[178] *Ibid.*, specifically CDDH/236/Rev. 1, p. 406.
[179] See ICRC, *Commentary*, p. 578.
[180] And thus, introducing a psychological element within a humanitarian text. On this point see specifically Percy, *Mercenaries*, pp. 178–179.
[181] 'A number of delegations thought that a person would not be a mercenary if he were enrolled in the armed forces of a State and that the definition of mercenary should therefore include the statement that he is not a member of the armed forces of a party to the conflict. Other delegations pointed to the fact that a State employing mercenaries

2.4 THE NOBILITY OF THE CAUSE MATTERS

From their side, Western states seemed to tacitly agree with the article voted on. The stronger criticism was directed towards the fact that Art. 47 did not contain any specific guarantees. The delegates of Australia, Switzerland, the United States, Ireland, Portugal, Italy, Sweden, Canada and the Netherlands reiterated their call for minimum protection to be granted to all types of combatants on the battlefield, even if unlawful ones. Perhaps the harshest comment came from the delegation of the Holy See, which also captured well the context in which Art. 47 was proposed: 'it was hardly admissible that an article relating to humanitarian law should be more the *expression of a passion* than of cold reason and justice, going so far as virtually to exclude from the human community men whose designation was unilateral and therefore, to say the least, questionable'.[182]

It is significant that, already at the time, Art. 47 was understood as a compromise between different states' attitudes towards mercenarism.[183]

---

could avoid having them lose combatant and prisoner-of-war status simply by making them members of the armed forces; they therefore opposed excluding members of the armed forces from the category of mercenaries.' Official Records, Vol. XV, CDDH/236/Rev. 1, p. 406.

[182] *See* Official Records, Vol. VI, p. 158. Emphasis added. Finally, the Dutch voiced their disagreement towards an article that did not get to the root of the mercenaries' problem but was only dealing with these actors once they were on the battlefield. For them, in fact 'the application of humanitarian law and the granting of humanitarian treatment should not be made dependent on some one's motivation for taking part on the armed conflict'. *Ibid.*, p. 194. For a similar argument in relation to the overall construction of API see Jessica Whyte, 'The "Dangerous Concept of the Just War": Decolonization, Wars of National Liberation, and the Additional Protocols to the Geneva Conventions' (2018) 9 *Humanity Journal* 313–341.

[183] The compromising nature of this article and its ambiguities were evident in many states' declarations after the vote. Although saluting the adoption of Art. 47 as a 'fatal blow to the mercenaries who wreaked endless havoc in Africa', the Nigerian delegation also recognized that '[this article] was a compromise text which had been carefully considered over a period of three years'. *See* Official Records, Vol. XV, p. 192. The delegate of Zaire was even more explicit. Stating that his delegation 'would have preferred a text that was more stringent in its provisions . . . and more detailed in the obligations placed on States in whose territories mercenaries were recruited', he also pointed out how it would have been difficult to collect the evidence proving the higher remuneration paid to mercenaries, so as to fulfil the requirement of sub-paragraph (c). Official Records, Vol. XV, p. 193. The very same concern was expressed by Mauritania, whose delegate suggested that the final article should have covered all types of mercenaries as '[they] were not always motivated by the desire for material gain'. Official Records, Vol. XV, p. 194. The Senegalese delegation, although praising the achievement made in defining a notion of mercenarism, also wished for a stronger text that 'would have obliged States to forbid the recruitment, training or assembling of mercenaries'. *See* Official Records, Vol.

Despite its evident loopholes, many recognized that the text was 'the most that could be achieved'[184] and that it 'contributed to the development of humanitarian law'.[185] For many, it seemed obvious that this represented the first natural step towards a more comprehensive treaty. As non-Western delegates expressed their wish that 'the new article would encourage Governments ... to take the necessary legislative action in order to eliminate the crime of the mercenary system',[186] they also recognized that 'although imprecise [the article] reflects the need to regulate all matters relating to the activities of mercenaries in an international convention'.[187] In other words, Art. 47 constituted a launching pad for the countries engaged in the struggle for self-determination. Nothing prevented a move towards a more detailed and complete convention in the years to come.

Things did not change much in the immediate aftermath of Geneva, however. Interestingly, the same problems evidenced throughout the Spanish Civil War resurfaced. Disagreement regarding whether mercenaries should have been distinguished from foreign volunteers is traceable in the writings of international legal scholars of the time, for instance.[188] Before the codification of Art. 47 much of the scholarly discussions

VI, p. 197. As the delegations of Libya, Vietnam, Czechoslovakia, Mozambique and Mali reiterated this point, Cuba lamented the lack of reference in the article to the responsibility of States in the whole business of mercenaries. See Official Records, Vol. VI, p. 197. While the Italian delegation did not hide the fact that the article 'was not altogether satisfactory, since it left some margin of discretion as to whether a person was a mercenary or not', the delegate of Syria reiterated the problem posed by sub-paragraph (e), probably the most striking loophole in the mercenaries' qualification. See Official Records, Vol. VI, p. 159 and Vol. XV, p. 197.

[184] See Official Records, Vol. XV, p. 200, specifically Ivory Coast.
[185] Ibid., p. 195, specifically Romania.
[186] Ibid., p. 194, specifically Hungary, and pp. 202–204, Soviet Union: 'The Soviet delegation expresses its deep satisfaction on the occasion of the adoption by consensus of the article on mercenaries. This article is one of the more important articles. of Protocol I, and is of great significance both politically and in the context of international law ... The article adopted on mercenaries is the result of prolonged work by Committee III, and it represents a compromise. It would of course have been more nearly perfect if it had included such elements as the establishment of the liability of States which permit or encourage the recruitment, training or use of mercenaries. We understand, however, that the article as worded represents the best compromise that could be achieved at the present time, and we accordingly endorsed it.'
[187] Ibid., p. 185, specifically Cuba.
[188] See Abdulqawi A. Yusuf, 'Mercenaries in the Law of Armed Conflicts', in Antonio Cassese (ed.), *The New Humanitarian Law of Armed Conflict* (Napoli: Editoriale Scientifica 1979) 113–127.

2.4 THE NOBILITY OF THE CAUSE MATTERS 149

focused on how to determine the status of mercenaries, comparable to today's struggle to find a suitable definition for foreign fighters.[189] Immediately after the Geneva talks, the debates shifted on whether mercenaries should have been granted POW rights, or at least a minimum amount of protection.[190] Overall, scholars tended to agree on the evident limits of the Luanda trial, yet failed to find a suitable solution to the mercenaries' problem. Many argued that the countries of origin should have exercised better control over their citizens, although recognizing the downside of hampering individual freedoms.[191] Others wondered whether specific duties and responsibilities could be imposed on states.[192] As much as with foreign volunteers in the Spanish case, mercenarism did not involve only the actors on the battlefield, but required mechanisms of recruitment, training and travel. The relevance of neutrality laws were once again put in question, especially by American legal scholars;[193] as was the case four decades earlier, many resorted to the founding fathers of international law.[194] Both Eric David and Antonio Cassese noted that 'le mercenaire c'est l'autre, c'est l'ennemi, c'est l'adversaire',[195] and thus questioned the problematic

---

[189] See specifically Robert E. Jr. Cesner and John W. Brant, 'Law of the Mercenary: An International Dilemma' (1977) 6 *Capital University Law Review* 339–370.

[190] See specifically John Robert Cotton, 'Comment: The Rights of Mercenaries as Prisoners of War' (1977) 77 *Military Law Review* 143–166; Josiane Tercinet, 'Les Mercenaires et le Droit international' (1977) 23 *Annuaire français de droit international* 269–293; Henry W. Van Deventer, 'Mercenaries at Geneva' (1976) 70 *American Journal of International Law* 811–816; and Riley Martin, 'Mercenaries and the Rule of Law' (1976) 17 *International Commission of Jurists Review* 51–57.

[191] 'The modern state can, and must exercise control over its nationals so as to prevent their involvement in activities contrary to international law and, in particular, so as to enable the state to fulfill its own obligation to respect the territorial integrity and political independence of other states.' H. C. Burmester, 'The Recruitment and Use of Mercenaries in Armed Conflict' (1978) 72 *American Journal of International Law* 37–56, p. 45.

[192] See Edwin I. Nwogugu, 'Recent Developments in the Law Relating to Mercenaries' (1981) 20 *Military Law & Law of War Review* 9–34.

[193] Grant E. Courtney, 'American Mercenaries and the Neutrality Act: Shortening the Leash on the Dogs of War' (1985) 12 *Journal of Legislation* 175–193 and Allaoua Layeb, 'Mercenary Activity: United States Neutrality Laws and Enforcement' (1989) 10 *New York Law School Journal of International and Comparative Law* 269–307.

[194] See specifically L. C. Green, 'The Status of Mercenaries in International Law' (1978–1979) 9 *Manitoba Law Journal* 201–246 and Tahar Boumedra, 'International Regulation of the Use of Mercenaries in Armed Conflicts' (1981) 20 *Military Law & Law of War Review* 35–87.

[195] David, 'Les Mercenaires en Droit International', p. 211.

reduction of these actors to the category of unlawful combatants.[196] Volunteers were not been spared such a characterization; they were accused of being more or less 'genuine' (and thus more or less legitimate) during the Spanish Civil War years. And such a portrayal would resurface even more dramatically in the decades to come under the threat posed by international terrorism.

In sum, the ambiguities that had characterized the 1975–1977 Geneva talks were not to be resolved easily, even when the work of the Ad Hoc Committee charged with drafting an international convention on mercenaries began. In particular, the Committee moved from the assumption that there was a fragmented approach on the issue of mercenarism and that 'municipal laws were ineffective ... and inadequate in stopping the recruitment and outfitting of mercenaries'.[197] Art. 47 was criticized for being too vague, and a stronger bond with the responsibility of states for the actions of mercenaries was requested by many delegations, including against states 'which acted tolerantly ... or failed to take effective measures against such activities'.[198] This call, however, collided with the will of Western countries, which refused to see codified a form of absolute responsibility for the actions of their citizens abroad.[199] After ten years of negotiations, the Convention was finally concluded in 1989. Entering into force in 2001, it expanded the scope and strengthened the definition of Art. 47. To date, however, only a handful of Western states have ratified it.[200] Doubts remain on the actual applicability of the law, particularly how and where mercenaries are to be sentenced. The recent appearance of private military companies has now put in question the

---

[196] Antonio Cassese, 'Mercenaries: Lawful Combatants or War Criminals?' (1980) 40 ZaöRV 1–30. See also W. Thomas Mallison, 'The Juridical Status of Irregular Combatants under the International Humanitarian Law of Armed Conflict' (1977) 9 Case Western Reserve Journal of International Law 39–78.

[197] See Report of the Ad Hoc Committee on the Drafting of an International Convention against the Recruitment, Use, Financing and Training of Mercenaries (1981). Official Records, 36th Session, Supplement 43 (A/36/43) p. 7.

[198] Ibid., p. 15.

[199] See Percy, Mercenaries, pp. 198–202.

[200] International Convention against the Recruitment, Use, Financing and Training of Mercenaries, adopted by A/44/49 (New York, 4 December 1989). For a compelling study regarding the ineffectiveness of the rules against mercenarism see specifically Hin-Yan Liu and Christopher Kinsey, 'Challenging the Strength of the Antimercenary Norm' (2018) 3 Journal of Global Security Studies 93–110.

relevance of the UN Convention and necessitates a complete reformulation of international norms on mercenarism.[201]

These issues fall outside the scope of this work. However, the cultural aspects surrounding Art. 47 of AP I should be highlighted. Throughout the Geneva talks the figure of the greedy, racist mercenary was not only opposed to that of the anti-colonial fighter, but particularly to the noble, idealistic volunteer of the previous time. These two figures stood in stark contrast to each other, with the latter being evoked to delegitimize the dishonourable enterprises of the white soldiers of fortune. As illustrated by the ICRC:

> Nowadays mercenaries only represent one section of the vast category of international volunteers who are defined *lato sensu* as individuals whose voluntary personal membership of an armed force involves certain elements of a foreign character ... In contrast to a volunteer who is moved by a noble ideal, the mercenary is considered to offer his services to the highest bidder, since he is essentially motivated by material gain [there is] a distinction between mercenaries pursuing their own 'interests' and selfless international volunteers.[202]

In other words, mercenaries came to represent the 'bad' or rotten side of foreign volunteers. And so, the perceived nobility of the latter's cause was still present in the imaginary of many delegations and was taken as a touchstone to differentiate the white soldiers of fortune from the heroes of the Spanish Civil War.

2.5 Conclusion

Throughout decolonization, mercenarism became a symbol of Western interference in the former European colonies. The Luanda trial (Section 2.1) captured the way in which the white, racist, right-wing mercenary was now seen as a professional soldier of fortune seeking to hamper self-determination. On the other side stood the freedom fighters sent by Russia and Cuba to help their Third World comrades. Beyond the

---

[201] See Katherine Fallah, 'Corporate Actors: The Legal Status of Mercenaries in Armed Conflict' (2006) 88 *International Review of the Red Cross* 599–611 and Juan Carlos Zarate, 'The Emergence of a New Dog of War: Private International Security Companies, International Law, and the New World Disorder' (1998) 34 *Stanford Journal of International Law* 75–162.
[202] See ICRC, *Commentary*, pp. 577–580.

ideological confrontation of the East–West blocs, however, the figure of the white mercenary was more ambivalent that one might think.

Section 2.2 retraced the discussions of state representatives at the United Nations, in a time span ranging from the Congo Crisis (1960–1967) to the Luanda trial (1976). There, we could see how the figure of the adventurer was still very much present in the imaginary of Western delegates. This is evidenced by Spaak's comparison of his compatriots in Congo with the heroes of the Spanish Civil War. Somehow a noble lineage connected the images of Byron, Lafayette, and the International Brigades to the soldiers of fortune active in Africa. On top of epitomizing a different conception of freedom from the one championed by the Soviets, these cultural references indicated a split in the consciousness of Europeans between the recognition of the right to self-determination and a nostalgic attitude towards their former colonies.

This vision clashed with the one informing the speeches of Third World states. For them, the figure of the mercenary carried completely different and more disturbing connotation: that of the former European masters. But the contrast between white mercenaries and anti-colonial freedom fighters was not straightforward either. The image of the cynical Comintern soldier resurfaced in the discourse of those states that were disapproving of the imperialist attitude of the Soviets in Africa. Alongside Byron and the heroes of the Spanish Civil War, other figures reappeared, contributing to the problematic systematization of foreign combatants in the categories of law.

Section 2.3 retraced the domestic debates in the United Kingdom as a reaction to the indictments of UK citizens in Angola. At the House of Commons, the discussions revolved around the question of how to distinguish mercenaries from other types of foreign volunteers. There, former figures came back to inform the position of the British legislator. As seen with Spaak at the Security Council, some British politicians believed that the so-called mercenaries were nothing more than individuals moved by political ideals. The figure of Byron re-emerged, alongside those colonial troops already encountered at The Hague in 1907. The British legislator was therefore the hostage of some long-standing images, through which was framed the difficult decision of whom to consider a mercenary and whom a volunteer. Aware of this, Prime Minister Wilson recognized that his government was mainly interested in outlawing the private actors who benefited from the mercenary business. The image of those freebooters who were condemned in the 1930s is still part of the story.

2.5 CONCLUSION

The chapter ended in Geneva. Section 2.4 retraced the *travaux préparatoires* of Art. 47 of Additional Protocol I. Even though the question of mercenarism was not originally included in the agenda, it resurfaced quite naturally during the discussions. A majority of Third World states pushed for a distinction to be made between new categories of combatants and Western soldiers of fortune. At the same time, the finalized text of Art. 47 was strongly influenced by the main figure that had characterized the discussions of the previous era: mercenaries in Geneva were in fact understood as one minor part of the larger category of foreign volunteers and as such, representing their 'bad' and immoral side.

Although four decades separated Spain from Angola, the Luanda trial once again made it clear that the law on foreign fighters was still largely vague and inadequate. The laissez-fare attitude, typical of the interwar period, was now being backed by the need to respect human rights. Beneath the surface of foreign policy concerns, however, ambivalent passions were at play. In particular, the ambiguous attitude of European countries towards their former colonies. Oscillating between a form of paternalism and the desire to keep possession over the African continent, this split in conscience contributed to a fundamental ambivalence in the law. Despite the developments reached at Geneva in 1977, the status of foreign fighters was still not clarified in the decades to come.

3

Enemies of Humanity or Freedom Fighters?

The Jihadist Combatant in the Syrian Civil War

3.1 Faceless, Nameless Enemies

Paris, 13 November 2015. Three groups of commandos perpetrate one of the bloodiest attacks on civilians in France's recent history. Soon after, the Islamic State (IS) releases a statement claiming responsibility and declaring that the actions were conducted in retaliation for French airstrikes in Syria and Iraq earlier that year. A few months later, on 22 March 2016, Brussels is hit by a series of bombings approved by the same organization. London, Istanbul, Nice, Berlin. The list grows longer and adds to a trail of bloodshed that bears the signature of the Islamic State. Little more than a decade after 9/11, a new threat to security seems to be menacing the international community.

Born from the ashes of the Sunni/Baathist Iraqi army of Saddam Hussein, the Islamic State had gradually moved away from Al-Qaeda and its affiliates to rise as a separate entity and take the leading role in the transnational jihad.[1] This self-proclaimed Caliphate quickly conquered vast areas of Syrian territory, launching an open war on its opponents and contenders. Most importantly, it started to attract a large number of foreign fighters to its ranks.[2] Conversely, the return of these fighters

---

[1] See Phyllis Bennis, *Understanding ISIS and the New Global War on Terror: A Primer* (Northampton, MA: Olive Branch Press 2015); Daniel Byman, *Al Qaeda, the Islamic State and the Global Jihadist Movement: What Everyone Needs to Know* (Oxford: Oxford University Press 2015); Micheal Weiss and Hassan Hassan, *Isis: Inside the Army of Terror* (New York: Regan Arts 2015); and Patrick Cockburn, *The Rise of the Islamic State: Isis and the New Sunni Revolution* (London: Verso Books 2015). See also Fawaz Gerges, *The Far Enemy: Why Jihad Went Global* (Cambridge: Cambridge University Press 2009).

[2] The actual numbers of foreign volunteers have of course shifted over the years. See Edwin Bakker and Mark Singleton, 'Foreign Fighters in the Syria and Iraq Conflict: Statistics and Characteristics of a Rapidly Growing Phenomenon', in A. de Guttry et al. (eds.), *Foreign Fighters under International Law* (The Hague: Asser Press 2016) 9–25.

from the battlefield soon raised serious concerns in their home countries.[3]

In a way, this situation is reminiscent of what we have seen in both Spain and Angola: a civil war attracting an influx of foreign nationals and reopening the unresolved issues outlined in previous chapters. To which is added the security concern posed by those individuals returning to their countries of origin – an aspect did not have serious consequences in the former instances, but that is now perceived as a serious threat in the new world order brought about by 9/11.[4]

However, foreign nationals enlisting within the ranks of the Islamic State were not the only foreign fighters present on Syrian soil. Many Western citizens joined other factions in the war, including Europeans arriving in Syria to take arms against the IS.[5] The landscape was therefore multifaceted, composed of many non-state armed groups, including contingents of mercenaries and contractors working alongside the

---

[3] At least one of the leading figures of the Paris plot had gone to Syria to receive military training, while other attacks were also perpetrated by returnees, or by individuals who had entered in contact with them. See specifically Kim R. Cragin, 'The November 2015 Paris Attacks: The Impact of Foreign Fighter Returnees' (2017) 61 *Orbis* 212–226. On the threat posed by returnees see Pokalova, *Returning Islamist Foreign Fighters Threats and Challenges to the West*; Kim R. Cragin, 'The Challenge of Foreign Fighters Returnees' (2017) 33 *Journal of Contemporary Criminal Justice* 292–312; Daniel Byman, 'The Jihadist Returnee Threat: Just How Dangerous?' (2016) 131 *Political Science Quarterly* 66–99; Edwin Bakker and Christoph Paulussen, 'Returning Jihadist Foreign Fighters Challenges Pertaining to Threat Assessment and Governance of this Pan-European Problem' (2014) 25 *Security and Human Rights* 11–32; and David Malet and Rachel Hayes, 'Foreign Fighter Returnees: An Indefinite Threat?' (2020) 32 *Terrorism and Political Violence* 1617–1635.

[4] This is of course an overgeneralization and the dynamics varied from country to country. Some of the Spanish Civil War volunteers were considered a danger upon their return by their own governments, as bearers of revolutionary and radical-leftist ideals. For the case of American volunteers see specifically Carroll, *The Odyssey of the Abraham Lincoln Brigade*, pp. 209–359. See also David Malet and Jason E. Fritz, 'Historical Responses to Foreign Fighters and Returnees', in Francesca Capone, Christophe Paulussen and Rebecca Mignot-Mahdavi (eds.), *Returning Foreign Fighters: Responses, Legal Challenges and Ways Forward* (The Hague: Asser Press 2023) 33–48.

[5] In the abundant literature concerning Western foreign fighters present on Syrian territory, and particularly those fighting against the Islamic State, see specifically: Kyle Orton, 'The Secular Foreign Fighters of the West in Syria' (2018) 20 *Insight Turkey* 157–178; Henry Tuck, Tanya Silverman and Candace Smalley, '"Shooting in the Right Direction": Anti-ISIS Foreign Fighters in Syria & Iraq' (2016) 1 *Institute for Strategic Dialogue* 1–55; Edoardo Corradi, 'Joining the Fight: The Italian Foreign Fighters Contingent of the Kurdish People's Protection Units' (2022) *Italian Political Science Review* 1–19; and Kyle Orton, 'The Forgotten Foreign Fighters: The PKK in Syria' (2017) The Henry Jackson Society, available at https://henryjacksonsociety.org/wp-content/uploads/2017/08/3053-PYD-Foreign-Fighter-Project-1.pdf.

Assad government.⁶ For the purposes of this study, the focus will be kept on the foreign fighters joining the Islamic State and Al-Nusra Front, and those joining the ranks of the Kurdish groups, such as the People's Protection Unit (YPG). As in the case of Spain and Angola, in the Syrian scenario an ideological battle unfolded, opposing different conceptions of freedom.

And yet a major shift had occurred. The attack on the Twin Towers and the war on international terrorism changed the cards on the table. In previous civil wars, groups of combatants were present on the ground; but never a transnational organization that altered the parameters of warfare to which international lawyers were accustomed.⁷ Similar to the case of Al-Qaeda, the international community engaged in an asymmetrical conflict, a continuation of the war on terror inaugurated by the Bush administration and revived by France in response to the terrorist attacks on its soil.⁸

This shift also had an effect on how foreign fighters were perceived. In particular, a new cultural type of foreign volunteer appeared. With a new history, a new genealogy, even a new aesthetic, this volunteer is portrayed very differently from the heroic idealists of the Spanish Civil War and the racist, right-wing mercenaries.⁹ Let's look into this aspect more closely. In September 2014, one year before the Paris attacks, the UN Security Council had criminalized those individuals willing to go

---

⁶ Micheal A. Rizzotti, 'Russian Mercenaries, State Responsibility, and Conflict in Syria: Examining the Wagner Group under International Law' (2020) 37 *Wisconsin International Law Journal* 571–614.

⁷ On this point see Raul A. Pedrozo and Daria P. Wollschlaeger, *International Law and the Changing Character of War* (Newport, RI: Naval War College 2011). For a critical assessment see Frédéric Mégret, '"War"? Legal Semantics and the Move to Violence' (2002) 13 *European Journal of International Law* 361–399. See also more generally Helen Duffy, *The 'War on Terror' and the Framework of International Law. 2nd Edition* (Cambridge: Cambridge University Press 2015).

⁸ American President G. W. Bush addressed a joint session of Congress nine days after the 9/11 attacks, claiming to be at war against terror, and characterizing the war against Al-Qaeda as a new kind of asymmetric warfare. After the November 2015 Paris attacks, French Prime Minister Manuel Valls reiterated the idea of being at war against terror. With reference to the Islamic State see specifically Michael Scharf, 'How the War against ISIS Changed International Law' (2016) *Case Western Reserve Journal of International Law* 1–54 and Antonio Coco and Jean-Baptiste Maillart, 'The Conflict with Islamic State: A Critical Review of International Legal Issues', in Annyssa Bellal (ed.), *The War Report. Armed Conflict in 2014* (Oxford: Oxford University Press 2015) 388–419.

⁹ It is important to stress that these are not the only foreign fighters present in contemporary warfare scenarios. See Kacper Rekawek, *Not only Syria: the Phenomenon of Foreign Fighters in a Comparative Perspective* (Amsterdam: IOS Press 2017).

fighting in Syria, classifying them as 'foreign terrorist fighters'. Resolution 2178 gave for the first time legal status to our actor as: 'individuals who travel to a State other than their States of residence or nationality for the purpose of the perpetration, planning, or preparation of, or participation in, terrorist acts or the providing or receiving of terrorist training, including in connection with armed conflict'.[10]

From the Hague Peace Conferences, through the 1949 Geneva Conventions (GC) and the Additional Protocol, foreign fighters seemed to have attained a concrete standing in the international arena. Leaving aside debates on whether the resolution can really be interpreted as creating any legal status at all, what is important to highlight is how different the landscape looks if compared with previous times.[11] Unlike the hesitant position of the League, and the confrontation of the East–West blocs during decolonization, in 2014 the Security Council undertook a clear decision. By unanimously adopting Resolution 2178 under Chapter VII, the Council had associated foreign fighters with international terrorists. Let's once again enter the UN, to see how the representatives of states characterized this new actor on the day of the vote on the text.

Ban Ki-moon opened the 7272nd meeting on 24 September. After having cheered the unanimous adoption of the resolution, the Secretary General commented: 'the world is witnessing a dramatic evolution in the nature of the terrorist threat ... those groups [the Islamic State and al-Nusra] have become a magnet for foreign terrorist fighters ... The growing phenomenon of foreign terrorist fighters is a consequence, not a cause, of the conflict in Syria'.[12] Another civil war, other foreign nationals involved in the battlefield, yet this time it was a short step to classify them as terrorists.

---

[10] S/RES/2178, preamble.

[11] On this aspect *see* specifically Vesselin Popovski and Trudy Fraser (eds.), *The Security Council as a Global Legislator* (New York: Routledge 2014). On the question concerning the legal status of foreign terrorist fighters derived from Resolution 2178 see specifically Anne Peters, 'Security Council Resolution 2178 (2014): The "Foreign Terrorist Fighter" as an International Legal Person, Part I' (20 November 2014) *EJIL:Talk!*, available at www.ejiltalk.org/security-council-resolution-2178-2014-the-foreign-terrorist-fighter-as-an-international-legal-person-part-i/, and, by the same author, 'Security Council Resolution 2178 (2014): The "Foreign Terrorist Fighter" as an International Legal Person, Part II' (21 November 2014) *EJIL:Talk!*, available at www.ejiltalk.org/security-council-resolution-2178-2014-the-foreign-terrorist-fighter-as-an-international-legal-person-part-ii/.

[12] UN Security Council Official Records, 7272nd meeting (24 September 2014) pp. 2–3.

It was then the turn of Barack Obama: 'what bring us together today ... is the unprecedented flow of fighters in recent years to and from conflict zones ... they may try to return to their home countries to carry deadly attacks'.[13] The speech almost sounds as a warning of what would happen about a year later in the heart of Paris. But Obama also wanted to make things clear in a legal sense: 'the historic resolution that we have just adopted ... it is legally binding. It establishes new obligations that nations must meet'.[14] In addition to providing a status, Resolution 2178 established a series of provisions aimed at preventing the recruitment, equipping, financing and travel of foreign fighters into war zones. In other words, the document highlighted the need for specific measures to control the flow of certain people towards certain areas of the world.[15]

As Obama concluded his speech with 'for if there was ever a challenge in our interconnected world ... is this one – terrorists crossing borders and threatening to unleash unspeakable violence',[16] the representative of Nigeria took this idea further: 'we now have mobile bands – thousands of terrorists sweeping across vast areas, destroying lives and even attempting to hold territory'.[17] Although the reference to mobile bands could recall those hostile military expeditions encountered decades earlier, it is evident that we are in a very different era from the one of the League. The ambiguity showed by many state representatives on how to stop volunteers has disappeared. A new, frightening transnational actor means everyone at the Council agreed: 'the events of 9/11 brought the fight against terrorism to the top of the global agenda ... foreign terrorist fighters ... they slip across borders to spread terror. They are a scourge to humankind ... the fight against faceless and nameless

---

[13] *Ibid.*, pp. 3–4.
[14] *Ibid.*, p. 4.
[15] In particular, Resolution 2178: '*Reaffirms* that all States shall prevent the movement of terrorists or terrorist groups by effective border controls and controls on issuance of identity papers and travel documents, and through measures for preventing counterfeiting, forgery or fraudulent use of identity papers and travel documents ... *Urges* Member States, in accordance with domestic and international law, to intensify and accelerate the exchange of operational information regarding actions or movements of terrorists or terrorist networks, including foreign terrorist fighters ... *Decides* that Member States shall ... prevent and suppress the recruiting, organizing, transporting or equipping of individuals who travel to a State other than their States of residence or nationality for the purpose of the perpetration, planning, or preparation of, or participation in, terrorist acts or the providing or receiving of terrorist training, and the financing of their travel and of their activities.' S/RES/2178, p. 4.
[16] UNSC, 7272nd meeting (24 September 2014) p. 4.
[17] *Ibid.*, p. 5.

terrorists without borders will not be easy', as the President of the Republic of Korea remarked.[18]

We have thus abandoned the heroic, honourable figures of Garibaldi, Byron and Lafayette. The Council is facing a 'faceless, nameless' enemy, an enemy that moves across borders spreading terror. Adopting the famous expression of Vattel, foreign terrorist fighters have now become the enemies of humanity of the post-9/11 world, an idea reiterated by China: 'terrorists defy the fundamental human rights and challenge the foundations of human civilization. As such, they are humankind's common enemy'.[19]

The image of the pirate evoked at the Council was not a new one. It had been utilized a decade earlier to designate those unlawful combatants fighting against the American forces in Afghanistan and Iraq; and during decolonization, when Third World countries wished to outlaw the actions of mercenaries on the African continent.[20] But there is more to the story. Foreign terrorist fighters are not just enemies of humanity with no names. They do have a tradition, they come with a genealogy. In the words of the Singaporean representative: 'an estimated 12,000 foreigners from over 70 countries have participated in the conflicts in Iraq and Syria. That is the largest mobilization of foreign militants since the Soviet–Afghan War in 1980s ... The Soviet–Afghan war drew in thousands of foreign fighters, led to the creation of Al-Qaida and inspired the creation of other terrorist groups'.[21] In the Council room one see some characters emerging that had not been encountered before. A few minutes earlier, the representative of Argentina had commented in a similar tone: 'Osama Bin Laden was trained by the Taliban to confront Russia during the Cold War ... as it turns out, many of these *freedom fighters* were fundamentalists who had received military training and who today are fighting under ISIS and recruiting young people.'[22]

---

[18] *Ibid.*, pp. 12–13.
[19] *Ibid.*, p. 17.
[20] See George C. Harris, 'Terrorism, War and Justice: The Concept of the Unlawful Enemy Combatant' (2003) 26 *Loyola of Los Angeles International & Comparative Law Review* 31–46. On the concept of enemy of humanity see specifically Walter Rech, *Enemies of Mankind: Vattel's Theory of Collective Security* (Leiden: Martinus Nijhoff 2013).
[21] Singapore representative's speech. UNSC, 7272nd meeting (24 September 2014) p. 36.
[22] UNSC, 7272nd meeting (24 September 2014). Emphasis added. Pointing to the same genealogy, see the speech of the Chadian representative: 'The phenomenon of foreign combatants, whether yesterday in Afghanistan or today in Syria and Iraq is sometimes exacerbated by outside interference.' *Ibid.*, p. 7.

This is a story probably heard before, as it often resonates in the political debates surrounding the 9/11 attacks and the subsequent war in Afghanistan.[23] What is significant is that a new genealogy – and a new figure – of the foreign fighter is evoked by the representatives of states sit at the Council. Its archetype is no longer represented by the Garibaldis, the Byrons, or the Lafayettes though, and certainly not by the heroes of the International Brigades. Rather, by the Mujahideen of the Soviet–Afghan war (Figure 3.1). What has been termed the 'Muslim foreign fighter', has now permeated the official discourse, and has entered the imaginary of international policymakers, replacing the memory of former virtuous volunteers.[24]

The point of this historical digression is not to enter the debates pertaining to another era, one in which the East–West confrontation was still influencing international politics. Nor is it to raise a wider point on the reversal of alliances between the United States, the Soviet Union and the Mujahideen, from the 1980s to the events of 2001.[25] Rather, it is to witness a change in the discourse on the foreign fighter, and to show how a different figure underpins the imaginary of world leaders adopting Resolution 2178. Finally, this reference is interesting precisely because it attests to a further important cultural detail: even if those volunteers

---

[23] Among the vast literature concerned with the role of the United States in funding the Mujahideen, and on the further links between the CIA and bin Laden, see specifically Steve Coll, *Ghost Wars: The Secret History of the CIA, Afghanistan, and bin Laden, from the Soviet Invasion to September 10, 2001* (New York: Penguin 2005).

[24] 'A salient feature of armed conflict in the Muslim world since 1980 is the involvement of so-called foreign fighters, that is unpaid combatants with no apparent link to the conflict other than religious affinity with the Muslim side ... most transnational jihadi groups today are by-products of foreign fighter mobilizations. Foreign fighters are therefore key to understanding transnational Islamist militancy.' Hegghammer, 'The Rise of the Muslim Foreign Fighters', p. 53. There is a vast literature on foreign fighters involved in armed struggles in the wider Muslim world. Here is a non-exhaustive list of some of the most significant works. For the case of Afghanistan: Brian Glyn Williams, 'On the Trail of the "Lions of Islam": Foreign Fighters in Afghanistan and Pakistan, 1980–2010' (2011) 55 *Orbis* 216–239. For the Yugoslavian wars: Darryl Li, 'Jihad in a World of Sovereigns: Law, Violence, and Islam in the Bosnia Crisis' (2016) 41 *Law & Social Inquiry* 371–401. On the Chechnyan war: Cerwyn Moore and Paul Tumelty, 'Foreign Fighters and the Case of Chechnya: A Critical Assessment' (2008) 31 *Studies in Conflict & Terrorism* 412–433. For other significant works on the role of foreign fighters in Iraq, Somalia and Yugoslavia please refer back to the Introduction.

[25] The Soviet–Afghan war has been the subject of extensive debates and Security Council resolutions. These culminated in the Geneva Accords (1988), where an agreement between Afghanistan and Pakistan was signed, with the United States and Soviet Union standing as guarantors.

Figure 3.1 Mujahid in Afghanistan (1985)
Source: Erwinlux (Courtesy of the author, Erwin Franzen).

could once have been perceived as freedom fighters, they have undergone a transformation, and are now depicted as enemies of humanity.

A new scenario is therefore drawn, made up of other places, actors and ideologies: from Afghanistan to the Balkans, from Chechnya to Somalia, the armed struggle in the wider Muslim world attracts a very different group of foreign combatants, who seemingly have nothing in common with former, honourable volunteers. The uneasiness of the leaders gathered at the Security Council was palpable. This was true of Western leaders in particular, especially when it came to admitting that many of their own citizens were leaving for Syria: 'but one of the most disturbing aspects is how [the Syrian Civil War] is sucking in our own young people from modern, prosperous societies ... let me say that from my own country, 500 of those *fanatics* have gone to Syria and Iraq', noted UK Prime Minister David Cameron.[26] And François Hollande stressed this point in relation to France: 'terrorism ... it has taken on another dimension ... to recruit a growing number of our citizens ... that is a threat to our own security. Earlier President Obama referred to 15,000 foreign fighters. Among them are 1,000 French nationals who are now in Syria or Iraq'.[27]

How troubling for secular countries such as the United Kingdom and France to see some of their nationals going to fight in distant conflicts, joining armed groups who use 'barbaric and medieval practices' to conduct warfare.[28] And how different the discourse of state representatives in September 2014 compared to the attitude towards the idealistic volunteers of the Spanish Civil War more than half a century earlier. The British and French citizens leaving for Syria were not a source of pride, but rather an alarming security threat. And the response of the international community was also clear. Having defined their tradition, their genealogy and their twisted ideals, all that remained was to implement legal measures: 'the fight against terrorism is also a fight for values. It is a fight that concerns the entire international community. We therefore welcome ... the resolution adopted today in the Council', remarked Belgian Prime Minister Di Rupo.[29] Even Russia, the country that had stood on the side of the Republicans in Spain, and of the liberation movements in Africa, seemed to have erased all memories of former political struggles: '[we have] consistently advocated the expansion of

---

[26] UNSC, 7272nd meeting (24 September 2014) p. 13. Emphasis added.
[27] *Ibid.*, p. 6. Other countries' representatives would join in and add to these numbers, reiterating the fear of seeing their citizens coming and going from and to Syria. See Australian Prime Minister Tony Abbott's speech, pp. 14–15. Also Gerard van Bohemen (New Zealand), p. 37, and Manuel Gomez-Acebo (Spain), pp. 37–38.
[28] 'The conflict in Iraq and Syria is shocking the world with its barbarity. The cruelty that is being meted out – beheadings, eyes being gouged out, rape – is horrific. It is literally medieval in its character ... The shocking murders of James Foley, Stephen Sotloff and David Haines by a fighter with an apparent British accent underlines the sinister and direct nature of the threat. The British people are sickened that a British citizen could be involved in murdering people in this way, including a fellow British citizen who had gone to Syria to help people. It is the very opposite of what our peaceful and tolerant country stands for.' Intervention by David Cameron. *Ibid.*, p. 13.
[29] UNSC, 7272nd meeting (24 September 2014) p. 29.

international cooperation to curb terrorism in all its forms, and abandoning double standards and the dividing of terrorists into *good* and *bad* terrorists'.[30]

No more double standards, no more ambivalence. The fight against international terrorism seems to have silenced every passion, censored every alignment, and it mirrors a world made up of pragmatists, seeking the best technical solutions to confront an absolute evil.[31] But is that so? To unpack this point further, one must not overlook a central aspect of Resolution 2178: the explicit request made to member states to take concrete steps in their national legislation to respond to the phenomenon of the foreign terrorist fighter.[32]

Many state representatives made this aspect clear the day of the adoption of the resolution. David Cameron for instance remarked that: 'in the United Kingdom, we are introducing new powers to strengthen our ability to seize passports and stop suspects from travelling; to allow us temporarily to prevent some British nationals from getting back into the country'.[33] For his part, François Hollande added that: 'France has in this respect adapted its legislation, and a bill is being discussed in the Parliament aiming to prevent, even prohibit, the departure of individuals when we have serious grounds to believe that they are travelling for terrorist purposes'.[34]

---

[30] *Ibid.*, p. 16. Emphasis added.

[31] See the speech of Herman Van Rompuy, President of the European Council: 'The Islamic State in Iraq and the Levant (ISIL) poses a dreadful threat to security not only in Syria and Iraq. Beyond the Middle East, ISIL is also a grave threat to us all. We must respond jointly by undertaking direct actions to destroy ISIL's military and economic capability, by increasing our support to affected countries and by stopping foreign fighters from joining ISIL. No doubt, ISIL will portray whatever we do as a fight against Islam, but this is a common fight against cruelty and barbarism.' *Ibid.*, p. 28. Along the same lines were the debates happening at the General Assembly the very same day as the adoption of Resolution 2178, see UN General Assembly Official Records, sixty-ninth plenary meeting (24 September 2014).

[32] Resolution 2178 has been the subject of extensive debates among international lawyers and experts, many of whom have highlighted its clear limits. In a nutshell, the resolution has been attacked under many different flags: from refugee law, to human rights standards and humanitarian principles. For a summary of these critiques see Cory Kopitzke, 'Security Council Resolution 2178 (2014): An Ineffective Response to the Foreign Terrorist Fighter Phenomenon' (2017) 24 *Indiana Journal of Global Legal Studies* 309–341.

[33] UNSC, 7272nd meeting (24 September 2014) p. 14.

[34] *Ibid.*, p. 6.

Western states had thus moved away from the laissez-faire attitude which had characterized the discussions of the previous decades. Starting with Resolution 2178, one can witness a flourishing of legislation targeting foreign fighters, their recruitment, attempts to travel abroad and their eventual return to their home countries. This legislation took the form of amendments to criminal codes and was introduced under the counterterrorism banner.[35] To close this first section, is important to reiterate that Resolution 2178 was adopted under the global counter-terrorism agenda, marking a clear shift from previous times. With this resolution, the Security Council introduced a legal status for foreign fighters. To do so, state representatives resorted to a new archetype. They identified the Mujahideen as the historical precedent to frame the struggle drawing volunteers to Syria. However, this actor was now accused of barbaric practices and singled out as an enemy of humanity. The jihadist fighter thus represents the 'bad' version of the freedom fighters of decolonization. Facing this unprecedented threat, all countries seemed finally to be coming together, abandoning their former political alignments. But what actually happens when new legislation is discussed in parliamentary venues? Are all foreign fighters seen in the same way, or are some distinctions still be drawn? And if so, by recurring to which cultural images? To attest once again to the ambivalences, we need to move to domestic debates in the immediate aftermath of the adoption of Resolution 2178.

3.2 Idealists or Fanatics?

In France, a draft law aimed at reinforcing the provisions relating to the fight against terrorism was presented at the National Assembly in July 2014.[36] Intended to hamper individuals from reaching terrorist groups and participating in terrorist activities abroad, this legislation echoed the neutrality laws passed by Western states to stop their citizens

---

[35] *See* generally Jessie Blackbourn, Deniz Kayis and Nicola McGarrity, *Anti-Terrorism Law and Foreign Terrorist Fighters* (London: Routledge 2019).

[36] Projet de Loi no. 2110 renforçant les dispositions relatives à la lutte contre le terrorisme (Procédure accélérée). Enregistré à la Présidence de l'Assemblée nationale le 9 juillet 2014. For a compelling study on French counter-terrorism and emergency laws see Vanessa Codaccioni, *Justice d'Exception: l'État Face aux Crimes Politiques et Terroristes* (Paris: CNRS Editions 2015). For a Franco-British perspective see Frank Foley, *Countering Terrorism in Britain and France: Institutions, Norms, and the Shadow of the Past* (Cambridge: Cambridge University Press 2013).

going to fight in Spain.³⁷ But much time had passed, with the legal machinery becoming much more refined and pervasive. Law 2014-1353 in fact introduced comprehensive administrative measures, including the cancellation of passports and national identity cards, together with specific terrorist offences.³⁸

A couple of weeks after the proposition of the draft, the socialist deputy Sébastien Pietrasanta presented a full report on it to the National Assembly. The aim was to summarize the salient points of the legislation, but also the proposed modifications in terms of human rights made by the Commission des Lois Constitutionnelles.³⁹ The report dealt quite extensively with the terrorist threat represented by those French citizens joining the ranks of the Islamic State: 'les volontaires partant de France constituent le plus fort contingent parmi les combattants européens dont le nombre est estimé à environ 1 500 – sur un total d'environ 9 000 combattants étrangers';⁴⁰ it referred to the 'filières djihadistes' (jihadist networks) present in French territory and more in general to the profiles of those combatants, before moving on to the discussions held within the Commission des Lois. It was in that venue that things became interesting.

Bernard Cazeneuve – at the time minister of the interior – reaffirmed the urgent need to pass relevant legislation, making clear, however, that

---

[37] *See* the final text of the legislation: Loi no. 2014-1353 du 13 novembre 2014 renforçant les dispositions relatives à la lutte contre le terrorisme. For a detailed analysis of Law 2014-1353 see Aurélie Cappello, 'L'interdiction de sortie du territoire dans la loi renforçant les dispositions relatives à la lutte contre le terrorisme' (2014) 12 *Actualité Juridique Pénal* 560–562; Hajer Rouidi, 'La loi no. 2014-1353 du 13 novembre 2014 renforçant les dispositions relatives à la lutte contre le terrorisme: quelles évolutions?' (2014) 12 *Actualité Juridique Pénal* 556–559; and Céline Godeberge and Emmanuel Daoud, 'La loi du 13 novembre 2014 constitue-t-elle une atteinte à la liberté d'expression?' (2014) 12 *Actualité Juridique Pénal* 563–566.

[38] For a detailed analysis of the administrative measures introduced under Law 2014-1353 see Sharon Weill, 'Terror in Courts, French Counter-Terrorism: Administrative and Penal Avenues', Report for the Official Visit of the UN Special Rapporteur on Counter-Terrorism and Human Rights' (May 2018). The law amended Article 421-1 of the French criminal code to include the crime of apology of terrorism. It also created a crime of 'individual terrorist enterprise' ('délit d'entreprise terroriste individuelle'. Art. 421-2-6, later modified). For an overview see Dorle Hellmuth, 'Countering Jihadi Terrorists and Radicals the French Way' (2015) 38 *Studies in Conflict & Terrorism* 979–997.

[39] *See* Rapport no. 2173, Fait au Nom de la Commission des Lois Constitutionnelles, de la législation et de l'administration générale de la République sur le projet de Loi (no. 2110), renforçant les dispositions relatives à la lutte contre le terrorisme. Enregistré à la Présidence de l'Assemblée nationale le 22 juillet 2014.

[40] *Ibid.*, p. 11.

'l'interdiction de sortir du territoire constitue naturellement une restriction à la liberté d'aller et venir ... Cette mesure est donc entourée de garanties. Elle ne pourra être prise qu'au vu d'éléments précis, solides et circonstanciés'.[41] One could recall that freedom of movement was the main counterargument towards the adoption of anti-mercenary legislation made by the British legislator in the 1970s.

Overlooking this point, the plan to prevent people from leaving for Syria was praised by a former anti-terrorism magistrate, Alain Marsaud: 'je craignais que des juges puissent s'interroger sur la politique étrangère actuelle de la France, consistant à aller combattre M. Assad sans faire la différence entre ceux qui s'en vont dans l'armée syrienne libre et ceux qui rejoignent Al-Qaïda ou Al-Nosra ... Heureusement, grâce à ce texte, nous n'en serons plus là'.[42] Hence, for some in the Commission, the draft law was to be applauded precisely because it avoided differentiating between those travelling to Syria to fight alongside the Free Syrian Army, and those joining the Islamic State. The mere fact of departing for certain war zones seemed now to override any political stance.

When it comes to discussing more thoroughly the article on the interdiction on leaving the national territory, things become more complicated. Jacques Myard, of the Republican Group, asserted that 'la participation de certains de nos concitoyens à des conflits armés sans autorisation expresse du Gouvernement est contraire à l'idée même de cohésion nationale',[43] Marsaud reaffirmed that 'ce délit nouveau irait dans le sens de la répression, en permettant – plus facilement que d'autres – d'incriminer tous ceux qui reviennent sur notre territoire après s'être livrés à des activités djihadistes'.[44]

Pietrasanta felt compelled to intervene at this point, making clear to his colleagues that 'tout d'abord, il n'existe pas de définition précise du "conflit armé", et demander au Quai d'Orsay de donner un avis sur tous les conflits dans le monde poserait des problèmes à notre diplomatie'.[45] The question of what counts as an armed conflict was far from being set, even in 2014. Consequently, how is it possible to decide who is a 'good' fighter, and in which theatre of war? It is Myard who seems to have the answer to this question: 'le conflit armé est un fait – c'est une notion

---

[41] *Ibid.*, p. 40.
[42] *Ibid.*, p. 54.
[43] *Ibid.*, p. 67.
[44] *Ibid.*
[45] *Ibid.*

politique, et non *juridique*! Le Quai d'Orsay publie d'ailleurs une carte des zones dangereuses'.[46]

In other words, it would be enough to indicate which conflicts are forbidden to understand which combatants should be criminalized. But Marie-Françoise Bechtel, a deputy from the Republican Left, noted: 'avec cet amendement, des Français n'auraient pu rejoindre la France libre ou combattre avec les républicains espagnols!'[47] This remark was immediately followed by Pascal Popelin, of the Socialist Party, who affirmed:

> La loi est faite pour répondre à toutes les situations. Je n'ai pour ma part aucune commisération pour ceux qui ne pourraient plus mener d'opérations mercenaires aux Comores ou ailleurs, mais j'ai une pensée émue pour ceux qui, en 1936, ont rejoint les Brigades internationales pour combattre le fascisme en Espagne!⁴⁸

Even in the age of counterterrorism, not all memories are lost. Cultural references appear to attest to the ambivalences, and the passions, still at play. The Spanish Civil War heroes were very much present in the imaginary of the French legislator, while mercenaries were now being referred to as the 'bad' foreign fighters in the story. Interestingly, the restrictive amendments to this article proposed by Myard and Marsaud were rejected by the Commission and referred to further discussion,[49] while Pietrasanta closed the meeting by stating that: 'le ministère des Affaires étrangères dresse effectivement une liste des zones de conflits, mais il ne saurait prendre position systématiquement'.[50]

In September 2014 the modified bill was presented to the National Assembly for the standard voting procedure. There, the same problems resurfaced. Cazeneuve once again began by presenting the worrying situation concerning French citizens going to fight in Syria, making no distinction between different types of combatants: 'À ceux et à celles qui songent au départ, que ce soit du fait d'une attirance morbide pour la violence, par désespérance, au nom d'un idéal religieux dévoyé, ou même par romantisme et par compassion pour les victimes du régime de Bachar

---

[46] *Ibid.*, p. 68. Emphasis added.
[47] *Ibid.*, p. 68.
[48] *Ibid.*
[49] In particular, Myard had proposed to ban the exit from the national territory 'ab initio', thus completely removing the question of where French citizens would go to fight, and especially with whom. On the same line was also the proposition of Marsaud, who envisaged creating a 'délit obstacle' in order to stop anyone willing to go abroad to fight. *Ibid.*, p. 67.
[50] *Ibid.*, p. 68.

el-Assad, je veux dire qu'ils commettent une erreur funeste, et une faute irréparable.'[51] Although recognizing the existence of a spectrum of motivations that could push French nationals to fight abroad (including fighting against the Assad regime), for the minister of the interior, when it comes to terrorism there can be no nuances in criminalization.[52]

Some minutes later Alain Marsaud took the floor. The anti-terrorism magistrate deplored the fact that his restrictive amendment had not been retained by the Commission. Pointing the finger at some of his colleagues, 'je me souviens que sur ces bancs, les députés socialistes – la gauche en général – criaient à la loi scélérate!',[53] Marsaud reiterates his disagreement with those who try to differentiate between jihadists: 'nous avons découvert les hésitations de la diplomatie française entre les bons et les mauvais djihadistes'.[54] Looking at the root of the problem, he emphasizes: 'L'un de nos collègues m'a objecté tout à l'heure qu'avec une telle disposition, André Malraux n'aurait pas pu aller combattre dans les brigades internationales.'[55] Marie-Françoise Bechtel, the leftist deputy at the Commission, responded: 'Exactement!'[56] A tense debate ensued, where the figure of the French intellectual André Malraux was used to introduce a differentiation in an otherwise one-sided debate. Perhaps the memories of Byron, Lafayette and Garibaldi had disappeared, but not those of the foreign fighters who fought on the 'good' side of the Spanish Civil War. Malraux's image conveyed the idea that the Syrian Civil War was a war of national liberation. Consequently, French citizens taking

---

[51] Journal officiel de la République française. Débats parlementaires, XIVe Législature, Deuxième session extraordinaire de 2013–2014. Séances du lundi 15 septembre 2014, p. 6310.

[52] Cazeneuve continues by stating that: 'À celles et ceux qui songent à partir, je le redis: le terrorisme n'est pas seulement un crime, c'est aussi un leurre, et c'est surtout une impasse, politique et morale. La manifestation la plus visible de cette mutation, c'est malheureusement le nombre élevé de citoyens français, ou d'étrangers résidant sur le territoire national, parmi les combattants enrôlés par les groupes djihadistes les plus radicaux. C'est la présence parmi eux de nombreux Français très jeunes, parfois mineurs, et également d'un nombre croissant de jeunes Françaises. Le nombre des jeunes Français radicalisés combattant sur le théâtre d'opérations syrien n'a cessé de croître.' Ibid.

[53] Ibid., p. 6316. Les Lois Scélérates was a set of repressive laws put in place during the French Third Republic in the years 1893–1894 in order to fight against anarchists. Due to their restrictions on individual liberties, they are usually associated with the present anti-terrorism legislation.

[54] Ibid., p. 6317.

[55] Ibid.

[56] Ibid.

Figure 3.2 Portrait of French intellectual André Malraux (1933)
Source: Agence de presse Meurisse: Bibliothèque Nationale de France.

part in it could be understood as freedom fighters and not categorized simply as terrorists (Figure 3.2).

Marsaud, however, was far from being satisfied: 'Pour vous, bien sûr, le cas de Malraux allant combattre en Espagne est tout à fait comparable à celui de Nemmouche portant la kalachnikov en djihadie!'[57] Looking at the

---

[57] *Ibid.* Mehdi Nemmouche was the Franco-Algerian dual national responsible for the attack to the Jewish Museum in Brussels in May 2014. For two accounts on the profiles of French jihadists see specifically David Thomson, *Les Français Jihadistes* (Paris: Éditions des Arènes 2014) and by the same author, *Les Revenants* (Paris: Seuil-Les Jours 2016).

issue from a technical angle – that of fundamental freedoms – another deputy intervened: 'Ce qui est en jeu, ce sont les principes généraux du droit!'[58] And yet, is this not further proof that, when it comes to foreign fighters, the issue cannot be solved only through the language of rights?

The tense discussion continued. While Marsaud regretted that a more restrictive amendment had not been approved, Marie-Françoise Bechtel remained firm in her position: 'cet amendement vise à criminaliser le fait de participer à des actions armées à l'extérieur du territoire'. Other deputies joined the debate: '[M. Claude Goasguen] C'est normal! C'était la loi: relisez le code pénal! [Mme Marie-Françoise Bechtel] C'est un amendement que j'ai, lors de la commission du 22 juillet, baptisé d'"anti-France libre" [M. Jacques Myard]. Quelle blague! [Mme Marie-Françoise Bechtel] Je maintiens que c'est un amendement "anti-France libre"! [M. Jacques Myard] Mais non! C'est ridicule!'[59]

It is thus clear that, more than half a century after the Spanish Civil War, the imaginary of the French legislator was still hostage to very precise images of the foreign combatant. The objectives of these discussions might be different from those encountered in the past: now the protection of fundamental freedoms has become a cornerstone against which to balance the counterterrorism legislation, for example. Yet the common denominator does not change. The creation of norms for the criminalization of foreign fighters passes through 'good' and 'bad' versions of the volunteer, embodying different ideals of freedom. A Report presented at the National Assembly a year after the abovementioned Parliamentary discussion sheds light on this ambivalence.[60] In this venue, focusing on the composition and functioning of the jihadist networks present on French territory, the thorny issue of foreign fighters' motivations resurfaced. While some policymakers remarked that jihadism is a 'perverted romantic ideal' coming from a misguided interpretation of Islam,[61] others challenged this view, putting the issue in a historical perspective:

---

[58] Journal officiel de la République française. Séances du lundi 15 septembre 2014.

[59] Ibid., p. 6320.

[60] See Rapport fait au nom de la commission d'enquête sur la surveillance des filières et des individus djihadistes (no. 2828). Enregistré à la Présidence de l'Assemblée nationale le 2 juin 2015.

[61] 'Idéal "romantique" perverti, souvent associé à une quête identitaire, il se nourrit à la fois du très proche – les humiliations dont seraient victimes les musulmans – et du très lointain. En effet, les conflits internationaux au Moyen-Orient, mais aussi, il faut bien le dire, les difficultés pour les jeunes de percevoir les lignes directrices de notre politique

3.2 IDEALISTS OR FANATICS?   171

> Il me semble qu'il s'était passé un phénomène identique, pendant la guerre d'Espagne, avec les Brigades internationales. Celles-ci pouvaient réunir à la fois des membres cyniques du Komintern, venus pour épurer leur propre camp républicain espagnol, ou des idéalistes comme Georges Orwell.[62]

The split between the 'good' and 'bad' foreign combatant is therefore also a split in the passions at the root of the engagement on the battlefield: jihadism can be understood both as a perverted romantic ideal and as a true political commitment. Significantly, these sentiments reconnect with specific figures which linger in the imaginary of the lawmakers: the cynical member of the Russian Comintern as representing the twisted side of idealism, and the committed intellectual (Orwell) fighting for a noble cause. But there is an additional layer to the story. As the policymakers involved in the preparation of the Report confronted the issue of the causes pushing French citizens to depart for Syria, some insisted that there was a need to include socio-cultural and historical elements in such a discussion:

> [il faut montrer] de manière beaucoup plus globale qu'à l'issue de la conquête, les peuples arabes ont retourné contre eux-mêmes leur énergie destructrice. On ne peut pas ne pas penser que ce phénomène a été alimenté par la politique des puissances occidentales depuis sinon les croisades, du moins la colonisation, au XIXe siècle, avec ses effets pervers au XXe: on a dans une large mesure détruit les nations existantes, on en a empêché d'autres d'exister.[63]

It is fascinating to see how the Arab people were seen as bearers of a destructive energy which they were now using 'against themselves'. Again, passions are always split, and so the jihadist combatant could be moved by a distorted form of idealism, or by a genuine political pledge. But also, the whole phenomenon of foreign volunteering in Syria cannot be detached from the colonial history of the West, guilty in some ways of 'having prevented others from existing'. And now these others were reappearing, willing to write history on their own terms. The paternalist

---

étrangère au cours des dix dernières années, constituent un terreau fertile pour ce phénomène.' *See* the intervention of M. Patrick Mennucci (rapporteur). *Ibid.*, p. 162.

[62] 'Bien sûr, la guerre d'Espagne est totalement différente sur de nombreux aspects. Mais si j'ai fait cette comparaison, c'est parce que vous y rencontriez également des jeunes gens venus de tous les continents se battre pour une cause plutôt que pour un pays.' *See* the intervention by Adrien Jaulmes and the subsequent answer of Joaquim Pueyo. *Ibid.*, pp. 399–400.

[63] *Ibid.*, p. 385.

stance embodied by Spaak at the United Nations some sixty years earlier might be outdated, but not its colonial undertone. This brings into the conversation another story: France's involvement in Syria through the League's Mandate, for instance, or the Sykes–Picot agreement drawing the boundaries of the Middle East.[64] It is thus clear that the problem of contemporary foreign fighters was coloured by more profound concerns haunting the French legislator, aside from legal technicalities.

And yet one must not overlook the fact that we are in the age of counterterrorism. As shown by the debates at the Security Council, a new enemy had appeared on the horizon. An enemy so frightening, that ambiguities were easily silenced. Let's return briefly to the French National Assembly, to conclude the debate on law 2014-1353.

> [M. Éric Ciotti] je voudrais souligner le caractère choquant des propos que vient de tenir Mme Bechtel ... Comparer le terrorisme que pratiquent les fanatiques de l'État islamique à ceux qui ont lutté pour nos libertés et pour la dignité de notre pays dans la France libre est particulièrement mal venu dans ce débat ... [M. Pascal Popelin] C'est pourtant comme cela que le gouvernement de Vichy les appelait! Il parlait de terroristes! [Mme Marie-Françoise Bechtel] Absolument! C'est l'Histoire![65]

---

[64] One of the claims put forward by the Islamic State was in fact to remove the Syria–Iraq border, thus rejecting the territorial divisions established with the 1916 Sykes–Picot Agreement signed by France and Great Britain. See Micheal Berdine, *Redrawing the Middle East: Sir Mark Sykes, Imperialism and the Sykes–Picot Agreement* (London: I. B. Tauris 2018).

[65] Journal officiel de la République française. Séances du lundi 15 septembre 2014, p. 6321. To describe once more the fundamental difference that many French politicians seem to draw between the past situation and the present terrorist threat, see the words of deputy Pierre Lellouche, in the subsequent discussion: 'À nos collègues de la majorité qui parlaient hier de Malraux, à ceux qui ce soir évoquent les victimes des banlieues françaises, je voudrais dire une chose: que vaut dans une démocratie la liberté d'aller et de venir quand cette liberté peut, à tout moment, se traduire par l'assassinat d'un membre de votre famille, de vos enfants, de vous-même, parce que vous prenez le métro, l'autobus, ou que vous vous rendez dans un grand magasin? Que représente la liberté d'aller et de venir si nous vivons dans un monde de danger immédiat très difficilement contrôlable par le Gouvernement? A toutes les belles âmes de cette assemblée qui parlent de la liberté d'aller et de venir, je demande de réaliser que nous avons changé de monde, que nous sommes confrontés à un état de guerre qui nous est imposé, qui n'est pas de notre fait, que la vie de nos concitoyens est en jeu. Il y aura des morts, des blessés. Il y en a déjà eu, d'ailleurs, à Boston, à Madrid, à Londres. Les Anglais parlent de *Homegrown terrorism* pour désigner ce terrorisme commis par des gens qui sont nés chez nous, qui sont allés à l'école chez nous, qui sont théoriquement intégrés à notre société et ont souvent poursuivi des études supérieures ... Quant à comparer les djihadistes d'aujourd'hui à André Malraux s'engageant dans la guerre d'Espagne ou aux compagnons de la Libération ...

3.2 IDEALISTS OR FANATICS? 173

Indeed, it is history. As seen in the case of both the Spanish volunteers and of mercenaries, history had judged foreign fighters. Or rather, the larger ideological landscape in which their struggles had occurred. And so, in the present age, marked by the fight against international terrorism, it does not seem apt to make distinctions between combatants when legislation needs to be passed: '[M. Éric Ciotti] Monsieur le ministre, notre pays est en guerre. Notre pays est en guerre contre le terrorisme et contre l'expression qu'il revêt aujourd'hui: celle du *fanatisme religieux* et de l'extrémisme, celle qui arbore le visage de l'État islamique, portant à un degré jamais égalé dans l'Histoire contemporaine.'[66] As the shouts of support for Ciotti's words filled the Assembly, the representative of the Republican right added:

> Se pose aussi la question du retour en France des individus qui sont montés au Djihad ... La question du retour est cruciale, car ces bombes humaines représentent une menace manifeste pour la sécurité de nos concitoyens ... David Cameron prévoit d'ailleurs la mise en place d'une mesure de confiscation, voire d'annulation de passeport pour éviter le retour de tels individus.[67]

Read with the November 2015 attacks in mind, these words make more sense than ever. However, the question of those combatants who did not necessarily go to fight in the ranks of jihadist groups remained open.[68]

---

pardonnez-moi mais nous sommes dans un autre monde! Cela n'a rigoureusement rien à voir. À cet égard, je pense que les services de renseignement français sont capables de faire la différence entre un combat terroriste et une cause noble.' See Journal officiel de la République française. Débats parlementaires, XIVe Législature, Deuxième session extraordinaire de 2013-2014. Deuxième séance du mardi 16 septembre 2014, p. 6393.

[66] Journal officiel de la République française. Séances du lundi 15 septembre 2014, p. 6321. Emphasis added.

[67] *Ibid.*

[68] The question of which armed group French citizens went to fight with resurfaced after the 2015 attacks. During a debate in the National Assembly on further counterterrorism legislation to be adopted, the same controversy over how and whom to criminalize among those returning from Syria arose again: '[M. Pascal Popelin] L'établissement de la matérialité des faits peut être rendue complexe du fait, par exemple, de la situation en Syrie où combattent plusieurs groupes, dont l'Armée syrienne libre, qui n'a pas un caractère terroriste [M. Olivier Marleix] Je regrette que l'on n'aille pas au bout de la logique, monsieur Popelin. Une solution pourrait être, c'est l'objet d'ailleurs d'une proposition de loi de Philippe Bas au Sénat, d'instaurer un délit qui serait constitué dès lors qu'on s'est rendu sur un théâtre d'opérations dans lequel la France est engagée ... Je pense qu'il faudrait faire d'un voyage en Syrie un motif suffisant d'incrimination.' Journal officiel de la République française. Débats parlementaires, XIVe Législature, Session ordinaire de 2015-2016, cent-trente-neuvième séance, séance du mercredi 2 mars 2016, pp. 1608-1611.

The discussions concerning the adoption of Law 1353 continued in the following weeks. The tones remained tense, with the extreme right trying to convey the message that those going to Syria were not really French citizens, and with the discussions shifting further on the issue of fundamental freedoms.[69] As already announced by Hollande during the session at the Security Council, Law 2014-1353 would finally pass on 13 November 2014, exactly one year before the Paris attacks. But the French legislation was not alone in being adopted in the aftermath of UNSC Resolution 2178. And it was no coincidence that at the National Assembly, some of the French deputies referred to the text presented by David Cameron. Let's move then once again across the Channel, to see what happened in the United Kingdom in the same period.

Contrary to the hesitant attitude shown during the Angolan crisis in the 1970s, Westminster took the issue of foreign fighters very seriously. As in France, in the United Kingdom the problem was seen through the lens of counterterrorism. Specifically, it was the Counter-Terrorism and Security Act (adopted in February 2015) that introduced a series of administrative measures, such as the seizure of travel documents and temporary exclusion orders from the country for those who had gone to fight in Syria.[70]

Revealing of the climate in which the legislation was discussed, the bill was accorded a fast-track procedure and lacked serious debate.[71] To give a sense of the practical attitude of the British government, it suffices to look at the words of David Cameron, presenting the bill in September 2014:

> We need to strengthen our powers to fill specific gaps in our armoury: preventing suspects from travelling; and dealing decisively with those

---

[69] '[Marion Le Pen] Il faut réformer les dispositions relatives à la déchéance de la nationalité française afin d'en assouplir l'application et de l'étendre, comme les Britanniques l'ont fait avec leurs binationaux. Il n'y a pas de scrupules à avoir: ces individus n'ont rien de français; ils combattent nos valeurs et notre République.' See Journal officiel de la République française. Débats parlementaires, XIVe Législature, Session ordinaire de 2014–2015, quarantième séance, deuxième séance du mercredi 29 octobre 2014, p. 8141.

[70] The Counter-Terrorism and Security Act of 2015. For an excellent review of the Act and its implications see Jessie Blackbourn and Clive Walker, 'Interdiction and Indoctrination: The Counter-Terrorism and Security Act 2015' (2016) 79 *Modern Law Review* 840–870. See also Helen Fenwick, 'Terrorism Threats and Temporary Exclusion Orders: Counter-Terror Rhetoric or Reality?' (2017) 3 *European Human Rights Law Review* 247–271.

[71] The Bill was scrutinized between December 2014 and early February 2015 in both British Houses. Additionally, various committees' reports, factsheets and impact assessments were taken into consideration through the various stages of the adoption of the legislation. These were, however, mainly technical debates.

already here who pose a risk ... it is abhorrent that people who declare their allegiance elsewhere can return to the United Kingdom and pose a threat to our national security ... To fill [the] gap, we will introduce specific and targeted legislation providing the police with a temporary power to seize a passport at the border.[72]

And when the Home Secretary Theresa May presented the bill to the Houses for the first round of consultations, her words left no doubt as to her government's attitude: 'ISIL and its western fighters now represent one of the most serious terrorist threats we face. They have shown their brutality by murdering, raping and torturing men, women and children in the territories they hold and by murdering western hostages – including British citizens – in the most savage way imaginable.'[73]

It is clear that this was a crucial turning point in the discourse concerning foreign fighters: the ambivalent laissez-faire attitude of the British government during the 1970s was over, and the words of two of its most important spokespersons were aligned with those already heard at the Security Council. The figure of the religious fanatic had settled in the imaginary of the British legislator, representing the dark counterpart of the freedom fighters of decolonization, and thus sweeping away any reference to the noble adventurers of previous times. The barbarism of which the Moorish troops were accused during the Spanish Civil War reappeared, here tinged with the new cultural universe brought by the jihadist struggle. As for the robbers and looters labelled as brutes by the German delegation in The Hague, the image of the fanatic epitomizes a fear of witnessing the dehumanization of warfare.

To give a further sense of the attitude at Westminster, Philip Hollobone, member of the Conservative Party, remarked during a subsequent session at the House of Commons: 'British jihadists who go abroad to support ISIS are aiding and abetting the Queen's enemies ... should it not be made clear to these people that it is worse than murder and terrorism – it is treason – and that should they ever be apprehended they should be prosecuted for such?'[74] The only sign of discomfort came from the Labour deputy Jeremy Corbyn, who tried to introduce some questions into an unidirectional debate: 'I have no truck whatever with

---

[72] HC Deb, 1 September 2014, Vol. 585, cc23–27.
[73] Home Office, Home Secretary Theresa May on counterterrorism (24 November 2014). The speech is available at www.gov.uk/government/speeches/home-secretary-theresa-may-on-counter-terrorism.
[74] HC Deb, 6 January 2015, Vol. 590, c154.

ISIS ... but if [British citizens] fight for the free Syrian army ... are they then deemed to be all right? Do they then have to prove which particular force they joined in Syria? [and] If someone fight with the Kurdish forces ... how [do] we decide who is a *good fighter* and who is *a terrorist*; who is struggling for liberation and who is a terrorist[?].'[75]

Other than that, the Parliamentary debates on the 2015 Counter-Terrorism Act mainly revolved around technical questions: whether existing legislation already covered the offences proposed in the new text, or how to tackle radicalization and more generally terrorism prevention. The great stumbling block of the discussion was fundamental rights. The bill was in fact scrutinized several times by the Joint Committee on Human Rights (an organ comparable to the French Commission des Lois), and the curtailing of fundamental freedoms entered the debates on various occasions.[76] It is not there, then, that one should look for ambivalence.

Interestingly, only two days after the adoption of Resolution 2178 at the Security Council, David Cameron reported to the House of Commons on the subject matter 'Coalition against ISIL'.[77] In his speech, the UK prime minister highlighted how his government 'recognises the threat ISIL poses to wider international security and the UK directly', and announced a plan to aid the Kurdish forces battling the Islamic State on the ground.[78] This announcement generated questions from the other

---

[75] HC Deb, 15 December 2014, Vol. 589, c1227. Emphasis added. However, Corbyn's remark fell into the void.

[76] *See* the following debates at the House of Lords: HL Deb, 13 January 2015, Vol. 758, cc651–698; HL Deb, 20 January 2015, Vol. 758, cc1197–1242; HL Deb, 26 January 2015, Vol. 759, cc1–48; HL Deb, 2 February 2015, Vol. 759, cc451–497; HL Deb, 4 February 2015, Vol. 759, cc643–689. Also significant in this respect was the work done by the Independent Reviewer of Terrorism Legislation. *See* specifically David Anderson, 'Report of the Independent Reviewer of Terrorism Legislation. The Terrorism Acts in 2015' (December 2016), which addressed the issue of foreign fighters under the current counterterrorism legislation.

[77] HC Deb, 26 September 2014, Vol. 585, cc1256–1366.

[78] *Ibid.* This plan was announced at the beginning of September, when Cameron reported to the House of Commons on the subject 'EU Council, Security and Middle East': 'So far we have received requests from the Kurds to facilitate the transfer and transport of arms and ammunition from Jordan and Albania to the Kurdish regional authorities. We have done that, and it is absolutely right that we have. I am not aware of a specific request directly from the Kurdish regional authorities for arms and military support, but as I have said before, we would look very favourably on such a request. They are our allies and friends, and we believe that they are helping to put the pressure on ISIL and to defend communities.' HC Deb, 1 September 2014, Vol. 585, c35.

deputies: 'also fighting ISIL on the ground is the Free Syrian Army. Given that last week the United States Congress voted to support the Free Syrian Army overtly with weapons, and given that the Free Syrian Army is conducting a ground war ... are [we] looking ... at the possibility of giving military hardware to the Free Syrian Army?'[79]

Some in the House tried to dissuade the prime minister from this possibility, fearing that 'The Free Syrian Army is a fiction that has been in the receipt of hundreds of millions of dollars and hundreds of tonnes of weapons, virtually all of which were taken from them by al-Qaeda, which has now mutated into ISIL';[80] while others put more strategic questions on the table: 'how can we attack ISIL in Syria without being seen as in some way supporting the Assad regime, when we are supporting the Free Syrian Army at the same time[?]'.[81] In sum, the wider geopolitical considerations seen in previous civil wars reappeared here. Although no longer read through the lens of neutrality, the decisions regarding whom to provide with military aid is not an easy one: 'Members today have said that the issue can be resolved only if we put more money and resources into the *freedom fighters*. Which of those freedom fighters will we support? The Muslim Brotherhood? Al Nusra? Will we support other extremist organisations that already exist? Will we support the un-Islamic state in the region?'[82] Far from being irrelevant, these pressing remarks were central to understanding which British citizens should be criminalized upon their return from Syria. Additionally, they testify to the complexity of the situation on the ground. A topic that would return again and again to the British Parliament in the years to come.[83]

On the same day that Cameron delivered his speech at the Commons, the topic of the Islamic State was also discussed in the House of Lords.[84] The tone of the debate were familiar: 'it is important we understand that ISIL is not simply another terrorist organisation. We have seen its hostage-taking, including innocent British and American citizens, the murder of David Haines and the holding of other British hostages ...

---

[79] HC Deb, 26 September 2014, Vol. 585, c1259.
[80] HC Deb, 26 September 2014, Vol. 585, George Galloway, cc1299–1300.
[81] *Ibid.* Sir James Paice, cc1335–1336.
[82] HC Deb, 26 September 2014, Vol. 585, Khalid Mahmood intervention, c1317. Emphasis added.
[83] *See* the debate held at the House of Lord in April 2016 on the subject 'UK Citizens Returning from Fighting Daesh'. The debate attests to the confusing situation regarding which British citizens to criminalize. HC Deb, 19 April 2016, Vol. 608, cc889–900.
[84] HC Deb, 26 September 2014, Vol. 755, cc1676–1746.

This is not Jihad – it is a war against all humanity', Lord Hunt of the Labour Party remarked.[85] Lord Alderice, of the Liberal Democrat, was however more cautious in his intervention, and put matters in context:

> I understand that for political reasons the Prime Minister and other colleagues speak passionately in terms of good and evil. We must beware of thinking about the conflict in entirely Manichean terms ... This is not simply a war like in the past ... There is also the possibility – indeed, almost the inevitability – of a whole new generation of young people being drawn into the jihadist orbit, just like the Arab Afghans going to Afghanistan in the 1980s.[86]

Although this is a confirmation of the shifting imaginary surrounding foreign fighters, Lord Alderice is suggesting introducing some nuance into the debate. As others reminded their peers of the mistakes made by Western interference in the Middle East, more haunting questions soon came back to the fore: 'ISIL [is] the harvest that we are reaping for not having armed the secular rebels in Syria at the beginning of the troubles there.'[87] As seen in both the Spanish and Angolan cases, civil wars do not happen in a vacuum, and states have often supported different groups, depending on their political alignments. But that has not helped in solving the question of foreign volunteers. Lord Desai then took the opportunity to make a compelling point about those British citizens leaving for the Syrian battlefield:

> the young men and women who go over there from here are *idealists*. After all, young men and women went to fight in the Spanish Civil War; they were doing a similar thing ... we have to understand the dynamics of what these young men and women are doing and not just say immediately, 'They are all terrorists and when they come back we will put them all in jail'.[88]

In the United Kingdom not all memories were lost then, or ambivalences appeased. The Spanish Civil War was recalled to better contextualize the struggle of contemporary foreign fighters, and to stress that their indiscriminate criminalization does not always represent a good plan. Or at least, that there should be some better assessment of which foreign volunteers should be treated as terrorists, and which as freedom fighters.

---

[85] *Ibid.* Lord Hunt of Kings Heath, cc1680–1681.
[86] *Ibid.* Lord Alderice, cc1682–1683.
[87] *Ibid.* Baroness Ramsay of Cartvale, cc1709–1710.
[88] *Ibid.* Lord Desai, c1716. Emphasis added.

As outlined in the speech by Jeremy Corbyn, different conceptions of freedom might indeed be at stake.

But as we saw in the case of France, such weighting is difficult to accomplish in the post-9/11 world order. As Baroness Stowell recalled: 'ISIL is a terrorist organisation unlike those with which we have dealt before. The brutality is staggering: beheadings, crucifixions, the gouging out of eyes, the use of rape as a weapon and the slaughter of children. All these things belong to the dark ages.'[89] And so, few moments later, a very explicit statement was made in response to Desai's intervention: 'the Spanish Civil War was an issue that we could understand in our terms. The caliphate is not like that. It is different from the Spanish Civil War in legitimising people going there'.[90]

For a majority of Western lawmakers the motivations and ideals championed by the Islamic State were too different; and the archetype of the volunteer called to join the ranks of the Caliphate was incomprehensible from their cultural tradition.[91] If some Lords had reminded the House that the Syrian battlefield was composed of different groups, at best those questions would gradually have been translated into the common human rights tropes. And as policymakers advanced with the voting procedures, the language of fundamental liberties would override more scorching, political questions.[92] Unlike in the case of

---

[89] *Ibid.*, Lord Privy Seal (Baroness Stowell of Beeston), cc1676–1680.

[90] *Ibid.* Lord Lea of Crondall intervention, c1720.

[91] On this point see the remark made by Viscount Hanworth: 'Seventy-five years ago, the threat was an external one. Those who had sympathised with the fascist ideology had been effectively sidelined and neutralised. Today, the circumstances are different. The jihadist movement has attracted a substantial number of British citizens. At least 500 have joined the movement in Syria and Iraq, and there may be three times that number. It is vital that we should understand the attractions of the ideology and that we should find ways of neutralising it. . . . What should be done to the returning jihadists? The answer is that we should handle them carefully and with discrimination. We should endeavour to distinguish between those who are dangerous to us and those who have been temporarily misled. To achieve that, we need to deploy adequate and appropriate resources within the border agency and elsewhere. The returning jihadists would be thoroughly vetted and debriefed. If they have been only weakly complicit in the activities of insurgents, they should be exonerated. However, if they have committed atrocities, they should be charged with war crimes.' *Ibid.*, c1729.

[92] Among the vast literature tackling the issue of foreign fighters from a human rights perspective see specifically Zubeda Limbada and Lynn Davis, 'Addressing the Foreign Terrorist Fighter Phenomenon from a Human Rights Perspective' (2016) 18 *International Community Law Review* 483–493; Letta Tayler, 'Foreign Terrorist Fighter Laws: Human Rights Rollbacks under UN Security Council Resolution 2178' (2016) 18 *International Community Law Review* 455–482; Alex Conte, 'States' Prevention and

mercenaries – when freedom of movement was mainly evoked as a pretext not to pass legislation – in the post-9/11 landscape, the tension between rights and security is at the centre of legislative debates on foreign fighters.

To conclude, while the counterterrorism discourse tended to assimilate all foreign fighters and encompassed a whole spectrum of motivations and affiliations, it was clear that a certain ambivalence subsisted in the mind of the Western legislator. Even if those nuances were not formally codified within the law, the question resurfaced when domestic courts had to take the difficult decision to allow individuals to leave, or to judge those returning from Syria. The next section asseses this aspect further, exploring some decisions concerning British and French foreign fighters, and the reasons for their prosecution or acquittal.

3.3 Barbarism versus Heroism

Flavien Moreau was the first French national to receive a prison sentence upon his return from Syria. This radicalized twenty-eight-year-old had travelled to the Middle Eastern country between November and December 2012, before making his way back to France. Preparing to leave again for the battlefield, he was stopped and put under arrest.[93] Moreau spent less than two weeks in Syria, and during his trial he claimed 'd'avoir rejoint un groupe ayant vocation à aider les blessés et

---

Responses to the Phenomenon of Foreign Fighters against the Backdrop of International Human Rights Obligations', in de Guttry et al. (eds.), *Foreign Fighters under International Law* 283–298; Tamara Laine, '"Passing the Buck": Western States Race to Denationalise Foreign Terrorist Fighters' (2017) 12 *Journal of Peacebuilding & Development* 22–35; and Shiva Jayaraman, 'International Terrorism and Statelessness: Revoking the Citizenship of ISIL Foreign Fighters' (2016) 17 *Chicago Journal of International Law* 178–216. On how the language of human rights tends to neutralize political questions, please refer to David Kennedy, 'The International Human Rights Movement: Part of the Problem?' (2002) 15 *Harvard Human Rights Journal* 101–125; Susan Marks, 'Human Rights and Root Causes' (2011) 74 *Modern Law Review* 57–78; Wendy Brown, '"The Most We Can Hope For..."': Human Rights and the Politics of Fatalism' (2004) 103 *South Atlantic Quarterly* 451–463; and Makau Mutua, 'The Ideology of Human Rights' (1996) 36 *Virginia Journal of International Law* 589–657. *See* also more generally Costas Douzinas, *The End of Human Rights: Critical Legal Thought at the Turn of the Century* (Oxford: Hart 2000).

[93] The facts regarding his radicalization, his journey to and from Syria are recounted in the Judgment of the Tribunal Correctionnel de Paris. *See* TGI de Paris, Jugement du 13/11/2014, no. parquet 12333060007.

à assurer la surveillance et la sécurité des populations civiles'.[94] Although his profile could be that of an idealist, the court circumvented the alleged humanitarian reasons put forward by the defence: 'sans exclure un objectif d'assistance à une partie de la population civile syrienne, Flavien MOREAU avait pour volonté de rejoindre un groupe de combattants dont le but était la mise en place par tout moyen d'un émirat islamique en Syrie et de combattre "les mécréants"'.[95] As such, the court charged him with terrorism offences and imposed a seven-year prison sentence.[96] It is significant to highlight that at the time of the relevant facts the Islamic State had not yet made declarations of sovereignty over Syrian territory. Things were different for subsequent judgments. This is the case for the trials concerning various jihadist networks responsible for recruiting volunteers to be sent to Syria.[97]

In a 2016 ruling concerning six French returnees, the court started by retracing the geopolitical situation between 2013 and 2014.[98] While acknowledging the presence of different jihadist groups 'qui luttaient contre les troupes de l'armée régulière',[99] the judges recognized that since June 2013 the Islamic State had proclaimed the city of Raqqa as its capital.[100] The court emphasized the criminal actions perpetrated by its combatants: 'exécutions sommaires, égorgements, crucifixions, amputations ... visaient manifestement ... à terroriser les populations civiles et militaires', before moving to the indictments for each of the accused.[101] Although some of them explained that they had never taken up arms,[102] or that if they did it was to fight against Assad,[103] the court

---

[94] Moreau responded about his affiliation to the jihadi cause: 'Pour moi, c'est la justice, comme les salafistes, c'est pour que les gens découvrent la religion, pour que la voie d'Allah soit la plus haute pour la justice.' *Ibid.*, p. 24.
[95] *Ibid.*, p. 40.
[96] Under Art. 421-1 of the French penal code.
[97] On these trials see specifically Antoine Mégie and Jeanne Pawella, 'Les procès correctionnels des filières djihadistes. Juger dans le contexte de la "guerre contre le terrorisme"' (2017) 2 *Les Cahiers de la Justice* 235–251.
[98] See TGI de Paris, Jugement du 07/01/2016, no. parquet 13205000228, p. 14.
[99] *Ibid.*
[100] *Ibid.*, p. 15.
[101] *Ibid.*
[102] [Prevenu no. 1]: 'si je me suis rendu en Syrie, ce n'était pas dans le but de faire le jihad mais, par contre, je voulais avoir une expérience de vie pour voir moi-même ce qu'il en était réellement ... par contre, tout ce que l'on m'a proposé sur place, j'ai refusé, faire l'entrainement, manier les armes.' Jugement du 07/01/2016, p. 18.
[103] [Prevenu no. 6]: '[La Syrie] c'est un pays en guerre. C'est dans ce genre de pays qu'on peut aider. Le combat est une éventualité ... j'avais envisagé de participer à des combats

rejected this line of defence. Their account of their stay in Syria was first dismissed on factual grounds.[104] Secondly, the fact that they were recruited through a jihadist network would have made the nature and purpose of their journey clear to them, the court explained.[105]

Indeed, some of these French foreign fighters could well have been moved by sincere political ideals. Yet the moment they joined a proscribed terrorist organization, courts would recognize that twisted motivation already singled out in parliamentary debates:

> Les convictions de ces personnes, leur fascination pour le djihad et leur admiration pour les figures du terrorisme international sont attestées par l'exploitation de leurs téléphones, ordinateurs et autres supports informatiques ... le fait de partir en SYRIE et d'y intégrer un group djihadiste pour combattre traduit l'adhésion aux buts poursuivis par l'organisation terroriste.[106]

The pursuit of a radical ideology with the aim of imposing a fundamentalist regime through violence also tends to dispel any humanitarian motivation beyond their journey: 'Il résulte des débats que [l'Etat islamique] en réunissant des individus partageant son idéologie religieuse radicale constituait bien un groupement ayant mis en œuvre, pour imposer par la violence un régime confessionnel fondamentaliste, une

---

mais ça ne s'est pas fait car l'opportunité ne s'est pas présentée ... j'ai appartenu à Jabhat Al Nosra à mon arrivée en Syrie ... je suis passé en Juin 2013 à l'E.I. car tous les étrangers s'y trouvaient. C'était l'EIIL à l'époque, dont l'objectif était de combattre Bachar.' *Ibid.*, p. 46.

[104] See the statement made in the case of Prevenu no. 6: 'Cette vision idéalisée de son séjour en Syrie sera contredite par nombre d'éléments de la procédure, notamment les écoutes téléphoniques évoquées ultérieurement, démontrant les motivations jihadistes de l'intéressé, sa participation effective à une opération militaire sur zone et au financement de la filière après son retour en France.' *Ibid.*, p. 33.

[105] Hence the indictment for mere participation in an 'association de malfaiteurs en vue de preparation d'un acte de terrorisme' (AMT), under Art. 421-2-1 of the French penal code. This offence can be translated as 'terrorist criminal association'. For an analysis see Henri Decœur, 'The Criminalisation of Armed Jihad under French Law: Guilt by Association in the Age of Enemy Criminal Law' (2017) 25 *European Journal of Crime, Criminal Law, and Criminal Justice* 299–326.

[106] *See* Arrêt Criminel du 22/06/2017, no. 16/0023. The Cour d'Assises dispelled any humanitarian motivation behind the of five of them travelling to Syria: 'la participation à une association de malfaiteurs terroriste peut être caractérisé par la simple adhésion volontaire au groupement dont les participants connaissent de manière générale le caractère intentionnel et ont favorisé l'action, sans forcément avoir eu connaissance de la totalité ou des détails des infractions projeté, mais en ayant simplement été informés des desseins poursuivis par le groupe dans ses grandes lignes et en y ayant adhéré volontairement' [Feuille de Motivation de la Sentence].

stratégie visant à troubler gravement l'ordre public par l'intimidation et la terreur.'[107] This approach was confirmed by subsequent judgments of the Tribunal de grande instance de Paris in other network cases.[108] One of the most famous was the trial of the filière de Strasbourg (July 2016). The seven men accused had left for Syria in December 2013, before making their way back to France in mid-2014.[109] The defence stressed that their clients went to fight Assad, and with a humanitarian intention: back in 2013, there was much indignation in the West about the massacres occurring in the city of Homs, for instance.[110] The commitment to fight injustice was backed by the argument that, at the time of their arrival, the various armed groups could not be clearly distinguished on the ground. The court, however, dismissed any philanthropic motivation: having been recruited within a jihadist network left no doubt about whom they were going to join. Additionally, the Islamic State had declared Raqqa as its capital in June 2013, months before the group left for Syria. Finally, the evidence showed that the accused had voluntarily integrated within the ranks of the Islamic State, and not with other groups fighting against Assad, such as the Free Syrian Army or the PKK.[111] In sum, the moment French foreign fighters joined the ranks of certain groups – no matter

---

[107] *See* Arrêt Criminel du 23/03/2018, no. 17/0048. The case of three French citizens who left for Syria between August and December 2013 and returned to France in November 2014. They were all charged with the crime of participation 'à une association de malfaiteurs établie en vue de la préparation d'actes de terrorisme' [Feuille de Motivation de la Sentence].

[108] *See* for instance TGI de Paris, Jugement du 23/03/2016, no. parquet 15033000932. Here, four French citizens willing to go to Syria had been stopped in Turkey and repatriated. The timeline of their recruitment was from July 2014 and March 2015. The court underlined how their departure to Syria took place about ten days after the attacks on Charlie Hebdo in Paris. Having established from the evidence that the four wanted to reach Syria to join the Islamic State 'pour rejoindre les rangs des combatants', the court concluded that their action was aggravated by the choice of 'quitter leur pays pour rallier une organisation terroriste à l'encontre de laquelle la France est engagée militairement ... et qui a pris la France pour cible avec le soutien, la preparation et la réalisation d'attentats sur le territoire national', pp. 27–33.

[109] *See* TGI de Paris, Jugement du 06/07/2016, no. parquet 15204000443, pp. 21–27.

[110] *Ibid.*, pp. 19–20

[111] 'Il apparait clairement que tous les prévenus sont volontairement partis en Syrie pour se battre dans les rangs de l'EIIL. La motivation humanitaire affichée par eux n'est qu'un système de défense qu'aucun élément objectif ne vient étayer. Leurs déclarations, comme les messages ou les conversations téléphoniques interceptés, font état d'entrainements militaires ... aucun acte de nature humanitaire n'est relaté.' *Ibid.*, p. 27. The sentences ranged from six to eight years, and were confirmed on Appeal. *See* Cour d'Appel de Paris, Sentence du 9/05/2017, Dossier no. 16/06145.

what had happened on the ground, or how long they remained in Syria – there was little that the defence could do to exculpate them.[112]

It is also significant to remember that law 1353-2014 – discussed in the previous section – had introduced a series of administrative measures to prevent suspects leaving for Syria: these included for instance house arrest, the annulment of passports and national identity cards. By looking at relevant jurisprudence from various administrative courts, it is evident how these sanctions applied particularly to those nationals willing to join jihadist armed groups, and who were profiled as radicalized.[113] Conversely, the story changed when foreign fighters joined groups professing a different ideology.

In July 2016 the Tribunal Administratif de Lyon convicted an individual who had travelled back and forth to Syria several times. The Tribunal rejected the man's plead for annulment of his house arrest, stating that: 'M. Y a effectué plusieurs allers-retours en Syrie entre décembre 2012 et mars 2014 ... et [le fait d'avoir rejoint depuis juin 2013] le groupe Ahrar al Sham favorable au salafisme et au jihade, le rend susceptible d'avoir acquis une expérience militaire de terrain dans le maniement des armes à feu et des explosifs.'[114]

There was a different approach in a decision by the Tribunal Administratif de Paris in March 2017. The defendant was free to travel to Syria, and his passport and identity card were returned to him. The

---

[112] This is the pattern observed in the cases analysed. See for instance TGI de Paris, Jugement du 22/09/2017, no. parquet 12355060014. The case of five French citizens who had gone to Syria between 2013 and 2014 and had later made their way back to France. The court found that even if some of them had at the beginning joined the Free Syrian Army, their subsequent passage into the Islamic State made them guilty: 'il n'est pas impossible qu'ils aient dans un premier temps combattu aux cotes de l'ASL mais certainement pas avec le même objectif d'aider la population syrienne à mettre fin au régime de Bachar al Assad et de gagner en liberté mais bien aux côtés de groupes jihadistes ... l'objectif était donc bien de mener la jihad armé aux côtés d'un groupe affilié à AL QAIDA', p. 39.

[113] See the following judgments, covering the period 2015–2018: TA Paris, Jugement du 07/07/2015, no. 1508213; TA Paris, Jugement du 27/11/2015, no. 1519030; TA Paris, Jugement du 28/11/2015, no. 1519404; TA Paris, Jugement du 12/02/2016, no. 1519389; TA Cergy-Pontoise, Jugement du 21/03/2016, no. 1602382; TA Rennes, Jugement du 4/06/2016, no. 1602381; TA Montreuil, Jugement du 4/07/2016, no. 1602647; CAA Paris, Jugement du 20/06/2016, no. 16PA01210; CAA Paris, Jugement du 8/07/2016, no. 16PA00305; CAA Paris, Jugement du 08/07/2016, no. 16PA01153; CAA Marseille, Jugement du 10/07/2017, no. 17MA01080; CAA Marseille, Jugement du 10/07/2017, no. 17MA01082; CAA Marseille, Jugement du 18/04/2017, no. 16MA04151 and CAA Douai, Jugement du 02/10/2018, no. 16DA01635.

[114] TA Lyon, Jugement du 29/07/2016, no. 1605634.

judge took into consideration the fact that the man had previously joined the ranks of the YPG – a group fighting against the Islamic State.[115] Yet the court had still to assess whether such a group was associated with the PKK, a proscribed terrorist organization.[116] The judge answered in the negative:

> si le [YPG] et le PKK combattent la même organisation terroriste dans la zone frontalière irako-syrienne, cette circonstance alléguée par le ministre ne suffit pas à démontrer que les activités du YPG, auxquelles M. B. pourrait participer, revêtiraient un caractère terroriste … En outre, le requérant fait valoir, sans être contredit, que le YPG coopère avec les forces armées françaises et alliées opérant en zone irako-syrienne.[117]

The cooperation between France and the YPG forces left little room to wonder about the basis of his acquittal. But there is more to the story. The defendant was in fact also cleared of representing a danger for national security. It had been argued that due to the military experience gained in the battlefield, he could have served 'left-wing radical projects' once back in France. In dismissing this point, the judge commented:

> Il ressort certes des pièces du dossier … que M. B. s'est déclaré partisan de la 'lutte pour l'édification du communisme et pour le peuple kurde' (MLKP) … qu'il s'est présenté comme un « militant marxiste

---

[115] TA Paris, Jugement du 31/03/2017, no. 1701210.
[116] 'Pour qualifier de terroristes les activités du YPG, le ministre de l'intérieur fait valoir que le "Parti de l'union démocratique" (PYD), dont le YPG constitue le démembrement combattant, est une émanation du "Parti des travailleurs du Kurdistan" (PKK), qui est inscrit sur la liste des personnes, groupes et entités terroristes, prévue au paragraphe 6 de l'article 1er de la position commune 2001/931/PESC du 27 décembre 2001 et actualisée par la décision (PESC) 2016/1136 du Conseil du 12 juillet 2016.' Ibid.
[117] The original transcript of the sentence: 'Toutefois, si le PYD [le "Parti de l'union démocratique" (PYD), dont le YPG constitue le démembrement combattant] et le PKK combattent la même organisation terroriste dans la zone frontalière irako-syrienne, cette circonstance alléguée par le ministre ne suffit pas à démontrer que les activités du YPG, auxquelles M. B. pourrait participer, revêtiraient un caractère terroriste. A cet égard, les pièces produites par le ministre n'établissent pas que des membres du YPG auraient commis des actes intentionnellement en relation avec une entreprise individuelle ou collective ayant pour but de troubler gravement l'ordre public par l'intimidation ou la terreur, qualifiables d'actes de terrorisme au sens des dispositions précitées des articles 421-1 et 421-2-1 du code pénal, ni que le YPG, qui n'est pas inscrit sur la liste européenne des entités terroristes mentionnée ci-dessus, constituerait un groupe terroriste au sens du droit de l'Union européenne et, notamment, de la position commune 2001/931/PESC du 27 décembre 2001. En outre, le requérant fait valoir, sans être contredit, que le YPG coopère avec les forces armées françaises et alliées opérant en zone irako-syrienne et que le PYD dispose depuis mai 2016 d'une antenne installée à Paris.' Ibid.

français ... et, enfin, qu'il a participé, à son retour en France, à une réunion organisée ... par le Nouveau parti anticapitaliste (NPA) sur la situation au 'Rojava' ... Toutefois, ces éléments ne suffisent pas à démontrer que les convictions et engagements politiques de M. B. sont susceptibles de le conduire à porter atteinte à la sécurité publique lors de son retour sur le territoire français.[118]

This type of reasoning is very different, in tone and content, from the previous ruling involving the jihadist group Ahrar al Sham. In light of what was discussed in the previous section, one could suggest that belonging to leftist factions which draw their inspiration directly from the International Brigades might inform the way French courts delivered their judgments.[119] It is also significant to highlight that these groups understood the fight against the Islamic State precisely as a struggle against a contemporary form of fascism, another clear indication of the historical parallels with the cultural universe of the Spanish Civil War

---

[118] Here is the passage in its entirety: '9. Le ministre de l'intérieur fait valoir que l'expérience opérationnelle acquise par M. B. en zone irako-syrienne est "susceptible d'être utilisée dans le cadre d'actions violentes de l'ultra-gauche révolutionnaire perpétrées contre les intérêts français". 10. Il ressort certes des pièces du dossier et, en particulier, des éléments contenus dans la note des services de renseignement produite par le ministre que M. B. s'est déclaré partisan de la "lutte pour l'édification du communisme et pour le peuple kurde" dans un courriel échangé le 10 mars 2015 avec des membres du "parti communiste marxiste-léniniste de Turquie/Kurdistan du Nord" (MLKP), qu'il s'est présenté comme un "militant marxiste français" dans un autre courriel du 6 juillet 2015, qu'il a rencontré des membres de l'organisation "Antifaschistische Aktion" (AFA) lors de son déplacement en zone irako-syrienne, qu'il a correspondu durant ce déplacement avec un "militant révolutionnaire de gauche" et, enfin, qu'il a participé, à son retour en France, à une réunion organisée le 15 décembre 2016 par le Nouveau parti anticapitaliste (NPA) sur la situation au "Rojava". 11. Toutefois, ces éléments ne suffisent pas à démontrer que les convictions et engagements politiques de M. B. sont susceptibles de le conduire à porter atteinte à la sécurité publique lors de son retour sur le territoire français. D'une part, si M. B. a entretenu des contacts avec des membres du MLKP et de l'AFA avant et pendant son déplacement en zone irako-syrienne, ces contacts apparaissent toutefois cantonnés à son engagement auprès de l'YPG dans cette zone. D'autre part, il ne ressort pas des pièces du dossier que M. B. aurait participé en France à des actions constitutives d'un trouble à l'ordre public, ni qu'il aurait fait l'objet d'un signalement auprès des services de police, y compris durant la période qui a suivi son retour en France. Enfin, il ressort des pièces du dossier que M. B. a coopéré de manière active avec les services de police français, en leur communiquant à son retour en France des pièces et informations collectées par lui lors de son déplacement en zone irako-syrienne.' Jugement du 31/03/2017.
[119] This point is further explained in François Doré, 'Champ d'application de l'interdiction de sortie du territoire' (2017) 23 *Actualités juridiques droit administratif* 1345–1348, p. 1345.

3.3 BARBARISM VERSUS HEROISM

heroes.[120] Overall, the cases analysed show a trend: if the administrative and criminal legislative tools were fully utilized by the French state, a distinction was maintained between combatants, and between groups.[121] As such, those fighters enrolling within the ranks of jihadist groups seemed to profess for the French judge that perverted romantic ideal outlined by policymakers at the National Assembly. Conversely, the motives pushing leftist combatants to leave for Syria might be perceived very differently in the courtroom.[122]

Let's move then one last time to the other side of the Channel to see if the same distinctions are applied there as well. The first conviction of a British foreign fighter was in May 2014, when the Kingston-upon-Thames Crown Court sentenced Mashudur Choudhury to four years' imprisonment for preparation of acts of terrorism.[123] This radicalized man from Portsmouth was arrested on 25 October 2013, upon his return from Syria. He was sentenced for acts taking place on UK soil, rather than abroad: his praise of martyrdom combined with preparations for travelling to join a jihadi group were the bases of his charges, rather than his actions in Syrian territory.[124] The same trend is found in two other cases, similar to the one of Choudhury: Mustafa Abdullah was sentenced to four years' imprisonment in December 2015, after having been

---

[120] See Charlotte Boitiaux, 'La "Task Force Lafayette": ces ex-soldats français face aux jihadistes de l'EI', France24 (13 October 2015), available at www.france24.com/fr/20151013-irak-soldats-militaires-francais-combattre-ei-jihadistes-kurdistan-peshmerga-terrorisme. See also André Hébert, *Jusqu'à Raqqa: avec les Kurdes contre Daech* (Paris: Les Belles Lettres 2019).

[121] See Sharon Weill, 'French Foreign Fighters: The Engagement of Administrative and Criminal Justice in France' (2018) 100 *International Review of the Red Cross* (2018) 211–236.

[122] For a compelling study on the topic see specifically Marc Hecker, '137 Shades of Terrorism: French Jihadists before the Courts' (April 2017) 79 *Focus Stratégique de l'Ifri*, available at www.ifri.org/en/publications/etudes-de-lifri/focus-strategique/137-shades-terrorism-french-jihadists-courts.

[123] Choudhury was sentenced under Section 5(1) of the UK Terrorism Act 2006. See International Criminal Database, *R v. Mashudur Choudhury*, available at www.internationalcrimesdatabase.org/Case/3286.

[124] The prosecutor commented: 'The prosecution's case against this defendant is that he was travelling to Syria to train to fight in pursuit of an ideological or religious cause. You are not being asked to determine who is right and who is at fault in Syria.' See Sandra Laville, 'First British Conviction for Syria-Related Terror Offence', *The Guardian* (20 May 2014) available at www.theguardian.com/uk-news/2014/may/20/briton-convicted-terror-offence-syria-jihadist-training-camp.

arrested at Gatwick Airport returning from Syria.[125] Mohammed Uddin was sentenced to seven years by Woolwich Crown Court in February 2016, after having spent only one month in Syria.[126] Both these British citizens were charged with preparatory acts of terrorism, rather than with acts that occurred abroad. The police found in their possession large quantities of material linked with jihadi propaganda.

In the case of Mohammed Khawaja, a prison sentence of twelve years was served by the Woolwich court, even if this British returnee had not taken a direct part in hostilities.[127] In this regard, the judge commented: 'although I am not satisfied that the evidence safely establishes that you took part in the fighting in Syria, I am satisfied ... that you were extremely close to one of the combat zones ... your intention in going to Syria, once you had completed your training, was to take part in the fighting on behalf of the Islamic State'.[128] In other words, where there was substantive proof of affiliation with jihadist groups, decisions were quite straightforward for the British courts.

This was the case for Tareena Shakil, sentenced to six years' imprisonment after she travelled to Syria with her son between October 2014 and January 2015.[129] Joining a proscribed terrorist group formed the basis of her sentence, on top of the charge of encouraging terrorist acts on social media.[130] Interestingly, when rendering the verdict, the judge

---

[125] Under Section 59 of the UK Terrorism Act 2000 and Section 5(b) of the UK Terrorism Act 2006. *See* 'Mustafa Abdullah of Stockwell Jailed over Terror Videos', BBC News (15 December 2015) available at www.bbc.com/news/uk-england-london-35103690. The case file with the summary of the indictments is available at www.thelawpages.com/.

[126] Under Section 5 of UK Terrorism Act 2006. *See* 'Man Held at Gatwick Jailed for Travelling to Syria to Join IS', BBC News (10 February 2016), available at www.bbc.com/news/uk-england-london-35542054. The summary of his case is available at www.thelawpages.com/.

[127] Specifically, Khawaja was indicted under three different charges: (1) Possessing an article/s for a purpose connected with terrorism (under section 57 of UK Terrorism Act 2000); (2) Engaging in conduct in preparation for acts of terrorism (under section 5 of the UK Terrorism Act 2006; (3) Conspiracy to attend or attendance at a place used for terrorist training (under section 8 of Terrorism Act 2006). *See* BBC News, 'British Jihadist Imran Khawaja Jailed for 12 Years' (6 February 2015) available at www.bbc.com/news/uk-31166062.

[128] The motivations are contained in Khawaja's case file, available at www.thelawpages.com/.

[129] *See* Steven Morris, 'British Woman Who Joined Isis Is Jailed for Six Years', *The Guardian* (1 February 2016) available at www.theguardian.com/uk-news/2016/feb/01/british-woman-tareena-shakil-convicted-being-isis-member-jailed-xx-years.

[130] Belonging to, or membership of a proscribed organization, under section 12 of UK Terrorism Act 2000; encouragement of terrorism, directly or indirectly, inciting or encouraging others to commit acts of terrorism, under section 1 of UK Terrorism Act

commented: 'You embraced ISIS ... Exactly what occurred in Raqqa is far from clear ... Your role as a woman in ISIS was different to that of a man but you embraced it and were willing to support those in Raqqa ... and were willing shamelessly to allow your son to be photographed in terms that could only be taken as a fighter of the future.'[131]

The constant reference to martyrdom and the willingness to enrol in an organization using barbaric warfare practices left no room for ambiguities in all of the above judgments. Even when different justifications for fighting abroad were presented, the result did not vary. In May 2014, the Old Bailey sentenced two brothers who pleaded guilty to having attended a terrorist training camp in Syria in 2013. This time, the charges were based on their actions on the battlefield.[132] Although the court recognized that the main purpose of their journey was to fight against the Assad regime, the judge stressed that: 'it is clear from the evidence from mobile phones that you both had been in a camp in Syria used for terrorist training. The evidence shows you were there for jihad, or holy war, and wanted to join an extremist group'.[133]

Another significant decision was rendered in the appeal judgment of *R* v. *Sarwar* in December 2015.[134] The case involved two male friends from Birmingham who had travelled to Syria to join Islamist forces fighting against Assad. Substantive evidence was brought to the court by the prosecutor, including pictures of them handling weapons.[135] Nonetheless, the defence lawyers stressed that their clients had not joined

---

2006. In *R* v. *Kahar (Mohammed Abdul)* Court of Appeal (Criminal Division), 17 May 2016, the court set out six categories/levels of offences with terrorism-related crimes. These standards will be used in subsequent cases. See *R* v. *Kahar (Mohammed Abdul)* [2016] EWCA Crim 568, [2016] 1 W.L.R. 3156, [2016] 5 WLUK 386.

[131] See Richard Vernalls, 'Woman Who Took Her Baby Son to Syria to Join IS Jailed for Six Years', *The Irish Independent* (1 February 2016) available at www.independent.ie/world-news/europe/woman-who-took-her-baby-son-to-syria-to-join-is-jailed-for-six-years/34413270.html and Tony Larner, 'Tareena Shakil Jailed for Six Years for Travelling to Syria to Join Islamic State', *The Birmingham Mail* (1 February 2016) available at www.birminghammail.co.uk/news/midlands-news/tareena-shakil-jailed-six-years-10817276.

[132] Specifically under section 1 of the Firearms Act 1968 and section 8(1) of the Terrorism Act 2006. The summary case file is available at www.internationalcrimesdatabase.org/Case/3285.

[133] See Dominic Casciani, 'British Brothers Jailed for Training at Syria Terror Camp', BBC News (26 November 2014) available at www.bbc.com/news/uk-30213771.

[134] See *R* v. *Sarwar*, Court of Appeal (Criminal Division) 9 December 2015, [2015] EWCA Crim 1886, [2016] 1 Cr. App. R. (S.) 54. Sentenced under section 5(1) of the UK Terrorism Act 2006.

[135] Their summary case file is available at www.internationalcrimesdatabase.org/Case/3305.

the ranks of the Islamic State, but rather those of the Al-Nusra Front, an organization not yet proscribed as terrorist by the British government.[136] Additionally, they had subsequently joined the ranks of the Free Syrian Army, once they had realized the brutal practices of Al-Nusra.[137] As such, their acts should have been regarded as a form of 'noble cause terrorism'.[138]

The court of appeal was not convinced by that line of defence. The judges stated that: 'to adopt such an approach would necessitate the court having to consider fine political arguments in a situation which is inherently fluid and uncertain, and where loyalties are not fixed or clear-cut [this] would involve a consideration of the policies of HM Government, an area which courts have hitherto been very wary of entering into'.[139] Based on the evidence and on the guilty pleas, the court did not take political motivation into account. It portrayed the accused as radicalized individuals likely to commit acts of terrorism abroad, no matter what they were directed against.[140] The verdict was a ten-year prison sentence for both.

On the one hand, the Sarwar ruling should be reassuring, given that the court set aside political matters. In contrast to the French cases, British courts seemed to adopt a more neutral stance when judging citizens going to fight in Syria. This approach is confirmed by a number of administrative judgments, all involving individuals who had direct links and affiliation with jihadist groups.[141] And yet the story is not as simple as it looks. For instance, a Swedish-born national Bherlin Gildo

---

[136] See R v. Sarwar, p. 5. The Al-Nusra Front became a proscribed terrorist organization while the two were in the battlefield.

[137] Ibid., p. 5.

[138] Ibid., p. 3.

[139] Ibid., p. 11.

[140] 'In so far as a similar point is taken on the basis that there was an intention to engage with Assad's armed troops rather than to direct activity against civilians the position is not that clear-cut ... If the appellants had fulfilled their intention of fighting whilst in Syria it would be unrealistic to conclude that there would be no harm caused to civilians. We can take judicial notice of the general nature of the conflict in Syria and the fact that there have been appalling consequences for the civilians of that country arising from the fighting. In our view the Crown is right. The likelihood of significant collateral damage being caused to civilians arising from armed engagement with Assad's forces would be great.' Ibid., p. 12.

[141] These are cases involving administrative sanctions (such as revocation of passports and other travel documents) for aspiring foreign fighters: *The Queen (on the application of Mr) v. Secretary of State for the Home Department* (High Court of Justice Queen's Bench Division Administrative Court, 10 March 2017). For reference: [2017] EWHC 469 (Admin) 2017 WL 00895282; *The Queen on the application of AS v. Secretary of State for the Home Department* (High Court of Justice Queen's Bench Division Administrative Court, 13 July 2018). For reference: [2018] EWHC 1792 (Admin) 2018 WL 03417238; *B, ND v. Secretary of State for the Home Department v. Commissioner of Police for the*

was arrested on charges of terrorist activities while transiting at Heathrow Airport in October 2014.[142] The case was subsequently dismissed: the Old Bailey in London recognized that Gildo was actively fighting in Syria in the years 2012–2013 on the side of resistance movements the United Kingdom was also supporting.[143] As Gildo's defence lawyer remarked: 'If it is the case that HM government was actively involved in supporting armed resistance to the Assad regime at a time when the defendant was present in Syria and himself participating in such resistance it would be unconscionable to allow the prosecution to continue.'[144] The case caused embarrassment in the government, and it points to the fact that not all foreign fighters are the same. This became more evident in subsequent incidents: in April 2016, two British citizens travelling from Syria after having fought alongside YPG forces were arrested at the border with Iraq.[145] Under diplomatic pressure from the government, the two men were freed with no charges. One of them, Jac Holmes, returned to Syria and died approximately a year later fighting in Raqqa against the Islamic State.[146] His death was widely reported in the British news, at a time when the UK government was holding discussions on whether to press charges on those going to fight alongside the YPG.[147]

Metropolis (High Court of Justice Queen's Bench Division Administrative Court, 12 October 2018). For reference: [2018] EWHC 2651 (Admin) 2018 WL 05112692.

[142] *See* Tom Whitehead, 'Old Bailey Trial of Terror Suspect Collapses after Security Services Refuse to Say Who They Helped in Syria', *The Telegraph* (1 June 2015) available at www.telegraph.co.uk/news/uknews/crime/11644227/Old-Bailey-trial-of-terror-suspect-collapses-after-security-services-refuse-to-say-who-they-helped-in-Syria.html.

[143] *See* Richard Norton-Taylor, 'Terror Trial Collapses after Fears of Deep Embarrassment to Security Services', *The Guardian* (1 June 2015) available at www.theguardian.com/uk-news/2015/jun/01/trial-swedish-man-accused-terrorism-offences-collapse-bherlin-gildo.

[144] *Ibid.*

[145] *See* Press Association, 'Two Britons Freed in Iraq on Way Home from Fighting Isis', *The Guardian* (26 April 2016) available at www.theguardian.com/world/2016/apr/24/two-britons-freed-in-iraq-after-arrest-on-way-home-from-fighting-isis.

[146] Lizzie Dearden, 'Jac Holmes: British Man Who Volunteered to Fight against Isis Killed in Syria', *The Independent* (24 October 2017) available at www.independent.co.uk/news/world/middle-east/jac-holmes-british-man-killed-fighting-isis-syria-raqqa-volunteer-dead-landmines-explosion-terrorism-a8016931.html.

[147] Matt Blake, '"Our Sons Were Heroes" Say Families of British Men Killed Fighting Isis', *The Guardian* (20 August 2017) available at www.theguardian.com/uk-news/2017/aug/20/our-sons-were-heroes-say-families-of-british-men-killed-fighting-isis. The question of British anti-ISIS volunteers was addressed several times in the British press. For instance see George Monbiot, 'Orwell Was Hailed a Hero for Fighting in Spain. Today He'd Be Guilty of Terrorism', *The Guardian* (10 February 2014) available at www.theguardian.com/commentisfree/2014/feb/10/orwell-hero-terrorism-syria-british-

If this foreign fighter was publicly praised as a hero, the British Parliament paid tribute to the fall of another British YPG volunteer, Erik Scurfield.[148]

Indeed, the issue of British anti-IS foreign fighters had been raised several times in Parliamentary debates, although it was almost completely overlooked in the discussions implementing the Counter-Terrorism Act of 2015. At that time, Jeremy Corbyn had tried to put the question on the table, wishing to introduce a differentiation between 'good' and 'bad' foreign fighters, but the issue fell on deaf ears. The problem was far from being set in practice. This is attested by the case of Joshua Walker (2017). The Welsh student had fought alongside the YPG and was charged with preparatory acts of terrorism upon his return from Syria.[149] The accusations were later on dropped. As he commented: 'I think arresting us [YPG volunteers] on suspicion of terror preparation is outrageous considering what we are doing.'[150] As recounted by the journalist who interviewed him at the beginning of his trial: 'Walker had read George Orwell's "Homage to Catalonia", which describes the author's journey to fight in the Spanish Civil War against fascist nationalists in the 1930s. He had also read stories about Welsh miners who – like Orwell and some 3,000 other Brits – travelled to Spain to take up arms against fascism.'[151] The Spanish Civil War was therefore still a reference for many of the

---

fighters-damned, and Emine Saner, 'Brits Abroad: Is It against the Law to Fight Isis?' *The Guardian* (25 February 2015) available at www.theguardian.com/world/shortcuts/2015/feb/25/brits-abroad-against-law-fight-isis.

[148] Dan Jarvis of the Labour Party addressed the issue in these terms: 'On a point of order, Madam Deputy Speaker. I should be grateful if you confirmed how this House could express our condolences to the family of Konstandinos Erik Scurfield, a constituent of mine who has been reported killed in Syria. Erik was a former Royal Marine who travelled to the region because he was horrified by Islamic State's brutal atrocities. His parents have asked me to pass on [a] brief message ... [Madam Deputy Speaker]: I thank the hon. Gentleman for his point of order. Let me first say on behalf of the whole House that we send to his constituent's family our most sincere sympathy at the loss of this brave young man.' HC Deb, 4 March 2015, Vol. 593, cc988. *See* also Ewen MacAskill, 'Erik Scurfield: The Former Marine Who Died in Someone Else's War', *The Guardian* (4 March 2015) available at www.theguardian.com/world/2015/mar/04/konstandinos-erik-scurfield-ex-marine-died-someone-elses-war-ypg-isis.

[149] Lizzie Dearden, 'Joshua Walker: Student Who Fought against Isis in Syria Cleared of Terror Charges over Book He Owned', *The Independent* (26 October 2017) available at www.independent.co.uk/news/uk/crime/joshua-walker-verdict-anarchists-cookbook-isis-syria-trial-uk-fighter-ypg-role-play-game-a8022126.html.

[150] *Ibid*.

[151] Ryan Gallagher, 'To Syria and Back', *The Intercept* (10 July 2017) available at https://theintercept.com/2017/07/10/josh-walker-isis-uk-terrorism-charge-ypg-syria/.

foreign fighters leaving for Syria, who understood their struggle as in the footsteps of their virtuous predecessors: 'Each generation gets only a limited amount of opportunities to actually make a difference in the world ... the Rojava revolution is the Spanish Civil War of our time.'[152] As such, these foreign fighters perceived the groups they enrolled in as being the ideal successors of those volunteers who had fought against the tyranny of authoritarian regimes on the Iberian Peninsula.[153]

The constant references made to the barbarity of the practices of certain factions active in Syria – in contrast to the acquittal of those volunteers enrolling in leftist battalions – is an indication that British courts did not operate in a cultural vacuum either. If judges were interested in the type of armed group volunteers had joined, they also placed particular emphasis on the means of conducting war. Finally, the radical, fanatic attitude recognized in the profiles of certain combatants could be compared to the perceived heroism of other foreign fighters.[154] Although the list of cases is longer, the point is sufficiently clear. What remains to be seen is how international law has developed on the subject. Humanitarian principles were in fact hardly ever mentioned by French or British courts. What happened to this branch of law after the 1977 Protocol and the norm against mercenaries? And how are foreign fighters understood in a time in which counterterrorism tends to overshadow any *jus in bello* consideration? To assess this aspect, we will move

---

[152] Shirin Jaafari, 'For some Americans, the Conflict in Syria is the Spanish Civil War of Our Time', *The World* (13 September 2017) available at www.pri.org/stories/2017-09-13/some-americans-conflict-syria-spanish-civil-war-our-time.

[153] Patrick Freyne, 'The Irish Man "Fighting Fascism" in Syria: "I Was Always Curious How I'd React to Battle"', *The Irish Times* (24 March 2018) available at www.irishtimes.com/news/world/middle-east/the-irish-man-fighting-fascism-in-syria-i-was-always-curious-how-i-d-react-to-battle-1.3435174. See also Sarah Leduc, 'Des Occidentaux Avec les Kurdes à Afrin: l'Ultra-Gauche Monte au Front', *France 24* (22 February 2018) available at www.france24.com/fr/20180220-syrie-turquie-kurdes-afrin-occidentaux-ultra-gauche-france-ypg-notre-dame-landes.

[154] This is attested for instance by the case of James Matthews (2018), an ex-British soldier coming back from Syria after having fought alongside the YPG. Matthews was charged with attending a terrorist training camp. His case was dropped for lack of evidence, and he walked out of the Old Bailey being cheered as a hero. See Mattha Busby, 'British Man Who Fought Isis in Syria Has Terror Charges Dropped', *The Guardian* (31 July 2018) available at www.theguardian.com/uk-news/2018/jul/31/james-matthews-who-joined-kurdish-forces-to-fight-isis-not-guilty. For an analysis of how British courts have differentiated between terrorist organizations and armed opposition movements see specifically Alexander Murray, 'Terrorist or Armed Opposition Group Fighter? The Experience of UK Courts and the Implications for Public International Law' (2018) 20 *International Community Law Review* 281–310.

to the last section, devoted to the application of IHL in some compelling returnees' cases.

3.4 Regular and Irregular Groups

At the beginning of this chapter, we saw how UNSC Resolution 2178 introduced a legal status for foreign fighters. This had not been possible at The Hague, while the problem did not really make the headlines in the subsequent Geneva talks. If on the former occasion the doctrine of neutrality had informed the debates, it was also agreed that foreign volunteers should not have been treated differently than other combatants. The Geneva text thus reaffirmed our actors as benefiting from POW status, provided they fulfilled the four criteria under Art. 4 of GC III. This, in a nutshell, was the situation before decolonization, when the question came dramatically back to the fore. Under strong pressure from newly independent states, it resulted in the codification of the norm against mercenaries. By employing the fighter terminology, and with its direct reference to warfare scenarios, UNSC Resolution 2178 had once again called into question the relevance and the application of IHL principles. This is attested by the vast amount of academic and expert literature on the subject, and by debates that resemble those already seen in the two previous historical moments.

If the classical doctrine of civil war is no longer part of today's discussions, it is interesting to note how contemporary experts hold very similar conversations to those of their predecessors. Naturally, these debates have been enriched by the developments of IHL in the last half-century, and so, alongside the various stages of a civil strife, one now finds the distinction between international and non-international armed conflict, the notion of direct participation in hostilities, or the idea of overall control, to name just few fundamental concepts.[155] What is evident is that the norm outlawing mercenaries contained in AP I has not put an end to the question of how to deal with third states' citizens going to fight in wars abroad. As the chapters have shown, each of those categorizations is inevitably permeated by the ideological contexts of a certain era. And it is so for our contemporary foreign fighters: Resolution 2178 was adopted in a precise timeframe and with a particular purpose,

---

[155] For an overview see Emanuele Sommario, 'The Status of Foreign Fighters under International Humanitarian Law', in de Guttry et al. (eds.), *Foreign Fighters under International Law* 141–160.

that of fighting international terrorism. By merging foreign volunteering with terrorism-related crimes, the Security Council produced a hybrid situation which circumvented the framework of humanitarian law and that contradicted some of its fundamental pillars.[156]

In the aftermath of the adoption of the resolution, many commentators started to hold discussions on how to deal with this new definition. The Geneva Academy of International Humanitarian Law in its Academic Briefing No. 7, for instance, proposed its own classification of foreign fighters as the following: 'A foreign fighter is an individual who leaves his or her country of origin or habitual residence to join a non-state armed group in an armed conflict abroad and who is primarily motivated by ideology, religion, and/or kinship.'[157] Avoiding the link with terrorism, this definition refers to an ideological/religious motivation behind foreign fighters' engagement in a conflict abroad, so as to distinguish them from mercenaries.[158] Conversely, the UN Working Group on the Use of Mercenaries suggested that the foreign fighter

---

[156] The 2014 report of the UN High Commissioner for Human Rights on countering terrorism highlighted a danger in the way the resolution was framed. Criminalization of the foreign terrorist fighter, the report explains, could amount to a pre-judgment of guilt or of criminal intent: for instance, it is unclear how states would distinguish between individuals travelling in certain areas of the world for business or family purposes, and someone embarking on a journey with a terrorist intent. *See* Report of the United Nations High Commissioner for Human Rights on the Protection of Human Rights and Fundamental Freedoms while Countering Terrorism, A/HRC/28/28 (14 December 2014) paragraphs 31–53. In the humanitarian field, many experts were uncomfortable with merging foreign fighters with terrorists. There was a presumption that engaging in acts of violence during an armed conflict could directly amount to terrorist offences, especially when joining certain groups. Overall, this would go as far as to undermine the principle of belligerent equality, one of the pillars of humanitarian law. On this point see specifically Sandra Kraehenmann, 'Foreign Fighters under International Law', Academic Briefing no. 7, *The Geneva Academy of International Humanitarian Law and Human Rights* (October 2014) pp. 15–20. For Kraehenmann, the resolution seemed to suggest that individuals joining a designated terrorist group in an armed conflict would in itself amount to receiving terrorist training. Additionally, it is unclear whether these individuals are understood as combatants in the sense of directly participating in hostilities, or whether they also take on non-combatant functions. For a further analysis see specifically Christopher Baker-Beall, 'The Concept of the Foreign Terrorist Fighter: An Immanent Critique' (2023) 8 *European Journal of International Security* 25–46.

[157] Kraehenmann, 'Foreign Fighters under International Law', p. 6.

[158] '[We] affirm that their primary motivation is ideology, religion, or kinship, not material gain; foreign fighters may be paid, but they are to be distinguished from mercenaries. (In fact, some armed groups, such as the Taliban and Islamic State, pay their fighters relatively generously.)' Kraehenmann, 'Foreign Fighters under International Law', p. 7.

phenomenon 'may be considered as contemporary forms of mercenarism or mercenary-related activities'.[159] As such, these actors could be accommodated under Art. 47 of AP I.[160] The latter position was echoed in the legislative discussions of some European countries (Belgium in particular) when it came to deciding on what basis to incriminate their own citizens who went to fight abroad.[161] The race to find the best classification for our actor extended to the academic world as well, with scholars trying to find the most encompassing and pertinent definition.[162] These

---

[159] Report of the UN Working Group on the Use of Mercenaries as a Means of Violating Human Rights and Impeding the Exercise of the Right of Peoples to Self-determination, A/70/330 (19 August 2015) paragraph 88.

[160] The topic has been further explored by some scholars: Simon Chesterman, 'Dogs of War or Jackals of Terror? Foreign Fighters and Mercenaries in International Law' (2016) 18 *International Community Law Review* 389–399 and José L. Gómez del Prado, 'Whether the Criteria Contained in the 1989 International Convention against the Recruitment, Use, Financing and Training of Mercenaries Notably Motivation Apply to Today's Foreign Fighters?' (2016) 18 *International Community Law Review* 400–417.

[161] *See* Chambre Des Représentants de Belgique, Projet de loi visant à renforcer la lutte contre le terrorisme (13 Juillet 2015) pp. 21–22: '[M. Koen Geens, ministre de la Justice] répond d'abord à la question de savoir pourquoi le gouvernement n'a pas opté en faveur d'une activation de la loi sur les mercenaires. Il explique que cette piste n'a pas été jugée idéale. D'une part, cette option présentait l'avantage qu'il ne fallait pas prouver qu'il y avait eu intention de commettre des actes terroristes, mais, d'autre part, son application risquait d'avoir des effets indésirables. Le ministre songe en particulier, à cet égard, aux combattants kurdes qui défendent la ville de Kobané, dans le nord de la Syrie, et qui sont soutenus par une coalition internationale. Ils risquaient de relever du champ d'application de la loi sur les mercenaires, ce qui n'est pas souhaitable. De plus, si l'on activait la loi sur les mercenaires uniquement en ce qui concerne le mouvement djihadiste, cela n'apporterait aucune valeur ajoutée par rapport à la législation antiterrorisme existante. Le ministre explique également que le parquet fédéral n'est pas favorable à l'activation de la loi sur les mercenaires, car il estime qu'une application combinée de cette législation et de la législation antiterrorisme pourrait donner lieu à des complications (juridiques). Il ne faut pas non plus oublier que l'application de la loi sur les mercenaires posera question à la lumière du droit humanitaire international.'

[162] David Malet provides a definition of foreign fighters as a 'non-citizen of conflict states who join insurgencies during civil war', and essentially distinguishes them from mercenaries and from private military companies. *See* Malet, *Foreign Fighters*, p. 9. Thomas Hegghammer differentiates foreign fighters from insurgents, terrorists, local rebels and independent global activists. Building on Malet's definition, he provides a narrower classification. The foreign fighter is someone who: (1) has joined, and operates within the confines of, an insurgency; (2) lacks citizenship of the conflict state or kinship links to its warring factions; (3) lacks affiliation to an official military organization; and (4) is unpaid. Hegghammer, 'The Rise of the Muslim Foreign Fighters', pp. 57–58. In this sense, Hegghammer excludes mercenaries who are normally paid and are motivated by private gain when they affiliate with a faction in a conflict. He also excludes soldiers who are part of a regular army, returning diaspora members or exiled rebels who might have affiliation to a previous conflict in the area. Finally, he distinguishes foreign fighters from

3.4 REGULAR AND IRREGULAR GROUPS 197

categorizations are not irrelevant, given that many experts have been called to advise Western governments when passing legislation on foreign fighters.[163] Now, a majority of those working in the humanitarian

> international terrorists as the latter are understood to operate outside an armed conflict zone. Other definitions exist in the academic literature regarding this phenomenon. They share some commonalities, such as the idea of fighting abroad, having a transnational identity and being distinct from mercenaries. For example, Cerwyn Moore and Paul Tumelty in a study on jihadis in Chechnya have adopted the definition for foreign fighters as of 'non-indigenous, non-territorialized combatants who, motivated by religion, kinship, and/or ideology rather than pecuniary reward, enter a conflict zone to participate in hostilities'. See Moore and Tumelty, 'Foreign Fighters and the Case of Chechnya', p. 412. Ian Bryan has described foreign fighters as 'not agents of foreign governments, but they leave home typically to fight for a transnational cause or identity'. See Ian Bryan, 'Sovereignty and the Foreign Fighter Problem' (2010) 54 *Orbis* 115–129, p. 116. Kristin Bakke classified them as 'transnational insurgents in armed intrastate conflicts, by which I refer to non-state actors that for either ideational or material reasons opt to participate in an intrastate conflict outside their own home country, siding with the challenger to the state. I do not consider as transnational insurgents foreign legions or private security companies that are hired by states or companies'. See Kristin M. Bakke, 'Copying and Learning from Outsiders? Assessing Diffusion from Transnational Insurgents in the Chechen Wars' (2010) American Political Science Association. Annual Meeting Paper, p. 3. Ciluffo, Cozzens and Ranstorp describe Western foreign fighters as 'violent extremists who leave their Western states of residence with the aspiration to train to take up arms against non-Muslim factions in Jihadi conflict zones'. See Franck J. Ciluffo, Jeffrey B. Cozzens and Magnus Ranstorp, 'Foreign Fighters: Trends, Trajectories and Conflict Zones', Homeland Security and Policy Institute (October 2010) p. 3, available at www.diva-portal.org/smash/get/diva2:380558/FULLTEXT01.pdf. Finally, while distinguishing foreign fighters from international terrorists, Mendelsohn maintains that the former are not citizens of the country where the conflict is fought and they are not part of the national military. See Barak Mendelsohn, 'Foreign Fighters – Recent Trends' (2011) 55 *Orbis* 189–202, pp. 192–194.

[163] Experts of course come with their own cultural biases in depicting good and bad versions of the foreign combatant, and thus in counselling how the contemporary phenomenon of foreign volunteering should be understood. In a nutshell, several figures inform these debates on foreign fighters (e.g., idealists, soldiers of fortune, religious fanatics), which have already been analysed in the previous sections. To offer an example, in 2014 Thomas Hegghammer briefed the British government on the contemporary phenomenon of foreign volunteering: 'When we asked Dr Hegghammer why British citizens fighting in the Syrian Civil War should be viewed differently to British citizens fighting in the Spanish Civil War he told us [that] the difference between the Islamist foreign fighter phenomenon today and a war like the Spanish Civil War is that today there are many cases of people moving on from this foreign fighter activity to international terrorism involving attacks against civilians in western cities. You did not have that at the time. There was not this sort of frequent and smooth transition from guerrilla warfare within the conflict at stake to more transnational terrorist operations. Whatever we think about the moral justification behind the initial involvement in the war, I think the reality that a substantial number of people move on to international

field pointed to the importance of distinguishing first and foremost whether these individuals were actors of an international (IAC) or a non-international armed conflict (NIAC).[164] Although it is sometimes problematic to draw a line between the two, the established doctrine portrays the former as an inter-state conflict, and the latter as one between a state and non-state armed groups.[165] The distinction between IAC and NIAC is crucial – experts argue – precisely because it defines the

terrorism from this activity should merit certain policy measures to prevent just that kind of violence.' See House of Commons, Home Affairs Committee Counter-terrorism, Seventeenth Report of Session 2013–14, p. 19. The Report is available at https://publications.parliament.uk/pa/cm201314/cmselect/cmhaff/231/231.pdf.

[164] On the distinction between IAC and NIAC see generally Jann K. Kleffner, 'Scope of Application of International Humanitarian Law', in Dieter Fleck (ed.), *The Handbook of International Humanitarian Law. 4th Edition* (Oxford: Oxford University Press 2021) 50–80. See also Sylvain Vité, 'Typology of Armed Conflicts in International Humanitarian Law: Legal Concepts and Actual Situations' (2009) 91 *International Review of the Red Cross* 69–94.

[165] More specifically, in order to distinguish NIACs from mere insurrections or internal disorders, one has to consider the level of intensity of fighting, together with the level or organization of the parties involved. These ideas were partially considered in Chapter 1, when exploring the classical doctrine of civil war. Naturally, the doctrine has evolved since then. As explained in the Introduction, it is not the purpose of this book to retrace those doctrines and concepts. However, the International Criminal Tribunal for the former Yugoslavia (ICTY) in the famous Tadic has provided a guidance in order to distinguish situations of internal violence from a NIAC. In this judgment, the ICTY stated that an armed conflict exists 'whenever there is a resort to armed force between States or protracted armed violence between governmental authorities and organized armed groups or between such groups within a State'. See *Prosecutor v. Dusko Tadic aka 'Dule'* (Decision on the Defence Motion for Interlocutory Appeal on Jurisdiction), IT-94-1, International Criminal Tribunal for the former Yugoslavia (ICTY), 2 October 1995, paragraph 70. Naturally, NIACs can later on become internationalized, thus triggering the application of the Geneva Conventions and of Additional Protocol I, specifically in terms of the combatants involved in the conflict. In the Nicaragua case (1986), the ICJ had set the effective control test to specify when a conflict takes an international character. According to this test, the conduct of the rebel armed forces is to be attributable to a state when the latter 'directed or enforced the perpetration of the acts contrary to human rights and humanitarian law'. See ICJ, *Nicaragua v. United States of America, Military and Paramilitary Activities*, Judgment of 27 June 1986, Merits, paragraph 115. Contrary to this high threshold, the ICTY (1999) instead elaborated the so-called overall control test, lowering the previous ICJ standard. In this case, a NIAC becomes internationalized not only when there is state financing or equipping of a rebel group, but also when a third state participates 'in the planning and supervision of military operations'. See *Prosecutor v. Dusko Tadic* (Appeal Judgment), IT-94-1-A, International Criminal Tribunal for the former Yugoslavia (ICTY), 15 July 1999, paragraph 104.

area of application of IHL in relation to the actors on the battlefield. As noted by the ICRC:

> The concept of 'foreign fighter' is not a term of art of IHL. The applicability of IHL to a situation of violence in which such fighters may be engaged depends on the facts on the ground ... In other words, IHL will govern the actions of foreign fighters, as well as any measures taken in relation to them, when they have a nexus to an ongoing armed conflict.[166]

Hence, the ICRC did not recognize foreign fighters as actors in warfare, emphasizing that 'nationality is irrelevant for determining whether a person qualifies as a combatant in an IAC'.[167] In other words, it does not matter which group one fights with, but rather what type of conflict (IAC or NIAC) these non-state actors engaged in. It is therefore crucial to see how IHL principles are applied in practice. Therefore, I propose to look at some court decisions (specifically in Belgium and the Netherlands), as they offer a window into the interconnections of humanitarian law and counterterrorism legislation in returnees' sentences.[168] It is here that some interesting distinctions are drawn.

At the beginning of our discussion, we saw how foreign fighters were mainly left free to enlist abroad. The only prohibition on states was not to aid the formation of organized groups of combatants (hostile military expeditions). This aspect was particularly emphasized during the Spanish Civil War, when the contingents sent by Italy and Germany were accused

---

[166] *See* International Committee of the Red Cross (ICRC), 'The Applicability of International Humanitarian Law to Terrorism and Counter-Terrorism' (2015), available at www.icrc.org/en/document/applicability-ihl-terrorism-and-counterterrorism.

[167] 'Under the Third Geneva Convention, nationality is irrelevant for determining whether a person qualifies as a combatant in an IAC, but may be important for determining whether a State will grant prisoner of war (POW) status to its own nationals captured fighting for a foreign army (State practice on this issue differs). Nationality is a decisive criterion for determining whether a detained person will benefit from "protected person" status under the Fourth Geneva Convention. This treaty, by its express terms (Article 4), does not apply to persons of the nationality of the detaining State or to the nationals of neutral or co-belligerent States, except where there is no "normal" diplomatic representation between such States and the detaining State.' *See* International Committee of the Red Cross (ICRC), 'International Humanitarian Law and the Challenges of Contemporary Armed Conflicts', document prepared by the ICRC for the 32nd International Conference of the Red Cross and Red Crescent (Geneva, Switzerland, 8–10 December 2015) p. 19, available at www.icrc.org/en/download/file/15061/32ic-report-on-ihl-and-challenges-of-armed-conflicts.pdf.

[168] On the application of humanitarian law in the domestic context see Sharon Weill, *The Role of National Courts in Applying International Humanitarian Law* (Oxford: Oxford University Press 2014).

of constituting formal battalions responding to a state's chain of command. Conversely, during decolonization, the foreign advisers dispatched by Cuba and Russia were contrasted with the unorganized (and thus unlawful) groups of Western mercenaries. In short, the organized/ unorganized nature of these combatants is one of the contrasting positions around which the legitimacy of foreign fighters has been played out. If technical debates in the aftermath of Resolution 2178 mainly revolved around the question of how FTF could be properly interpreted in light of the Geneva Conventions and their Protocols, court rulings uncover an additional layer to this story.

In the trial of Sharia4Belgium (February 2015), the Court of First Instance of Antwerp convicted several individuals belonging to this jihadist network with sentences imposed ranging between three and fifteen years.[169] The court found that the acts were committed between 2010 and 2014 (in both Belgium and Syria) and included: incitement to terrorist action, participation in terrorist activities and sending people to fight in Syria with terrorist groups (notably Al-Nusra and Majlis Shura Al Mujahidin).[170] What is crucial for the sake of the analysis, however, is a specific section of the Belgian criminal code. Under terrorist offences and the relevant punishable acts, article 141*bis* specifies in fact that:

> Le présent titre ne s'applique pas aux activités des forces armées en période de conflit armé, tels que définis et régis par le droit international humanitaire, ni aux activités menées par les forces armées d'un Etat dans l'exercice de leurs fonctions officielles, pour autant qu'elles soient régies par d'autres règles de droit international.[171]

This article can be understood as a saving clause, because in case of war it shifts the applicability of Belgian law to humanitarian law .[172] In other

---

[169] *Sharia4Belgium*, Court of First Instance of Antwerp, 11 February 2015, Case file: FD35.98.47-12-AN35.F1.1809-12. See also 'Sharia4Belgium Trial: Belgian Court Jails Members', BBC News (11 February 2015) available at www.bbc.com/news/world-europe-31378724.

[170] For a good overview of the trial see specifically Christophe Paulussen and Eva Entenmann, 'National Responses in Select Western European Countries to the Foreign Fighters Phenomenon', in de Guttry et al. (eds.), *Foreign Fighters under International Law* 391–422, pp. 395–397.

[171] Article 141*bis* of the Belgian Criminal Code (Law of 8 June 1867, as amended).

[172] For an analysis see specifically Vaios Koutroulis, 'Le Jugement du Tribunal Correctionnel d'Anvers dans l'Affaire dite "Sharia4Belgium" et l'Article 141bis du Code Pénal Belge', in Anne Jacobs and Daniel Flore (eds.), *Les Combattants Européens en Syrie* (Paris: L'Harmattan 2015) 85–103.

3.4 REGULAR AND IRREGULAR GROUPS

words, the Antwerp court had to assess whether the activities of the members of Sharia4Belgium could have been exempted from terrorist charges, given that these offences might have occurred during an armed conflict. The court thus had to clarify if an armed conflict existed (and where), and to interpret the meaning of armed forces, in this case the groups into which the defendants were integrated.

While recognizing that a conflict of non-international character was carried out in Syria, the tribunal made clear that no armed conflict was being fought in Belgium, so some of the accused could still be incriminated for terrorist acts committed in their home country.[173] Yet for those individuals who had actually gone to the battlefield the question remained whether or not humanitarian law applied.[174] Having recognized the existence of a NIAC in Syria, the court had to elucidate the problematic question of defining armed forces in such a conflict. The tribunal took the view that both Al-Nusra and Majlis Shura Al Mujahidin were armed groups lacking a definitive organization. More precisely: (a) they did not have an organized command structure, or an identifiable leadership, and (b) they were unwilling to respect IHL principles.[175] As such, humanitarian law would not apply in their case, and the defendants could still be prosecuted for terrorism offences under Belgian law.[176]

A similar issue arose in the case of *Federal Prosecutor* v. *Hamza B. et al.* (November 2015). The Tribunal de Première Instance de Bruxelles sentenced several individuals for recruitment and travel to war zones to rejoin jihadist groups.[177] As one of the returnees from Syria brought in his defence the application of Art. 141*bis*, the court was again confronted with the question of establishing its application.[178] In this case, the Brussels Tribunal started by elucidating the developments of the various

---

[173] The tribunal limited itself to listing the requirements for the existence of a NIAC: that the parties in the Syrian conflict were distinguishable from the civilian population; that the conflict had reached a certain degree of intensity; that the duration of the conflict was somehow significant. See *Sharia4Belgium*, p. 32.

[174] As the defence lawyers suggested, their clients could have been convicted of war crimes for actions in Syria, but not for terrorism in Belgium. See Koutroulis, 'Le Jugement du Tribunal Correctionnel d'Anvers, pp. 85–87.

[175] See Paulussen and Entenmann, 'National Responses', pp. 397–398.

[176] *Ibid.*

[177] *Federal Prosecutor* v. *Hamza B et al.*, Tribunal de Première Instance Francophone de Bruxelles, 6 November 2015, Case file: FD.35.98.212/11.

[178] In particular, the accused had travelled to Syria in mid-2013. He had joined and fought on behalf of Al-Nusra before returning to Belgium in 2014,

jihadist groups in the Syrian Civil War. It recalled specifically UNSC Resolution 2170 and its criminalization of the Al-Nusra Front and of other groups associated with Al-Qaeda, before assessing the relevance of IHL norms.[179] Analysing the jurisprudence of the ICTY and the work of humanitarian experts, the court first drew its own assessment of non-international armed conflict as of: 'conflits armés qui opposent de manière prolongée sur le territoire d'un Etat les autorités du government de cet Etat et des *groupes armés organisés*'.[180] Then it considered whether the groups joined by the defendant could be understood as organized, and therefore legitimate to participate in a NIAC. Here, the Brussels court dwelt more precisely on the characteristics of these groups, which were described as functioning 'par nature, dans une certaine clandestinité ... le terme "nébuleuse" ... illustre parfaitement le mode de fonctionnement de ces groups qui sont composes de cellules éparses inconnues les unes des autres'.[181] The court further explained that these battalions did not have an established headquarters, they were not able to set up a disciplinary regime respecting IHL norms, they did not engage in common actions, nor did they speak with a single voice.[182] The differentiation between an organized armed group and a terrorist one was thus drawn. Once again, Art. 141*bis* was found not applicable, and the returnee was charged with terrorism offences.

Clandestine, nebulous, without a clear chain of command, these characterizations are anything but neutral. On the contrary, they are indicative of a negative image underlying the criminalization of certain armed groups. The reasoning used by Belgian courts closely resembles the one used by the Bush administration to deny POW status to Taliban prisoners during the first decade of the war on terror.[183] Beyond the applicability of certain articles in fact, what is evident is how the dichotomy between organized and unorganized groups haunts these courts' reasoning. This juxtaposition speaks of a deeper bias behind the conceptualization of international humanitarian law.[184] Already in 1874, the German delegation feared that the occupied population could not be

---

[179] See *Federal Prosecutor v. Hamza B et al.*, pp. 6–9.
[180] Ibid., p. 9. Emphasis added.
[181] Ibid., p. 13.
[182] Ibid., p. 14.
[183] See John C. Yoo, 'The Status of Soldiers and Terrorists under the Geneva Conventions' (2004) 3 *Chinese Journal of International Law* 135–150.
[184] For instance a colonial bias at the root of the combatant status. On this point see Mégret, 'From "Savages" to "Unlawful Combatants"'.

distinguished from normal state troops. The idea of seeing 'adventurers of all sorts' flocking to the battlefield was reiterated by the same delegation at The Hague in 1907. And one should not forget that combatant status was based on the idea that volunteer corps had to resemble the army of a state. In other words, the figure that lurks in this conception of war is that of the irregular combatant.[185] This figure's alleged lack of organization, failure to follow the dictates of humanitarian law and fear of the 'good' conduct of hostilities being corrupted permeates IHL principles. Its image keeps reappearing at different times and under different guises, as evidenced by the examples of the German delegations, of mercenaries in the 1970s, or by the use made of it during the war on terror. And Belgian courts used this very image to delegitimize the presence of certain groups in the Syrian Civil War.

There is one final point that deserves attention. As emphasized by the ICRC, the combatant's status is always related to the type of armed conflict being fought. This aspect reveals another significant cultural bias at the heart of humanitarian law. If experts generally insist on the difference between IAC and NIAC, the relevance of such a distinction becomes clear in practice.

In the case of *Maher H.* (December 2014), the defendant had travelled to Syria to join a jihadi armed group, remaining on site for several months before making his way back to the Netherlands.[186] During the hearings of the trial, his defence raised the compelling point that if Syria was in a situation of civil strife, members of armed groups in such a conflict should have been exempted from prosecution for terrorism under Dutch criminal law.[187] Maher could have been charged for breaking basic IHL provisions, but not tried under terrorism law.

The District Court in the Hague took this line of defence seriously, and first assessed that the conflict in Syria was indeed a NIAC.[188] Nonetheless, the court stressed that in such conflicts, members of non-state armed groups were not justified to use violence (unlike those joining government forces). The judges made clear that individuals participating in hostilities alongside armed groups did not enjoy a status comparable

---

[185] On this point see Berman, 'Privileging Combat?' and Scheipers, *Unlawful Combatants*.
[186] See *Prosecutor* v. *Maher H.*, District Court of The Hague, 1 December 2014, Case file: 09/767116-14.
[187] Even if the actual actions undertaken by Maher on the battlefield remained unclear, the respondent was still charged with preparatory acts linked with armed jihad and for disseminating proscribed material. *Ibid.*, paragraph 3.
[188] *Ibid.*

to the combatant privilege in IACs.¹⁸⁹ And finally, that it was irrelevant whether these acts were conducted by freedom fighters waging war against an oppressive government.¹⁹⁰

A slightly different take was followed in a subsequent judgment by the same Hague court. In *Prosecutor v. Imane B. et al.* (December 2015), several individuals received sentences for incitement and dissemination of terrorist material, recruiting for terrorist groups (notably Al-Nusra and the Islamic State) and travelling to Syria to join those groups.¹⁹¹ The events having taken place over two years (2012–2014), all defendants were found guilty of participating in an armed jihadist struggle. Yet the tribunal was called once again to assess which legal system applied to the case at stake, whether international humanitarian law or Dutch anti-terrorism law.¹⁹²

Here the defence argued that the Syrian war could be described as a situation of international armed conflict, as 'many countries have joined in the conflict in Syria ... also on the side of the insurgents ... this support to the insurgents is more than just financial or logistical support and that other countries effectively exercise control over certain groups'.¹⁹³ The card played was clear: to afford their clients protection under the combatant's privilege. The court was thus asked to assess whether the Syrian conflict had reached a certain level of intensity and whether third states exercised overall control over these armed groups: which would have shifted the NIAC to an IAC.¹⁹⁴ Although the judges answered affirmatively to the first question, they were not convinced on

---

[189] Ibid. The court added that the existence of a NIAC did not render inapplicable other legal systems/regimes. Furthermore, that terrorist acts were also punishable under IHL.

[190] Ibid.

[191] *Prosecutor v. Imane B et al.*, District Court of The Hague, 10 December 2015, Case files: 09/842489-14, 09/767038-14 and 09/767313-14, 09/767174-13 and 09/765004-15, 09/767146-14, 09/767256-14, 09767238-14 and 09/827053-15, 09/767237-14, 09/765002-15, 09/767077-14.

[192] For IHL 'determines which individuals are entitled to perform certain acts of violence ... indemnifying them against criminal prosecution'. *Prosecutor v. Imane B et al.*, paragraph 7.2.

[193] Ibid., paragraph 7.4.

[194] Here is the relevant formulation given in Tadic: '[A]n armed conflict exists whenever there is a resort to armed force between States or protracted armed violence between governmental authorities and *organized armed groups* or between such groups within a State.' Emphasis added. See *Prosecutor v. Dusko Tadic aka 'Dule'*, paragraph 70. Subsequently, the ICTY clarified that these groups must have some hierarchical structure, laying down five constitutive elements: (1) The existence of a command structure; (2) The fact that the group could carry out operations in an organized manner; (3)

the second point: 'the defence failed to assert which power allegedly exercised overall control over which groups and therefore did not, or at least insufficiently concretely, substantiate on the basis of which facts and circumstances [the conflict] was internationalized'.[195] The court was of the opinion that at the time of the relevant facts (2012–2014), there existed a consensus in the international community which saw the Syrian conflict as a civil strife.[196]

Having established the existence of a NIAC in Syria, the Hague court followed the same line of reasoning as it did in *Maher*. Pointing out that in civil conflicts 'combatant status does not exist' and that only 'members of state armed forces are entitled to use violence', the court reaffirmed that 'during armed conflicts various legal regimes apply, including ... the domestic law of a state'.[197] Additionally, it highlighted the fact that groups such as Al-Nusra and the Islamic State systematically violated IHL. From there, it was only a short step before the judges found that the

---

Elements indicating a level of sophistication with respect to logistics; (4) The existence of internal discipline; and (5) The ability to speak with one voice. See *Prosecutor* v. *Ljube Boškoski and Johan Tarčulovski* (Judgment), IT-04-82-T, International Criminal Tribunal for the former Yugoslavia (ICTY), 10 July 2008, paragraphs 199–203. See also Tilman Rodenhäuser, 'Armed Groups, Rebel Coalitions, and Transnational Groups: The Degree of Organization Required from Non-State Armed Groups to Become Party to a Non-International Armed Conflict' (2016) 19 *Yearbook of International Humanitarian Law* 3–35.

[195] *Prosecutor* v. *Imane B et al.*, paragraph 7.12.

[196] 'The court did, also on its own motion, not find plausible any facts or circumstances which could have led to any other opinion. The court does not ignore the involvement of other powers in the conflict in Syria and acknowledges the possibility that the conflict may be classed as an international armed conflict in the future. However, the court cannot conclude that in the period stated in the charges the requirement of "overall control" was already fulfilled. In its report of 13 August 2015, the IICIS also concludes with regard to the armed conflict in Syria: While fought mostly by Syrians and largely contained within Syrian territory, the war is increasingly driven by international and regional powers, primarily in accordance with their respective geostrategic interests. Syrian stakeholders, on all sides of the conflict, have gradually lost control over the course of events due to a variety of external factors that have obscured the internal dimension of the war. As the war endures, it displays worrying signs of becoming internationalized. The competition among regional powers for influence has resulted, among other consequences, in alarming exacerbation of the sectarian dimension, instigated by the intervention of foreign fighters and extremist clerics. On the basis of the above the court concludes that during part of the period stated in the charges – from July 2012 through 31 October 2014 – there was a non-international armed conflict in Syria. In this period, the Syrian armed forces on the one hand and the fighters of the organized armed opposition groups on the other hand were engaged in an intensive and long-term armed struggle.' *Ibid.*, paragraphs 7.12 and 7.13.

[197] *Ibid.*, paragraphs 7.17–24.

defendants could not be granted protection under IHL and should have been prosecuted solely under Dutch criminal law.[198]

To conclude, the cases analysed in this section highlight some of the cultural biases underlying humanitarian law. On a purely technical standpoint, they showed that contemporary counterterrorism legislation largely overshadows IHL norms. The fact that foreign fighters can be criminalized more easily at the national level through anti-terrorist laws takes away the basic protection offered by humanitarian law, for instance.[199] They also highlighted that in the context of NIACs, fighters who join the ranks of insurgent groups are less protected than those joining government forces, another imbalance at the core of IHL. Finally, even if individuals who fight with these groups could potentially be freedom fighters, that does not change much in practice.[200] Naturally, the cases examined involved only certain armed groups. It would have been interesting to see whether the same argumentation regarding the applicability of IHL norms were used for those foreign fighters joining the ranks of the YPG or of the Free Syrian Army.

---

[198] *Ibid.*, paragraphs 7.26–29.

[199] There is a vast amount of literature analysing the problematic merging of IHL with terrorism-related offences. See, for example, Agathe Sarfati, 'International Humanitarian Law and the Criminal Justice Response to Terrorism: From the UN Security Council to the National Courts' (2021) 103 *International Review of the Red Cross* 267–293; Jan Klabbers, 'Rebel with a Cause? Terrorists ad Humanitarian Law' (2003) 14 *European Journal of International Law* 299–312; Marco Sassoli, 'Use and Abuse of the Laws of War in the War on Terrorism' (2004) 22 *Law & Inequalities* 195–221; Gabor Rona, 'Interesting Times for International Humanitarian Law: Challenges from the "War on Terror"' (2005) 17 *Terrorism and Political Violence* 157–173; Laura M. Olson 'Prosecuting Suspected Terrorists: The War on Terror Demands Reminders about War, Terrorism, and International Law' (2010) 24 *Emory International Law Review* 479–496. *See also* Andrea Bianchi and Yasmin Q. Naqvi (eds.), *International Humanitarian Law and Terrorism* (Oxford: Hart 2011).

[200] The question of differentiating between members of terrorist groups and freedom fighters is a long-standing one. On how some domestic courts have dealt with this issue, see Marina Mancini, 'Defining Acts of International Terrorism in Time of Armed Conflict: Italian Case Law in the Aftermath of September 11, 2001 Attacks' (2009) 9 *Italian Yearbook of International Law* 115–128; Lucia Alieni, 'Distinguishing Terrorism from Wars of National Liberation in the Light of International Law: A View from Italian Courts' (2008) 6 *Journal of International Criminal Justice* 525–539; Pierre-Emmanuel Dupont, 'International Terrorism, Resistance and the Just in Bello before French Courts: The Case of the Iranian Militant Opposition' (2013) 11 *Journal of International Criminal Justice* 441–462; and Antonio Coco, 'The Mark of Cain: The Crime of Terrorism in Times of Armed Conflict as Interpreted by the Court of Appeal of England and Wales in R v. Mohammed Gul' (2013) 11 *Journal of International Criminal Justice* 425–440.

In a wider sense, the dichotomy between 'good' and 'bad' combatants outlined throughout this book is here replaced by the distinction made between state armies and non-state armed groups, and more precisely between organized and unorganized groups. Even when humanitarian law is applied, these decisions point to the state-centric bias at the core of the laws of war. This is evident in the unwillingness to recognize non-state armed groups as legitimate actors on the battlefield, either because they are not organized as formal armies, or because they do not respect the basic principles of IHL. The dichotomy played between organized and unorganized group is however affected by the figure of the irregular combatant. This figure haunts the reasoning of the courts and the characterization of certain groups seen as barbaric and uncivilized, and thus not worthy of the protection of IHL. It comes from afar, as we saw in the context of the Brussels Conference. It has a similar trajectory to the history of the foreign combatant. As such, it remains part of the imagination of the legal actors in the present and will likely be used to delegitimize other foreign fighters in the future.

3.5 Conclusion

The Syrian Civil War represents one of the current scenarios of conflict where foreign fighters have reappeared on a large scale. In a rush to stop the influx of nationals of third states joining the ranks of the Islamic State and other jihadist groups, the Security Council criminalized these individuals as foreign terrorist fighters. This chapter opened with the debates underlying the adoption of Security Council Resolution 2178 (Section 3.1). In this venue a new figure has arisen, that of the jihadist combatant. Perceived as a security threat in home states, this contemporary version of the enemy of humanity represents the 'bad' side of the freedom fighter of decolonization. As seen on previous occasions, however, the Syrian Civil War also took place amidst tense ideological struggles: those fighting in support of the global jihad, but also against the Assad regime and the Islamic State itself. Different conceptions of freedom were thus at stake on the battlefield.

The ambiguities surrounding the criminalization of contemporary foreign fighters under the banner of counterterrorism became evident at the national level. Section 3.2 retraced the debates underlying the adoption of legislation in France and the United Kingdom in the aftermath of SC Resolution 2178. The figures of French intellectual André

Malraux and British writer George Orwell were evoked to question the terrorist label used to indiscriminately criminalize all foreign fighters. For some, however, it was questionable that the leftist heroes of the Spanish Civil War could be compared to present-day terrorists. The figure of the jihadist was thus split in two: on the one hand, policymakers recognized a 'good' version of this combatant, seen as a committed political individual. On the other, jihadism was understood as a 'perverted romantic ideal'; these individuals were therefore compared to those cynical, opportunist members of the Comintern army already singled out as the 'bad' version of the virtuous volunteers during the Spanish Civil War.

But the figure of the jihadist called into question deeper aspects connected with Western involvement in the Arab world. The mixed feeling of guilt and paternalism encountered at the United Nations during decolonization is echoed in the present day, as evidence of those colonial ghosts that are part of the modern history of the foreign volunteer. Despite these ambivalences, a major shift seemed to have occurred in the Western cultural imaginary. In the United Kingdom, there was a sense of how the references to the romantic adventurers à la Byron were being replaced by a more powerful image: that of the religious fanatic. A dark, brutal, version of former freedom fighters, the religious fundamentalist was portrayed as an actor who dehumanizes warfare, washing away the memory of previous, virtuous volunteers.

Section 3.3 retraced significant judgments in France and the United Kingdom. In both countries, courts of law made a clear differentiation between radicalized individuals willing to join jihadist groups and those who instead joined the 'good' side. In the former cases, tribunals emphasized the inclination towards martyrdom, along with the choice to join armed factions that used barbaric practices. As such, these fighters represented for the judges that perverted romantic ideal outlined in parliamentary venues. On the other hand, those French and British citizens fighting alongside Kurdish groups were either left free to go, or were acquitted upon their return. Overall, membership of left-wing battalions directly inspired by the International Brigades had an influence on these judgments: the cultural universe of the Spanish Civil War still had a role to play in the way French and British courts understood the struggle fought in Syria.

The chapter ended with a digression regarding the developments of humanitarian law (Section 3.4). The focus was kept on experts' discourse and courts' decisions, foregrounding the figures which informed the conversation and particularly the adjudication of returnees. The images of the *bon sauvage* and of the scary adventurer encountered a century earlier gave way to technical references to the armed conflict fought and to the type of armed groups on the ground. Here, the split into 'good' and 'bad' fighters was replaced by the distinction made between organized and unorganized groups. Clandestine battalions lacking a clear chain of command were singled out as endangering the good conduct of hostilities. The figure of the irregular combatant, already found in previous decades, reappeared to epitomize one of the fundamental biases underlying the application of IHL. The law on foreign fighters is thus destined to remain contextual, uncertain, ambiguous. Above all, it is based on fragmented cultural figures, which influence the understanding of the legitimacy or illegitimacy of the foreign fighters' cause and, as such, contribute to making the foreign combatant an undefined category whose legacy will continue to haunt international law.

BACK TO THE FUTURE

The problem of foreign fighters does not, of course, end with Syria. Many conflicts witness the presence of third-state nationals on the ground. The most recent example being the Russo-Ukrainian War. The question of how these foreign fighters will be categorized remains open. Will they be seen as mercenaries, freedom fighters, or as something else? This book offered an analytical grid to trace the persistence and the modifications of the cultural archetypes utilized to define who is a 'lawful' and who is an 'unlawful' foreign volunteer.

First, it showed how the figure of the foreign fighter emerges from precise historical contexts. Hence, it is crucial to understand the ideological battles unfolding around a specific civil war. It is there that figures rise to their partial, contextual meaning. But the image of the foreign fighter also travels in time and reappears in subsequent periods, affecting the way in which actors in subsequent historical moments think and produce norms on volunteers. Take for instance the war in Ukraine. What are the conceptions of freedom at stake, and how should European citizens fighting on either side of the conflict be classified? Which cultural references appear in lawmaking venues and in courts of law? Will the image of the soldier of fortune be opposed to that of the freedom fighter? In this sense, a line of continuity (and of rupture) could be established between the figures studied here, and new ones emerging from this and future conflicts.

Secondly, it would be useful to expand the repertoire of images by tracing those coming from a non-Western tradition. The method developed in this book could be applied to other contexts, outside of a Eurocentric paradigm. The cultural history of the foreign fighter would as such be doubly enriched. On the one hand, multiple trajectories could be found, in Asia, Africa or Latin America. Other wars and characters will be added alongside Byron, Orwell and Malraux. This could eventually lead to a comparison of recurrences and alterations with the archetypes seen in this book. Because these figures epitomize fantasies and ideas about warfare, its actors, and not ultimately about freedom, gathering a repertoire of non-Eurocentric images could also help uncover different worldviews. What about other ways of understanding the nobility (or the illegitimacy) of fighting abroad? What other tales of war, liberation and sovereignty are out there?

A third way of expanding the project is to go back in history. How did the figure of the adventurer reach The Hague Peace Conferences, for instance? If foreign volunteering did not have much resonance in 1874 the issue appeared pressing in 1907. Did the Second Boer War have anything to do with that? Following the method of this book, one could trace the history of the foreign volunteer using a nineteenth-century archive: Greece, Latin America, the United States. Is there a connection between these civil wars? What cultural images are evoked by British and French state representatives, foreign diplomatic officers, and legislators to categorize their citizens fighting abroad in the long nineteenth century? The freebooter, the noble adventurer, the *bon sauvage*: the figures seen in the interwar years originate in the previous historical period, and it could be noteworthy to understand their cultural matrix. Such a study would represent a prequel to the current monograph.

In conclusion, the three expansions of the project might well serve the purpose of expanding the history of foreign volunteering. But not only that. As pointed out in the Introduction, using a cultural approach means pushing the traditional ways of writing about international law. International law is not just about power struggles, foreign policy and diplomatic concerns. Fantasies, fears and desires are also part of the story, as is the conscious and unconscious recourse to cultural archetypes. These embody different conceptions of freedom, of war, and not ultimately of sovereignty claims. Cultural images are constitutive of our discipline and should not be cast aside as simply irrational, or superfluous. We have been told to live in post-ideological times. The response to the acknowledgement that law is politics was fleeing to expertise. But foreign fighters challenge such escapism. And so do the actors who judge them. They are still taken into a network of passions and moral dilemmas. The images of the foreign fighter are fractured because *we* are fractured. Social, political and historical considerations are part of our split identities. Desires, fears and fantasies keep inhabiting us. Let's restart there to imagine different ways of looking at the world. Let's write our passions back into international law.

BIBLIOGRAPHY

Books

Alpert M., *A New International History of the Spanish Civil War* (London: Macmillan 1994).
  The Republican Army in the Spanish Civil War, 1936–1939 (Cambridge: Cambridge University Press 2013).
Anghie A., *Imperialism, Sovereignty and the Making of International Law* (Cambridge: Cambridge University Press 2006).
Arielli N., *From Byron to Bin Laden: A History of Foreign War Volunteers* (Cambridge, MA: Harvard University Press 2018).
Arielli N., Collins B. (eds.), *Transnational Soldiers: Foreign Military Enlistment in the Modern Era* (London: Palgrave Macmillan 2013).
Armitage D., *Civil Wars: A History in Ideas* (New York: Alfred A. Knopf 2017).
Arnold G., *Mercenaries: The Scourge of the Third World* (Basingstoke: Macmillan 1999).
Baudens S., Dupré M., Terrom H. (eds.), *Les Combattants Érangers: Approches Culturelles et Juridiques* (Paris: Mare et Martin 2021).
Baxell R., *British Volunteers in the Spanish Civil War: The British Battalion in the International Brigades, 1936–1939* (London: Routledge 2004).
Belsey C., *Poststructuralism: A Very Short Introduction* (Oxford: Oxford University Press 2002).
Bennis P., *Understanding ISIS and the New Global War on Terror: A Primer* (Northampton, MA: Olive Branch Press 2015).
Berdine M., *Redrawing the Middle East: Sir Mark Sykes, Imperialism and the Sykes–Picot Agreement* (London: I. B. Tauris 2018).
Berman N., *Passions and Ambivalence: Colonialism, Nationalism, and International Law* (Leiden: Brill 2011).
Bernanos G., *Les Grands Cimetières Sous la Lune* (Paris: Plon/Seuil 1995).
Bianchi A. (ed.), *Non-state Actors and International Law* (Aldershot: Ashgate 2009).
Bianchi A., Naqvi Y. Q. (eds.), *International Humanitarian Law and Terrorism* (Oxford: Hart 2011).
Birmingham D., *A Short History of Modern Angola* (London: Hurst 2015).

Blackbourn J, Kayis D., McGarrity N., *Anti-Terrorism Law and Foreign Terrorist Fighters* (London: Routledge 2019).
Bott Spillius E., Milton J., Garvey P., Couve C., Steine D. (eds.), *The New Dictionary of Kleinian Thought* (New York: Routledge 2011).
Boyd White J., *The Legal Imagination* (Chicago: University of Chicago Press 1985).
Brenan G., *The Spanish Labyrinth* (Cambridge: Cambridge University Press 2014).
Brown Scott J. (ed.), *The Hague Conventions and Declarations of 1899 and 1907: Accompanied by Tables of Signatures, Ratifications and Adhesions of the Various Powers, and Texts of Reservations.* 2nd edition (New York: Oxford University Press/Humphrey Milford 1915).
  The Proceedings of the Hague Conferences. Vol. 1 (Oxford: Oxford University Press 1920).
  The Proceedings of the Hague Conferences. Vol. 3 (Oxford: Oxford University Press 1921).
Brownlie I., *International Law and the Use of Force by States* (Oxford: Clarendon Press 1963).
Burchett W., Roebuck D., *The Whores of War: Mercenaries Today* (Harmondsworth: Penguin Books 1977).
Burke P., *The French Historical Revolution: The Annales School 1924–2014* (Cambridge: Polity Press 2015).
Butler J., *The Psychic Life of Power: Theories in Subjection* (Stanford, CA: Stanford University Press 1997).
Byman D., *Al Qaeda, The Islamic State and the Global Jihadist Movement: What Everyone Needs to Know* (Oxford: Oxford University Press 2015).
  Road Warriors: Foreign Fighters in the Armies of Jihad (New York: Oxford University Press 2019).
Carroll P., *The Odyssey of the Abraham Lincoln Brigade: Americans in the Spanish Civil War* (Stanford, CA: Stanford University Press 1994).
Cassese A., *The Human Dimension of International Law: Selected Papers* (Oxford: Oxford University Press 2008).
Castoriadis C., *The Imaginary Institution of Society* (Cambridge, MA: MIT Press 1997).
  World in Fragments: Writings on Politics, Society, Psychoanalysis, and the Imagination (Stanford, CA: Stanford University Press 1997).
Castrén E., *The Present Law of War and Neutrality* (Helsinki: Suomalainev Tiedeakemia 1954).
Chakrabarty D., *Provincializing Europe: Postcolonial Thought and Historical Difference* (Princeton, NJ: Princeton University Press 2000).
Chesterman S., Lehnardt C. (eds.), *From Mercenaries to Market: The Rise and Regulation of Private Military Companies* (Oxford: Oxford University Press 2007).
Clark E. A., *History, Theory, Text: Historians and the Linguistic Turn* (Cambridge, MA: Harvard University Press 2004).

Cockburn P., *The Rise of the Islamic State: ISIS and the New Sunni Revolution* (London: Verso 2015).
Codaccioni V., *Justice d'Exception: l'État Face aux Crimes Politiques et Terroristes* (Paris: CNRS Editions 2015).
Coll S., *Ghost Wars: The Secret History of the CIA, Afghanistan, and bin Laden, from the Soviet Invasion to September 10, 2001* (New York: Penguin 2005).
Collingwood R. G., *The Idea of History* (Oxford: Oxford University Press 1994).
Constable M., *Our Word Is Our Bond: How Legal Speech Acts* (Stanford, CA: Stanford University Press 2014).
Coverdale J. F., *Italian Intervention in the Spanish Civil War* (Princeton, NJ: Princeton University Press 1975).
Craven M., Fitzmaurice M., Vogiatzi M. (eds.), *Time, History and International Law* (Leiden: Brill 2007).
Cunningham V. (ed.), *The Spanish Front: Writers on the Civil War* (Oxford: Oxford University Press 1986).
Damasio A. R., *Descartes' Error: Emotion, Reason, and the Human Brain* (New York: Avon Books, 1995).
D'Aspremont J. (ed.), *Participants in the International Legal System: Multiple Perspectives on Non-State Actors in International Law* (London: Routledge 2011).
Deák F., Jessup P. C. (eds.), *A Collection of Neutrality Laws, Regulations and Treaties of Various Countries* (2 vols.) (New York: Columbia University Press 1939).
De Certeau M., *Heterologies: Discourse on the Other* (Minneapolis: University of Minnesota Press 1986).
  Histoire et Psychanalyse Entre Science et Fiction (Paris: Gallimard 1987).
  The Writing of History (New York: Columbia University Press 1992).
De Guttry A., Capone F., Paulussen C. (eds.), *Foreign Fighters under International Law and Beyond* (The Hague: Asser Press 2016).
Dempster C., Tomkins D., *Fire Power* (London: Corgi Books 1978).
Deshpande G. P., Gupta H.K., *United Front against Imperialism: China's Foreign Policy in Africa* (Bombay: Somaiya Publications 1986).
Derrida J., *Spectres of Marx: The State of the Debt, the Work of Mourning and the New International* (New York: Routledge 1994).
Douzinas C., *The End of Human Rights: Critical Legal Thought at the Turn of the Century* (Oxford: Hart 2000).
Duffy H., *The 'War on Terror' and the Framework of International Law*. 2nd edition (Cambridge: Cambridge University Press 2015).
Dumont S., *Les Mercenaires* (Berchem: EPO 1983).
Fenwich C. G., *The Neutrality Laws of the United States* (Washington, DC: Carnegie Endowment for International Peace 1913).
Fitzsimmons S., *Mercenaries in Asymmetric Conflicts* (Cambridge: Cambridge University Press 2012).

Foley F., *Countering Terrorism in Britain and France: Institutions, Norms, and the Shadow of the Past* (Cambridge: Cambridge University Press 2013).
Ford J. D., *The Emergence of Privateering* (Leiden: Brill/Nijhoff 2023).
Foucault M., *The Order of Things* (New York: Routledge 2001).
The Archeology of Knowledge (Abingdon: Routledge 2002).
Freud S., *Civilization and Its Discontents* (New York: Norton 2010).
Garcia-Mora M. R., *International Responsibility for Hostile Acts of Private Persons against Foreign States* (The Hague: Martinus Nijhoff 1962).
George E., *The Cuban Intervention in Angola, 1965–1991: From Che Guevara to Cuito Cuanavale* (London: Frank Cass 2005).
Gerges F., *The Far Enemy: Why Jihad Went Global* (Cambridge: Cambridge University Press 2009).
Goodrich P., *Oedipus Lex: Psychoanalysis, History, Law* (Berkeley: University of California Press 1995).
Goodrich P., Carlson D. G. (eds.), *Law and the Postmodern Mind: Essays on Psychoanalysis and Jurisprudence* (Ann Arbor: University of Michigan Press 1998).
Greenspan M., *The Modern Law of Land Warfare* (Berkeley: University of California Press 1959).
Gurski P., *Western Foreign Fighters: The Threat to Homeland and International Security* (Lanham, MD: Rowman & Littlefield 2017).
Harsch E., Malik M., *Angola: The Hidden History of Washington's War* (New York: Pathfinder Press 1976).
Hébert A., *Jusqu'à Raqqa: avec les Kurdes contre Daech* (Paris: Les Belles Lettres 2019).
Heffes E., Kotlik M. D., Ventura M. J. (eds.), *International Humanitarian Law and Non-State Actors: Debates, Law and Practice* (The Hague: Asser Press 2020).
Heller-Roazen D., *The Enemy of All: Piracy and the Law of Nations* (New York: Zone Books 2009).
Hemingway E., *For Whom the Bell Tolls* (London: Vintage Books 2005).
Hermet G., *La Guerre d'Espagne* (Paris: Éditions du Seuil 1989).
Hoare M., *The Road to Kalamata: A Congo Mercenary's Personal Memoir* (Lexington, MD: Lexington Books 1989)
Hobsbawm E., *Bandits*. Revised edition (New York: Pantheon Books 1981).
Iggers G. G., *Historiography in the Twentieth Century: From Scientific Objectivity to the Postmodern Challenge* (Middletown, CT: Wesleyan University Press 2005).
Jenkins K., *Re-Thinking History* (New York: Routledge 2003).
Johns F., Joyce R., Pahuja S. (eds.), *Events: The Force of International Law* (London: Routledge 2010).
Keene J., *Fighting for Franco: International Volunteers in Nationalist Spain during the Spanish Civil War* (London: Hambledon Continuum 2007).

Kennedy D., *Of War and Law* (Princeton, NJ: Princeton University Press 2006).
  A World of Struggle. How Power, Law and Expertise Shape Global Political Economy (Princeton, NJ: Princeton University Press 2016).
Kenwood A. (ed.), *The Spanish Civil War: A Cultural and Historical Reader* (Providence, RI: Berg , 1993).
Khun T., *The Structure of Scientific Revolutions* (Chicago: University of Chicago Press 1970).
Kinsella H. M., *The Image before the Weapon: A Critical History of the Distinction between Combatant and Civilian* (Ithaca, NY: Cornell University Press 2011).
Kirschenbaum L. A., *International Communism and the Spanish Civil War: Solidarity and Suspicion* (Cambridge: Cambridge University Press 2015).
Klein M., *The Psychoanalysis of Children* (New York: Grove Press 1932).
  Contributions to Psychoanalysis 1921–1945 (London: Hogarth Press 1948).
Koskenniemi M., *The Gentle Civilizer of Nations: The Rise and Fall of International Law 1870–1960* (Cambridge: Cambridge University Press 2004).
  From Apology to Utopia: The Structure of the International Legal Argument. Reissued with a New Epilogue (Cambridge: Cambridge University Press 2005).
  The Politics of International Law (Oxford: Hart 2011).
Koskenniemi M., Rech W., Jimenez Fonseca M. (eds.), *International Law and Empire: Historical Explorations* (Oxford: Oxford University Press 2017).
Kruger C., Levesen S. (eds.), *War Volunteering in Modern Times: From the French Revolution to the Second World War* (London: Palgrave Macmillan 2013).
Lacan J., *Écrits: The First Complete Edition in English* (New York: Norton 2010).
Lawrence T. E., *The Seven Pillars of Wisdom* (London: Penguin Classics 2000).
Le Fur L., *La Guerre d'Espagne et le Droit* (Paris: Les Editions Internationales 1938).
Lennon K., *Imagination and the Imaginary* (New York: Routledge 2015).
Li D., *The Universal Enemy: Jihad, Empire, and the Challenge of Solidarity* (Stanford, CA: Stanford University Press 2019).
Lieblich E., *International Law and Civil War* (New York: Routledge 2013).
Malet D., *Foreign Fighters: Transnational Identity in Civil Conflicts* (Oxford: Oxford University Press 2013).
Malraux A., *L'Espoir* (Paris: Gallimard 1937).
Mantilla G., *Lawmaking under Pressure. International Humanitarian Law and Internal Armed Conflict* (Ithaca, NY: Cornell University Press 2020).
Mazurel H., *Vertiges De La Guerre: Byron, Les Philhellènes et Le Mirage Grec* (Paris: Les Belles Lettres 2013).
Mockler A., *Gli Ultimi Mercenari* (Milano: Sugarco 1987).
Moore-Gilbert B., *Postcolonial Theory: Contexts, Practices, Politics* (London: Verso 1997).

Muggeridge M., Hood S. (eds.), *Ciano's Diplomatic Papers* (London: Odhams Press 1948).
Neff S. C., *The Rights and Duties of Neutrals: A General History* (Manchester: Manchester University Press 2000).
Noortmann M., Ryngaert C. (eds.), *Non-State Actor Dynamics in International Law: From Law-Takers to Law-Makers* (London: Routledge 2016).
Norton M. J., Perkovich J. (eds.), *Law and Civil War in the Modern World* (Baltimore, MD: Johns Hopkins University Press 1974).
O'Connor S., Piketty G. (eds.), *Foreign Fighters and Multinational Armies: From Civil Conflicts to Coalition Wars, 1848–2015* (Abingdon: Routledge 2022).
Oppenheim L., *International Law: A Treatise, Fifth Edition Vol. II*. Edited by Hersch Lauterpacht (New York: Longmans, Green and Company 1935).
Orford A., *International Law and the Politics of History* (Cambridge: Cambridge University Press 2021).
Ortnoy A., Clore G. L., Collins A. (eds.), *The Cognitive Structure of Emotions* (Cambridge: Cambridge University Press 1988).
Orwell G., *Homage to Catalonia* (London: Penguin 2013).
Othen C., *Franco's International Brigades. Adventurers, Fascists and Christian Crusaders in the Spanish Civil War* (London: C. Hurst 2013).
Padelford N. J., *International Law and Diplomacy in the Spanish Civil Strife* (New York: The Macmillan Company 1939).
Pahuja S., *Decolonizing International Law: Development, Economic Growth and the Politics of Universality* (Cambridge: Cambridge University Press 2011).
Payne S. G., *The Spanish Civil War, the Soviet Union, and Communism* (New Haven, CT: Yale University Press 2004).
The Spanish Civil War (Cambridge: Cambridge University Press 2012).
Pearce H. A., *The Hague Peace Conferences and Other International Conferences Concerning the Laws and Usage of War. Texts of Conventions with Commentaries* (Cambridge: Cambridge University Press 1909).
Pedrozo R. A., Wollschlaeger D. P., *International law and the Changing Character of War* (Newport, RI: Naval War College 2011).
Percy S., *Mercenaries: The History of a Norm in International Relations* (Oxford: Oxford University Press 2007).
Pictet J. (ed.), *Commentary to the Geneva Convention III Relative to the Treatment of Prisoners of War* (Geneva: ICRC 1960).
Pokalova E., *Returning Islamist Foreign Fighters: Threats and Challenges to the West* (Cham: Springer International Publishing 2020).
Popovski V., Fraser T. (eds.), *The Security Council as a Global Legislator* (New York: Routledge 2014).
Rech W., *Enemies of Mankind: Vattel's Theory of Collective Security* (Leiden: Martinus Nijhoff 2013).

Rekawek K., *Not only Syria: the Phenomenon of Foreign Fighters in a Comparative Perspective* (Amsterdam: IOS Press 2017).
Richardson D., *Comintern Army: The International Brigades and the Spanish Civil War* (Lexington: University of Kentucky 1982).
Rodriguez M. E., *Freedom's Mercenaries: British Volunteers in the Wars of Independence of Latin America. Vol. I: Northern South America and Vol. II: Southern South America* (Lanham, MD: Hamilton Books 2006).
Under the Flags of Freedom: British Mercenaries in the War of the Two Brothers, the First Carlist War, and the Greek War of Independence (1821–1840) (Lanham, MD: Hamilton Books 2009).
Rongier S., *Theories des Fantomes. Pour une Archeologie des Images* (Paris: Les Belles Lettres 2016).
Roussillon S., *Les 'Brigades Internationales' de Franco. Les Volontaires Étrangers du Côté National* (Versailles: Via Romana 2012).
Scheipers S., *Unlawful Combatants. A Genealogy of the Irregular Fighter* (Oxford: Oxford University Press 2015).
Schillings S., *Enemies of All Humankind* (Hanover, NH: Dartmouth College Press 2016).
Schmitt C., *The Concept of the Political*. Expanded edition (Chicago: University of Chicago Press 2007).
Schramme J., *Le Bataillon Leopard : Souvenirs d'un Africain Blanc* (Paris: Laffont 1969).
Schwarz H., Ray S. (eds.), *A Companion to Postcolonial Studies* (Malden, MA: Blackwell 2005).
Scott J., *Théorie Critique de l'Histoire. Identités, Expériences, Politiques* (Paris: Fayard 2009).
Simpson G., *The Sentimental Life of International Law: Literature, Language, and Longing in World Politics* (Oxford: Oxford University Press 2021).
Singer P. W., *Corporate Warriors: The Rise of the Privatized Military Industry* (Ithaca, NY: Cornell University Press 2007).
Skoutelsky R., *L'Espoir Guidait Leur Pas: Les Volontaires Français Dans les Brigades Internationales* (Paris: Grasset & Fasquelle 1998).
Skouteris T., *The Notion of Progress in International Law Discourse* (The Hague: Asser Press 2010).
Spivak G. C., *A Critique of Postcolonial Reason: Toward a History of the Vanishing Present* (Cambridge, MA: Harvard University Press 1999).
St. Clair W., *That Greece Might Still Be Free: The Philellhenes in the War of Independence* (Oxford: Oxford University Press 1972).
Steiner R., *Carre Rouge: Du Biafra au Soudan, Le Dernier Condottiere* (Paris: Laffont 1976).
Stéphane R., *Portrait de l'Aventurier : T. E. Lawrence, Malraux, Von Solmon* (Paris: Points Editeur 2014).

Stockwell J., *In Search of Enemies: A CIA Story* (New York: Norton 1978).
Stone J., *Legal Controls of International Conflict: A Treatise on the Dynamics of Disputes and War-Law* (New York: Rinehart 1954).
Stremlau J. J., *The International Politics of the Nigerian Civil War, 1967–1970* (Princeton, NJ: Princeton University Press 1977).
Taylor C., *Modern Social Imaginaries* (Durham, NC: Duke University Press 2004).
Thomas H., *The Spanish Civil War: Third Edition. Revised and Enlarged* (London: Penguin 1977).
Thomson, D., *Les Français Jihadistes* (Paris: Éditions des Arènes 2014).
  Les Revenants (Paris: Seuil-Les Jours 2016).
Thomson J. E., *Mercenaries, Pirates, and Sovereign: State-Building and Extraterritorial Violence in Early Modern Europe* (Princeton, NJ: Princeton University Press 1994).
Tremlett G., *The International Brigades: Fascism, Freedom and the Spanish Civil War* (London: Bloomsbury 2020).
Van der Esch P. A. M., *Prelude to War. The International Repercussions of the Spanish Civil War (1936–1939)* (The Hague: Martinus Nijhoff 1951).
Vivó R. V., *Angola: Fim do Mito dos Mercenários* (Luanda: África editora 1976).
Warren R., *Terrorist Movements and the Recruitment of Arab Foreign Fighters. A History from 1980s Afghanistan to ISIS* (Oxford: Bloomsbury 2021).
Weintraub S., *The Last Great Cause: The Intellectuals and the Spanish Civil War* (New York: Weybright and Talley 1968).
Weill S., *The Role of National Courts in Applying International Humanitarian Law* (Oxford: Oxford University Press 2014).
Weiss M., Hassan H., *Isis: Inside the Army of Terror* (New York: Regan Arts 2015).
Whealey R. H., *Hitler and Spain: The Nazi Role in the Spanish Civil War, 1936–1939* (Lexington: University of Kentucky Press 1989).
White H., *Metahistory: The Historical Imagination in Nineteenth-Century Europe* (Baltimore, MD: Johns Hopkins University Press 1973).
  The Content of the Form: Narrative Discourse and Historical Representation (Baltimore, MD: Johns Hopkins University Press 1987).

Journal Articles

Alexander A., 'International Humanitarian Law, Postcolonialism and the 1977 Geneva Protocol I' (2016) 17 *Melbourne Journal of International Law* 15–50.
Allard E. B., 'The Crescent and the Dagger: Representations of the Moorish Other during the Spanish Civil War' (2016) 93 *Bulletin of Spanish Studies* 965–988.
Alieni L., 'Distinguishing Terrorism from Wars of National Liberation in the Light of International Law: A View from Italian Courts' (2008) 6 *Journal of International Criminal Justice* 525–539.

Allot P., 'International Law and the Idea of History' (1999) 1 *Journal of History of International Law* 1-21.

Al Tuma A., 'The Participation of Moorish Troops in the Spanish Civil War (1936-39): Military Value, Motivations, and Religious Aspects' (2011) 30 *War & Society* 91-107.

Arielli N., Frei G. A., Van Hulle I., 'The Foreign Enlistment Act, International Law, and British Politics, 1819-2014' (2016) 38 *International History Review* 636-656.

Baker-Beall C., 'The Concept of the Foreign Terrorist Fighter: An Immanent Critique' (2023) 8 *European Journal of International Security* 25-46.

Bakker E., Paulussen C., 'Returning Jihadist Foreign Fighters: Challenges Pertaining to Threat Assessment and Governance of This Pan-European Problem' (2014) 25 *Security and Human Rights* 11-32.

Berman N., 'Between "Alliance" and "Localization": Nationalism and the New Oscillationism' (1994) 26 *New York University Journal of International Law & Politics* 449-492.

  'Legalizing Jerusalem or, of Law, Fantasy, and Faith' (1996) 45 *Catholic University Law Review* 823-835.

  'Nationalism "Good" and "Bad": The Vicissitudes of an Obsession' (1996) 90 *Proceedings of the Annual Meeting of the American Society of International Law* 214-218.

  'In the Wake of Empire' (1999) 14 *American University International Law Review* 1515-1569.

  'Privileging Combat? Contemporary Conflict and the Legal Construction of War' (2004) 43 *Columbia Journal of Transnational Law* 1-71.

Bianchi A., Saab A., 'Fear and International Law-Making: An Exploratory Inquiry' (2019) 32 *Leiden Journal of International Law* 351-365.

Blackbourn J., Walker C., 'Interdiction and Indoctrination: The Counter-Terrorism and Security Act 2015' (2016) 79 *Modern Law Review* 840-870.

Blank Y., 'The Reenchantment of Law' (2011) 63 *Cornell Law Review* 633-670.

Borchard E., 'The Power to Punish Neutral Volunteers in Enemy Armies' (1938) 32 *American Journal of International Law* 535-538.

Boumedra T., 'International Regulation of the Use of Mercenaries in Armed Conflicts' (1981) 20 *Military Law & Law of War Review* 35-87.

Brown W., '"The Most We Can Hope For...": Human Rights and the Politics of Fatalism' (2004) 103 *South Atlantic Quarterly* 451-463.

Brownlie I., 'Volunteers and the Law of War and Neutrality' (1956) 5 *International and Comparative Law Quarterly* 570-580.

  'International Law and the Activities of Armed Bands' (1958) 7 *International and Comparative Law Quarterly* 712-735.

Bruyère-Ostells W., 'La Révolte Des Mercenaires Contre Mobutu en 1967' (2012) 247 *Guerres mondiales et conflits contemporains* 91-104.

'L'Influence Français Dans la Sécession Katangaise: Naissance d'Un Système Mercenaire' (2015) 162 *Relations internationales* 157–172.

Bryan I., 'Sovereignty and the Foreign Fighter Problem' (2018) 54 *Orbis* 115–129.

Buchanan T., 'Edge of Darkness: British "Front-Line" Diplomacy in the Spanish Civil War, 1936–1937' (2003) 12 *Contemporary European History* 279–303.

Burmester, H. C., 'The Recruitment and Use of Mercenaries in Armed Conflict' (1978) 72 *American Journal of International Law* 37–56.

Byman D., 'The Jihadist Returnee Threat: Just How Dangerous?' (2016) 131 *Political Science Quarterly* 69–99.

Cassese A., 'Mercenaries: Lawful Combatants or War Criminals?' (1980) 40 *ZaöRV* 1–30.

Cesner R. E., Brant J. W., 'Law of the Mercenary: An International Dilemma' (1977) 6 *Capital University Law Review* 339–370.

Chadwick E., 'Neutrality Revised' (2013) 22 *Nottingham Law Journal* 41–52.

Charlesworth H., 'International Law: A Discipline of Crisis' (2002) 65 *Modern Law Review* 377–392.

Chesterman S., 'Dogs of War or Jackals of Terror? Foreign Fighters and Mercenaries in International Law' (2016) 18 *International Community Law Review* 389–399.

Chimni B. S., 'Third World Approach to International Law: A Manifesto' (2006) 8 *International Community Law Review* 3–27.

'The Past, Present and Future of International Law: A Critical Third World Approach' (2007) 8 *Melbourne Journal of International Law* 499–514.

Churchill W., 'U.S. Mercenaries in Southern Africa: The Recruiting Network and U.S. Policy' (1980) 27 *Africa Today* 21–46.

Coco A., 'The Mark of Cain: The Crime of Terrorism in Times of Armed Conflict as Interpreted by the Court of Appeal of England and Wales in R v. Mohammed Gul' (2013) 11 *Journal of International Criminal Justice* 425–440.

Corradi E., 'Joining the Fight: The Italian Foreign Fighters Contingent of the Kurdish People's Protection Units' (2022) *Italian Political Science Review* 1–19.

Cotton J. R., 'Comment: The Rights of Mercenaries as Prisoners of War' (1977) 77 *Military Law Review* 143–166.

Courtney G. E., 'American Mercenaries and the Neutrality Act: Shortening the Leash on the Dogs of War' (1985) 12 *Journal of Legislation* 175–193.

Cragin K. R., 'The Challenge of Foreign Fighters Returnees' (2017) 33 *Journal of Contemporary Criminal Justice* 292–312.

'The November 2015 Paris Attacks: The Impact of Foreign Fighter Returnees' (2017) 61 *Orbis* 212–226.

Crawford E., 'Regulating the Irregular: International Humanitarian Law and the Question of Civilian Participation in Armed Conflicts' (2011) 18 *UC Davis Journal of International Law and Policy* 163–190.

Curtis R. E., 'The Law of Hostile Military Expeditions as Applied by the United States' (1914) 8 *American Journal of International Law* 1–37.
David E., 'Les Mercenaires en Droit International (Développements récents)' (1977) 13 Revue Belge de Droit International 197–237.
Davidson B., 'Angola: A Success That Changes History' (1976) 28 *Race and Class* 23–37.
d'Aspremont J., 'Critical Histories of International Law and the Repression of Disciplinary Imagination' (2019) 7 *London Review of International Law* 98–115.
De Bustamante A. S., 'The Hague Convention Concerning the Rights and Duties of Neutral Powers and Persons in Land Warfare' (1908) 2 *American Journal of International Law* 95–120.
De la Rasilla del Moral I., 'In the General Interest of Peace? British International Lawyers and the Spanish Civil War' (2016) 18 *Journal of the History of International Law* 197–238.
De St. Jorre J., 'Looking for Mercenaries (and Some Pen-Portraits of Those We Found)' (1967) 33 *Transition* 19–25.
Decœur H., 'The Criminalisation of Armed Jihad under French Law: Guilt by Association in the Age of Enemy Criminal Law' (2017) 25 *European Journal of Crime, Criminal Law, and Criminal Justice* 299–326.
Dowdeswell T. L., 'The Brussels Peace Conference of 1874 and the Modern Laws of Belligerent Qualification' (2017) 54 *Osgoode Hall Law Journal* 805–850.
Dupont P.-E., 'International Terrorism, Resistance and the Just in Bello before French Courts: The Case of the Iranian Militant Opposition' (2013) 11 *Journal of International Criminal Justice* 441–462.
Elaigwu J. I., 'The Nigerian Civil War and the Angolan Civil War Linkages between Domestic Tensions and International Alignments' (1977) 12 *Journal of African and Asian studies* 215–235.
Elder D. A., 'The Historical Background of Common Article 3 of the Geneva Convention of 1949' (1979) 11 *Case Western Reserve Journal of International Law* 37–69.
Esenwein G., 'Freedom Fighters or Comintern Soldiers? Writing about the "Good Fight" during the Spanish Civil War' (2010) 12 *Civil Wars* 156–166.
Ettinger A., 'The Mercenary Moniker: Condemnations, Contradictions and the Politics of Definition' (2014) 45 *Security Dialogue* 174–191.
Fenwich C., 'Can Civil Wars Be Brought under the Control of International Law' (1938) 32 *American Journal of International Law* 538–542.
Fenwick H., 'Terrorism Threats and Temporary Exclusion Orders: Counter-Terror Rhetoric or Reality?' (2017) 3 *European Human Rights Law Review* 247–271.
Finch G. A., 'The United States and the Spanish Civil War' (1937) 31 *American Journal of International Law* 74–81.

Forcese C., Mamikon A., 'Neutrality Law, Anti-Terrorism, and Foreign Fighters: Legal Solutions to the Recruitment of Canadians to Foreign Insurgencies' (2015) 48 *University of British Columbia Law Review* 305–360.

Friedmann W., 'The Growth of State Control over the Individual, and Its Effect upon the Rules of International State Responsibility' (1938) 19 *British Yearbook of International Law* 118–150.

Garner J. W., 'Questions of International Law in the Spanish Civil War' (1937) 31 *American Journal of International Law* 66–73.

Genin V., 'La France et le Congo ex-Belge (1961–1965). Intérêts et Influences en Mutation' (2013) 91 (4) *Revue Belge de Philologie et d'Histoire* 1057–1110.

Gleijeses P., '"Flee! The White Giants are Coming!": The United States, Mercenaries, and the Congo, 1964–1965' (1994) 18 *Diplomatic History* 207–237.

Goetschel L., 'Neutrality, A Really Dead Concept?' (1999) 34 *Cooperation and Conflict* 115–139.

Gómez del Prado J. L., 'Whether the Criteria Contained in the 1989 International Convention against the Recruitment, Use, Financing and Training of Mercenaries Notably Motivation Apply to Today's Foreign Fighters?' (2016) 18 *International Community Law Review* 400–417.

Gordon R. W., 'Critical Legal Histories' (1984) 36 *Stanford Law Review* 56–125.

Green L. C., 'The Status of Mercenaries in International Law' (1978–1979) 9 *Manitoba Law Journal* 201–246.

Griffin C., 'French Military Policy in the Nigerian Civil War, 1967–1970' (2015) 26 *Small Wars & Insurgencies* 114–135.

Harris G. C., 'Terrorism, War and Justice: The Concept of the Unlawful Enemy Combatant' (2003) 26 *Loyola of Los Angeles International and Comparative Law Review* 31–46.

Hayes R., Malet D., 'Foreign Fighter Returnees: An Indefinite Threat?' (2020) 32 *Terrorism and Political Violence* 1617–1635.

Hegghammer T., 'The Rise of the Muslim Foreign Fighters: Islam and the Globalization of Jihad' (2011) 35 *International Security* 53–94.

Hellmuth D., 'Countering Jihadi Terrorists and Radicals the French Way' (2015) 38 *Studies in Conflict & Terrorism* 979–997.

Hesford V., Diedrich L., 'On "The Evidence of Experience" and Its Reverberations: An Interview with Joan W. Scott' (2014) 15 *Feminist Theory* 197–207.

Hewitt C., Kelley-Moore J., 'Foreign Fighters in Iraq: A Cross-National Analysis of Jihadism' (2009) 21 *Terrorism and Political Violence* 211–220.

Hoover M. J., 'The Laws of War and the Angolan Trial of Mercenaries: Death to the Dogs of War' (1977) 9 *Case Western Reserve Journal of International Law* 323–406.

Hughes G., 'Soldiers of Misfortune: The Angolan Civil War, the British Mercenary Intervention, and UK Policy towards Southern Africa, 1975–6' (2014) 36 *International History Review* 493–512.

Ip J., 'Reconceptualising the Legal Response to Foreign Fighters' (2020) 69 *International and Comparative Law Quarterly* 103–134.

Jayaraman S., 'International Terrorism and Statelessness: Revoking the Citizenship of ISIL Foreign Fighters' (2016) 17 *Chicago Journal of International Law* 178–216.

Jessup P. C., 'The Spanish Rebellion and International Law' (1937) 15 *Foreign Affairs* 260–279.

Jochnick C., Normand R., 'The Legitimation of Violence: A Critical History of the Laws of War' (1994) 35 *Harvard International Law Journal* 49–95.

Joenniemi P., 'Two Models of Mercenarism; Historical and Contemporary' (1977) 7 *Instant Research on Peace and Violence* 184–196.

Jouannet E., 'Universalism and Imperialism: The True–False Paradox of International Law?' (2007) 18 *European Journal of International Law* 379–407.

Kemmerer A., '"We Do Not Need to Always Look at Westphalia…" A Conversation with Martti Koskenniemi and Anne Orford' (2015) 17 *Journal of the History of International Law* 1–14.

Kennedy D., 'The International Human Rights Movement: Part of the Problem?' (2002) 15 *Harvard Human Rights Journal* 101–125.

Klabbers J., 'Rebel with a Cause? Terrorists and Humanitarian Law' (2003) 14 *European Journal of International Law* 299–312.

Komarnicki T., 'The Problem of Neutrality under the United Nations Charter' (1952) 38 *Transactions of the Grotius Society* 77–91.

Kopitzke C., 'Security Council Resolution 2178 (2014): An Ineffective Response to the Foreign Terrorist Fighter Phenomenon' (2017) 24 *Indiana Journal of Global Legal Studies* 309–341.

Koskenniemi M., 'Histories of International Law: Significance and Problems for a Critical View' (2013) 27 *Temple International and Comparative Law Journal* 215–240.

'Expanding Histories of International Law' (2016) 56 *American Journal of Legal History* 104–112.

Laine T., '"Passing the Buck": Western States Race to Denationalise Foreign Terrorist Fighters' (2017) 12 *Journal of Peacebuilding & Development* 22–35.

Lauterpacht H., 'Revolutionary Activities by Private Persons against Foreign States' (1928) 22 *American Journal of International Law* 105–130.

'Recognition of Insurgents as a de facto Government' (1939) 3 *Modern Law Review* 1–20.

Layeb A., 'Mercenary Activity: United States Neutrality Laws and Enforcement' (1989) 10 *New York Law School Journal of International and Comparative Law* 269–307.

Legendre P., 'Introduction to the Theory of the Image: Narcissus and the Other in the Mirror' (1997) 8 *Law and Critique* 3–35.

Li D., 'Jihad in a World of Sovereigns: Law, Violence, and Islam in the Bosnia Crisis' (2016) 41 *Law & Social Inquiry* 371–401.
Limbada Z., Lynn D., 'Addressing the Foreign Terrorist Fighter Phenomenon from a Human Rights Perspective' (2016) 18 *International Community Law Review* 483–493.
Liu H.-Y., Kinsey C., 'Challenging the Strength of the Antimercenary Norm' (2018) 3 *Journal of Global Security Studies* 93–110.
Lockwood G. H., 'Report on the Trial of Mercenaries: Luanda, Angola – June, 1976' (1977) 7 *Manitoba Law Journal* 183–202.
Mackenzie S. P., 'The Foreign Enlistment Act and the Spanish Civil War, 1936-1939' (1999) 10 *Twentieth Century British History* 52–66.
Mallison W. T., 'The Juridical Status of Irregular Combatants under the International Humanitarian Law of Armed Conflict' (1977) 9 *Case Western Reserve Journal of International Law* 39–78.
Mancini M., 'Defining Acts of International Terrorism in Time of Armed Conflict: Italian Case Law in the Aftermath of September 11, 2001 Attacks' (2009) 9 *Italian Yearbook of International Law* 115–128.
Marcum J. A., 'Lessons of Angola' (1976) 54 *Foreign Affairs* 407–425.
Marks S., 'Human Rights and Root Causes' (2011) 74 *Modern Law Review* 57–78.
Martin R., 'Mercenaries and the Rule of Law' (1976) 17 *International Commission of Jurists Review* 51–57.
McNair A., 'The Law Relating to the Civil War in Spain' (1937) 53 *Law Quarterly Review* 471–500.
Mégret F., '"War"? Legal Semantics and the Move to Violence' (2002) 13 *European Journal of International Law* 361–399.
   'The Laws of War and the Structure of Masculine Power' (2018) 19 *Melbourne Journal of International Law* 200–226.
Mendelsohn B., 'Foreign Fighters–Recent Trends' (2011) 55 *Orbis* 189–202.
Moore C., Tumelty P., 'Foreign Fighters and the Case of Chechnya: A Critical Assessment' (2008) 31 *Studies in Conflict & Terrorism* 412–433.
Murray A., 'Terrorist or Armed Opposition Group Fighter? The Experience of UK Courts and the Implications for Public International Law' (2018) 20 *International Community Law Review* 281–310.
Mustapha J., 'The Mujahideen in Bosnia: The Foreign Fighter as Cosmopolitan Citizen and/or Terrorist' (2013) 17 *Citizenship Studies* 742–755.
Mutua M., 'The Ideology of Human Rights' (1996) 36 *Virginia Journal of International Law* 589–657.
Mutua M., Anghie A., 'What Is TWAIL?' (2000) 94 *Proceedings of the Annual Meeting (American Society of International Law)* 31–40.
Norton P. M., 'Between the Ideology and the Reality: The Shadow of the Law of Neutrality' (1976) 17 *Harvard International Law Journal* 249–312.

Nwogugu E. I., 'Recent Developments in the Law Relating to Mercenaries' (1981) 20 *Military Law & Law of War Review* 9-34.

Okafor O. C., 'Newness, Imperialism, and International Legal Reform in Our Time: A TWAIL Perspective' (2005) 43 *Osgoode Hall Law Journal* 171-191.

'Critical Third World Approaches to International Law (TWAIL): Theory, Methodology, or Both?' (2008) 10 *International Community Law Review* 371-378.

Olson L. M., 'Prosecuting Suspected Terrorists: The War on Terror Demands Reminders about War, Terrorism, and International Law' (2010) 24 *Emory International Law Review* 479-496.

Orford A., 'On International Legal Method' (2013) 1 *London Review of International Law* 166-197.

O'Rourke V., 'Recognition of Belligerency and the Spanish War' (1937) 31 *American Journal of International Law* 398-413.

Padelford N. J., Seymour H. J., 'Some International Problems of the Spanish Civil War' (1937) 52 *Political Science Quarterly* 364-380.

Rizzotti M. A., 'Russian Mercenaries, State Responsibility, and Conflict in Syria: Examining the Wagner Group Under International Law' (2020) 37 *Wisconsin International Law Journal* 571-614.

Rodenhäuser T., 'Armed Groups, Rebel Coalitions, and Transnational Groups: The Degree of Organization Required from Non-State Armed Groups to Become Party to a Non-International Armed Conflict' (2016) 19 *Yearbook of International Humanitarian Law* 3-35.

Rona G., 'Interesting Times for International Humanitarian Law: Challenges from the "War on Terror"' (2005) 17 *Terrorism and Political Violence* 157-173.

Rousseau C., 'La Non-Intervention en Espagne' (1939) 19 *Revue de Droit International et de Législation Comparée* 217-280.

Roy A., 'Postcolonial Theory and Law: A Critical Introduction' (2008) 29 *Adelaide Law Review* 315-357.

Rubin A. P., 'The Concept of Neutrality in International Law' (1988) 16 *Denver Journal of International Law & Policy* 353-375.

Sassoli M., 'Use and Abuse of the Laws of War in the War on Terrorism' (2004) 22 *Law & Inequalities* 195-221.

Scelle G., 'La Guerre Civile Espagnole et le Droit des Gens' (1939) 13 *Revue Générale de Droit International Public* 197-228.

Scharf M., 'How the War against ISIS Changed International Law' (2016) 48 *Case Western Reserve Journal of International Law* 1-54.

Schwarzenberger, G., 'Images and Models of International law' (1966) 19 *Current Legal Problems* 192-207.

Scott, J., 'Fantasy Echo: History and the Construction of Identity' (2001) 27 *Critical Inquiry* 284-304.

Smith H. A., 'Some Problems of the Spanish Civil War' (1937) 18 *British Yearbook of International Law* 17-31.

Tayler L., 'Foreign Terrorist Fighter Laws: Human Rights Rollbacks under UN Security Council Resolution 2178' (2016) 18 *International Community Law Review* 455–482.
Tercinet J., 'Les Mercenaires et le Droit international' (1977) 23 *Annuaire français de droit international* 269–293.
Thobhani A. H., 'The Mercenary Menace' (1976) 23 *Africa Today* 61–68.
Thuo Gathii J., 'Imperialism, Colonialism and International Law' (2007) 54 *Buffalo Law Review* 1013–1066.
  'TWAIL: A Brief History of Its Origins, Its Decentralized Network, and a Tentative Bibliography' (2011) 3 *Trade Law and Development* 27–64.
Vagts D. F., 'The Traditional Legal Concept of Neutrality in a Changing Environment' (1998) 14 *American University Interntational Law Review* 83–102.
Valenta J., 'The Soviet–Cuban Intervention in Angola, 1975' (1978) 9 *Studies in Comparative Communism* 3–33.
Van Deventer H. W., 'Mercenaries at Geneva' (1976) 70 *American Journal of International Law* 811–816.
Vidino L., Pantucci R., Kohlmann E., 'Bringing Global Jihad to the Horn of Africa: al Shabaab, Western Fighters, and the Sacralization of the Somali Conflict' (2010) 3 *African Security* 216–238.
Voß K., 'Plausibly Deniable: Mercenaries in US Covert Interventions During the Cold War, 1964–1987' (2016) 16 *Cold War History* 37–60.
Walker W. L., 'Recognition of Belligerency and Grant of Belligerent Rights' (1937) 23 *Transactions of the Grotius Society* 177–210.
Whyte J., 'The "Dangerous Concept of the Just War": Decolonization, Wars of National Liberation, and the Additional Protocols to the Geneva Conventions' (2018) 9 *Humanity Journal* 313–341.
Wilcox F. O., 'The League of Nations and the Spanish Civil War' (1938) 198 *Annals of the American Academy of Political and Social Science* 65–72.
  'The Localization of the Spanish War' (1938) 32 *American Political Science Review* 237–260.
Wilkinson J. D., 'Truth and Delusion: European Intellectuals in Search of the Spanish Civil War' (1987) 76 *Salmagundi* 3–52.
Williams B. G., 'On the Trail of the "Lions of Islam": Foreign Fighters in Afghanistan and Pakistan, 1980–2010' (2011) 55 *Orbis* 216–239.
Yoo J. C., 'The Status of Soldiers and Terrorists under the Geneva Conventions' (2004) 3 *Chinese Journal of International Law* 135–150.
Zarate J. C., 'The Emergence of a New Dog of War: Private International Security Companies, International Law, and the New World Disorder' (1998) 34 *Stanford Journal of International Law* 75–162.

Chapters

Abrams K., Keren H., 'Who's Afraid of Law and the Emotions', in Bandes S. A. et al. (eds.), *The Edward Elgar Research Handbook on Law and Emotion* (Northampton, MA: Edward Elgar 2021) 566–600.

Bakker E., Singleton M., 'Foreign Fighters in the Syria and Iraq Conflict: Statistics and Characteristics of a Rapidly Growing Phenomenon', in de Guttry A. et al. (eds.), *Foreign Fighters under International Law and Beyond* (The Hague: Asser Press 2016) 9–25.

Becker-Lorca A., 'Eurocentrism in the History of International Law', in Fassbender B., Peters A. (eds.), *The Oxford Handbook of the History of International Law* (Oxford: Oxford University Press 2012) 1034–1057.

Bottici C., 'From Imagination to the Imaginary and Beyond: Towards a Theory of Imaginal Politics' in Bottici C., Challand B. (eds.), *The Politics of Imagination* (London: Birkbeck Law Press 2011) 16–37.

Cardinal P.-A., Mégret F., 'The Other "Other": Moors, International Law and the Origin of the Colonial Matrix' in de la Rasilla del Moral I., Shahid A. (eds.), *International Law and Islam: Historical Explorations* (Leiden: Brill/Nijhoff 2018) 165–198.

Coco A., Maillart J-B., 'The Conflict with Islamic State: A Critical Review of International Legal Issues', in Bellal A. (ed.), *The War Report. Armed Conflict in 2014* (Oxford: Oxford University Press 2015) 388–419.

Conte A., 'States' Prevention and Responses to the Phenomenon of Foreign Fighters against the Backdrop of International Human Rights Obligations', in de Guttry A. et al. (eds.), *Foreign Fighters under International Law and Beyond* (The Hague: Asser Press 2016) 283–298.

Craven M., 'Theorizing the Turn to History in International Law', in Hoffmann F., Orford A. (eds.), *The Oxford Handbook of the Theory of International Law* (Oxford: Oxford University Press 2016) 21–37.

Flores M., 'Foreign Fighters Involvement in National and International Wars: A Historical Survey', in de Guttry A. et al. (eds.), *Foreign Fighters under International Law and Beyond* (The Hague: Asser Press 2016) 27–47.

Foucault M., 'Nietzsche, Genealogy, History', in Bouchard D. F. (ed.), *Language, Counter-Memory, Practice: Selected Essays and Interviews* (Ithaca, NY: Cornell University Press 1977) 139–164.

Freud S., 'Delusion and Dream in Jensen's Gradiva', in Strachey J., Freud A., Strachey A., Tyson A. (eds.), *The Standard Edition of the Complete Psychological Works of Sigmund Freud. Vol. IX* (London: Hogarth Press 1959) 7–93.

Jouannet E., 'A Critical Introduction', in Berman N. (ed.), *Passion and Ambivalence: Colonialism, Nationalism, and International Law* (Leiden: Brill 2006) 1–38.

'Koskenniemi: A Critical Introduction', in Koskenniemi M. (ed.), *The Politics of International Law* (Oxford: Hart 2011) 1–32.

Kleffner J. K., 'Scope of Application of International Humanitarian Law', in Fleck D. (ed.), *The Handbook of International Humanitarian Law*. 4th edition (Oxford: Oxford University Press 2021) 50–80.

Koutroulis V., 'Le Jugement du Tribunal Correctionnel d'Anvers dans l'Qffaire dite "Sharia4Belgium" et l'Qrticle 141bis du Code Pénal Belge', in Jacobs A., Flore D. (eds.), *Les Combattants Européens en Syrie* (Paris: L'Harmattan 2015) 85–103.

Lacan J., 'The Mirror Stage as Formative of the I Function as Revealed in Psychoanalytic Experience', in Lacan (ed.), J., *Écrits: The First Complete Edition in English* (New York: Norton 2010) 75–81.

Lieber F., 'On Guerrilla Parties', in Lieber F. (ed.), *The Miscellaneous Writings of Francis Lieber: Contributions to Political Science, Vol. II* (Philadelphia: J. B. Lippincott 1881) 275–292.

Lloydd M., 'Framing Foreign Fighting: Exploring the Scope of Prevention and the Categorisation of Fighters in International Law', in Paulussen C., Scheinin M. (eds.), *Human Dignity and Human Security in Times of Terrorism* (The Hague: Asser Press 2020) 207–238.

Malet D., Fritz J. E., 'Historical Responses to Foreign Fighters and Returnees', in Capone F. et al. (eds.), *Returning Foreign Fighters: Responses, Legal Challenges and Ways Forward* (The Hague: Asser Press 2023) 33–48.

McNemar D. W., 'The Postindependence War in the Congo', in Falk R. (ed.), *The International Law of Civil War* (Baltimore: Johns Hopkins University Press 1971) 244–302.

Mégret F., 'From "Savages" to "Unlawful Combatants": A Postcolonial Look at International Humanitarian Law's "Other"', in Orford A. (ed.), *International Law and Its Others* (Cambridge: Cambridge University Press 2006) 265–317.

'Theorizing the Laws of War', in Hoffmann F., Orford A. (eds.), *The Oxford Handbook of the Theory of International Law* (Oxford: Oxford University Press 2016) 762–778.

Orford A., 'International Law and the Limits of History', in Werner W. et al. (eds.), *The Law of International Lawyers: Reading Martti Koskenniemi* (Cambridge: Cambridge University Press 2015) 297–320.

Paulussen C., Entenmann E., 'National Responses in Select Western European Countries to the Foreign Fighters Phenomenon' in de Guttry A. et al. (eds.), *Foreign Fighters under International Law* (The Hague: Asser Press 2016) 391–422.

Simpson G., 'Piracy and the Origins of Enmity', in Craven M. et al. (eds.), *Time, History and International Law* (Leiden: Brill 2007) 219–230.

Sommario E., 'The Status of Foreign Fighters under International Humanitarian Law', in de Guttry A. et al. (eds.), *Foreign Fighters under International Law and Beyond* (The Hague: Asser Press 2016) 141–160.

Wynen A. V., Thomas A. J., 'International Legal Aspects of the Civil War in Spain, 1936–39', in Falk R. (ed.), *The International Law of Civil War* (Baltimore: Johns Hopkins University Press 1971) 111–175.

Van Waas L., 'Foreign Fighters and the Deprivation of Nationality: National Practices and International Law Implications', in de Guttry A. et al. (eds.), *Foreign Fighters under International Law and Beyond* (The Hague: Asser Press 2016) 469–487.

Xifaras M., 'Comment rendre le passé contemporain?', in Laurent-Bonne N., Prévost X. (eds.), *Penser l'ancien droit privé, Vol. II* (Paris: LGDJ 2018) 13–38.

Yusuf A. A., 'Mercenaries in the Law of Armed Conflicts', in Cassese A. (ed.)., *The New Humanitarian Law of Armed Conflict* (Napoli: Editoriale Scientifica 1979) 113–127.

Reports, Reviews and Policy Papers

Anderson D., 'Report of the Independent Reviewer of Terrorism Legislation. The Terrorism Acts in 2015' (December 2016).

Bakke K. M., 'Copying and Learning from Outsiders? Assessing Diffusion from Transnational Insurgents in the Chechen Wars' (2010) American Political Science Association. Annual Meeting Paper.

Cappello A., 'L'interdiction de sortie du territoire dans la loi renforçant les dispositions relatives à la lutte contre le terrorisme' (2014) 12 *Actualité Juridique Pénal* 560–562.

Ciluffo F. J., Cozzens J. B., Ranstorp M., 'Foreign Fighters: Trends, Trajectories and Conflict Zones', Homeland Security and Policy Institute (October 2010) available at www.diva-portal.org/smash/get/diva2:380558/FULLTEXT01.pdf.

Doré F., 'Champ d'application de l'interdiction de sortie du territoire' (2017) 23 *Actualités juridiques droit administratif* 1345–1348.

Fallah K., 'Corporate Actors: The Legal Status of Mercenaries in Armed Conflict' (2006) 88 *International Review of the Red Cross* 599–611.

Godeberge C., Daoud E., 'La loi du 13 novembre 2014 constitue-t-elle une atteinte à la liberté d'expression?' (2014) 12 *Actualité Juridique Pénal* 563–566.

Hecker, M., '137 Shades of Terrorism: French Jihadists before the Courts' (April 2019) 79 *Focus Stratégique de l'Ifri*.

International Committee of the Red Cross (ICRC), 'The Applicability of International Humanitarian Law to Terrorism and Counter-Terrorism' (2015), available at www.icrc.org/en/document/applicability-ihl-terrorism-and-counterterrorism.

'International Humanitarian Law and the Challenges of Contemporary Armed Conflicts', document prepared by the ICRC for the 32nd International

Conference of the Red Cross and Red Crescent (Geneva, Switzerland, 8–10 December 2015) available at www.icrc.org/en/download/file/15061/32ic-report-on-ihl-and-challenges-of-armed-conflicts.pdf.

Kraehenmann S., 'Foreign Fighters under International Law', Academic Briefing no. 7, Geneva Academy of International Humanitarian Law and Human Rights (October 2014).

Lloydd M., 'Retrieving Neutrality Law to Consider "Other" Foreign Fighters under International Law' (2017) 9 *ESIL Conference Paper Series* 1–28.

Mégie A., Pawella J., 'Les procès correctionnels des filières djihadistes. Juger dans le contexte de la "guerre contre le terrorisme"' (2017) 2 *Les Cahiers de la Justice* 235–251.

Orton K., 'The Forgotten Foreign Fighters: The PKK in Syria' (2017) The Henry Jackson Society, available at https://henryjacksonsociety.org/wp-content/uploads/2017/08/3053-PYD-Foreign-Fighter-Project-1.pdf.

'The Secular Foreign Fighters of the West in Syria' (2018) 20 *Insight Turkey* 157–178.

Peters A., 'Security Council Resolution 2178 (2014): The "Foreign Terrorist Fighter" as an International Legal Person, Part I' (20 November 2014) *EJIL:Talk!*, available at www.ejiltalk.org/security-council-resolution-2178-2014-the-foreign-terrorist-fighter-as-an-international-legal-person-part-i/.

'Security Council Resolution 2178 (2014): The "Foreign Terrorist Fighter" as an International Legal Person, Part II' (21 November 2014) *EJIL:Talk!*, available at www.ejiltalk.org/security-council-resolution-2178-2014-the-foreign-terrorist-fighter-as-an-international-legal-person-part-ii/.

Rouidi H., 'La loi n° 2014-1353 du 13 novembre 2014 renforçant les dispositions relatives à la lutte contre le terrorisme: quelles évolutions?' (2014) 12 *Actualité Juridique Pénal* 556–559.

Sarfati A., 'International Humanitarian Law and the Criminal Justice Response to Terrorism: From the UN Security Council to the National Courts' (2021) 103 *International Review of the Red Cross* 267–293.

Tuck H., Silverman T., Smalley C., '"Shooting in the Right Direction": Anti-ISIS Foreign Fighters in Syria & Iraq' (2016) 1 *Institute for Strategic Dialogue* 1–55.

Vité S., 'Typology of Armed Conflicts in International Humanitarian Law: Legal Concepts and Actual Situations' (2009) 91 *International Review of the Red Cross* 69–94.

Weill S., 'French Foreign Fighters: The Engagement of Administrative and Criminal Justice in France' (2018) 100 *International Review of the Red Cross* 211–236.

'Terror in Courts, French Counter-Terrorism: Administrative and Penal Avenues', Report for the Official Visit of the UN Special Rapporteur on Counter-Terrorism and Human Rights' (May 2018).

Zelin A. Y., 'The Others: Foreign Fighters in Libya', (2018) 44/45 *Washington Institute for Near East Policy: Policy Notes* 1–2.

Newspaper Articles

BBC News, 'British Jihadist Imran Khawaja Jailed for 12 Years' (6 February 2015).
  'Mustafa Abdullah of Stockwell Jailed Over Terror Videos' (15 December 2015).
  'Sharia4Belgium Trial: Belgian Court Jails Members' (11 February 2015).
  'Man Held at Gatwick Jailed for Travelling to Syria to join IS' (10 February 2016).
Blake M., '"Our Sons Were Heroes" Say Families of British Men Killed Fighting Isis', *The Guardian* (20 August 2017).
Boitiaux C., 'La "Task Force Lafayette": ces ex-soldats français face aux jihadistes de l'EI', France24 (13 October 2015).
Busby M., 'British Man Who Fought Isis in Syria Has Terror Charges Dropped', *The Guardian* (31 July 2018).
Casciani D., 'British Brothers Jailed for Training at Syria Terror Camp', *BBC News* (26 November 2014).
Dearden L., 'Jac Holmes: British Man Who Volunteered to Fight against Isis Killed in Syria', *The Independent* (24 October 2017).
  'Joshua Walker: Student Who Fought against Isis in Syria Cleared of Terror Charges over Book he Owned', *The Independent* (26 October 2017).
Freyne P., 'The Irish Man "Fighting Fascism" in Syria: "I Was Always Curious How I'd React to Battle"', *The Irish Times* (24 March 2018).
Gallagher R., 'To Syria and Back', *The Intercept* (10 July 2017).
George M., 'Orwell Was Hailed a Hero for Fighting in Spain. Today He'd be Guilty of Terrorism', *The Guardian* (10 February 2014).
Jaafari S., 'For Some Americans, the Conflict in Syria Is the Spanish Civil War of Our Time', *The World* (13 September 2017).
Larner T., 'Tareena Shakil Jailed for Six Years for Travelling to Syria to Join Islamic State', *The Birmingham Mail* (1 February 2016).
Laville S., 'First British Conviction for Syria-Related Terror Offence', *The Guardian* (20 May 2014).
Leduc S., 'Des Occidentaux Avec les Kurdes à Afrin: l'Ultra-Gauche Monte au Front', *France 24* (22 February 2018).
MacAskill E. K., 'Erik Scurfield: The Former Marine Who Died in Someone Else's War', *The Guardian* (4 March 2015).
Morris S., 'British Woman Who Joined Isis Is Jailed for Six Years', *The Guardian* (1 February 2016).
Norton-Taylor R., 'Terror Trial Collapses after Fears of Deep Embarrassment to Security Services', *The Guardian* (1 June 2015).
Press Association, 'Two Britons Freed in Iraq on Way Home from Fighting Isis', *The Guardian* (26 April 2016).
Saner E., 'Brits Abroad: Is It against the Law to Fight Isis?' *The Guardian* (25 February 2015).

Vernalls R., 'Woman Who Took Her Baby Son to Syria to Join IS Jailed for Six Years', *The Irish Independent* (1 February 2016).
Whitehead T., 'Old Bailey Trial of Terror Suspect Collapses after Security Services Refuse to Say Who They Helped in Syria', *The Telegraph* (1 June 2015).

Online Sources

www.internationalcrimesdatabase.org/.
www.thelawpages.com/.

League of Nations Documents

League of Nations, Official Journal, Special Supplement 155, 17th Ordinary Session. Sixth Plenary Meeting (1936).
League of Nations, Official Journal 18, 95th Session of the Council. Third Meeting (1936).
League of Nations, Official Journal, Special Supplement 165, White Book (1937).
League of Nations, Official Journal, Special Supplement 169, 18th Ordinary Session. Fifth Plenary Meeting (1937).
League of Nations, Official Journal, Special Supplement 169, 18th Ordinary Session. Eleventh Plenary Meeting (1937).
League of Nations, Official Journal, Special Supplement 175, 18th Ordinary Session. Sixth Committee, Eighth Meeting (1937).
League of Nations, Official Journal, Special Supplement 175, 18th Ordinary Session. Sixth Committee, Ninth Meeting (1937).
League of Nations, Official Journal 18, 97th Session of the Council. Fifth Meeting (1937).
League of Nations, Official Journal 19, 101st Session of the Council. Seventh Meeting (1938).
League of Nations, Official Journal 19, 101st Session of the Council. Fourth Meeting (1938).
League of Nations, Official Journal 19, 103rd Session of the Council. Second Meeting (1938).
League of Nations, Official Journal 20, 104th Session of the Council. Provisional Report of the International Military Commission Entrusted with the Verification of the Withdrawal of Non-Spanish Combatants from Spain (1939).
League of Nations, Covenant of the League of Nations (Paris, 28 April 1919).

UN Documents

UNSC Official Records

UNSC Official Records, 974th meeting (15 November 1961).
UNSC Official Records, 975th meeting (16 November 1961).

UNSC Official Records, 976th meeting (17 November 1961).
UNSC Official Records, 1376th meeting (10 July 1967).
UNSC Official Records, 1900th meeting (26 March 1976).
UNSC Official Records 1901st meeting (29 March 1976).
UNSC Official Records 1902nd meeting (29 March 1976).
UNSC Official Records 1904th meeting (30 March 1976).
UNSC Official Records 1906th meeting (31 March 1976).
UNSC Official Records, 1932nd meeting (23 June 1976).
UNSC Official Records, 1987th meeting (8 February 1977).
UNSC Official Records, 2005th meeting (14 April 1977).
UNSC Official Records, 2049th meeting (24 November 1977).
UNSC Official Records, 7272nd meeting (24 September 2014).

UNGA Official Records

UNGA Official Records, 967th plenary meeting (24 March 1961).
UNGA Official Records, 975th plenary meeting (4 April 1961).
UNGA Official Records, 977th plenary meeting (5 April 1961).
UNGA Official Records, 978th plenary meeting (6 April 1961).
UNGA Official Records, 980th plenary meeting (7 April 1961).
UNGA Official Records, 983rd plenary meeting (14 April 1961).
UNGA Official Records, 987th plenary meeting (18 April 1961).
UNGA Official Records, 995th plenary meeting (21 April 1961).
UNGA Official Records, 1035th plenary meeting (13 October 1961).
UNGA Official Records, 1060th plenary meeting (21 November 1961).
UNGA Official Records, 1292nd plenary meeting (7 December 1964).
UNGA Official Records, 1293rd plenary meeting (7 December 1964).
UNGA Official Records, 1307th plenary meeting (18 December 1964).
UNGA Official Records, 1575th plenary meeting (2 October 1967).
UNGA Official Records, 1590th plenary meeting (13 October 1967).
UNGA Official Records, 1743rd plenary meeting (16 December 1968).
UNGA Official Records, 1749th plenary meeting (19 December 1968).
UNGA Official Records, 1751st plenary meeting (20 December 1968).
UNGA Official Records, 84th plenary meeting (1 December 1976).
UNGA Fourth Committee, 46th meeting (13 December 1976).
UNGA Fourth Committee, 49th meeting (14 December 1976).
UNGA, Official Records, 69th plenary meeting (24 September 2014).

Security Council Resolutions

S/RES/161 (21 February 1961).
S/RES/169 (24 November 1961).

S/RES/239 (10 July 1967).
S/RES/2178 (24 September 2014).

General Assembly Resolutions

A/RES/1514 (14 December 1960).
A/RES/2395 (29 November 1968).
A/RES/2465 (20 December 1968).
A/RES/2548 (11 December 1969).
A/RES/2625 (24 October 1970).
A/RES/3103 (12 December 1973).
A/RES/3314 (14 December 1974).

OAU

AHG/Res. 49 (IV), 14 September 1967.
CM/St. 6 (15 June 1971).

International Conventions

Convention (III) Relative to the Treatment of Prisoners of War (Geneva, 12 August 1949).
Convention (V) Respecting the Rights and Duties of Neutral Powers and Persons in Case of War on Law (The Hague, 18 October 1907).
Convention de Genève du 27 juillet 1929 Relative au Traitement des Prisonniers de Guerre (Geneva, 27 July 1929).
Convention for the Definition of Aggression (London, 3 July 1933).
International Convention against the Recruitment, Use, Financing and Training of Mercenaries, adopted by A/44/49 (New York, 4 December 1989).
Protocol Additional to the Geneva Conventions of 12 August 1949, and Relating to the Protection of Victims of International Armed Conflicts (Protocol I) (Geneva, 8 June 1977).

Final Records, Reports and Miscellaneous

Actes de la Conférence de Bruxelles de 1874 sur le Projet d'Une Convention Internationale Concernant la Guerre. Protocoles des Séances Plenieres. Protocoles de la Commission Déléguée par la Conférence. Annexes (Paris: Librairie Des Publications Législatives 1874).
Final Record of the Diplomatic Conference of Geneva of 1949, Vol. II A.
Final Record of the Diplomatic Conference of Geneva of 1949, Vol. II B.

Institut de Droit International, Resolution. 'De la Condition Juridique Internationale des Étrangers Civils ou Militaires, au Service des Belligérants' (Florence, 28 September 1908).
Instructions for the Government of Armies of the United States in the Field (Lieber Code) 24 April 1863, originally Issued as General Orders No. 100 (Washington, DC: Government Printing Office 1898).
International Committee of the Red Cross, *Commentary on the Additional Protocols of 8 June 1977 to the Geneva Conventions of 12 August 1949* (The Hague: Martinus Nijhoff 1987).
International Committee of the Red Cross, *Draft Additional Protocols to the Geneva Conventions of August 12, 1949: Commentary* (Geneva, 1973).
Official Records of the Diplomatic Conference on the Reaffirmation and Development of International Humanitarian Law Applicable in Armed Conflicts. Geneva (1974–1977), Vol. III, Vol. V, Vol. VI, Vol. XIV, Vol. XV.
Project of an International Declaration Concerning the Laws and Customs of War (Brussels, 27 August 1874).
Report of the Ad Hoc Committee on the Drafting of an International Convention Against the Recruitment, Use, Financing and Training of Mercenaries (1981). Official Records, 36th Session, Supplement 43 (A/36/43).
Report of the United Nations High Commissioner for Human Rights on the Protection of Human Rights and Fundamental Freedoms while Countering Terrorism, A/HRC/28/28 (19 December 2014).
Report of the UN Working Group on the Use of Mercenaries as a Means of Violating Human Rights and Impeding the Exercise of the Right of Peoples to Self-determination, A/70/330 (19 August 2015).

Parliamentary Records

France

Journal officiel de la République française. Débats parlementaires. Chambre des députés. Séance du samedi 5 Décembre 1936.
Journal officiel de la République française. Débats parlementaires. Chambre des députés. Séance du vendredi 15 Janvier 1937.
Journal officiel de la République française. Débats parlementaires, XIVe Législature, Deuxième session extraordinaire de 2013–2014. Séances du lundi 15 septembre 2014.
Journal officiel de la République française. Débats parlementaires, XIVe Législature, Deuxième session extraordinaire de 2013–2014. Deuxième séance du mardi 16 septembre 2014.

Journal officiel de la République française. Débats parlementaires, XIVe Législature, Session ordinaire de 2014–2015, quarantième séance, deuxième séance du mercredi 29 octobre 2014.

Journal officiel de la République française. Débats parlementaires, XIVe Législature, Session ordinaire de 2015–2016, cent-trente-neuvième séance, séance du mercredi 2 mars 2016.

United Kingdom

HC Deb, 1 December 1936, Vol. 318, c1068.
HC Deb, 1 December 1936, Vol. 318, cc1148–1149.
HC Deb, 25 November 1936, Vol. 318, c394.
HC Deb, 18 December 1936, Vol. 318, c2826.
HC Deb, 19 January 1937, Vol. 319, cc98–110.
HC Deb, 1 February 1937, Vol. 319, cc1272–1273.
HC Deb, 17 March 1937, Vol. 321, c2143.
HC Deb, 19 December 1975, Vol. 902, c819.
HC Deb, 10 February 1976, Vol. 905, cc236–247.
HC Deb, 28 January 1976, Vol. 904, c411.
HC Deb, 9 February 1976, Vol. 905, c47.
HC Deb, 10 February 1976, Vol. 905, c412.
HC Deb, 19 February 1976, Vol. 905, c814.
HC Deb, 10 March 1976, Vol. 907 cc409–410.
HC Deb, 1 September 2014, Vol. 585, cc23–27.
HC Deb, 6 January 2015, Vol. 590, c154.
HC Deb, 15 December 2014, Vol. 589, c1227.
HC Deb, 26 September 2014, Vol. 585 cc1256–1366.
HC Deb, 1 September 2014, Vol. 585, c35.
HC Deb, 19 April 2016, Vol. 608, cc889–900.
HC Deb, 4 March 2015, Vol. 593, cc988.
HL Deb, 10 February 1976, Vol. 368, cc22–30.
HL Deb, 17 February 1976, Vol. 368, cc423–426.
HL Deb, 17 February 1976, Vol. 368, cc437–438.
HL Deb, 9 March 1976, Vol. 368, cc1201–1207.
HL Deb, 13 January 2015, Vol. 758, cc651–698.
HL Deb, 20 January 2015, Vol. 758, cc1197–1242.
HL Deb, 26 January 2015, Vol. 759, cc1–48.
HL Deb, 2 February 2015, Vol. 759, cc451–497.
HL Deb, 4 February 2015, Vol. 759, cc643–689.
HD Deb, 26 September 2014, Vol. 755, cc1676–1746.

Belgium

Chambre Des Représentants de Belgique, Projet de loi visant à renforcer la lutte contre le terrorisme (13 Juillet 2015).

Hearings, National Reports, Draft Laws

Angola

O Povo Acusa: Julgamento dos Mercenários: Alegações Finais do Procurador Popular (Luanda: I.N.A. 1976).

France

Loi no. 2014-1353 du 13 novembre 2014 renforçant les dispositions relatives à la lutte contre le terrorisme.
Projet de Loi no. 2110 renforçant les dispositions relatives à la lutte contre le terrorisme (Procédure accélérée). Enregistré à la Présidence de l'Assemblée nationale le 9 juillet 2014.
Rapport no. 2173, Fait au Nom de la Commission Des Lois Constitutionnelles, de la législation et de l'administration générale de la République sur le projet de Loi (no. 2110), renforçant les dispositions relatives à la lutte contre le terrorisme. Enregistré à la Présidence de l'Assemblée nationale le 22 juillet 2014.
Rapport fait au nom de la commission d'enquête sur la surveillance des filières et des individus djihadistes (no. 2828). Enregistré à la Présidence de l'Assemblée nationale le 2 juin 2015.

United Kingdom

Home Office, Home Secretary Theresa May on counter-terrorism (24 November 2014).
House of Commons, Home Affairs Committee Counter-terrorism, Seventeenth Report of Session 2013–14.
'Mercenaries in Africa': Hearing before the Special Subcommittee on Investigations of the Committee on International Relations, House of Representatives, Ninety-fourth Congress, Second Session (9 August 1976).
Report of the Committee of Privy Counsellors appointed to inquire into the recruitment of mercenaries ('Diplock Report'), Cmnd. 6569 (August 1976).

Domestic and International Cases

Belgium

Sharia4Belgium, Court of First Instance of Antwerp, 11 February 2015, Case file: FD35.98.47-12 –AN35.F1.1809-12.

Federal Prosecutor v. Hamza B et al., Tribunal de Première Instance Francophone de Bruxelles, 6 November 2015, Case file: FD.35.98.212/11.

France

Arrêt Criminel du 22/06/2017, n°16/0023.
Arrêt Criminel du 23/03/2018, n°17/0048.
Cour d'Appel de Paris, Sentence du 9/05/2017, Dossier n° 16/06145.
TA Paris, Jugement du 07/07/2015, n° 1508213.
TA Paris, Jugement du 27/11/2015, n° 1519030.
TA Paris, Jugement du 28/11/2015, n° 1519404.
TA Paris, Jugement du 12/02/2016, n° 1519389.
TA Cergy-Pontoise, Jugement du 21/03/2016, n° 1602382.
TA Rennes, Jugement du 4/06/2016, n° 1602381.
TA Montreuil, Jugement du 4/07/2016, n° 1602647.
TA Lyon, Jugement du 29/07/2016, n° 1605634.
TA Paris, Jugement du 31/03/2017, n° 1701210.
CAA Paris, Jugement du 20/06/2016, n° 16PA01210.
CAA Paris, Jugement du 8/07/2016, n° 16PA00305.
CAA Paris, Jugement du 08/07/2016, n° 16PA01153.
CAA Marseille, Jugement du 10/07/2017, n° 17MA01080.
CAA Marseille, Jugement du 10/07/2017, n° 17MA01082.
CAA Marseille, Jugement du 18/04/2017, n° 16MA04151.
CAA Douai, Jugement du 02/10/2018, n° 16DA01635.
TGI de Paris, Jugement du 13/11/2014, n° parquet 12333060007.
TGI de Paris Jugement du 07/01/2016, n° parquet 13205000228.
TGI de Paris, Jugement du 23/03/2016, n° parquet 15033000932.
TGI de Paris, Jugement du 06/07/2016, n° parquet 15204000443.
TGI de Paris, Jugement du 22/09/2017, n° parquet 12355060014.

Netherlands

Prosecutor v. Maher H., District Court of The Hague, 1 December 2014, Case file: 09/767116-14.
Prosecutor v. Imane B et al., District Court of The Hague, 10 December 2015, Case files: 09/842489-14, 09/767038-14 and 09/767313-14, 09/767174-13 and 09/765004-15, 09/767146-14, 09/767256-14, 09767238-14 and 09/827053-15, 09/767237-14, 09/765002-15, 09/767077-14.

United Kingdom

R v. Kahar (Mohammed Abdul) [2016] EWCA Crim 568, [2016] 1 W.L.R. 3156, [2016] 5 WLUK 386.

R v. Sarwar, Court of Appeal (Criminal Division) 9 December 2015, [2015] EWCA Crim 1886, [2016] 1 Cr. App. R. (S.) 54.

The Queen (on the application of Mr) v. Secretary of State for the Home Department (High Court of Justice Queen's Bench Division Administrative Court, 10 March 2017). For reference: [2017] EWHC 469 (Admin) 2017 WL 00895282;

The Queen on the application of AS v. Secretary of State for the Home Department (High Court of Justice Queen's Bench Division Administrative Court, 13 July 2018). For reference: [2018] EWHC 1792 (Admin) 2018 WL 03417238;

B, ND v. Secretary of State for the Home Department v. Commissioner of Police for the Metropolis (High Court of Justice Queen's Bench Division Administrative Court, 12 October 2018). For reference: [2018] EWHC 2651 (Admin) 2018 WL 05112692.

International Tribunals

Prosecutor v. Dusko Tadic aka "Dule" (Decision on the Defence Motion for Interlocutory Appeal on Jurisdiction), IT-94-1, International Criminal Tribunal for the former Yugoslavia (ICTY), 2 October 1995.

Prosecutor v. Dusko Tadic (Appeal Judgment), IT-94-1-A, International Criminal Tribunal for the former Yugoslavia (ICTY), 15 July 1999.

Prosecutor v. Ljube Boškoski and Johan Tarčulovski (Judgment), IT-04-82-T, International Criminal Tribunal for the former Yugoslavia (ICTY), 10 July 2008.

ICJ, *Nicaragua v. United States of America, Military and Paramilitary Activities*, Judgment of 27 June 1986, Merits.

INDEX

Al-Qaeda, 154, 156, 159, 177, 202
American Civil War, 2, 8, 48, 84
Arab–Israeli War, 90, 136
archetype, 16, 160, 164, 179, 210–211
assistance, 49, 75, 96, 111–112, 126, 181

Blum, Leon, 61–64, 66
Bolshevism, 45, 64, 92
bon sauvage, 81, 83, 93, 132, 209, 211
Brownlie, Ian, 83, 89–91, 94
Brussels Peace Conference, 84, 93
Byron, Lord, 4–5, 7–8, 21, 25, 63, 68, 93, 127, 132, 152, 159, 168, 208, 210

Callan, Colonel, 95, 98, 100, 105, 107, 122, 125, 144
Cameron, David, 162–163, 173–174, 176–177
Castoriadis, Cornelius, 18–20
Ciano, Galeazzo, 43
civilization, 39, 64, 92, 159
Cochrane, Thomas, 5
Cold War, 91, 96, 159
colonialism, 13, 102–103, 115, 126, 128
Comintern, 27, 93, 152, 171, 208
communism, 8, 33, 38–39, 92, 96, 185
Congo crisis, 110, 117
Counter-Terrorism Act, 174, 176, 192
cultural image, 10, 14, 21, 76, 164, 211
Curtis, Emerson, 53, 55

D'Annunzio, Gabriele, 91, 94
de Certeau, Michel, 15
del Vayo, Julio Álvarez, 36–38, 40, 42–43, 46, 81, 92, 103
Delbos, Yvon, 40, 43

den Beer Poortugael, Jacobus Catharinus Cornelis, 80
Denard, Robert, 110, 127–128
Derrida, Jacques, 15
Diplock Report, 130, 136
discontinuity, 14, 22–24

Eagle Squadrons, 136
Eden, Anthony, 40, 63, 65–67
emotion, 17
enemy of humanity, 27, 35, 107, 164, 207
episteme, 22
Eurocentrism, 11, 210
evil, 30, 111, 163, 178

faith, 4, 67, 92–93, 114–115, 121, 133
fantasy, 14
fascism, 8, 33, 38–39, 47, 92, 102–103, 167, 186, 192
Federal Prosecutor v. *Hamza B. et al.*, 201
filibuster, 53, 58, 133
Foreign Enlistment Act, 50, 66–67, 130, 138
Foucault, Michel, 22, 24
francs-tireurs, 87
Free Syrian Army, 166, 176–177, 183, 190, 206
freedom fighter, 6–7, 19, 25, 151–152, 159, 161, 164, 169, 175, 177–178, 204, 206–208, 210
Freud, Sigmund, 17–18

Garcia-Mora, Manuel, 91
Garibaldi, Giuseppe, 5, 8, 63, 68, 93, 159, 168
genealogy, 15, 22, 64, 93, 104, 156, 159–160, 162

Greek War of Independence, 2, 8
Gurkhas, 132, 136, 146

Hague Peace Conferences, 34, 68, 93, 157, 211
hauntology, 15
Hemingway, Ernest, 5, 39
Hoare, Mike, 110
Hollande, François, 162–163, 174
hostile military expedition, 52–53, 67, 71, 93, 158, 199
House of Commons, 65, 130–131, 152, 175–176
House of Lords, 67, 177
humanitarian intervention, 27

idealism, 4, 126, 171
ideology, 97, 131, 182, 184, 195
imperialism, 13, 43, 96, 102–103, 125
International Brigades, 11, 34, 43, 45, 89, 99, 132, 136, 152, 160, 186, 208
International Criminal Tribunal for the Former Yugoslavia, 202

Jessup, Philip, 47–49, 51, 92
jus ad bellum, 146
jus in bello, 146, 193

Kipling, Rudyard, 114
Klein, Melanie, 12, 14–15
Korean War, 90
Kurdistan Workers' Party, 183, 185

Lacan, Jacques, 17
Lafayette, Marquis de, 5, 8, 63, 68, 93, 127, 152, 159, 168
laissez-faire, 56, 82, 91, 130, 139, 164, 175
Lauterpacht, Hersch, 47, 52–53, 56, 77, 92
Lawrence, T. E., 4–5
levée en masse, 85
Lieber Code, 83

Malraux, André, 4–5, 7, 39, 168, 208, 210
McNair, Arnold, 47, 49–52, 93
Middle East, 172, 178

Moors, 42, 64, 175
mujahideen, 3, 160, 164

National Assembly, 66, 164–165, 167, 170, 172, 174, 187
national liberation, 35, 96, 101, 108, 110, 127, 140–142, 168
neutrality laws, 19, 22, 27, 49, 53, 57, 69, 80, 149, 164
Noel-Baker, Philip, 65, 67

Obama, Barack, 158, 162
Old Bailey, 189, 191
Oppenheim, Lassa, 55, 70
Orwell, George, 5, 7, 39, 171, 192, 208, 210
otherness, 26

Padelford, Norman, 47, 59
paternalism, 21, 114, 127, 153, 171, 208
People's Protection Unit, 156, 185, 191–192, 206
Péri, Gabriel, 63–64
pirate, 27, 55, 159
post-structuralism, 22
privateer, 53, 59
Prosecutor v. Maher H., 203, 205

Raqqa, 181, 183, 185, 189
resistance movements, 87–88, 141, 191
ressortissants, 75, 77–78, 80
Rojava, 186, 193

Schramme, Jean, 110, 120, 127
Scott, Joan, 14
Second Boer War, 2, 211
Sharia4Belgium, 200–201
signifier, 7
soldier of fortune, 34, 101, 113, 121, 132, 151, 210
Soviet–Afghan War, 3, 159–160
Spaak, Paul-Henri, 113–119, 121, 132, 152, 172
splitting, 12–16, 171
Steiner, Rolf, 110, 121, 127

Taliban, 159, 202
Taylor, Charles, 20–21

United Nations Mercenary
 Convention, 110
United Nations Working Group on the
 use of mercenaries, 195
Universal Declaration of Human
 Rights, 124, 137

von Bieberstein, Adolf Marschall,
 74, 76

Westminster, 70, 164, 174
Wilson, Harold, 130–133, 152
World War II, 87, 96, 119, 136, 138

CAMBRIDGE STUDIES IN INTERNATIONAL AND COMPARATIVE LAW

Books in the Series

191 *Ghosts of International Law: The Figure of the Foreign Fighter in a Cultural Perspective*
Alberto Rinaldi

190 *Merchants of Legalism: A History of State Responsibility (1870-1960)*
Alan Tzvika Nissel

189 *The Functions of International Adjudication and International Environmental Litigation*
Joshua Paine

188 *Demystifying Treaty Interpretation*
Andrea Bianchi and Fuad Zarbiyev

187 *International Law-Making by the International Court of Justice and International Law Commission: Partnership for Purpose in a Decentralized Legal Order*
Omri Sender

186 *The Rebirth of Territory*
Gail Lythgoe

185 *Reimagining Sustainable Development in International Law: Perspectives from African Legal Cosmologies*
Godwin Eli Kwadzo Dzah

184 *Collective Self-Defence in International Law*
James A. Green

183 *Weaponising Evidence: A History of Tobacco Control in International Law*
Margherita Melillo

182 *The Justice Factory: Management Practices at the International Criminal Court*
Richard Clements

181 *A Communitarian Theory of WTO Law*
Chi Carmody

180 *Drones and International Law: A Techno-Legal Machinery*
Mignot-Mahdavi

179 *The Necessity of Nature: God, Science and Money in 17th Century English Law of Nature*
Mónica García-Salmones

178 *Making the World Safe for Investment: The Protection of Foreign Property 1922-1959*
Andrea Leiter

177 *National Governance and Investment Treaties*
Josef Ostřanský and Facundo Pérez Aznar

176 *Who Owns Outer Space? International Law, Astrophysics, and the Sustainable Development of Space*
Michael Byers and Aaron Boley

175 *Intervening in International Justice: Third States before Courts and Tribunals*
    Brian McGarry
174 *Reciprocity in Public International Law*
    Arianna Whelan
173 *When Environmental Protection and Human Rights Collide*
    Marie-Catherine Petersmann
172 *The International Law of Sovereign Debt Dispute Settlement*
    Kei Nakajima
171 *The Everyday Makers of International Law: From Great Halls to Back Rooms*
    Tommaso Soave
170 *Virtue in Global Governance: Judgment and Discretion*
    Jan Klabbers
169 *The Effects of Armed Conflict on Investment Treaties*
    Tobias Ackermann
168 *Investment Law's Alibi: Colonialism, Imperialism, Debt and Development*
    David Schneiderman
167 *Negative Comparative Law: A Strong Programme for Weak Thought*
    Pierre Legrand
166 *Detention by Non-State Armed Groups under International Law*
    Ezequiel Heffes
165 *Rebellions and Civil Wars: State Responsibility for the Conduct of Insurgents*
    Patrick Dumberry
164 *The International Law of Energy*
    Jorge Viñuales
163 *The Three Ages of International Commercial Arbitration*
    Mikaël Schinazi
162 *Repetition and International Law*
    Wouter Werner
161 *State Responsibility and Rebels: The History and Legacy of Protecting Investment Against Revolution*
    Kathryn Greenman
160 *Rewriting Histories of the Use of Force: The Narrative of 'Indifference'*
    Agatha Verdebout
159 *The League of Nations and the Protection of the Environment*
    Omer Aloni
158 *International Investment Law and Legal Theory: Expropriation and the Fragmentation of Sources*
    Jörg Kammerhofer
157 *Legal Barbarians: Identity, Modern Comparative Law and the Global South*
    Daniel Bonilla Maldonado
156 *International Human Rights Law Beyond State Territorial Control*
    Antal Berkes

155 *The Crime of Aggression under the Rome Statute of the International Criminal Court*
Carrie McDougall
154 *Minorities and the Making of Postcolonial States in International Law*
Mohammad Shahabuddin
153 *Preclassical Conflict of Laws*
Nikitas E. Hatzimihail
152 *International Law and History: Modern Interfaces*
Ignacio de la Rasilla
151 *Marketing Global Justice: The Political Economy of International Criminal Law*
Christine Schwöbel-Patel
150 *International Status in the Shadow of Empire*
Cait Storr
149 *Treaties in Motion: The Evolution of Treaties from Formation to Termination*
Edited by Malgosia Fitzmaurice and Panos Merkouris
148 *Humanitarian Disarmament: An Historical Enquiry*
Treasa Dunworth
147 *Complementarity, Catalysts, Compliance: The International Criminal Court in Uganda, Kenya, and the Democratic Republic of Congo*
Christian M. De Vos
146 *Cyber Operations and International Law*
François Delerue
145 *Comparative Reasoning in International Courts and Tribunals*
Daniel Peat
144 *Maritime Delimitation as a Judicial Process*
Massimo Lando
143 *Prosecuting Sexual and Gender-Based Crimes at the International Criminal Court: Practice, Progress and Potential*
Rosemary Grey
142 *Capitalism As Civilisation: A History of International Law*
Ntina Tzouvala
141 *Sovereignty in China: A Genealogy of a Concept Since 1840*
Adele Carrai
140 *Narratives of Hunger in International Law: Feeding the World in Times of Climate Change*
Anne Saab
139 *Victim Reparation under the Ius Post Bellum: An Historical and Normative Perspective*
Shavana Musa
138 *The Analogy between States and International Organizations*
Fernando Lusa Bordin

137 *The Process of International Legal Reproduction: Inequality, Historiography, Resistance*
   Rose Parfitt
136 *State Responsibility for Breaches of Investment Contracts*
   Jean Ho
135 *Coalitions of the Willing and International Law: The Interplay between Formality and Informality*
   Alejandro Rodiles
134 *Self-Determination in Disputed Colonial Territories*
   Jamie Trinidad
133 *International Law as a Belief System*
   Jean d'Aspremont
132 *Legal Consequences of Peremptory Norms in International Law*
   Daniel Costelloe
131 *Third-Party Countermeasures in International Law*
   Martin Dawidowicz
130 *Justification and Excuse in International Law: Concept and Theory of General Defences*
   Federica Paddeu
129 *Exclusion from Public Space: A Comparative Constitutional Analysis*
   Daniel Moeckli
128 *Provisional Measures before International Courts and Tribunals*
   Cameron A. Miles
127 *Humanity at Sea: Maritime Migration and the Foundations of International Law*
   Itamar Mann
126 *Beyond Human Rights: The Legal Status of the Individual in International Law*
   Anne Peters
125 *The Doctrine of Odious Debt in International Law: A Restatement*
   Jeff King
124 *Static and Evolutive Treaty Interpretation: A Functional Reconstruction*
   Christian Djeffal
123 *Civil Liability in Europe for Terrorism-Related Risk*
   Lucas Bergkamp, Michael Faure, Monika Hinteregger and Niels Philipsen
122 *Proportionality and Deference in Investor-State Arbitration: Balancing Investment Protection and Regulatory Autonomy*
   Caroline Henckels
121 *International Law and Governance of Natural Resources in Conflict and Post-Conflict Situations*
   Daniëlla Dam-de Jong
120 *Proof of Causation in Tort Law*
   Sandy Steel

119 *The Formation and Identification of Rules of Customary International Law in International Investment Law*
   Patrick Dumberry
118 *Religious Hatred and International Law: The Prohibition of Incitement to Violence or Discrimination*
   Jeroen Temperman
117 *Taking Economic, Social and Cultural Rights Seriously in International Criminal Law*
   Evelyne Schmid
116 *Climate Change Litigation: Regulatory Pathways to Cleaner Energy*
   Jacqueline Peel and Hari M. Osofsky
115 *Mestizo International Law: A Global Intellectual History 1842–1933* Arnulf Becker Lorca
114 *Sugar and the Making of International Trade Law*
   Michael Fakhri
113 *Strategically Created Treaty Conflicts and the Politics of International Law*
   Surabhi Ranganathan
112 *Investment Treaty Arbitration As Public International Law: Procedural Aspects and Implications*
   Eric De Brabandere
111 *The New Entrants Problem in International Fisheries Law*
   Andrew Serdy
110 *Substantive Protection under Investment Treaties: A Legal and Economic Analysis*
   Jonathan Bonnitcha
109 *Popular Governance of Post-Conflict Reconstruction: The Role of International Law*
   Matthew Saul
108 *Evolution of International Environmental Regimes: The Case of Climate Change*
   Simone Schiele
107 *Judges, Law and War: The Judicial Development of International Humanitarian Law*
   Shane Darcy
106 *Religious Offence and Human Rights: The Implications of Defamation of Religions*
   Lorenz Langer
105 *Forum Shopping in International Adjudication: The Role of Preliminary Objections*
   Luiz Eduardo Salles
104 *Domestic Politics and International Human Rights Tribunals: The Problem of Compliance*
   Courtney Hillebrecht

103 *International Law and the Arctic*
   Michael Byers
102 *Cooperation in the Law of Transboundary Water Resources*
   Christina Leb
101 *Underwater Cultural Heritage and International Law*
   Sarah Dromgoole
100 *State Responsibility: The General Part*
   James Crawford
 99 *The Origins of International Investment Law: Empire, Environment and the Safeguarding of Capital*
   Kate Miles
 98 *The Crime of Aggression under the Rome Statute of the International Criminal Court*
   Carrie McDougall
 97 *'Crimes against Peace' and International Law*
   Kirsten Sellars
 96 *Non-Legality in International Law: Unruly Law*
   Fleur Johns
 95 *Armed Conflict and Displacement: The Protection of Refugees and Displaced Persons under International Humanitarian Law*
   Mélanie Jacques
 94 *Foreign Investment and the Environment in International Law*
   Jorge E. Viñuales
 93 *The Human Rights Treaty Obligations of Peacekeepers*
   Kjetil Mujezinović Larsen
 92 *Cyber Warfare and the Laws of War*
   Heather Harrison Dinniss
 91 *The Right to Reparation in International Law for Victims of Armed Conflict*
   Christine Evans
 90 *Global Public Interest in International Investment Law*
   Andreas Kulick
 89 *State Immunity in International Law*
   Xiaodong Yang
 88 *Reparations and Victim Support in the International Criminal Court*
   Conor McCarthy
 87 *Reducing Genocide to Law: Definition, Meaning, and the Ultimate Crime*
   Payam Akhavan
 86 *Decolonising International Law: Development, Economic Growth and the Politics of Universality*
   Sundhya Pahuja
 85 *Complicity and the Law of State Responsibility*
   Helmut Philipp Aust

84 *State Control over Private Military and Security Companies in Armed Conflict*
   Hannah Tonkin
83 *'Fair and Equitable Treatment' in International Investment Law*
   Roland Kläger
82 *The UN and Human Rights: Who Guards the Guardians?*
   Guglielmo Verdirame
81 *Sovereign Defaults before International Courts and Tribunals*
   Michael Waibel
80 *Making the Law of the Sea: A Study in the Development of International Law*
   James Harrison
79 *Science and the Precautionary Principle in International Courts and Tribunals: Expert Evidence, Burden of Proof and Finality*
   Caroline E. Foster
78 *Transition from Illegal Regimes under International Law*
   Yaël Ronen
77 *Access to Asylum: International Refugee Law and the Globalisation of Migration Control*
   Thomas Gammeltoft-Hansen
76 *Trading Fish, Saving Fish: The Interaction between Regimes in International Law*
   Margaret A. Young
75 *The Individual in the International Legal System: Continuity and Change in International Law*
   Kate Parlett
74 *'Armed Attack' and Article 51 of the UN Charter: Evolutions in Customary Law and Practice*
   Tom Ruys
73 *Theatre of the Rule of Law: Transnational Legal Intervention in Theory and Practice*
   Stephen Humphreys
72 *Science and Risk Regulation in International Law*
   Jacqueline Peel
71 *The Participation of States in International Organisations: The Role of Human Rights and Democracy*
   Alison Duxbury
70 *Legal Personality in International Law*
   Roland Portmann
69 *Vicarious Liability in Tort: A Comparative Perspective*
   Paula Giliker
68 *The Public International Law Theory of Hans Kelsen: Believing in Universal Law*
   Jochen von Bernstorff

67 *Legitimacy and Legality in International Law: An Interactional Account*
   Jutta Brunnée and Stephen J. Toope
66 *The Concept of Non-International Armed Conflict in International Humanitarian Law*
   Anthony Cullen
65 *The Principle of Legality in International and Comparative Criminal Law*
   Kenneth S. Gallant
64 *The Challenge of Child Labour in International Law*
   Franziska Humbert
63 *Shipping Interdiction and the Law of the Sea*
   Douglas Guilfoyle
62 *International Courts and Environmental Protection*
   Tim Stephens
61 *Legal Principles in WTO Disputes*
   Andrew D. Mitchell
60 *War Crimes in Internal Armed Conflicts*
   Eve La Haye
59 *Humanitarian Occupation*
   Gregory H. Fox
58 *The International Law of Environmental Impact Assessment: Process, Substance and Integration*
   Neil Craik
57 *The Law and Practice of International Territorial Administration: Versailles to Iraq and Beyond*
   Carsten Stahn
56 *United Nations Sanctions and the Rule of Law*
   Jeremy Matam Farrall
55 *National Law in WTO Law: Effectiveness and Good Governance in the World Trading System*
   Sharif Bhuiyan
54 *Cultural Products and the World Trade Organization*
   Tania Voon
53 *The Threat of Force in International Law*
   Nikolas Stürchler
52 *Indigenous Rights and United Nations Standards: Self-Determination, Culture and Land*
   Alexandra Xanthaki
51 *International Refugee Law and Socio-Economic Rights: Refuge from Deprivation*
   Michelle Foster
50 *The Protection of Cultural Property in Armed Conflict*
   Roger O'Keefe

49 *Interpretation and Revision of International Boundary Decisions*
   Kaiyan Homi Kaikobad
48 *Multinationals and Corporate Social Responsibility: Limitations and Opportunities in International Law*
   Jennifer A. Zerk
47 *Judiciaries within Europe: A Comparative Review*
   John Bell
46 *Law in Times of Crisis: Emergency Powers in Theory and Practice*
   Oren Gross and Fionnuala Ní Aoláin
45 *Vessel-Source Marine Pollution: The Law and Politics of International Regulation*
   Alan Khee-Jin Tan
44 *Enforcing Obligations Erga Omnes in International Law*
   Christian J. Tams
43 *Non-Governmental Organisations in International Law*
   Anna-Karin Lindblom
42 *Democracy, Minorities and International Law*
   Steven Wheatley
41 *Prosecuting International Crimes: Selectivity and the International Criminal Law Regime*
   Robert Cryer
40 *Compensation for Personal Injury in English, German and Italian Law: A Comparative Outline*
   Basil Markesinis, Michael Coester, Guido Alpa and Augustus Ullstein
39 *Dispute Settlement in the UN Convention on the Law of the Sea*
   Natalie Klein
38 *The International Protection of Internally Displaced Persons*
   Catherine Phuong
37 *Imperialism, Sovereignty and the Making of International Law*
   Antony Anghie
36 *Principles of the Institutional Law of International Organizations*
   C. F. Amerasinghe
35 *Necessity, Proportionality and the Use of Force by States*
   Judith Gardam
34 *International Legal Argument in the Permanent Court of International Justice: The Rise of the International Judiciary*
   Ole Spiermann
33 –
32 *Great Powers and Outlaw States: Unequal Sovereigns in the International Legal Order*
   Gerry Simpson

31 *Local Remedies in International Law (second edition)*
   Chittharanjan Felix Amerasinghe
30 *Reading Humanitarian Intervention: Human Rights and the Use of Force in International Law*
   Anne Orford
29 *Conflict of Norms in Public International Law: How WTO Law Relates to Other Rules of International Law*
   Joost Pauwelyn
28 –
27 *Transboundary Damage in International Law*
   Hanqin Xue
26 –
25 *European Criminal Procedures* Edited by Mireille Delmas-Marty and J. R. Spencer
24 *Accountability of Armed Opposition Groups in International Law*
   Liesbeth Zegveld
23 *Sharing Transboundary Resources: International Law and Optimal Resource Use*
   Eyal Benvenisti
22 *International Human Rights and Humanitarian Law*
   René Provost
21 *Remedies against International Organisations*
   Karel Wellens
20 *Diversity and Self-Determination in International Law*
   Karen Knop
19 *The Law of Internal Armed Conflict*
   Lindsay Moir
18 *International Commercial Arbitration and African States: Practice, Participation and Institutional Development*
   Amazu A. Asouzu
17 *The Enforceability of Promises in European Contract Law*
   James Gordley
16 *International Law in Antiquity*
   David J. Bederman
15 *Money Laundering: A New International Law Enforcement Model*
   Guy Stessens
14 *Good Faith in European Contract Law*
   Reinhard Zimmermann and Simon Whittaker
13 *On Civil Procedure*
   J. A. Jolowicz
12 *Trusts: A Comparative Study*
   Maurizio Lupoi and Simon Dix

11 *The Right to Property in Commonwealth Constitutions*
   Tom Allen
10 *International Organizations before National Courts*
   August Reinisch
 9 *The Changing International Law of High Seas Fisheries*
   Francisco Orrego Vicuña
 8 *Trade and the Environment: A Comparative Study of EC and US Law*
   Damien Geradin
 7 *Unjust Enrichment: A Study of Private Law and Public Values*
   Hanoch Dagan
 6 *Religious Liberty and International Law in Europe*
   Malcolm D. Evans
 5 *Ethics and Authority in International Law*
   Alfred P. Rubin
 4 *Sovereignty over Natural Resources: Balancing Rights and Duties*
   Nico Schrijver
 3 *The Polar Regions and the Development of International Law*
   Donald R. Rothwell
 2 *Fragmentation and the International Relations of Micro-States: Self-Determination and Statehood*
   Jorri C. Duursma
 1 *Principles of the Institutional Law of International Organizations*
   C. F. Amerasinghe

Printed in the United States
by Baker & Taylor Publisher Services